Better Off Dead

Better Off Dead

THE EVOLUTION OF THE ZOMBIE AS POST-HUMAN

Edited by

DEBORAH CHRISTIE AND SARAH JULIET LAURO

FORDHAM UNIVERSITY PRESS

New York 2011

Copyright © 2011 Fordham University Press

All rights reserved. No part of this publication may be reproduced, stored in a retrieval system, or transmitted in any form or by any means—electronic, mechanical, photocopy, recording, or any other—except for brief quotations in printed reviews, without the prior permission of the publisher.

Fordham University Press has no responsibility for the persistence or accuracy of URLs for external or third-party Internet websites referred to in this publication and does not guarantee that any content on such websites is, or will remain, accurate or appropriate.

Fordham University Press also publishes its books in a variety of electronic formats. Some content that appears in print may not be available in electronic books.

Library of Congress Cataloging-in-Publication Data

Better off dead : the evolution of the zombie as post-human / edited by Deborah Christie and Sarah Juliet Lauro.—1st ed.
  p. cm.
Includes bibliographical references and index.
ISBN 978-0-8232-3446-2 (cloth : alk. paper)
ISBN 978-0-8232-3447-9 (pbk. : alk. paper)
ISBN 978-0-8232-3448-6 (epub)
 1. Zombies. 2. Zombies in popular culture. 3. Zombies in literature. 4. Zombies in motion pictures. I. Christie, Deborah. II. Lauro, Sarah Juliet.
 GR581.B48 2011
 398.21—dc22
 2011007494

Printed in the United States of America
14   5 4
First edition

CONTENTS

Acknowledgments   vii

Introduction
    SARAH JULIET LAURO AND DEBORAH CHRISTIE   1

And the Dead Shall Rise
Part introduction by Kevin Boon   5

1. "They are not men . . . they are dead bodies": From Cannibal to Zombie and Back Again
    CHERA KEE   9
2. "We are the mirror of your fears": Haitian Identity and Zombification
    FRANCK DEGOUL (TRANSLATED BY ELISABETH M. LORE)   24
3. Undead Radio: Zombies and the Living Dead on 1930s and 1940s Radio Drama
    RICHARD HAND   39
4. The Zombie as Other: Mortality and the Monstrous in the Post-Nuclear Age
    KEVIN BOON   50

And the Dead Shall Walk
Part introduction by Deborah Christie   61

5. A Dead New World: Richard Matheson and the Modern Zombie
    DEBORAH CHRISTIE   67
6. Nuclear Death and Radical Hope in *Dawn of the Dead* and *On the Beach*
    NICK MUNTEAN   81

7. Lucio Fulci and the Decaying Definition of Zombie Narratives
   STEVEN ZANI AND KEVIN MEAUX 98
8. Imitations of Life: Zombies and the Suburban Gothic
   BERNICE MURPHY 116
9. All Dark Inside: Dehumanization and Zombification in Postmodern Cinema
   SORCHA NÍ FHLAINN 139

And the Dead Shall Inherit the Earth
Part introduction by Peter Dendle 159

10. Slacker Bites Back: *Shaun of the Dead* Finds New Life for Deadbeats
    LYNN PIFER 163
11. Zombie Movies and the "Millennial Generation"
    PETER DENDLE 175
12. "Off the page and into your brains!": New Millennium Zombies and the Scourge of Hopeful Apocalypses
    MARGO COLLINS AND ELSON BOND 187
13. Playing Dead: Zombies Invade Performance Art... and Your Neighborhood
    SARAH JULIET LAURO 205

Afterword: Zombie (R)evolution
   SARAH JULIET LAURO 231

Notes 237
Selected Bibliography 277
List of Contributors 285
Index 289

ACKNOWLEDGMENTS

Our impulse is to try to thank everyone who has ever influenced or supported our study of zombies, but in the interest of saving some room to actually talk about said zombies we will limit ourselves to as small a list as we can manage.

SJL: Many people advised me as we began to put together a collection of this type, and others offered their sage advice as we endeavored to find the right home for it. Peter Dendle, Simon Sadler, and Eric Smoodin offered invaluable advice about the art of editing and publishing. I am so grateful that my advisers didn't balk when I told them I was taking this on: Claire Waters, Scott Simmon, and Michael Ziser were encouraging and full of wisdom to share; Timothy Morton offered invaluable editorial advice; Colin Milburn was a constant source of support on all fronts—my contributions to this collection would have looked very different without his steadying guidance. Without the example, advice, and friendship of Caleb Smith, I doubt very much that I would have had the moxie to take on a project of this scope and size. In this, and every other endeavor, the late Marc Blanchard was my rock: He will be sorely missed. Last, however, I have to acknowledge the unflagging support of my darling husband and my lovely children, who sometimes endure nightmares, because Mommy works on zombies.

DC: Years ago, at a pivotal point in my graduate studies, I nearly turned away from the study of monsters, thinking that nobody would ever take that research seriously. Walter Kendrick convinced me otherwise and supported the idea that studying the things we fear is ultimately a liberating and uplifting experience. The world is a smaller place without Dr. Kendrick, who passed away in 1998, but it is my fondest hope that he would have been proud of the scholarship represented in this collection and of my continued pursuit of the darker mysteries of life and all things after. Ken Monteith, Margo Collins, and Mark Cantrell have been my support and my sounding boards throughout this project. I also need to thank

Patrick McCarthy, the English department, and the library staff at the University of Miami for providing me with the resources and encouragement to see this project through to completion. Much like my coeditor, I have to acknowledge the amazing support of my husband and my children, who have frequently had to do without me because of this collection. I could not do what I do without their support, and I would not be who I am without their love.

The editors would be remiss if they didn't acknowledge that Steven Zani and Kevin Meaux are the biological parents of this collection. They conceived of the project of assembling a collection of scholarly essays on the zombie and solicited many of our contributors. We are so grateful that they allowed us to adopt the project, give it our own name and shape, and develop it as we saw fit, but we owe them an especial debt of gratitude for having first breathed life into it. Besides, we think it fitting that the collection has been reanimated.

We are grateful to the editorial board at Fordham University Press and all the hard work the staff—particularly Josh Jones, Tom Lay, Eric Newman, Nicholas Taylor, Kathleen Sweeney, and Kathleen O'Brien—has done on our behalf. We are immensely appreciative that editor Helen Tartar was willing to consider having such an acclaimed scholarly press publish a collection devoted to such an unusual topic.

This project has undergone many transformations, and in the process we have had the benefit of exchanging work and ideas with many scholars. We would like to thank Jillian Mcdonald, Alexandre Joseph, Christopher Zealand, Kyle Bishop, Jennifer Cooke, John Kitterman, Kriscinda Meadows, Dion Turbrette, Shelley O'Brien, and Martin Carter for sharing their insights with us.

Death is not the end . . . in fact, in this collection, it is quite literally the beginning.

INTRODUCTION

Sarah Juliet Lauro and Deborah Christie

That the zombie is ubiquitous in popular culture cannot be disputed: From popular literature and comic books to video games and performance art, in smartphone applications and in homemade films, zombies are all around us. Though horror film has been of interest to scholars for decades, some critics have heralded a resurgence of the zombie in popular culture and, subsequently, inaugurated a new boom of scholarly investigation of this fearsome figure of living death.[1] Perhaps we can say with certainty that the zombie is more popular now than ever before; it has even seemed to have crashed the boundaries of narrative and stepped into real life. Newspapers are full of stories of large-scale games of zombie tag, of zombie proms, of zombie warnings posted on road signs by cheeky hackers: this transgression from the screen to the street is but one of the many types of "zombie evolution" we discuss herein.[2] Assembling this collection in the year marking the bicentennial of Charles Darwin's birth, and the sesquicentennial of his publication of *On the Origin of Species* (1859)—the seminal text describing the principle of evolution and postulating that humans and apes descended from a common ancestor—we felt that our project was haunted by the zeitgeist, for this collection charts the evolution of the zombie, establishing how this myth has developed along with human civilization. With an eye toward the future (and perhaps a tongue in cheek), we question whether the zombie resembles our prehistoric past, acts as a mirror reflecting our present anxieties, or suggests whether the future will house a more evolved post-humanity or merely the graves of a failed civilization.

We structured our collection around a basic rising—or evolving—principle. The book consists of three parts, representing the three most recognizable stages of twentieth- and twenty-first-century zombie configurations: the classic mindless corpse, the relentless instinct-driven newly dead, and the millennial voracious and fast-moving predator. Our dissection of the zombie myth is concerned with it not only as a fictive monster on which we stamp our society's latest fears, but also as a model to which we have applied modes and methods of reading. This collection is a survey of the zombie's cinematic history, but also an investigation of the zombie from an interdisciplinary perspective, with an emphasis on deep analytical engagement with diverse kinds of narratives. Just as we approach the zombie from many different points of view, looking across history and across media, we also employ diverse theoretical perspectives. Our collection's deep engagement with narratives that reach beyond those found in film and literature to investigate zombies in art, life, and cyberspace reveals that the zombie has not just evolved within narratives—it has evolved in a way that transforms narrative. In this way, we feel our collection acknowledges the possibility that the zombie is post-human, and also illustrates that we are already living in the period of the post-zombie. Yet, for all this evolutionary progress, we acknowledge that any use of the word "post" is, as Neil Badmington writes, "forever tied up with what it is post-ing."[3]

The zombie may therefore be an apt icon for the post-human in its frustrating antipathy: Just as the post-human will always assert what the human is by that which it supposes itself to be beyond, the zombie both is, and is not, dead and alive.[4] It was its complex sense of transformation, more than any other aspect of the "Millennial Zombie" (a category that Peter Dendle fleshes out in his essay here), that called for this collection. The zombie auteur George Romero, who was himself responsible for guiding the zombie from one iteration to another, has cast aspersions in a number of interviews as to whether the ravenous creatures in works like *28 Days Later* are "dead" enough to be legitimately called zombies. If the zombie has evolved so much over the course of the twentieth century that, at the beginning of the twenty-first, it is nearly unrecognizable, then surely there is a need to define exactly what we mean when we call something a zombie, to chart the evolution of this concept, and to map out the ways that this monster has been and will continue to be a useful theoretical apparatus—most recently as an expression of our own evolving relationship to new technologies.

The first section of the book grounds our examination of the zombie in its cultural, anthropological, and historical origins as a monster that comes to the United States by way of Haitian folklore. Chera Kee charts both the zombie's evolution as a myth developing out of African religions and its migration to the United States in travel narratives and film. Frank Degoul's essay presents his firsthand research on zombification and what this association does for Haitian identity. Richard Hand delves into the radio archives for examples that betray how the early zombie morphed from exotic to evil. Kevin Boon provides a historical overview that illustrates how the zombie came to take on the kinds of characteristics we associate with later horror films.

The second part of the book concentrates on what we might consider to be the period wherein the classic horror zombie developed, from the 1950s to the late 1970s. Anchored in the literature and film of these decades, this section portrays various kinds of evolution in tracing different mutations among the zombie's divergent origin stories. Deborah Christie illustrates how what we consider the modern-day zombie evolved from vampires within a narrative of violent social renewal. Nick Muntean presents the traumatized zombie that is the product of the atomic age. Steven Zani and Kevin Meaux give an overview of one of the zombie myth's most potent strains, its development into a viral infection. Bernice Murphy discusses the evolution of a suburban zombie, from the automatons of *The Stepford Wives* (1975) to *Fido* (2006). Sorcha Ní Fhlainn expands the theme of dehumanization into the removal of individual thought, explicitly characterized by the soldiers of modern warfare in films like *28 Days Later* (2002), *28 Weeks Later* (2007), and *Jacob's Ladder* (1990).

The third part of the book propels zombie scholarship into the future by looking at the most recent iterations of the zombie narrative and investigating zombies in unlikely places. In discussing the most recent wave of zombie films, Peter Dendle considers the much bandied-about question "Why are zombies getting faster?," and Lynn Pifer looks at the tendency toward zombie comedy, dissecting *Shaun of the Dead* (2004) as a revisionist zombie film for a new generation of fans. Margo Collins and Elson Bond continue the investigation into "zom com" by looking at the recent and popular appearance of zombies in novels—original and spoofed—and blogs, as well as the proliferation of real-life zombie survival groups, as emblematic of the zombie's millennial role as "monstrous placeholders" for an anomic society at odds with itself. Finally, Sarah Juliet Lauro argues that zombies in performance art and public demonstrations elucidate a further type of zombie evolution: the spectator has become participant in, and even creator of, his own zombie stories.

Across an ever-broadening array of media, zombies are making their presence known, and in several variations they are learning, adapting to their altered circumstances with frightening rapidity, and evolving into a rather perplexing ontological problem for humans.[5] As the demarcating line between us and them, and subject and object, recedes, confusion arises. We must ask ourselves: Are zombies becoming more human, or are humans becoming more like zombies? If we are, might that resolve some of our uniquely humanist problems? Will the equalizing force of the zombie horde undergo gender trouble, identity politics, and disparities between the haves and the have-nots? Might we not all be *better off dead*?

And the Dead Shall Rise

Part introduction by Kevin Boon

> Death is a very serious matter, Mrs. Fiske. People who go through it are never the same.
>
> LAURELL K. HAMILTON, "Those Who Seek Forgiveness"

Discourse in contemporary popular American culture concerning zombie mythology is colored by George Romero's fusion of the zombie with the ghoul in his monumental film *Night of the Living Dead* in 1968. Nearly every film made after Romero's first sequel to *Night*, *Dawn of the Dead* (1978), can be linked back to Romero's characterization of the zombie. And it is quite difficult to find a zombie novel or short story released after Romero's third film in his zombie series, *Day of the Dead* (1985), that does not follow the director's lead. It is not surprising, then, that contemporary discussions of the zombie often ground themselves in Romero's vision and begin their examinations during the period Peter Dendle labels the "Golden Age."[1] But zombie mythology, as the essays in this section show, possesses a rich history and a much broader relevance to contemporary cultures than customarily attributed to it.

Unlike other iconic creatures in horror narratives—Frankenstein's monster, werewolves, vampires, and other monstrous manifestations in European fictional narratives—the zombie proper emerges from religious and cultural origins of the African diaspora. The chapters in this section go a long way toward tracking that journey through fields of Haitian sugarcane to American popular culture. The two chapters that frame this section, Chera Kee's "'They are not men . . . they are dead bodies!': From

Cannibal to Zombie and Back Again" and Franck Degoul's "'We are the mirror of your fears': Haitian Identity and Zombification," both examine zombie mythology's ineluctable relationship to Haiti. Kee traces the myth through the nineteenth century and up to the 1968 appearance of Romero's *Night of the Living Dead*, illustrating a predominately Western view of voodoo[2] and the zombie, while Degoul contrasts that view with an illumination of these same myths "within the Haitian context."

We might further credit Romero's influence by privileging film over other forms of media in discussions of the zombie, despite the zombie myth's permeation of American media and culture. Richard J. Hand's "Undead Radio: Zombies and the Living Dead on 1930 and 1940s Radio Drama" helps to offset this shortcoming by chronicling the zombie's presence in the early days of radio and its appearance on such iconic programs as *The Shadow* and *Inner Sanctum Mysteries*. Film does not hold exclusive domain over the zombie. The zombie has lumbered into every American art form, including theater, music, literature, performance art, painting, and sculpture.

Most approaches to zombie studies fall into two broad categories. The first examines the sociohistorical evolution of the myth through and across cultural landscapes. The zombie (as Degoul clearly illustrates) is primarily a political, cultural, and religious product, and how it is defined depends on who is looking; thus Western and Haitian characterizations of the zombie differ. Further, contemporary characterizations (American and Haitian) largely differ from early nineteenth-century characterizations, so much so that no single perspective can contain the whole of the myth. Parts of the myth may, at times, even contradict one another. Just as voodoo and tales of zombies were employed by colonial forces to dehumanize Haitians (as Kee outlines), they are also, as Franck Degoul points out, a source of empowerment for Haiti and its citizens, a "valorizing sign of Haitianness."

The second category involves psycho-philosophical critiques of the zombie designed to clarify the nature of the myth and its relationship to human consciousness. My own offering in this section, "The Zombie as Other: Mortality and the Monstrous in the Post-nuclear Age," falls into this category in its attempt to illustrate the existential nature of the zombie and the myth's relationship to the self before and after the introduction of nuclear weapons into American consciousness.

A sociohistorical approach is bound to the label "zombie," but a psycho-philosophical approach can be more liberal in this regard. The first approach dates the beginning of the zombie film to the 1932 production of *White Zombie*, but the second might date the first zombie film to the 1920 production of *Das Cabinet des Dr. Caligari*, by arguing that Cesare, the somnambulated assassin, has lost his volition and is largely indistinguishable from the zombies we encounter in *White Zombie* and later films, such as *Ouanga* (1935), *Revolt of the Zombies* (1936), and *I Walked with a Zombie* (1943).

The term "zombie" is often equated with terms such as "the undead" and discussed as if returning from the dead is an indispensible characteristic of the zombie. Yet, if we are to use that characteristic to define zombies, we encounter numerous complications. The story of Jesus's crucifixtion and resurrection becomes a story of zombification, as does every ghost story ever told, and the zombies Wade Davis refers to in *The Serpent and the Rainbow* and *Passage of Darkness: The Ethnobiology of the Haitian Zombie* cease to be zombies.

What is still needed in zombie studies is a clear articulation of what constitutes a zombie. While Hollywood zombies since the mid-eighties have largely been reanimated corpses, not all reanimated corpses have been zombies. Frankenstein's monster, for example, is reanimated dead flesh, but the monster has never, to my knowledge, been referred to as a zombie, while the infected in *28 Days Later*, who do not return from the dead, are nearly always classified as zombies.

My colleague Peter Dendle claims that "the substantial overlap among the various movie monsters precludes the possibility of an all-encompassing definition of a zombie,"[3] a point that easily extends to the representation of zombies in literature and other cultural manifestations. Nevertheless, zombies do all share a common characteristic: the absence of some metaphysical quality of their essential selves. This may be the soul, the mind, the will, or, in some cases, the personality. But every zombie experiences a loss of something essential that previous to zombification defined it as human. Usually this entails a loss of volition, though not always. The zombies in Brian Keene's *The Rising* are intelligent and act with purpose. They have volition, but it is not the volition of the bodies' original occupants. The original self has been altered in a way that guts its essence. The person is no longer a person in either an existential or metaphysical sense. While this characteristic is not an all-encompassing definition, it is a uniform criterion that makes classification possible. When we apply this criterion to zombie mythology as it appears in art, film, literature, radio, and culture, we can identify nine major categories of zombies, seven of which cover zombies that exhibit the necessary loss of self, and two additional categories which are necessary because the term "zombie" is sometimes employed to identify non-zombies.[4]

The nine types, briefly defined, are as follows: (1) *zombie drone*: a person whose will has been taken from him or her, resulting in a slavish obedience; (2) *zombie ghoul*: fusion of the zombie and the ghoul, which has lost volition and feeds on flesh; (3) *tech zombie*: people who have lost their volition through the use of some technological device; (4) *bio zombie*: similar to tech zombies, except some biological, natural, or chemical element is the medium that robs people of their will; (5) *zombie channel*: a person who has been resurrected and some other entity has possessed his or her form; (6) *psychological zombie*: a person who has lost his or her will as a result of some psychological conditioning; (7) *cultural zombie*: in general, refers to the type of zombie we locate within popular culture; (8) *zombie ghost*: not actually a zombie, rather someone who has returned from the dead with all or most of his or her faculties intact; and (9) *zombie ruse*: slight of hand common in young adult novels where the "zombies" turn out to not be zombies at all.[5]

It should be noted that these categories often overlap. The zombies in the 1998 film *I, Zombie*, for example, are both tech zombies (because of their implants) and zombie drones (because they are shambling slave labor like the Haitian zombies of earlier works). Cesare in *Caligari* is both a psychological zombie, by dint of his mesmerization, and a zombie drone, because of his complete servitude to Caligari's will. The zombies in Romero's series are zombie ghouls and bio zombies. Yet despite the sometimes-fluid boundaries between these categories, this system of classification offers some foundation as we enter into discussions of zombies in their many artistic and cultural incarnations. In this collection, which examines zombie evolution, we might focus especially on where the flux between categories suggests a kind of development, mapping the zombie's transformations throughout the twentieth century both diachronically and synchronically in order to determine where there has been teleological transformation, and where several kinds of zombies have coexisted, peopling a kind of zombie nation.

CHAPTER 1

"They are not men ... they are dead bodies!": From Cannibal to Zombie and Back Again

Chera Kee

Contemporary American zombies[1] are remarkably similar: They are born of infection, are the dead returned to life, and have a taste for human flesh. But this hasn't always been the popular imagining of the zombie. When zombies were first introduced into U.S. culture, they were radically different. The earliest zombies were neither sick nor cannibalistic; they were victims of an exotic religion, used as slaves, forced to submit to the will of a zombie master. While it is widely accepted that modern zombies were born in George Romero's 1968 film *Night of the Living Dead*, discussion of the ties that bind modern zombies to their Haitian ancestors is sometimes forgotten. Yet this ignores the zombie's cannibalistic roots.

The zombie is one of the few popular Hollywood monsters that come from outside Europe; rather, it arises out of stories connected to Haitian Voodoo, and early zombie fiction in the United States owes much to fears of Haiti as an independent black republic. From the time of the Haitian Revolution onward, stories of Voodoo circulated throughout the Americas and Europe. Anxiety about Haiti in the United States translated into an anxiety about Voodoo, which was increasingly linked to cannibalism in the U.S. popular press to underscore supposed Haitian primitivism. Yet, after the tumultuous U.S. occupation of Haiti from 1915 to 1934, cannibalism began to fade out of the discourse surrounding Voodoo in favor of zombies.

The nineteenth- and twentieth-century cannibalistic discourse surrounding Haitian Voodoo was transformed into a racialized discourse in early zombie films, but it becomes evident that over time, as the zombie matured, the overt link to Haiti and to Voodoo dissolved so that zombies came to represent any ethnic group.[2] Zombie fiction changed to produce a more diffuse definition of the self and the Other[3] as it evolved into its modern form. Thus Hollywood's zombie films from the late 1930s to 1968, when *Night of the Living Dead* enacted its radical break in the genre, were increasingly confusing the boundaries between "us" and "them." To understand the significance of these changes to the zombie, it is important to explore the pre-zombie imaginings of Haiti and Voodoo in the United States, how the zombie entered the U.S. imaginary, and how it came to be defined in U.S. film up to 1968.[4] From its introduction into U.S. popular culture in the late 1920s to the present, the zombie has never quite managed to shake its Haitian heritage. Therefore, to understand the zombie in the United States, one must go back to Haiti.

They Eat Their Children

Following a series of slave revolts in the 1790s, in 1804 Haiti became the first black-ruled independent nation in the Western Hemisphere. Voodoo gatherings were integral to the beginnings of the revolts: As C. L. R. James observes, these clandestine gatherings[5] provided the future leaders of the revolts with the opportunity to meet and gather supporters, and it was, in fact, at a Voodoo meeting that the revolution began.[6] From nearly the beginning, external commentary painted Voodoo as central to the revolts, and merely the possibility of a connection between the revolution and Voodoo presented opponents of Haitian independence with a means to disparage revolutionary ideas by linking them to a supposedly barbaric, superstitious belief system.

The heroes of Haiti's revolution were also heroes to slaves throughout the Americas, who in some areas shared Voodoo beliefs. Logically, slaveholders feared similar revolts and mistrusted slave gatherings, especially those connected to Voodoo. Most of the fears connected to Haiti centered on stories of revolutionary atrocities directed toward white peoples. As David Brion Davis reports, "In general, the Haitian Revolution reinforced the conviction that slave emancipation in any form would lead to economic ruin and to the indiscriminant massacre of white populations."[7]

There was some justification to these fears: reports indicate that Jean Jacques Dessalines, Haiti's new emperor, did order the massacre of the whites remaining in Haiti only a few months after the nation's declaration of independence.[8] Further, while in 1789 Saint-Domingue was overwhelmingly the most important French colony in terms of trade, by the time it became Haiti and was independent, the richest colony in the world had been reduced to ruins by more than a decade of fighting—and the impact on the global economy was immense.

As the hemisphere's only black-ruled republic, Haiti naturally spawned much curiosity, which was fueled by the fact that the island existed in virtual isolation: trade embargoes and the lack of international diplomatic recognition[9] effectively sealed Haiti off from the rest of the world. Thus, what little information was available about Haiti wasn't subject to much critical interrogation. Much of the nineteenth- and early-twentieth-century material available in English was written by those with only a passing familiarity with the nation, or by those who wanted to use Haiti to further their own ideological causes.[10] They tended to paint Haiti as either corrupt and gradually devolving or shakily trying to stand on its own.

Haiti was a pawn in battles between abolitionists and slavers, used by both to prove their respective points. In *Sketches of Hayti: From the Expulsion of the French to the Death of Christophe* (1827), W. W. Harvey, in many ways an admirer of Haiti, nevertheless remarks that the country's history since the revolution "presents to us the picture of a people newly escaped from slavery, yet still suffering and exhibiting in their character, its pernicious and demoralizing effects."[11] Harvey's views were typical of the abolitionists and missionaries writing on Haiti during the early nineteenth century. Yet those opposed to abolition were much more critical. In an 1805 letter from French Foreign Minister Charles Talleyrand to U.S. Secretary of State James Madison, for instance, Talleyrand observes, "The existence of a Negro people in arms, occupying a country it has soiled by the most criminal acts, is a horrible spectacle for all white nations. . . . There are no reasons . . . to grant support to these brigands who have declared themselves the enemies of all government."[12]

Haiti's revolution deprived white Europeans and Americans of the ability to "civilize" the black world formerly known as Saint-Domingue; therefore, Haiti had to be demonized so as to create a situation where the civilizing forces of the white world could save the nation from itself. Therefore, the revolution and the nation it produced could never be seen as successful.

Following colonialist discourse elsewhere, many writers tended to portray Haiti as a country in ruins. Unlike other colonial holdings, however, Haiti's ruins were not evidence of a once-great empire, but rather evidence of French colonialism left to waste. Voodoo was often cited as the root cause for the devolution these authors saw at play in Haiti; it was rarely viewed as anything other than malicious black magic. For example, a 1920 article on Haiti in *National Geographic* reported, "Here, in the elemental wildernesses, the natives rapidly forgot their thin veneer of Christian civilization and reverted to utter, unthinking animalism, swayed only by fear of local bandit chiefs and the black magic of voodoo witch doctors."[13]

Nineteenth-century texts on Haiti devoted many pages to descriptions of Voodoo ceremonies and beliefs. Many of these reports were fictitious, but they were repeated nonetheless. Spencer St. John, for instance, devoted a great deal of his 1884 book *Hayti, or the Black Republic* to Voodoo. Although he never actually attended a Voodoo ceremony, relying instead on gossip and newspaper articles as sources, St. John tied it to cannibalism, human sacrifice, and grave robbing in what would become one of the most-read texts on Haiti in the nineteenth century.[14]

Interestingly, St. John was careful to claim that cannibalism was not endured under the French, asserting that it was never mentioned in French colonial accounts of Haiti and that it would have been difficult to perform when colonial masters kept such a close eye on their property: one missing slave would have raised suspicions. Of course, inherent in St. John's argument was the idea that cannibalism was the result of Haitian self-rule. Writings on Haitian Voodoo continued on themes of cannibalism, often claiming that Haitians ate their children in sacrifice to Voodoo gods, as many books and articles either borrowed directly from St. John or built on his assertions.[15]

Voodoo was seen as an intrinsic part of Haitian life, something that corrupted Haiti's people because it was allowed to operate without restraint. This led outside observers to conclude that Haitians were unable to govern themselves. In his 1900 book *Where Black Rules White: A Journey across and about Hayti*, Hesketh Pritchard noted that Voodoo was a central part of every Haitian's life and that its power would remain undaunted "as long as Hayti retains an entirely negro government."[16] Voodoo corrupted Haiti, so much so that even those institutions that might grant it the appearance of civilization were tainted.

Yet there was a practical side to concerns relating to Haitian independence as well. The revolution disrupted markets and created a massive shortfall in the supply of tropical products like sugar and coffee. It also forced waves of refugees and migrants into neighboring countries.

Upon the assassination of Jean-Jacques Dessalines in late 1806, the country was divided between a kingdom in the north, ruled by Henri Christophe, and a republic in the south, run by Alexandre Pétion. By 1822, Jean-Pierre Boyer had reunified Haiti, but a series of coups and armed revolts followed his departure from office in 1843. The impoverished nation was often in a state of near rebellion.

As Haiti came to represent a sort of self-destruction that could someday spill over into the rest of the Americas, the belief that Haiti had to be saved—and in its saving, contained—was prominent. Although sentiment like this may not have been the only excuse, it did play a part in the U.S. occupation of Haiti in 1915 and was most certainly an important justification for a continued presence there. The occupation is described in greater detail in Franck Degoul's chapter, "'We are the mirror of your fears': Haitian Identity and Zombification." Yet it is worth noting here that, to most Americans, the United States occupied Haiti under the pretense of civilizing it, and a negative image of Haitians and of Voodoo in particular were instrumental in gaining and keeping support for the action. Thus, as Joan Dayan notes, "it should not surprise us that during the American occupation . . . tales of cannibalism, torture, and zombies were published in [the United States]. What better way to justify the 'civilizing' presence of marines in Haiti than to project the phantasm of barbarism?"[17]

Enter the Zombie

The term "zombie" was virtually unknown outside Haiti until 1929. At that time, though, zombies entered U.S. culture quite forcefully in William Seabrook's book *The Magic Island*. Seabrook lived in Haiti and had developed a close friendship with a Voodoo priestess. In *The Magic Island*, he gave detailed accounts of Voodoo rituals and folklore, and one being in particular captured his interest. He wrote, "I recalled one creature I had been hearing about in Haiti, which sounded exclusively local—the zombie."[18] Seabrook devoted a chapter of his book to the zombie. Titled ". . . Dead Men Working in the Cane Fields," the chapter described zombies in detail: "The zombie, they say, is a soulless human corpse, still dead, but taken from the grave and endowed by sorcery with a mechanical semblance of life—it is a dead body which is made to walk and act and move as if it were alive."[19] Seabrook continued, explaining that zombies were used as slaves by those who raised them; he then described the physical traits of zombies he had supposedly seen, who were "plodding like brutes, like automatons," and whose faces were "expressionless" and "vacant" with eyes "like the eyes of a dead man, not blind, but staring, unfocused, unseeing."[20] Seabrook's descriptions, coupled with Alexander King's powerful accompanying illustrations, came to codify zombie behavior in U.S. imaginations for years to come.

Interestingly, just as the zombie entered the U.S. imagination, tales of cannibalism tied to Voodoo began to fade. Thus, linking the zombie to Haiti simply traded the idea of an overt threat (cannibalism) for a fantasy marking the entire country as a nation of eternal slaves. Moreover, the zombie was transplanted into the United States almost exactly as the Great Depression began. For the first time since the Civil War and emancipation, much of the United States felt dispossessed. Many Americans were made aware of just how powerless they were in the capitalist system. Identification with zombies, then, may have been particularly resonant in the 1930s United States, as zombies became an ideological critique of modernity in the form of capitalist exploitation.

Further, the depression exacerbated racial tensions, and stereotypes of peoples of color thrived in this sort of environment. In film and the other arts, such individuals were often cast as delinquents, criminals, or mentally challenged. They became the monsters, so to speak. Zombies could thus also operate within a discourse that maintained whiteness as the norm and constructed those of color as monstrous. Moreover, zombies were something created outside the experience of white, middle-class America: they literally happened "over there." And further fitting with earlier colonialist discourse that generally accorded white persons an individual identity, zombies were faceless masses: a new means of robbing the Other of its individuality in order to keep it as the Other.

One of the earliest appearances of the zombie after *The Magic Island* was Kenneth Webb's stage play *Zombie*, which opened in New York in February 1932. By all accounts, the story line of *Zombie* borrowed liberally from *The Magic Island*, and the zombies of the play were portrayed in a fashion similar to Seabrook's descriptions. With its links to people of color, the zombie was a natural emblem for the slave, easily expendable and under the control of a powerful master. Yet, as exotic as the zombie may have been, the similarities between its plight and that of of many of these "everyday" Americans were not lost on observers. As J. Brooks Atkinson wrote in his review of the play in the *New York Times*, "If zombies are those who work without knowing why and who see without understanding, one begins to look around among one's fellow countrymen with a new apprehension. Perhaps those native drums are sounding the national anthem."[21]

Zombie had a very limited New York run and then played in Chicago. What impact it had on U.S. culture is hard to discern. Yet, in examining some of the ads for the play, one can begin to see a theme that will recur throughout early zombie fiction: a white woman is being threatened by a black figure with arms outstretched. The zombie threat to the white woman became an almost universal theme in early zombie fiction, and even as zombies moved out of Haiti, the image of the white woman endangered by a zombie would remain.

Examining race in early horror films, Elizabeth Young has noted, "In the racist iconography that sustained such [stereotypes], the most common cultural image was that of a black man, 'a monstrous beast, crazed with lust,' assaulting a white woman."[22] Both black men and white women were imprisoned in sexual stereotypes as a means of controlling them. Thus early zombie films used the Other as a means of knowing and defining the white self, while allowing the white female to be corrupted by that Other to show exactly what harm mixing with the Other could cause. Yet these films rarely were so overt as to cast a black man as the corrupting force and the white woman as susceptible to his advances; rather, black zombies were often background and filler, and it was the "black" magic of Haitian Voodoo, utilized by zombie masters, that openly threatened white femininity. Thus, without being explicit, these films managed to use the zombification of the white woman to speak to fears of miscegenation. But *Zombie* and the zombie fiction that would follow postulated that there was a solution to the zombie problem, that things could be returned to normal. The white male could defeat black "corruption"; the white female could be saved.

Many of the ads for the first feature-length zombie film, *White Zombie* (1932), were similar to those for *Zombie*: A white woman reclines in peril, either from zombies or the zombie master. In many of these ads, it is the zombie master's (sexual) desire that puts the woman in peril, and she is powerless against it. For instance, in one ad, under ominous eyes, text read, "With these zombie eyes he rendered her powerless . . . ," while under hands clasped together, the text warned, "With this zombie grip he made her perform his every desire!" Another ad contained the tagline "She was not ALIVE . . . nor DEAD . . . just a WHITE ZOMBIE . . . performing his every desire!"[23] White slavery became an implicit undercurrent in the film's advertising.

As long as zombification was connected to Haiti or other foreign lands and was performed only on Haitians or other people of color, it could be dismissed as something primitive, so the implication of zombifying a white woman had several dimensions. First, it implied that a primitive nature lurked inside the civilized white person: the zombie inhabited a space in which the white person feared there was no difference between him and the Other, that he was really dark, or primitive, at heart. As previously mentioned, it also spoke to fears of miscegenation. In an era when interracial coupling was still largely prohibited, or at least strongly frowned upon, there was a sense that zombification could represent the intermingling of "black" magic and white bodies. Finally, it implicated the female: primitivism might be associated with one's gender. To borrow from Freud, women might really be "the dark continent."[24]

Here, we see that as traditional Other-ing breaks down in one sense, a new form of Other-ing takes its place. Whereas under colonialism the boundaries between self and Other, black and white, civilized person and cannibal, seemed sharply defined,[25] at this point that sharpness began to blur. In zombifying white people, in essence turning them into slaves and corrupting them with black magic, *White Zombie* begins to ask: How does one define the Other if the Other looks just like you or me? Things hadn't quite reached a point of blurring whereby the Other and the self became largely indistinguishable, but there were traces of anxiety that perhaps the self (at least in the form of the female) was not so different from the Other.

In *White Zombie*, the female succumbs to the powers of black magic, prompting the question: What does it say about the white woman, that bastion of civilization, if she can so easily be corrupted by zombification? The idea that the white female zombie somehow represents that which is both black and white implicitly spoke to fears of miscegenation that were rather explicitly dealt with in *White Zombie*: When it becomes clear that Madeline, the zombified white heroine of the film, is not in her grave as her friends thought she was, Neil, her distraught fiancé, remarks, "Surely you don't think she's alive, in the hands of natives. Oh no! Better dead than that!"[26] Thus it is better for a white woman to be destroyed than to intermix with the "natives."

Of course, zombification also created a situation in which victims of a zombie master were feminized. Typically, under patriarchal systems, the female is under the power of the male—she is supposed to be ready to serve his will. This relationship is replayed with zombie masters and their zombies.[27] Still, this would be complicated in most zombie films, as white men also eventually fell prey to zombie masters. Yet these same white men were usually the only ones with the power to reverse the effects of zombification and defeat the zombie master.

While zombiism seemed to strip those afflicted of their humanity, white males, in being able to overcome zombification, retained their humanity, or at least regained it—and this is key. In the opening scene of *White Zombie*, a group of pale figures lumber toward the road where a coach has stopped; the coachman spies them, then spurs his horses into action, yelling "Zombies!" As he later helps his two passengers from the coach, he explains his haste in leaving the earlier scene: "They are not men, monsieur," he says. "They are dead bodies. Zombies! The living dead. Corpses taken from their graves and made to work in the sugar mills and fields at night." Here, we get to the very heart of zombies: They are not men.

In one phrase, the coachman has summarized one possible reason the zombie fascinated 1930s America: it cast an entire group of people as beings without humanity.[28] It reduced them to an animalistic state and fantasized that these beings could then be made to work endless hours, supplying the rest of the world's needs. It represented the ultimate Othering, casting the perceived opposite as a nonentity. Soon after this scene, the zombies are seen working in a sugar mill. Following Seabrook's descriptions, these zombies silently shuffle through the Haitian night, and in perhaps the most chilling moment of the film, one accidentally falls into the sugar grinder, eliciting no response from his fellow zombies as he is ground to death: life is cheap on the sugar plantation.

David Skal writes, "The shuffling spectacle of the walking dead in films like *White Zombie* (1932) was in many ways a nightmare vision of a breadline. . . . Millions already knew that they were no longer completely in control of their lives; the economic strings were being pulled by faceless, frightening forces."[29] Thus, while zombies seem to represent a very real fear of the return of the colonial master, they also offer a critique of both slavery and the abuse of the worker under the capitalist system. Yet, while the zombie could thus be seen as a critique of empire, zombie films also replayed a fantasy of empire. For example, zombifying white people was a very literal reenactment of what happened in Haiti during the revolution when the colonial masters were overthrown and at the mercy of their former slaves. But early zombie fiction postulated a solution to the zombie "problem." In the end, the zombie master would be defeated (and his zombies with him) and the status quo restored: black Voodoo was no match for white reason. Thus *White Zombie* and much of the zombie fiction that would follow implicitly asserted the need to reimpose control over Haitians and the rest of the colonies.

This may have been very resonant with some audiences of the 1930s. At the turn of the twentieth century, socioeconomic changes preceding from industrialization and increasing immigration had marked a perceptible change in the face of the United States, so much so that some white peoples could have seen this change as a threat to the racial purity of the nation. By the 1920s and 1930s, African Americans had been moving to the industrialized North in large enough numbers that similar perceptions of a threat arose, which were exacerbated by the Depression. Films like *White Zombie* may have provided a fantasy of reclaiming a sense of white control over society.

This need to reclaim control was a current throughout early zombie films. For instance, the 1935 film *Ouanaga*[30] follows a Haitian Voodoo priestess in her attempt to win the love of a white man. The priestess is a mulatto, and with a tag line that claims, "Her skin is white but her heart is black," the film speaks to fears implicitly addressed in *White Zombie* related to miscegenation and the possibility of the primitive lurking within. Of course, this film is much more explicit in placing primitivism in the female body, yet here it is not the body of the white woman that is used; rather, it is the body of a mulatto woman that is inherently wicked because she has a "black" heart. This is why she uses evil spells to corrupt both a white woman and a white man. But the white man will defeat the priestess and free his (white) love. Although this film is one of only a handful to use a female zombie master, as the priestess uses two black male zombies to abduct her rival, the film falls back on a visual trope seen in much of the *Zombie* and *White Zombie* advertising: the white female in peril from the black male zombie.

The Halperin brothers, producers of *White Zombie*, returned to the genre in 1936 with *Revolt of the Zombies*. The plot of the film centers on eliminating a zombie spell so it won't fall into the wrong (nonwhite) hands. Things are fine as long as zombiism only affects the natives, but it is clearly not acceptable when the zombie master begins to zombify the white members of an archaeological expedition.[31] *Revolt of the Zombies* capitalized on the idea of a "zombie army," and the film implied that these zombie masses, if in the control of the wrong people, could present the world with a serious threat. That this film was released just prior to World War II would seem to indicate that there were certain groups (perhaps the

Nazis or the Japanese?) who could use the power to zombify against white America even if they didn't succeed in zombifying white peoples.[32]

The next major American film to feature zombies was 1940's *The Ghost Breakers*, starring Paulette Goddard and Bob Hope. This film transported Voodoo and zombies to Cuba, where Goddard's character inherited a haunted castle guarded by "an old Negro woman with a zombie son."[33] When Bob Hope asks a native Cuban what zombies are, the man answers: "Yes, that's more Voodooism, and not very pleasant. When a person dies and is buried, it seems there are certain Voodoo priests who have the power to bring him back to life." This is met by the exclamation, "How horrible!," to which the man continues: "It's worse than horrible because a zombie has no will of his own. You see them sometimes, walking around blindly with dead eyes. Following orders. Not knowing what they do. Not caring."

Zombies, according to this definition, don't realize what they are doing; they are pawns in someone else's game, and this reinforces the idea of some sort of outside control over zombies. In earlier depictions of Haiti, when the Voodoo-cannibalism duality was being used to describe the nation, Voodoo was something under almost exclusive Haitian control. It didn't operate as effectively (according to outside observers) under the French, and it was hoped that it wouldn't operate as effectively under some other outside civilizing force. Here, though, with the Voodoo-zombie combination, there is the idea that a malevolent practice once used by Haitians on Haitians, then used by Haitians (or other people of color) on Haitians and white peoples, could now be used by unscrupulous groups of any race or belief system on peoples of color to work against American interests. The Other becomes split into two forms: it can be the Other who holds some form of power, or the Other who is used by that power holder.

The lone zombie seen in *The Ghost Breakers* is simply one more character haunting Goddard's castle.[34] But the film is intriguing in that it suggests that the ghosts haunting Goddard's castle and the malignant Voodoo practices associated with it have to do with a slaveholding legacy: at least one character asserts that Goddard's castle is haunted in revenge for Goddard's great-grandfather being the largest slaveholder in Cuba.[35]

The Zombie Codified, Then Changed

By the early 1940s, zombies were becoming a somewhat familiar concept.[36] Conventions within the genre began to become evident. For instance, zombies were under the control of a physically locatable outside force. In the early films, this control came via a Voodoo priest or sorcerer. During the 1950s, when fears connected to burgeoning space exploration became more prevalent, zombie control was also via mad scientists or aliens. Still, zombies never acted of their own accord: there was always some sort of zombie master pulling the strings.[37]

At a very basic level, the lure of the zombie was an idea of the exotic. Many zombie films during this period were set in foreign lands (e.g., Haiti, Cambodia, Cuba, Africa, the West Indies), and even the zombie fiction set in the United States tended to be located in exotic spaces, like carnivals or the Louisiana bayous. Joseph Maddrey, in analyzing reactions to Tod Browning's 1932 film *Freaks*, notes that the strong reactions to that film were due in part to the fact that "audiences were unable to dismiss the horrors as eccentricities of backward countries across the globe."[38] In this light, zombies of the early period could be read as "safe" monsters, fueling a fear of the Other while also implying that when compared to it, people in the United States were normal. If the cannibal had been used during much of the nineteenth century as a means of separating the world into civilized and non-civilized, the zombie was continuing this work in films of the 1930s, '40s, '50s, and '60s.

Although most of the zombie films from 1932 to 1968 share similarities, probably the most defining characteristic of the zombie genre was its mutability. Unlike other creatures of the undead, like Dracula or Frankenstein's monster, the zombie was not born of a preexisting literary tradition. As Peter Dendle notes, the zombie was "one of the few screen creatures in the Hollywood menagerie not of European origin."[39] He also observes that the zombie moved from folklore to film without much other mediation.[40] In other words, there were no strong preexisting mythologies connected to the zombie in the United States—no rules or conventions with which U.S. audiences would have been familiar. As S. S. Prawer further notes in *Caligari's Children*, "This has . . . so rapidly become a genre, has so rapidly established conventions and expectations, that gifted film makers have been able to use the conventions as a kind of grid against which to draw their own rather different pictures—as something to be at once alluded to and subverted."[41] What zombie conventions there were could be considered more like guidelines than fixed rules. Therefore, there was room to play.

For instance, whether zombies were reanimated corpses or merely hypnotized or drugged persons varied. In some films, like *Plan 9 from Outer Space* (1958) or *Bowery at Midnight* (1942), having the dead return to life was crucial to the plot. In other films, like *King of the Zombies* (1941) or *The Incredibly Strange Creatures Who Stopped Living and Became Mixed-Up Zombies* (1964), the zombies weren't dead but rather living people under mind control. How a person was zombified also varied: from the beginning, drugs and potions were a popular choice; hypnotism, spells, and special alien powers were also used to create zombies. Generally, however, the effects were the same: the human being lost control of his body and was directed to work for the will of another.

Yet this changed in 1968 with *Night of the Living Dead*. The established ability to play with the rules of the zombie genre may have contributed to the radical break with the Voodoo-style zombie enacted by *Night of the Living Dead*, as with it, zombies moved from being automatons used as slave labor to being mindless killers.[42] Now, rather than following the will of a specific master, zombies were following the drive to eat. They were now explicitly cannibals.

From Cannibal to Zombie and Back Again

Operating within a system that assumed a knowable world and that fed on an impulse to categorize and classify, the Other was created. At first, this Other was the primitive, the savage, or the cannibal, but over time the Other became a monster. It is no coincidence that Dracula, Frankenstein's monster, and the zombie all became popular movie monsters at roughly the same time. With each variation, American audiences could say, "I am what the Other is not." Yet the zombie consistently presented the further fantasy of being tainted by the Other but then being saved. Zombiism, as it was first presented to U.S. audiences, was not a disease, nor was it irreversible; it was a state, not unlike being under hypnosis, that could be experienced and then abandoned, and most often, with the death or defeat of the zombie master, all the zombies the master controlled awoke from the spell.[43]

Whereas cannibalism was the symbol of Haitian regression to the primitive in the United States's pre-zombie imaginings of Haiti and Voodoo, it was contained and remained well within Haitian borders. Zombies hinted that Voodoo could corrupt those outside Haiti as well. And yet, while at one level the zombie represents a separation from the cannibal in regard to how people in the United States were thinking about Haiti, Voodoo, and the Other, the concept of cannibalism was still present in early zombie films.[44] It wasn't the literal cannibalism of the earliest discourse surrounding Haitian Voodoo, but rather a cannibalism in which those notions one held to be true, the very mechanisms that one used for defining the self, were slowly eaten away: if an average, ordinary American could become a zombie, just like the Haitians did, what really differentiated "us" from "them" anyway? Further, the zombie did the same kind of ideological work as the cannibal—it was a new means of separating the world into its civilized and barbaric categories.

Early zombie fiction might also invite links to bell hooks's concept of eating the Other, the one-way consumption of other cultures. hooks states, "It is by eating the Other that one asserts power and privilege," and this sort of "cultural cannibalism" concerns power relations that grant white peoples the ability to enjoy the privilege of being able to appropriate, utilize, and borrow from other cultures without having to experience what it is actually like to be a member of another culture.[45] In a sense, it is being able to try on other cultural forms at will with no real lasting effect. This is very similar to what characters were able to do in early zombie films. Before 1968, zombiism was a reversible state that could be experienced then discarded. In a sense, zombification granted one the ability to try on the culture of the Other without any real fear that one would truly become like the Other. It allowed one to have all of the pleasures associated with being the Other without any of the frustrations. Thus it was a slice of Haitian exoticism (and later, exoticism in general) that allowed one to get rid of the veneer of white "civilization" temporarily but postulated that eventually the status quo would be restored.

But what constituted the Other became more and more confused as the zombie matured, leaving more and more room for skepticism as to what constituted the self. Zombies stopped being exclusively Haitian and became the province of any exotic group, but as time passed, the zombie's explicit ties to the exotic and the Other were also weakened. Without a clearly recognized Other against which to define the self, it became that much harder to draw the line between "us" and "them."

In *The Philosophy of Horror*, Noël Carroll claims that what creates fear is evidence of "things out of place."[46] Indeed, many of the fears one could associate with zombies have to do with things being out of place in relation to the human body. With very few exceptions, in early zombie fiction, the physical body of a victim of zombification rarely showed any signs of harm; further, the physical changes engendered by zombification were usually not overly dramatic or permanent. It was rather the mind, the embodied self, that was most affected. One's free will was at stake, as it could be devoured at any time, and in this light zombies became an allegory for the larger societal self: the Depression, the world wars, the Cold War, and the atomic age were all potent reminders that people were caught up in events essentially in someone else's control. Zombies reflected a fear of the anarchy or monster inside us all.

As zombies increasingly entered less exotic and much more mundane, white middle-class territory, their effectiveness as the new cannibals was threatened; by the time they came to reside in the rural Pennsylvania countryside with *Night of the Living Dead*, however, cannibalism was coupled with the zombie overtly. The cannibal, as an element of a strange religion called Voodoo, worked to separate the world into "us" and "them." For a time, the zombie, another fantastic element of Voodoo, ostensibly worked to do the same. But over time, the boundaries drawn by the zombie ceased to produce the meaning they once had: any "us" had the potential to become a "them," and new groups began to inhabit the world once solely the province of the racial Other. Yet while conventions became flexible and abstract enough to allow the zombie to become a sort of all-purpose form for mediating a wide range of concerns, it continued to carry its past with it, and that past caught up to the zombie in 1968. With the zombies of *Night of the Living Dead*, cannibalism reentered the picture and could once again work to divide the world into "us" and "them," but this time it would do so overtly tied to the form of the zombie. The zombie needed to become an obvious cannibal if it was going to continue to be put to the same kind of work.

In the end, both cannibalism and the zombie as channeled through Voodoo were an attempt to cast Haitians, and by extension any peoples of color, as less than human. "They are not men," the coachman in *White Zombie* had declared. Yet, over time, it became more and more apparent that the audience secretly feared he could say the same of any of them as well.

CHAPTER 2

"We are the mirror of your fears": Haitian Identity and Zombification

Franck Degoul (translated by Elisabeth M. Lore)

How does the outside world perceive Haiti in light of its practice of zombification, and how does Haiti position itself in relation to this "exteriority" by making use of the way the practice is imagined?[1] These are the questions that will be addressed in this article. Though the group that I designate as the "exteriority" is, of course, variable in nature, the essential relationship in question here will be that which concerns Haiti and the United States. While this relationship appears to write itself into contemporary history, it is the object of numerous representations in various discourses that one encounters in Haiti. Further, it is during the American occupation of Haiti in the first third of the twentieth century that the figure of the Haitian zombie, and with it the "phenomenon" of zombification, enters into quasi-anthropological literature, as well as Hollywood and eventually European cinema. Overflowing the borders of its initial sociocultural context in this way, the mythology of zombification intervened immediately, through the attribution of a system of beliefs and practices, to play a determinant role in how the Haitian reality was regarded.

Because of this, it seems to me judicious to make use of the qualitative inscription "exogenous"—inasmuch as it is a description coming from outside the sociocultural Haitian context—in order to give an account of this image of Haiti, constituted through the interpretive prism that defines zombification and witchcraft as unfailingly linked. Coming from outside its sociocultural space, this association of magical zombification with the "Haitian being"—which is most notably developed in film and literature made about Haiti—encases, in a remarkable manner, the phenomenon within the Haitian context. Yet it is an encasement that, in return, is not without ramifications for the way the practice is thought of and practiced by Haitians.

The term exogenous in question here, in fact corresponds to the notion of the "hetero-image" proposed by Jean-Pierre Jardel,[2] in which he illustrates, in the register of representation of self by Others, the image of the Caribbean constructed by Western authors. In the case of this particular alterity (the relation of the Other and the same), the self-image constructed by others is opposed to the "auto-image," the image of the West Indian constructed by West Indians. The Haitian indigenous movement, born precisely in reaction against the American occupation, tentatively boasts the successful production of an auto-image opposed to the depreciative hetero-image—of Vaudou, and of Haitian folklore—constructed by Westerners under the category of travel writing. Further, Jardel notes that "the Haitian anthropologist E. C. Paul highlighted again, in 1956, the negative influence of the prejudices driven by generations of authors and scholars, prejudices often interiorized by the implicated populations who had been submitted to the process of colonial acculturation, as Roger Bastide has illustrated in several of his works."[3] Therefore, the question that we will address here is not exactly how to understand zombification as it is inscribed within the Haitian context, but rather how to understand its modes of inscription, according to the foreigner, and, in Haiti, in the same context, in response. After reviewing some necessary historical background, we will explore the world of local discourse on the subject, for which I will rely on interview excerpts from some of my Haitian sources.

"Haiti is Vaudou; Vaudou: witchcraft; and witchcraft . . . is zombification": The Exogenous Inscription of Zombification in the Haitian Sociocultural Context

In the years that followed its declaration of independence in 1804, the Republic of Haiti found itself quickly exhausted by an exorbitant colonial debt demanded by France in compensation for the losses, notably of slaves, suffered by the colonists, and asked for as a demonstration of the nascent country's gratitude. The loans incurred from sources both inside and outside the country were necessary to recover, but they weakened the young economy considerably over the following century. In 1913, the inhabitants of the North (the "Cacos") demanded a reduction in the cost of living and more regulation of social justice (following the unexpected, massive expropriation of land from 1911 to 1913 for a railroad that was never even mapped out). This led to a revolt that, when added to the chronic political instability and the economic depression, would serve as the pretext for American intervention in Haiti.[4] "If nothing can contest the reality of the pretext that brings the United States to intervene in Haiti," notes André-Marcel d'Ans, "neither can anyone seriously doubt that it is neither more nor less than pretext."[5] As a result, the United States occupied Haiti from 1915 to 1934, securing its hold on Haiti's economy, guiding its politics, and going even so far as modifying the country's constitution to its advantage. The national bank, commerce, industry, the administration, the army: all these sectors would be placed under American control.

During this époque, this type of American intervention was not an isolated incident—far from it. During the first half of the twentieth century (and afterward, as we know), the United States had, in fact, militarily intervened a number of times in Central America and in the Caribbean. They occupied Cuba from 1900 to 1902, intervened there again from 1906 to 1909, as well as from 1912 to 1917; in 1903, they intervened in Panama. As for the Dominican Republic, it was equally the object of several interventions: in 1904, 1911, 1914, and from 1916 to 1924, an eight-year run in which the marines were permanently stationed there. In 1909, it was Honduras's turn. In 1910, and then from 1912 to 1913, diverse military actions took place in Nicaragua that would be repeated from 1922 to 1924, and later, from 1926 to 1933. Veracruz, in Mexico, was occupied for seven months in 1914 before the Americans, represented by General Pershing, penetrated the Mexican territory again in 1946 to "punish" Pancho Villa. Thirty-five years earlier, in 1911, American forces came to exercise pressure on Honduras, Nicaragua, and the Dominican Republic to recover some financial assets for the United States.[6] The Republic of Haiti was occupied from 1915 to 1934, which represents, among all the others, the longest uninterrupted occupation of this period of America's involvement in the Caribbean.

It is with this particular American occupation that the zombie theme first appeared in quasi-anthropological literature. As Charles Najman notes, "It is the American, Seabrook, in his book entitled *The Magic Island*, who gives birth to the legend of zombies."[7] Najman writes that Seabrook speaks of Haiti as a country that

> breathes the spirit of the old, faraway Africa with its myths, terrors, superstitions and its terrified adoration of the forces of nature. A fantasy that stimulates and reinforces the old prejudices of slavery: "black, despotic and cannibalistic," such was the generic definition of the Haitian. The myth of the living dead grew, but it occupied a new function: to justify the "civilization mission" of the United States in Haiti. Until this time, in fact, practically no author had spoken about zombies. With Seabrook's book, the living dead became, sadly, celebrated across the United States and Europe.[8]

Let us not forget the story of Ti-Joseph the Zombi Maker that was mentioned numerous times in Najman's study, and which was taken from Seabrook's work.

Not long after the book's appearance, the first film adaptation of the zombie theme was born. In the book, Seabrook recounted the story of "Ti-Joseph," and, in 1932, the film *White Zombie* came out in which "the bulging eyes under his black mask, the master of zombies transformed a young American into a living-dead girl. . . . The zombie theme entered Hollywood never to leave again."[9] Haiti is thus instantiated as a country of Vaudou, sacrifices, and barbarism in this representation of the black sorcerer and the young white female that he chooses as his victim, who "needs to be saved from zombification in order that she not be assaulted by racially impure hands."[10] The American imagination appropriates, then, a theme that issued from the Haitian imagination, racializes and eroticizes it, all the while associating it in quasi-symbolic fashion with the Haitian situation, with Negro Haitianness more broadly, as marked by witchcraft. But the phenomenon had already been at work for several years, as Najman reveals: "The Haitian zombie knew, from the beginning of the 20th century, a 'global success.' The great powers, which had never accepted the birth of the completely new black republic, would instantly associate Vaudou and witchcraft before making the zombie the incarnation of the 'bad Haitian.'"[11]

In 1943, as Lizbeth Paravisini-Gebert tells us, Hollywood returned to the zombie theme with the film *I Walked with a Zombie*, which, despite its confessed ambition to be more "historical," putting into perspective the tragic slave history of the fictive island (San Sebastián) where the plot is set, nonetheless maintains this racial white/black division and continues to identify Négritude with "Vaudou," and Vaudou with "what is half-incomprehensible, half-frightening."[12] We can see more clearly, then, what role zombification, and its association with Vaudou, plays in the relationship maintained between the United States and Haiti. According to an interactionist lecture inspired by the works and concepts of Fredrik Barth,[13] we can say that it serves as a sort of indicator and differentiator of culture, but also, and above all, of race—in that these cultural traits are, as I have said, racialized, for their basis is more located in nature than in culture. In this interplay of Same and Other, which can be reduced to the interplay between us and them, the practice of zombification (attributed, fantasized, generalized) constitutes a fundamental sign of distinction between Americans—of white race, the possessors of civilization—and Haitians—of African origin, bloodthirsty barbarians. Vaudou practices and zombification, from the etic point of view of the outside observer who disregards his own interactive intervention in the construction, insist therefore on the substantial difference of the nature of the Haitian Other.

This process, moreover, is coupled with another ideological mechanism. As the anthropologist Paul Farmer points out, we distinguish in these negative representations of the Other, in political discourses as well as in literary and cinematographic expression, a process of "blaming the victim":

> The artisans of the American occupation barely try to hide their widely shared feelings: the country's problems came, in reality, from the fact that blacks were incapable of governing themselves. Robert Lansing, American Secretary of State, wrote in 1918, "The experience of Liberia and Haiti shows that the African races are devoid of any capacity for political organization and lack genius for government." The American occupation was brutal and shamelessly racist; since then, the way of doing things has changed; we have updated the victim-accusation process.[14]

In 1919, adds Najman, "the American propaganda doubled in intensity. In *Black Bagdad*, Craige tries to explain Haiti's history since its independence through its witchcraft practices. Vaudou is a superstition, a neurosis, hysteria, and collective epilepsy similar to the 'Dark Africa' of which the peasants were not yet delivered."[15] While Seabrook's work had not yet been published, the framework in which the zombification motif would be ensconced was most certainly already established: Haiti, a Negro country, was characterized by its barbarism and its inhumane and bloodthirsty witchcraft practices. Zombification would be, from this point on, situated and inscribed in the Haitian context as a symbol of the congenital obscurantism that reigned supreme, and as a sign of the Negro atavism that pushed the Haitian to cruelty, as revelatory of his incapacity to access the "civilization," to which, at the time, the Americans were trying to guide him. This exogenous instantiation of zombification in the Haitian context thus operated by a systematic and general classification of a practice conceived of as inherent and indicative. The imagination, which is at the source of the expression of this theme, is not taken in account, or rather, is taken literally, "realized," made real, tacked on to the Haitian reality as if it were intrinsically linked to the Haitian. Haiti: it is Vaudou; Vaudou: witchcraft; and witchcraft . . . zombification.

But we can ask what were, and what could still be, the repercussions of this exogenous ascription for certain Haitian representations of zombification. For, as I suggested earlier, it seems to me that the latter representations, in turn, were not without effects on the endogenous discourses concerning the relationship between Haiti and the United States. The American occupation at the beginning of the last century had direct repercussions on the imagination of zombification. This "practice" thus becomes a central issue, inscribed right at the heart of representations of this relationship.

The Instantiation of Zombification within the Domain Defining Collective Haitian Identity

> Colbert: At the time of the American occupation . . . well, there was an old saying, an old story saying that the first general or colonel—I don't know—who had walked on the soil still works at Léogâne, in the sugar fields. . . . That's why those whites there fear our country.[16]

Haiti had been occupied, but it defended itself by means of zombification, a practice that scared the "blancs"—that is to say, in the Haitian sense of the term, the "outsiders." This anecdote is conjoined to the very principle of "occupation," testifying that one of the first generals of the American army to have walked on Haitian soil was transformed into a zombie. This first step onto Haitian soil becomes a symbol of the sudden emergence of whites in the affairs of the first black republic in the world, and a symbol of this violation of its sovereignty. Everything continues as if the fear of zombification displayed in North American literature and cinema had been confirmed in Haiti, legitimated by an affirmation of the reality of the object of terror. Americans fear zombification, express it in all sorts of mediums, and are right to perceive the object of their fear in this way: zombification is precisely that which escapes them, and which simultaneously constitutes Haiti's mysterious power amid the neocolonial effort by which the North American hegemony had attempted to establish itself. We have, then, in this matter, a certain representation of a particular period of history and of the power relations that were inscribed at the heart of the relationship between Haiti and the foreign American force of the époque; the representation continues to mobilize zombification as a vehicle to metaphorize the character of Haiti's relationships to the outside world.

In fact, even today, or at the very least in the framework of contemporary history, this tense relationship between Haiti and the United States persists at the political and economic level. Further, a similar relationship also exists between Haiti and the Dominican Republic. In this second case, it is notably a question of both official and clandestine immigration to the neighboring nation, for the purposes of economic gain, that is at the center of the tension: not a month passes in which the Dominican border police do not shoot down several immigrants who hope to "seek a living," as they say in Haiti, on the other side of the border, which never fails to inflame Haitian public opinion. But there is more, because to this source of antagonism is added another that bears witness to the imagination of zombification as it is studied here. Jean-Marie Théodat reminds us, "In the respective collective memories of the two groups, the neighboring country continues to be comprehended through a prism of old clichés. . . . There is, from Haiti's point of view, especially since the dissolution of the army in 1995, the specter of a plot of invasion and occupation to be orchestrated by the Dominican Republic."[17]

Certain representations confirm this even further. We must recognize that the situation is conducive to the development and perpetuation of stereotypes and of diverse mutual fears. Are we not dealing with, as the aforementioned author highlights, two nations sharing an insular territory, or two identities separated by a border and yet coexisting in a common, encompassing, inclusive space?[18] Throughout history, this coexistence has not always been peaceful: troops from the newly formed Haitian republic invaded and annexed the eastern part of the island, which they occupied from 1822 to 1844; in 1937, the dictator Leónidas Trujillo ordered the massacre of tens of thousands of Haitians, which constituted three-quarters of the agricultural workforce in the Dominican Republic at the time, even while exportations of sugar and rum were essential elements of the national economy. The reasons: fear of territorial invasion, and "explosively sensitive exchanges [with the other nation] concerning the implied risks of racial impurities,"[19] such as those that were produced at

Haitian Identity and Zombification 31

the time. As a result, "contention lives on in the collective memory of the two peoples."[20]

Thus it is inadvisable to neglect this major dimension of the problem, concerning Haiti's position among surrounding fields of power—be they political, economic, or geopolitical. Set between the Dominican Republic (rich, touristy, and supported by the United States) and Cuba (with its Castro supporters, and so near the American superpower), Haiti (one of the poorest countries in the world, and the poorest in the Caribbean) finds itself at the very center of a sort of triangulation that explains a number of facts of recent postcolonial history. The Haitian imagination takes note of these forces and makes an account of them, notably through the prism that constitutes zombification, which is considered, as a practice, a privileged marker of Haitianness:

> Colbert: Dominicans are afraid of us: It is for this reason [zombification]. You haven't seen the video of Koudjay [a Haitian "roots" musical group]? The video from last year? (I say no. He begins to sing.) "Nap tann yo! Mwen tandé Sendomeng ap vin okipé nou! Mwen di yo: la yé! Nap tann yo."[21] You see, and then in the video we see a Dominican who (armed, demonstrating his power) is armed, and then the Haitian holds in his hand (mimes a powder that he blows in this person's direction, who is clearly a soldier).
> Q: And the other one becomes a zombie? Is that right?
> Colbert: Yes! Yes! It is a reality; they are afraid of us!
> Q: And in the words of the song, what does it say? "We are waiting for you," right?
> Colbert: "We are waiting for you!" Yes. "We are waiting for you!" "Keep your armored tanks and your weapons . . . we are waiting for you." At the same time, when the Americans penetrated Haitian soil, in 1994, it was us who had invited them. It was the people who had invited them. If this had not been the case, they couldn't have. . . . It was the country's power that had invited them . . . if it hadn't been for that, they wouldn't have been able to do it. Because . . . we have Vaudou . . . we have devils.

Concerning the connection to the United States, the following fragment from Claudel[22] offers us a new illustration of the idea that, although penniless and deprived of military strength, the Haitian nation knows how to defend itself by using distinctively characteristic means that strike fear into the hearts of other nations: the principle of zombification and its "powders": "Americans make weapons, but us, our weapon is the principle of zombification! In the same way, if we cannot zombify you, if we see that we cannot zombify you, we'll try another route that we call 'pyès,' that we call 'powders.'"

If the North American chroniclers of the first years of the occupation established zombification as an emblem of Negro Haitian savagery, this same zombification is equally associated in Haiti by drawing the same connection, but in a way that, in fact, reverses the terms of discourse. Positively reappropriated, this allocation of practices conditions an affirmation of Haitian power that, simultaneously, protects Haiti from the iniquity of all involuntary occupation of its soil and imposes respect for its sovereignty outside its natural borders—all by means of the fear that zombification instills. It is by these means that the Americans were able to land in 1994 to reinstate President Jean-Bertrand Aristide to power while evicting the dictator Raoul Cédras—whom they would, however, continue to support secretly—for the good reason that the people of Haiti demanded it. Had popular opinion opposed the intervention, the Americans would not have been able, in any way, to intervene in Haitian business and disembark on the soil as they did. This secret, free weapon derived from a strictly Haitian knowledge, zombification, could have been employed in battle and used to chase the invaders. In a like manner, Vaudou, in general, could be used defensively:

> Fène: We ourselves fight with our mysterious "blacks" and with our red handkerchiefs. You can possess weapons, big guns, but us, we have, between our hands, our red handkerchief! . . .
> Q: So, if I understand correctly, even if Haiti no longer has an army . . .
> Fène: No, but we have an army! We have an army! Vaudou is the army! We kill people without batons, without pistols, without rifles! . . . It is inevitable. Vaudou is the only richness that we have.
> Q: You don't see any other richness for Haiti?
> Fène: We have nothing else! Moreover, we occupied the Dominican Republic for a long time, for nineteen years, and now they want to occupy Haiti today in return! But they are afraid of Vaudou. It is Vaudou they fear, because if not, they are afraid of nothing: They possess weapons and everything else needed to declare war, enter Haiti, and invade us. But Vaudou, how do you fight against that?

It is thus that we must regard zombification, as it can be interpreted in Haiti, as a cultural trait used by certain Haitians to mark a fundamental difference between Haiti and the surrounding nations with whom it has, or has had in the past, less peaceable relations, as in the cases with the Dominican Republic and the United States. As a "cultural marker"—to use a term borrowed from Barth[23]—the zombification practice acquires, in this context, the value of a manifest sign that the agents exhibit as a component of their identity: a sign of Haitianness dependent on a witchcraft arsenal, which, first and foremost, includes transforming individuals into zombies. As Barth explains, the conscious separation between "us" and "them" can emerge only if there is interaction in a common social context. The American occupation, of which traces persist in the collective memory, established such an interaction—although an unequal one. To this, we can add a contemporary "common context"—different, but less problematic—the one that the Haitians of the "diaspora" share with members of their host societies in Miami, New York, Montréal, or Paris. Many stories describe recourse to the zombificatory practice undertaken abroad, at the heart of these great megalopolises, where a good number of Haitians often suffer exploitation of all types, most notably in their salaries. In these stories, zombification often occurs in situations that address conflict between Haitians over employment or competition for a job. But a number of others also use this practice to help Haitian victims of injustice (real or declared) at the hand of their "blanc" employer, who invariably becomes a zombie in the end.

As for the situation with the neighboring Dominican Republic, with which there already exists a passive history, the social context is mostly produced in a unique way: one that involves Haitian travelers, clandestine or official, who come by the thousands to "Dominicanie" to harvest sugarcane, and who are often subjected to scorn from the local population. Many Dominicans still maintain outmoded racist and xenophobic sentiments in opposition to these "followers of barbaric cults," these "representatives of an inferior race," who are "bloodthirsty and with loose morals."[24] How, in the face of the United States and Dominican Republic—who absorb their workforce, using up their resources while belittling them, often simultaneously—can the Haitians defend themselves and affirm their identity, even though they no longer have an army and even while the rhetoric of invasion/occupation (be it past or future, American or Dominican) endures? Because of Vaudou and zombification, the people have a means of representing themselves.

Zombification, from the outside observer's point of view and as a cultural practice, demonstrated Haitian barbarism and, simultaneously, served as a deep founding anchor at the heart of this relationship, establishing the racial and cultural difference of the Haitian people. The presentation of this vision to the entire world, notably through means of the cinema, returned it, in the end, to the context from which it had been taken—that is to say, back to Haiti. There, by a display of positive reappropriation, what had been an outside indicator becomes an inside marker: not a marker of Haitian barbarism, but rather of Haitianness, relying simultaneously on a knowledge of witchcraft that is completely Haitian and jealously protected—the knowledge that gives one the power to turn an individual into a zombie—and the related power to put this knowledge into practice, particularly if Haiti were to be invaded or occupied. By this interactive process, what had been a depreciative trait abroad became, within Haitian society, and in relation to other nations, a valorizing sign of Haitianness: its secret weapon envied by all the researchers of the world who have tried to penetrate its secret.

The Exogenous Production of Knowledge about Vaudou and Zombification as a Threat to the Haitian Nation

In effect, zombification is represented as the fruit of a jealously guarded secret knowledge. This is what we come to understand from the following quote, which explains that, under a more recent and more peaceable form, the strategic mobilization of zombification evidenced in the imaginary is likewise incarnated in fields relating to knowledge and power. The occupation in question is no longer at the political-military level, but is here raised to the level of knowledge—the knowledge of zombification as it was researched by the Americans in an attempt to reconstitute it. The following story, collected in the countryside of Haiti, tells of a curious student who had come from the United States—all this was explained to me in the discussions that took place after the story's narration—and met a "bôkô" (sorcerer):

> He was a curious person who had come to Haiti, wanting some facts—just like you! (laughter) . . . about zombification. And someone told me that this guy went to see a bôkô, and then, well, he offered him money for a demonstration of zombification. The "oungan" [Vaudou priest] asked him if he wanted to experience the zombification himself. So he answered, "Okay, no problem. I simply want to know exactly what it entails. I really want to know what zombification is." And then he paid a portion of the fee for the experience, and then fully accepted the fact that the demonstration would be performed on his person. And then, indeed, I'm not sure how they proceeded—if it was by means of a powder, if it was done with a powder, or if by . . . anyway, some sort of ritual, I don't know—but actually the foreigner had been . . . was found dead! And then after some time, well, the oungan brought him back to life, and then afterward, he paid the rest of his

fee, and then . . . but, he said that it was a terrible experience, that he would never want to do it again! (laughter) He felt a need to leave right away! (laughter) Maybe, he had some sort of pain, I don't know exactly![25]

If our student/seeker did not succeed in exposing the secret of zombification, he, at the very least, succeeded in paying the price of observing the real existence of the practice. The moral of the story is that a sly, crafty bôkô will always be a sly, crafty bôkô, and that, moreover, his powers are truly effective: he grew rich at the expense of a young guinea pig who can no longer deny that zombification exists. The student/seeker's trip to Haiti was exclusively motivated by the production of a knowledge that clearly established a serious issue at the local level—the possibility of an underground Haitian power existing among the forces that had been delimited from above. Also, has not the bôkô acted in a way that adapts this power relationship in a manner that exemplifies the Foucauldian knowledge/power dynamic? Is not all knowledge produced abroad about the making of zombies operating under the conditions of power as they are defined "elsewhere"—by American definitions of power in this case, which are imposed on Haiti? In demonstrating the effectiveness of this practice—by a demonstration of force—and without revealing the secret, the bôkô of the story affirms a Haitian supremacy, all the while protecting this supremacy from its possible annihilation by the "Other," non-Haitian, with whom, by means of intervention, Haiti experiences constant conflict and tension. The American political-military occupation occasioned, moreover, from the point of view of their narrative structure and driving message, the production of similar accounts. Jean Kerboull tells us one of them, collected during the 1970s from one of his sources:

> "Have there been any foreign witnesses to these metamorphoses?," someone will say incredulously, like Fontenelle. A Haitian student verified this for me. He tells the story of his father, an upstanding gentleman who never tells it himself. The critical witness is a marine, a sergeant of American brigades sent to occupy Haiti. Around 1920, in Grand-Goâve, in the Western district, the non-commissioned officer makes a bet with a Vaudou priest that he cannot transform men into cattle before his very eyes. High stakes . . . guards bring into the public square four prisoners of common law, recognizable by their black-and-white striped uniforms. The priest holds his sacred staff in his hand. He begins to come to life . . . enters into a trance, speaks out several incantations, gesticulates. All of a sudden, the marine sees, instead of the four guinea-pig prisoners, four magnificent bulls that begin to bellow lamentably, snouts aimed to the heavens! . . . The American is disconcerted, struck dumb, and the oungan pockets his money.[26]

Replace this soldier with a researcher, the period of occupation with today, zoomorphic powers with the practice of zombification through secret knowledge, the financial loss with an issue no less negative, but this one physiologically and mentally damaging, and we see that these two stories share a common structure and identical discursive impact. In each of these stories, the Other, the foreigner, enters into the domain of Haitian magical knowledge and witchcraft, which he wants to experience and benefit from. Sure of themselves, the solicited oungans succeed in demonstrating the factual reality of the questioned operations, but all the while keeping secret the arcane mystery of how this is accomplished. Moreover, they benefit from the initial request, pocketing the promised sum of money in exchange for providing the experience. The losers find themselves, in fact, close to, yet not within, this strange, invasive (both literally and figuratively), enviable alterity, which, along with loss and terror, brings proof of the existence of a magical witchcraft power that is uniquely Haitian.

This collective conception relative to the Other, this definition of a particular form of alterity, explains that the anthropological research completed on zombification and Vaudou, as well as the desire demonstrated by certain "blancs" to be initiated in its rites, takes on the quality of suspicious intrusions into the very core of their Haitianness. What have they come to learn? What exactly are they searching for, these foreigners with their tape recorders, notebooks, unceasing questions, sometimes even trying to become an oungan or mambo by lending themselves to the secret rites of passage? Their interference remains suspect in the eyes of collective public opinion:

> Colbert: Those men [the Americans] are very wise. They are very intelligent! Don't forget. They have done a lot of research on zombification and Vaudou in Haiti.
> Madison: There are whites, especially Americans, who come to perform "Kanzo" [who are initiated into Vaudou in order to achieve a certain goal] . . . simply to find out how we "spin"! [become entranced] . . . Because they earn a lot of money with that, yes.
> Q: Because they want to use this technique?
> Madison: Yes. A lot of doctors know how to do it with medicines, but the oungan also know how to do it with plants.

These two excerpts, in their own way, illustrate the point: it doesn't escape anyone that the "whites," the foreigners, and especially the Americans, have been interested in the popular Haitian religion and its magical-religious aspects and elements of sorcery for a very long time; they come to this—to understand, to know, to dominate—by means of strategic "intelligence" or by bribery. Whatever its exact nature, their marked interest in this field of expression, which has become symbolic of the sociocultural Haitian, masks an undeniable desire to seize hold of that which the Haitian national identity is founded on, and which gives it its strength and power. For it is clearly national identity that is at stake in opposing these self-interested alterities, as an audience member at an interview once made clear to me: "To know certain things [concerning zombification], it is necessary to enter into what we call 'Makaya' [the rite]. And when you are a foreigner and you enter into it, you must stay there and not leave. Well, you might make several short visits to your home, but then you must return to that land and no longer leave it. Because it is a matter of a national contract, a national commitment! It is the chiefs, the highest rank of the 'Makaya' society, who possess these secrets."

Entering into this field of knowledge amounts to a "national commitment," a "contract" with the Haitian nation; one gains access to secret knowledge of the practice of zombification, which far exceeds the framework of academic interest, of curiosity about the Other. Whoever finds himself the keeper of the secrets is bound to the very existence of the nation; the knowledge is considered like a secret military, a collection of inherited operations that must not become known by foreign powers. That is why the person initiated in Haiti would forever reside there, in order that he never divulge the precious information that has fallen into his possession. The stakes are national because zombification holds an essential place in this structure constituting a particular form of collective identity. Zombification is Haitian, uniquely Haitian, exclusively Haitian. But do these foundations reveal only a national dimension? "No," explained several of my sources, coupling this aspect with a determinant racial inscription:

> Colbert: There was a woman, an American, she worked at the American consulate: today, she is a mambo, she lives at Cyvadier. . . . But, I don't really believe she possesses all the knowledge necessary.
> Q: Do you believe that in this case . . . what you're trying to say is, that it is a thing rather . . . profoundly Haitian?
> Colbert: Haitian and Negro. That is . . . it's really . . . special: It is Haitian and Negro.

Vaudou, and zombification as a result, is strictly of a Haitian nature, but it is also "Negro." That is why this famous mambo, a white American, whose peristyle is found not far from Jacmel, cannot be a priestess like Haitian women. According to Colbert, only African descendants are capable of practicing Vaudou completely and correctly. This is specifically due to their racial, "Negro" identity; this makes sense in terms of a certain lineage, and, of course, is not lacking historical basis, but this notion has, in addition, a mythical value in this framework. Those who cannot claim ancestry from the old and faraway "Guinea Africa" cannot know how to master perfectly the popular Haitian religion or its associated practices. Based on this point, we understand that it is through this racialization that the cultural practice is elaborated and a border is put in place that restricts access to mastery. The criteria for discrimination and for inclusion/exclusion is not only sought through nationality, but also through the order of "nature," of essence, and of race, which prohibits, by the same token, all "foreign" claims to appropriate the popular Haitian religion.

The effect of such a division on the basis of this racial criteria places Vaudou and zombification, by discursive means, beyond the reach of the white foreigners, to whom is attributed a fundamental, natural incapacity to possess the knowledge required to completely and entirely master those Vaudou practices. Participating in an explicitly racialized Haitianness, these practices, in fact, go beyond their initial signification and, in this discursive context, begin to hold value and meaning as key elements in the creation of a collective Haitian identity—and, finally, in the interaction of macro-social relations between the republic and its surrounding nations, or at least in the manner in which we perceive them.

Finally, then, the hermeneutic reading of stories and interview excerpts contained in the present chapter has led us to highlight a singular mode of inscription of zombification within the Haitian context. This practice, as we have seen, intercedes in Haitian representations of the relationships maintained between Haiti and its surrounding nations. Expressed in the social imagination within a framework that questions a dynamic and communal identity, zombification is used as a cultural marker that establishes Haitianness by means of positive reappropriation, through a "symbolic reversal" of those traits that were previously attributed in an exogenous manner. Zombification, as a symbol of negative Haitianness—an exogenous vision centering on barbarism—is transformed into a symbol of positive Haitianness. This positive Haitianness is an endogenous vision focusing on the national power conferred by zombification and foundational knowledge of the Vaudou religion, as the objects of a particularly vibrant and intense strategy of protection and preservation.

CHAPTER 3

Undead Radio: Zombies and the Living Dead on 1930s and 1940s Radio Drama

Richard Hand

The so-called golden age of live radio drama in the United States from the 1930s to the 1950s may have only been a little more than two decades in duration, but in that relatively short period of time an enormous and remarkable body of work was created.[1] One of the first genres to be established in the broad canon of radio drama was horror. Probably the most famous example of horror radio is *The Mercury Theater on the Air*'s "War of the Worlds" (October 30, 1938). John Houseman and Howard Koch's inventive adaptation of H. G. Wells's *The War of the Worlds* (1898) in a consummate pastiche of live news broadcasting caused panic on the streets ("1.7 million believed it to be authentic news")[2] and a major media and political furor, and yet it was simply designed as a timely Halloween "trick." Orson Welles, the twenty-one-year-old actor-director of the Mercury Theater, announces at the end of the broadcast that the play was simply a "radio version of dressing up in a sheet and jumping out of a bush and saying 'Boo!'": with the benefit of hindsight, a supremely ironic epilogue to the most potent demonstration of the potential of horror radio ever broadcast.

As important as the "War of the Worlds" broadcast remains, it has perhaps unduly eclipsed the broad achievement and sheer quantity of other examples of horror radio. After all, as Martin Grams Jr. explains, in the 1930s it became immediately evident that "radio listeners favored spine-chilling terrors over situation comedies," with the direct consequence that by the late 1940s, "US Radio ... fired at least 80 programs of horror and bloodcurdling adventure at its listeners every week."[3] This prolific body of work represents one of the most fascinating yet woefully neglected areas in the study of popular horror culture. The vast body of horror radio presents an extraordinarily rich and diverse range of plays. Sometimes the horror plays are clichéd or predictable, occasionally they are innovative and audacious, but frequently American horror radio of the 1930s and 1940s presents numerous icons from the broadest spectrum of horror: vampires, werewolves, ghosts, witches, mummies, mad scientists, serial killers, aliens, and monstrous creatures are all brought to life in the listener's mind through narrative, description, and sound effects. The zombie and the living dead are also to be found in the panoply of horror radio, not least in the shows that will, in due course, be analyzed in this chapter.

From the rise of radio broadcasting in the United States in the 1920s, radio became the dominant communication media with unparalleled rapidity. Radio was embraced with extraordinary enthusiasm and soon infused and permeated the living space of its listeners. People lived their lives by the sound of the radio. By the early 1950s, there were around forty-five million households in the United States, forty-three million of which owned radios. Radio was not restricted to the home environment either: as early as 1938 more than four million American cars had radios. The sound of the radio was omnipresent, and indelible moments of U.S. history and identity were forged live on the airwaves: President Franklin D. Roosevelt's "Fireside Chats" between 1933 and 1944 (a daring experiment that would forever change the nature of political broadcasting all over the world), Herbert Morrison's eyewitness account of the *Hindenburg* airship disaster in May 1937, and the boxer Joe Louis's defeat of Max Schmeling in June 1938 are just a few examples of monolithic "radio events."

But it was not just news, sports, and current events that were broadcast "as they happened": all radio broadcasting was live. This was not a technical issue but rather a deliberate strategy on the part of the major networks so that all the voices, music, and sound effects the audience heard were broadcast contemporaneously. In particular, NBC and CBS adopted anti-recording policies to preserve the public perception of live, "factual" broadcasting. Consequently, radio also exploited its "escapist" potential with a similar literal simultaneity. Shows such as the situation comedy

Amos 'n' Andy (1926–60) enjoyed a massive and sustained popularity, the scale of which we struggle to comprehend—at the peak of its popularity in 1931, 53.4 million listeners tuned in to its live episodes each weekday night.[4]

The insatiable demands of the audience and the fiercely competitive nature of the competing radio stations in the pioneering years of network radio led to the creation of many new formats and genres. Not only were many of these subsequently adopted by television, but in fact they remain largely unchanged in the twenty-first century: news and current affairs coverage, political reportage, and sports broadcasting have scarcely changed since radio invented them. Likewise, quiz shows, soap operas, situation comedies, crime drama, and serialized drama were all invented by radio and have changed very little since migrating to television. Of the numerous genres inaugurated by radio, horror and suspense radio was particularly popular.

The first specific horror drama series on radio was Alonzo Deen Cole's groundbreaking *The Witch's Tale*, which was first produced in 1931 and enjoyed several years of great popularity before terminating in 1938. This program marked the beginning of a hugely popular era of horror radio. Each episode of *The Witch's Tale* featured a host called Old Nancy, the Witch of Salem, who, accompanied by her sinisterly mewling cat, Satan (played by Alonzo Deen Cole himself), would provide a sardonic introduction, interlude, and conclusion as a framing narrative to each self-contained play, which ranged from adaptations of popular or obscure Gothic literature to original horror plays. Humor was an extremely important component to Old Nancy's narrative frame, as she would chuckle at her own ironic jokes and take morbid delight in the fate of the benighted victims in her tales. The role and persona of Old Nancy had an immediate impact on copycat horror radio shows, many of which created mordantly humorous character-hosts of their own, but it also cast a long shadow of influence over the history of American popular horror culture, including horror comics from the pre-code era onward (consider EC Comics' Crypt-Keeper, Vault-Keeper, and Old Witch) and television horror show hosts in the 1950s and 1960s (such as Vampira, Zacherley, and Ghoulardi).

The horror shows that followed in the wake of *The Witch's Tale* included programs that used a very similar formula, such as *The Hermit's Cave* (1935–44) with its cackling character-host, the Hermit. But other series proved highly original and distinctive, presenting works of horror radio that range from the knowingly ironic to the genuinely unsettling, and providing stylistic examples from classic storytelling and literary adaptation to unique and innovative experimentation.[5] Particularly noteworthy examples include *Lights Out* (1934–47), *Inner Sanctum Mysteries* (1941–52), *The Mysterious Traveler* (1943–52), and *Quiet, Please* (1947–49). In addition to these shows that specialized in horror, or, as John Dunning says of *Quiet, Please*, "dark fantasy,"[6] there are other programs that ventured into similar territory, albeit on a sporadic basis. Although the long-running series *Suspense* (1942–62) may have predominantly offered hard-boiled crime dramas, a kind of "radio noir," it occasionally presented examples of horror, such as an impressive H. P. Lovecraft adaptation, "The Dunwich Horror" (November 1, 1945), and "The House in Cypress Canyon" (December 5, 1946), a masterful tale of lycanthropy. *Escape* (1947–54) specialized in adventure yarns, including adaptations of Joseph Conrad and Robert Louis Stevenson, but plays such as "Three Skeleton Key" (March 17, 1950), in which a lighthouse is besieged by a plague of giant rats, remain paradigms of audio horror.

Given the huge popularity of horror radio, the pressure placed on creative teams was enormous. Networks competed for the lion's share of listeners—and sponsors—on increasingly packed airwaves. Producers and writers needed to develop distinctive aspects to their particular brand of audio horror as a kind of "trademark" to their show, using the skills of their voice actors, composers and musicians, and sound effects technicians to the fullest degree. In addition, there is only a certain number of times a listener would want to hear yet another adaptation of *Dracula* or *Frankenstein*, so writers and producers were obliged to develop new stories that would hook their listeners enough to hold them for the entire broadcast and encourage them to tune in for a brand-new play the following week. After all, repeats were highly unusual in this era, as only the plays that received exceptional critical or popular approbation were revived for rebroadcasting.[7]

Zombies and the living dead were present on the all-live radio networks, in a variety of guises. In the Himan Brown–produced series *Inner Sanctum Mysteries*, for example, "The Island of Death" (March 13, 1945) is set in Haiti and exploits voodoo myths, including zombies. In this radio play, an American couple, John and Muriel, are traveling in "the secret, magic island Haiti" during a tropical storm, and the husband scornfully dismisses the concept of "voodoo" even when the natives' drums start to pound. When Muriel is drawn into a voodoo ritual, John kills the witch doctor before the ceremony is complete, believing that he has saved her. But soon thereafter he is told that Muriel is dead. He ridicules the idea but a Haitian explains, "Her heart is still beating, yes. But she is not really alive. Her soul left her body." Moreover, no "white doctor" can help her soul return to its rightful place. Drawn into another voodoo ritual, John breaks off the ceremony and flees, taking the still-unconscious Muriel with him. Later that night Muriel awakes in a daze, and shortly afterward she hears the scream of John outside. He is found dead, lying beside the corpse of the witch doctor he had slain. The sardonic host of *Inner Sanctum Mysteries* concludes this tale of soulless zombies and vengeful corpses with characteristic irony: "Now if you should happen to get into an argument with anyone about whether the dead come back from the grave, about goats without horns, black magic, conjuring, whatnot . . . remember the old saying: 'Voodoo to others as you would have them voodoo to you!'"

A few months later, in the *Inner Sanctum Mysteries* episode "The Undead" (December 18, 1945), a woman believes she has married an undead man. Although she comes to believe he is possibly a vampire, what is remarkable is that far from being a Transylvanian or heavily Gothic tale, the play is set in 1940s New York City. Like the best examples of American horror radio of the 1930s and 1940s, the play has great resonance and can be interpreted as a reflection of postwar angst, paranoia, and guilt: a society emerging from a global conflict that had created thousands of war widows or families attempting to readjust to the return of their menfolk.

When it comes to the live radio zombie, in some cases the radio medium dictated that the living dead had a surprising degree of consciousness, with zombies able to think and talk. In other examples, the soundscape is utilized to make the living dead a formidable presence through the sound of their movements or through the reactions of their horrified witnesses or victims. Sometimes the monsters on horror radio are zombies by implication. For example, *The Hermit's Cave*'s "Spirit Vengeance" (no specific broadcast date extant, but circa early 1940s) features a mad scientist conducting evil experiments on lost travelers who stumble into his isolated mansion. The scientist, Professor Rommel Santo,[8] dreams of finding a way to make "the heart beat on forever." A married couple, Mr. and Mrs. Kenton, arrive at Santo's house during a fierce storm, having become lost while trying to visit their recently married daughter and son-in-law at their new village home. Forced to stay the night in Santo's home, Mrs. Kenton hears her daughter eerily call out her name and we realize that Santo has probably used her and her husband as specimens for vivisection. Later, as Santo is about to experiment on his new victims, we hear a door swing open and the undead daughter and husband murder Santo and his evil assistant. Ostensibly, the undead couple, corpses with beating hearts, are the vengeful "spirits" of the title, but the sound of their feet scraping awkwardly across the wooden floor as they creep away to their tomb make it clear that these are living dead zombies, as fetid and decaying as the listener cares, or dares, to imagine. Even if *The Hermit's Cave*'s "Spirit Vengeance" talks of "spirits," its sound effects afford another interpretation, and other horror radio plays are more explicit in their description and audacious in their treatment of the living dead, such as plays produced by *Lights Out*.

Two of the finest living-dead dramas in American horror radio belong to the *Lights Out* repertoire and were both written and produced by Arch Oboler. Curiously, the two plays in question, "Scoop" (December 8, 1942) and "Knock at the Door" (December 15, 1942), were broadcast just a week apart from each other. "Scoop" is set in a newspaper office in which the unscrupulous editor Mr. Bridge callously fires the office clerk Mr. Roberts, who then commits suicide by leaping out the window. The undead Roberts returns from the grave and drags Bridge to his family vault in the cemetery. Inside the tomb, Bridge fully beholds the living dead man, declaring "I can't bear to look at you!" This is hardly surprising:

> Bridge: Roberts, your face!
> Roberts: My coffin was a poor one. Worms and maggots worked quickly . . .
> Bridge: No!
> Roberts: The dead are dead they told me . . .
> Bridge: Stay back!
> Roberts: The dead can't walk they told me . . .
> Bridge: No closer!
> Roberts: The dead can't talk they told me . . .
> Bridge: Stay back!
> Roberts: And yet I walk, I talk . . .
> Bridge: Back!

The undead figure that Arch Oboler creates in his listener's mind is less like the somnambulant creatures of Hollywood's contemporaneous *I Walked with a Zombie* (Val Lewton, 1943) than a precursor to the explicitly decaying living dead in pre-code horror comics or the zombies of the George A. Romero generation of 1968 and beyond.[9] Roberts is driven by a desire for revenge so strong that it made him crawl from the tomb:

> Roberts: There's hate in me now. Hate that wants to tear the eyes that saw only profit . . . from your head . . .
> Bridge: No! Please! I beg of you!

> Roberts: Hate that wants to rip that trapped and pitiful tongue from out your head. Hate that wants to rip the skin from off your flesh . . .
> Bridge: Stop!

Bridge decides he can only evade the undead Roberts by hiding in a coffin and, in a great sequence of audio horror, he becomes trapped and suffocates. The coda to the play offers its listeners a suitably grisly finale. The newspaper staff are impatiently awaiting the editor when they discover a proof sheet has arrived that announces Bridge's suicide, printed on "a piece of human skin."

In the following week's *Lights Out* play, "Knock at the Door," a woman called Ella, who is the narrator of the story, becomes increasingly resentful of her mother-in-law, who wields enormous influence over Jay, her "mommy's boy" husband, who regards his mother as the "greatest woman in the world." Ella eventually pushes her interfering mother-in-law into a disused well that lies in the basement of the house: significantly, prior to the murder Ella thinks the well is a "sewer" (an apt place to dispose of her despised mother-in-law). Jay is distraught and recruits the police to solve the mystery of his disappeared "Momma." It is as Ella is planning the murder of Jay in a similar fashion that the couple hears knocking on the basement door. According to Ella, "Yeah. It was her alright. There she was. Eyes glittering. Dirty gray old hair plastered wet around her face . . . I could see her with my own eyes. She was dead I tell you. Dead. Jay didn't know that. No. He took that dead thing by the arm and he led her into the room. And he sat her down in a chair." Jay is thrilled to see his mother again and asks her where she has been. The mother merely croaks indistinctly in reply: it is a vocal utterance that is meant to match the decaying body that Ella beholds. The next morning the undead mother-in-law has disappeared and Ella races down to the basement to slide the iron manhole cover off the well to see the "big fat" corpse of the mother-in-law floating in the water, thus convincing herself that the evening before was just a nightmare. But when Jay returns home there is a knock on the basement door again, and in creeps the mother-in-law.

Once again, Jay does not notice that his mother is undead. As Ella puts it with suggestive use of ellipsis, "He didn't see her face was . . . uh . . ." and "the water had . . . uh . . ." Ella's halting speech allows the listeners to create the most dreadful picture of reanimated putrefaction in their minds. Jay notices only that his mother is icy cold and decides he needs to fetch the doctor. As he leaves, he tells his wife, "Ella, you take momma right upstairs and put her to bed. Lie down with her. Keep her warm till

I get back." As if this was not appalling enough, tonight the zombie has begun to regain the power of speech, uttering with difficulty, "My son said put me to bed . . . He said to keep me warm. Come upstairs, Ella, to keep me warm." Ella is aghast, again using effective ellipsis: "Her wet, cold, dripping skin against . . . NO! I wouldn't do it! She thought she'd make me crazy that way. Hold me in her bony arms until all the sense in me ran out like the well water was running out of her." Eventually Ella is driven insane and commits suicide, hanging herself in the basement, after which we hear the undead mother-in-law chortle. In a fine example of inventive radio ambiguity, we hear a splash and the manhole cover closing: either the undead mother-in-law has descended back into the well or she has cast the corpse of Ella into the well in order to remain with her doting son.

"Knock at the Door" uses sexualized horror to shocking effect, most emphatically when we are presented with the mother-in-law in bed with her murderer, but it also functions as a powerful study of guilt (the reappearance of the mother may simply be a psychological manifestation of the guilt that leads the killer to her gruesome suicide). The play also serves as a complex metaphor of the dysfunctional American family and a possible reflection of the Second World War context when many families were forced, sometimes problematically, to reconfigure themselves into closer relationships with in-laws and extended family networks due to the demands of the war effort. Of course, the play is sardonically humorous, being perhaps the ultimate mother-in-law joke. Arch Oboler is aware of this when he takes the opportunity in his introduction to plead with any mothers-in-law that may be listening not to send him poison pen letters with the words "I'm really not responsible for what happens in the twisted brains of my characters, am I?"

Lights Out was typically broadcast well into the evening if not late at night. But zombies and the concept of the undead also had a presence in more obviously "mainstream" time slots. *The Shadow* (1930–54) was one of the most popular family adventure series on radio and featured the crime-fighting escapades of Lamont Cranston, a quasi-superhero with a disguise, sense of justice, and the ability to become invisible by hypnotizing whomever he needs to. Over its near quarter of a century run, the Shadow was played by a variety of notable radio actors, including Orson Welles, Frank Readick, and Bill Johnstone, and the Shadow's female sidekick Margo Lane was portrayed by, among others, Agnes Moorehead. *The Shadow* could command a huge family audience with the thrilling adventures of its eponymous hero confronting a diverse range of villains. But in contrast to the other, more orthodox, superhero dramas of the era—such as *The Green Hornet* (1936–52) and *The Adventures of Superman* (1940–50)—*The Shadow* is distinguished by its macabre and even horrific story lines, which generally feature human atrocity and scientific abuse rather than the supernatural, and always conclude with the Shadow's sage and rational explanations. As an example of its hideous inventiveness, in the classic episode "The Gibbering Things" (September 26, 1943), the Shadow confronts a Frankenstein-style scientist who transplants human brains into monkeys. For the critic Gerald Nachman, *The Shadow* "was a total aural experience, taking place in the dark night of the soul," and was quite possibly "the ultimate radio show."[10] Overall, as Dunning writes, "Lamont and Margo confronted the maddest assortment of lunatics, sadists, ghosts, and werewolves ever heard on the air."[11] To this list we can add the "living dead," which, in the broadest terms, was a favorite for the program. Some of the titles of episodes reveal this predilection: "Society of the Living Dead" (January 23, 1938), "Valley of the Living Dead" (January 22, 1939), "Isle of the Living Dead" (October 13, 1940), "Undead" (December 14, 1941), "Ship of the Living Dead" (December 16, 1945), and "The Case of the Living Dead" (May 17, 1953). We are fortunate that three recordings of *The Shadow*'s "living dead" adventures survive—"Society," "Valley," and "Isle"—and the concept of the "living dead" is interpreted quite differently in each of the episodes.

In "Society of the Living Dead," the Shadow uncovers an international fake passport scam in which the identities of presumed-dead victims are stolen. In "Valley of the Living Dead," the Shadow and Margo arrive in a village that they initially consider might be a kind of "state poor farm." They are informed, however, that it is strictly "private": a cult rather than an example of welfare, held under the control of a millionaire called Mr. Maxim. Described as "the kindest man there ever was," the aptly named Maxim lives by the motto "It is the privilege of all strong people . . . to take care of the weaker" in order to "avoid the corruption of the outside world." But far from being a socialistic paradise, Maxim's world is one of total oppression: everyone lives by the benevolence of Maxim with no need to work, no need to hunger, but with absolutely no freedom. As the Shadow explains, "The villagers sleep, Margo, but they do not rest. Come. I'll show you how their tortured, subconscious minds react." Leading Margo through the village, he lets her hear their sleeping thoughts: "I've become as soft as something that lies rotting in the sun. There is no hope. I am dead, dead"; and "This place of living death, this silence, beats on my ears like the drums of eternity." The Shadow proclaims that he will take it on himself to "free them from the bondage of submission": "Their suffering has been great enough. I'll make them help themselves. . . . Everyone has been asleep too long, but with luck, I hope to awaken their minds to this . . . this living death!" Talking to each citizen, the Shadow encourages them to express their liberty by returning to work, and to "fight out of the weakness to strength and freedom." The success of this is signified through an effective technical device: the citizens have spoken into an echo chamber, but once released from the torpor of living death they speak with clear, open voices. Interestingly, compared to the many diabolical adversaries *The Shadow* has confronted, Maxim is not evil but merely deluded: his communistic idealism was founded on good intentions but proved utterly tyrannical. The Shadow successfully teaches him that the stealing of liberty is as depraved as the stealing of money, and Maxim is genuinely delighted when he eventually hears "the cheers of the living and the free people!" *The Shadow*'s critique of the "cult" of Maxim can clearly be seen as a reflection of its political context and as serving a propagandist function: broadcast in 1939, the episode reflects anxieties about the rise of fascist and communist totalitarianism in the world, or, more cynically, about the perceived risks of an overdependence on welfare.

The final surviving recording of *The Shadow* that concerns the living dead takes as its theme the original folkloric zombie. In "Isle of the Living Dead," the Shadow and Margo are enjoying a cruise to the West Indies when they disembark on a small island during a tropical storm. The ship's pilot tells them that the island, Saint June, is cursed: "One half of island good, other half belong to devil." Asking for an explanation leads to the following exchange:

Pilot: You ever hear of zombies?
Margo: Zombies?
The Shadow: Zombies are supposed to be dead men here in the tropics
    who walk about with no mind or soul. Native superstition.

Soon afterwards, they hear native drums and see fires on the island's plantation. The pilot warns, "Drums bring death!" Undeterred, the Shadow and Margo explore the island, meeting a stranger with a "weird half-dark face" in the road who runs off in despair screaming "Keep away!" Arriving at a villa, they meet Mrs. Nesbitt, the seemingly charming plantation owner, a "white woman living alone" among the natives. But the Shadow hears eerie moaning coming from the cellar. Unsurprisingly, Mrs. Nesbitt is the "devil" of the island and has created an army of "zombies." Talking to the moaning horde, she declares, "Quiet, you fools. Now listen to me, all of you. I don't expect you to know what I'm saying but listen anyway. You understand that you're no longer men: you're slime in chains, bound together, just as cattle labor in the cane fields under my command. . . . I only keep all of you alive because I save money using you to labor for me instead of native help. And fortunately the silly superstition of zombies has kept all people away." In fact, Nesbitt has exploited zombie folklore to create a culture of terror on the island. The Shadow compels her to reveal what she has done to turn "these poor creatures into living dead men. Slaves who move and act like animals!" Nesbitt explains she has used a drug to control their minds and actions, although it will wear off if not administered regularly.[12] She receives a brutal comeuppance—in an extremely vivid radio sequence—when she dies of fright, locked in the cellar surrounded by the increasingly "restless" and groaning "living dead." Margo is afforded the punch line to "Isle of the Living Dead": "The only zombies that I want to see again are the type they serve in a nightclub in a long, cool glass."

Like the "Valley of the Living Dead," the anxieties regarding "mind control" in "Isle of the Living Dead" can be interpreted as propaganda about fascist or communist totalitarianism. As we have seen in this chapter, American radio drama of the 1930s and 1940s offered a surprisingly rich and diverse range of plays based on themes of zombies and the living dead. Whether exploiting the voodoo folklore of the zombie or the reanimation of corpses, horror radio offered tales of the living dead that could mix and merge social and political comment, ironic humor, and experiential thrills. The "living dead" in 1930 and 1940s radio shows such as *The Shadow* could draw on the distinctly modern anxieties of "mind control," exploitation of the worker, and the denial of liberty. As the Shadow himself exclaims in "Valley of the Living Dead," "This is a fight for freedom!," a comment that demonstrates the blatant politicization of the concept of the living dead, even for family listening. When it comes to the supernatural undead, the maggot-eaten or water-bloated animated corpses brought to life on *Lights Out* may have crawled into the pre-code horror comics artwork of Johnny Craig, Jack Davis, and Graham Ingels in the 1950s, but they were unthinkable on the screen in their fully realized state of decay until the late 1970s onward.

CHAPTER 4

The Zombie as Other: Mortality and the Monstrous in the Post-Nuclear Age

Kevin Boon

The zombie has gained substantial cultural currency since George Romero's influential 1968 film *Night of the Living Dead*, spawning numerous films, novels, comics, graphic novels, and websites dedicated to the undead. The proliferation of zombie mythology into mainstream culture during the past three decades has established the zombie as the predominate symbol of the monstrous other. Zombie mythology and its relationship to Western culture, however, predate its infusion into mainstream discourses, falling into three overlapping periods, beginning with its presence in African tribal mythology, moving through its transformation within Caribbean religious practices, and concluding with its current incarnation as an aggressive, flesh-eating threat to the survival of the individual. Metaphysical, epistemological, and ontological issues distinguish these three periods and link the evolution of zombie mythology to shifts in Western thought during the past several centuries. The increased appeal of the zombie in the later twentieth century is linked to the mythology's ability to stir existential anxieties about our own mortality within the larger context of cultural attitudes about the nature of self.

One of the earliest traceable predecessors of the zombie is found in the character of the "Nzambi," an invisible being with origins in the Bantu and Bankongo tribes in the Nzambi Mpungu region of the lower Congo

River area, who reportedly oversaw the people of the region. R. P. Van Wing, writing in 1921 about his experiences among the African people, describes the Nzambi as "above all . . . the sovereign Master, unapproachable, who has placed man here below to take him away some day, at the hour of death. He watches man, searches him out everywhere and takes him away, inexorably, young or old. . . . Among the laws there are *nkondo mi Nzambi*, 'God's prohibitions,' the violation of which constitutes a *sumu ku Nzambi* [a sin against Nzambi], and an ordinary sanction of this is *lufwa lumbi* 'a bad death.'"[1] The Nzambi is a religious figure, a spiritual entity with superhuman abilities, and an object of religious faith. The term "Nzambi" dates to 1600 and is associated in its various linguistic incarnations with the idea of spirit. E. Torday claims that the term "Nzambi Mpungu" "appears . . . to mean 'the chiefly spirit of the first man'" and points out that the term was "revived by the advent of Christianity,"[2] when it was used to describe God. This is in some opinions a misuse of the term. One writer argues in 1906 that the term in use north of the French Congo literally means "Terrible Earth" and links the term to Mother Earth, "the fountain of all life and, in turn, also the home of the dead."[3] Despite varying definitions, there is no question that the Nzambi was a spiritual creature.

The relationship between the Bantu and Bankongo tribes and the Nzambi was religious and dependent on faith among tribal members. Similar to faith in Western religious traditions, faith in the Nzambi depended on the belief that the origin of truth was external, that truth came from gods and demigods, and that validation of that truth was subjective. Subjective validation of an external truth enables one to make a claim of certainty, such as "I know God is real," wholly in the absence of any empirical evidence. This is the same epistemological system that dominated religious thought in Western civilization prior to the Enlightenment, as articulated in the "Proslogion" of Anselm of Canterbury, where he writes, "Come on now little man, get away from your worldly occupations for a while, escape from your tumultuous thoughts. Lay aside your burdensome cares and put off your laborious exertions. Give yourself over to God for a little while, and rest for a while in Him. Enter into the cell of your mind, shut out everything except God and whatever helps you to seek Him once the door is shut."[4] Thus the religious traditions of Western belief and African tribal practices posited spiritual beings and the truth they presumably possessed outside of self. The early modern rationalism of Leibniz, Spinoza, and Descartes, and the empiricism of Locke, Berkeley, and Hume supplanted this religious faith with reason and began a perceptual shift among the general population, which ultimately led to the Enlightenment. Rationalism mandates that truth is uncovered within self (that is, within the mind where self resides), that what we know to be true is a matter of what our mind can reason, and that the more accurately we reason with respect to the physical universe, the closer our beliefs approximate what is true. This is the rationalism to which Blaise Pascal refers when he argues that "reason is the slow and torturous method by which those who do not know the truth discover it," and the empiricism to which Da Vinci refers when he argues that "it is necessary for us . . . to commence with experience and from this to proceed to investigate the reason."

Liebniz's "principle of sufficient reason" implies these two differing viewpoints (religious faith and faith in reason), claiming that anything that exists must have a reason and that that reason (or cause) must necessarily be one of two options: either (1) a necessary "God" or (2) infinity. A necessary God (or gods) belongs to the domain of religion. Infinity, principally, results from an exercise of reason. The period of Western civilization before the Enlightenment is dominated by the first conclusion—that a necessary God is the source of truth. The period after is increasingly dominated by reason and the belief that truth is realized through the exercise of rational thought. Significant to this change is the shift in the locus of control that it represents. Faith in internal reason replaces faith in an external God as the arbiter of truth, thus the shift from religious faith (or God) to reasoned truth (or science) moves truth from an external source (God) to an internal source (reason).[5] The validation of truth also shifts location. What was verified internally under the dominion of religious faith (I know God exists) became externally verifiable under science (what I reason to be true can be verified in the physical world).

For most people, however, dependence on an "other" as the source of truth did not change. One needed to be a scientist in order for the locus to move internally. For the greater population (nonscientists and nonphilosophers), faith remained situated with an "other." Just as God had been the other source of truth, and faith in God as the source of truth represented faith in something that is other than self, science became the other source of truth, and faith in science as the source of truth represented faith in something that is other than self. Most people did not engage in reasoned experimentation and were therefore left to accept on faith what scientists and philosophers were telling them. For these people, the source of truth remained just as external as it had been prior to the Enlightenment. Science became their God (as an abstract concept, not as a procedure), and what science said was perceived as true and accepted on faith.

The movement of zombie mythology from its first period to its second period, which is rooted in the African diaspora, mirrors the shift from faith in God to faith in science. When tribal members settled in the Caribbean, specifically in Saint-Domingue (i.e., Haiti), the term "zombi" still referred to a spirit, as indicated in M. L. E. Moreau de Saint-Méry's 1789 definition of the term as a "Creole word which means spirit, revenant."[6] But during the nineteenth century, as African religious beliefs collided with Western influences and zombie mythology underwent the vicissitudes of cultural migration, the term came to represent a spirit that can occupy people (still an external). Eventually, in Haiti, the external disappeared and the term came to refer to a person for whom internal consciousness and volition were absent—a "zombie drone" (one of the nine classifications of zombies found in literature, film and culture that are fleshed out at the end of this chapter). The empirical (pro-science) view that took root among the general population toward the end of the nineteenth century ironically resulted in an increased objectification of self. The self, which to medieval sensibilities had been perceived as a whole, was transformed into an object of inquiry. Rationalism made it possible for the self to examine the self; thus it became possible to ask questions such as "I believe that I am X, but am I really X?" In situating the source of truth internally, rationalism divided the self between what is "me" and what is not "me," and imbued the self with uncertainty. It became philosophically possible to make claims such as "I am not behaving like myself today," an assertion that requires a divided self and is necessary to understanding the epistemological and ontological issues surrounding the emergence of the zombie drone in the late nineteenth and early twentieth centuries. The self, apparently, could occupy both subjective and objective positions, and it could occupy them simultaneously.

Jean-Paul Sartre points out that "self" necessarily occupies consciousness inasmuch as consciousness is always conscious of itself. For Sartre, perceptions of self are bifurcated into being-for-itself (conscious experience) and being-in-itself; thus self can consider self. Key to Sartre's argument and our understanding of the zombie drone that emerges from Haitian culture in the nineteenth century and is apprehended by Western culture during the opening of the twentieth is Sartre's notion of negation and its relationship to what he labels the figure and ground. Negation, Sartre tells us, is the ability to identify something as not being something else. If, for example, you are supposed to meet a friend at a restaurant and your friend is not there, negation is the process by which you identify his absence. When this occurs, the entire restaurant becomes "ground" to the absent "figure" of your friend. If we imagine that in place of a restaurant we have a person, we come to understand the transformation that the mythological zombie came to represent—a person who is all ground and no figure; that is, an absence of conscious self, a person for whom identity, self, personhood, and so on are absent from the body.

In lacking consciousness, the zombie is incapable of examining self. It is emptied of being, a receptacle of nothingness, wholly other. This is the philosophical foundation of the zombie as it was when introduced to Western culture in the early twentieth century. Woodrow Wilson's aggressive policies toward Latin America between 1914 and 1918 made possible a discourse between American and Haitian culture. In 1915, Wilson seized political control of the island for the purpose of establishing hegemony and increasing American control in the region, after which Americans were exposed to Haitian culture, mythology, and religious practices. The stories that Americans brought back from Haiti—such as those of Captain John Houston Craige, who wrote *Black Bagdad* (1933) about his second visit to Haiti in 1925 (his first was in 1912)—fascinated the reading public with tales of strange voodoo practices and helped to spread new myths into Western culture. The zombie that entered American culture as a result of increased political contact with Haiti in the first part of the twentieth century was a drone, a mindless, soulless worker returned from the dead for the purposes of cheap labor. The fear that the Haitian zombie drone engenders comes from more than its unusual origins. The potential loss of self leads to existential despair and dread. The idea of a human body absent of Sartre's figure, a body that is only ground, stirs the most primal, instinctual fear: the possibility that we could be absent from ourselves, that we could look into the body and find only an absence, is ontologically terrifying because it denies humans that which makes us human.

The zombie as it appears in literature and film during the first half of the twentieth century is primarily a physical body occupied by nothingness—a human shell lacking whatever properties are presumed to constitute self to our consciousness. This is the zombie found in films such as *White Zombie* (1932), *King of the Zombies* (1941), *I Walked with a Zombie* (1943), and *Revenge of the Zombies* (1943), and in literature such as "The Country of the Comers-Back" (1889) by Lafcadio Hearn, "The Hollow Man" (ca. 1920–45) by Thomas Burke, *The Whistling Ancestors* (1936) by Richard E. Goddard, and *Tell My Horse* (1937) by Zora Neale Hurston.

These two periods of zombie mythology—the zombie as spirit followed by the zombie as human shell—mirror shifts in Western thought. The zombie emerged in Africa as an external being, which functioned as an object of faith. In the Caribbean, it became the absence of spirit (self) within the human body. Under the directive of faith, the zombie represented an external force that invaded human form; under the directive of reason, when faith shifted to rationalism and an increased confidence in the physical world, the zombie came to represent a loss of internal reliability, a loss of being, which results in a human shell occupied by nothingness.

On August 6, 1945, the United States dropped the atomic bomb on Hiroshima, giving birth to the nuclear age and clearing the ground for the third zombie period. The bomb resulted in the disillusionment of a generation and a shift away from modernism. Prior to the bomb, faith still existed; it had merely shifted from external gods to science. People had confidence that science (reason and empiricism) and its practitioners could potentially bring about a human utopia. Irving Howe sums up Western attitudes in the pre-nuclear twentieth century when he notes that modern writers, though strongly influenced by World War I, still continued to "believe in the quest, sometimes the grail too," but the modern writer was "no longer persuaded that a quest is necessarily undertaken through public action and . . . is unsure as to where the grail can be found."[7] The modern heroic attitude that Howe describes changed after the bomb, which destroyed all faith in external science. Kurt Vonnegut articulates this ideological shift when he says, "I was a great believer in the truth, scientific truth, and then . . . truth was dropped on Hiroshima. . . . I was hideously disappointed."[8] Confidence in external reason—that is, what is outside the self (e.g., faith in science and scientists)—evaporated, leaving the individual with no reliable external referent on which to base his faith, no source of truth beyond self. Therefore, the individual was left with the bifurcated state of being and nothingness (what he is and what he isn't), the yin/yang of self residing in consciousness in a lone, existential state. People could only rely on their reason for the definition of self, and that definition, as Sartre pointed out, is never complete. Because self was all that remained after the bomb, the loss of self became the greatest fear. If self is lost, all that remains is an abyss of nothingness—precisely what the post-nuclear zombie came to signify.

The world into which this postnuclear individual was thrust was one in which the self became an existential agent whose attitude toward self was determined by the self's practical engagement with the world. Yet this engagement, in the absence of any external locus of truth—that is, in the absence of a reliable "other" in whom/which faith can be placed—must face the threat of engulfment by the world. The self's greatest fear is that it will be absorbed by the other and thus be irretrievably lost. This existential predicament underscores the post-nuclear zombie, which fused the aggressiveness of the ghoul mythology with the absent shell zombie from the second period of zombie mythology (i.e., the Haitian zombie or zombie drone). This new zombie, which I have labeled the "zombie ghoul," symbolizes the malignant universe surrounding the existential self. Unlike the zombie drone, which functions as slave labor, the zombie ghoul is an other that aggressively seeks to deprive the individual of his or her unique self, to excise the figure from human identity, leaving only an abyss of nothingness. The loss of essential self in a malignant universe was terrifyingly real after the bomb. Coupled with the instinctual fear of physical death was the fear of continued existence in absence of self. Post-nuclear anxiety resides in consciousness, in the self, which the rise of rationalism bifurcates into being and nothingness, and which the advent of nuclear technology has left without an object of faith. This divided self resembles the schizoid personality that R. D. Laing describes in *A Divided Self*:

> The schizoid self [in objectifying others] is not erecting defenses against the loss of a part of his body. His whole effort is rather to preserve his self. This . . . is precariously established; he is subject to the dread of his own dissolution into non-being, into what William Blake described in the last resort as "chaotic non-entity." His autonomy is threatened with engulfment. He has to guard himself against losing his subjectivity and sense of being alive. In so far as he feels empty, the full, substantial, living reality of others is an impingement which is always liable to get out of hand and become implosive, threatening to overwhelm and obliterate his self completely. . . . The schizoid individual fears a real live dialectical relationship with real live people. He can relate himself only to depersonalized persons, to phantoms of his own phantasies (imagos), perhaps to things, perhaps to animals.[9]

Laing's definition of a schizoid self describes the post-nuclear human condition that made fertile ground for the zombie ghoul, which has dominated zombie films since *Night of the Living Dead* (1968), moving increasingly toward zombies as hoards of dangerous undead during the 1970s with Amando de Ossario's Blind Dead trilogy (which began in 1971), Romero's sequel to *Night*, *Dawn of the Dead* (1978), and the films of Lucio Fulci. This transformation stabilized somewhat in the 1980s with the current mythology of zombie survival fiction. The purest manifestation of the paranoia Laing attributes to the schizoid self—and which has dominated zombie fiction since the mid-1980s when novels and anthologies such as Gary Bradner's *Carrion* (1986), Joe R. Lansdale's *Dead in the West* (1986), Peter Haining's *Zombie: Stories of the Walking Dead* (1985), and Candace Caponegro's *The Breeze Horror* (1987)—shifted the course of zombie fiction away from the zombie drone of Haitian folklore toward the flesh-eating, brain-hungry dead that Romero devised. The postnuclear zombie is the manifestation of the post-nuclear hero's greatest ontological insecurity: the loss of the "figure" of self in his or her engulfment by the "other." Thus we find in the post-nuclear world that the instinctual human fear of being dead occupies second place to a more intimate fear of being undead, and that the living death of the zombie is more monstrous than the grave.

The Nine Classifications of Zombies

ZOMBIE DRONE

The zombie drone is the classic zombie. Whether dead first or not, it is robbed of its self and becomes a witless shell used for slave labor. The Haitian zombie falls into this category. This is the zombie we find in films such as *White Zombie* (1932), *King of the Zombies* (1941), and *I Walked with a Zombie* (1943), and novels such as Peter Tremayne's *Zombie!* (1981). The zombie drone's appearance in literature dates back to the nineteenth century.

ZOMBIE GHOUL

The zombie ghoul is Romero's creation, a fusion of the Haitian undead zombie with the flesh-eating ghoul. The zombie ghoul, like the zombie drone, is missing an essential self and operates to varying degrees as an eating machine. This is the most common zombie found in film and literature, present in nearly every zombie film or novel made after the mid-eighties. Romero's zombies in *Night of the Living Dead* are certainly the first film versions of the zombie ghoul, but a few instances of the zombie ghoul in literature predate Romero's film. The most notable is H. P. Lovecraft's "Herbert West—Reanimator," which was published as a serial in *Home Brew* (1921–22). Lovecraft's story contains the earliest fictional linking of the zombie to cannibalism. The reanimated corpse in that story is said to have "done cannibal things before it had been captured."[10]

Tech Zombie

Found both in film and literature, the tech zombie is someone robbed of volition by technology. Ira Levin's 1972 novel *The Stepford Wives* contains this type of zombie, though the 1975 film version does not.[11] In the film, robotic duplicates replace the wives completely; in the novel, technology alters the wives, depriving them of their essential selves. Curt Selby's *I, Zombie* (1982), a science fiction zombie novel, reanimates the dead by implanting them with technological devices called "packs" before shipping them off to work as slave labor on other planets. The "Martians" in Kurt Vonnegut's *The Sirens of Titan* (1959), which are people who have been implanted with antennae so they can be controlled, would also qualify as tech zombies.

Bio Zombie

The bio zombie is one that has been deprived of its essential self or its volition by some external substance, either temporarily, as is the case in Richard Layman's novel *One Rainy Night* (1991), in which something in the black rain turns people into psychotic creatures until the water is washed off, or permanently, as in Wilson Yip's film *Bio-Zombie* (1998), in which biochemicals in a soft drink create flesh-eating zombies. The course of zombification can vary from chemicals to viruses, but some substance has caused the loss of self. The zombies in the films *28 Days Later* (2002) and *Quarantine* (2008) are bio zombies.

Zombie Channel

Primarily found in literature, the zombie channel is a zombie that has been taken over by another consciousness. The zombies in Brian Keene's novel *The Rising* (2003), for example, are cogent and organized, but the entities that inhabit them are not the original occupants of those bodies. We also find the zombie channel in Lucius Shephard's *Green Eyes* (1984) and Daniel Ksenych's clever story "The Other Side of Theory."[12] The zombies in Stephen King's *Cell* (2006) might also qualify as zombie channels.

Psychological Zombie

It is the psychological zombie that I would argue first appeared in film, in *Das Cabinet des Dr. Caligari* (1920). This zombie has been robbed of will through some psychological means such as hypnotism, as in the case of Cesare in *Caligari*, or brainwashing, as in Richard Condon's 1959 novel *The Manchurian Candidate* and its subsequent film adaptations.

Cultural Zombie

Cultural zombies have not yet received the attention they deserve, yet they offer a fascinating bridge between zombie mythology and the wider, general culture. Two of the best literary examples of the cultural zombie can be found in Brad Gouch's novel *Zombieoo* (2000), in which the main character identifies himself as a zombie and narrates his personal journey from Truckstown, Pennsylvania, to Haiti, and Joyce Carol Oates's *Zombie* (1995). Brad Anderson's Kafkaesque film *The Machinist* (2004), in which the emaciated machinist is eaten away by subconscious guilt and becomes a wasted, corpse-like creature, is an excellent film example of the cultural zombie. The main characteristics of cultural zombies are that they acquire the basic qualities associated with zombies, though they occupy narratives that do not employ fantasy, science fiction, or the supernatural.

Zombie Ghost

The zombie ghost does not qualify as a zombie proper, but the category is necessary because so many stories that are essentially ghost stories are included in zombie anthologies or mentioned in discussions of zombies. We might attribute this misnomer to the overemphasis often placed on returning from the dead. Stephen Jones's 1993 collection *The Mammoth Book of Zombies*, for example, includes Edgar Allan Poe's "The Facts in the Case of M. Valdemar," a story in which the spirit of a man is trapped between this world and the next by an unscrupulous hypnotist. But the essence of Valdemar is not absent, thus it is a ghost story rather than a zombie story. The same can be said for Clive Barker's "Sex, Death, and Starshine" (from the same collection), in which Shakespearean actors continue to perform after their death. Note the cogency and the presence of self in the following exchange from Barker's story:

> Her voice was a ghost's voice: thin, forlorn. Her skin, which he had thought so flatteringly pale, was, on second view, a waxen white.
> "You are dead?" he said.

"I'm afraid so. Two hours ago: in my sleep. But I had to come, Terry; so much unfinished business. I made my choice. You should be flattered. You are flattered, aren't you?"[13]

Returning from the dead is not enough to qualify someone as a zombie, and examples such as the ones we find in Barker's story belong more properly to the domain of ghosts.

Zombie Ruse

The category of zombie ruse is necessary primarily because of books made for children, which use the word "zombie" to entice readers though the work does not contain any zombies. Chapter books, such as *The Gorgonzola Zombies in the Park* (1994) and *The Zombie Zone* (2005), and novels, such as *Bill, the Galactic Hero: On the Planet of Zombie Vampires* (1991), among numerous others, present themselves as zombie works but turn out to not to have zombies in them. It is, essentially, a marketing ploy that exploits the popularity of zombie stories by invoking it in the title without presenting actual zombies in the plot. This trick is so prevalent that these works warrant their own category.

And the Dead Shall Walk

Part introduction by Deborah Christie

> I wander among the dead, awaiting the moment when I shall pass imperceptibly from the stumbling of the living into the stumbling of the dead. Avaunt.
>
> BRIAN EVENSON, "Prairie"

The essays in this section address a radical shift in the popular culture of the zombie. No longer the benign sleepwalker or the organic puppet of a voodoo master, here the zombie becomes a force of nature that moves under its own autonomy, propelled forward by its own instinctual needs.

Initiating the section, Deborah Christie examines the roots of the modern zombie in, of all places, a story about vampires, tracing the development of what is now an iconic image of the shambling dead from its genesis in Richard Matheson's novel *I Am Legend* through its representation in a number of films, including the classic works of George A. Romero. Drawing on Aldous Huxley's paradigmatic example of societal evolution—of one society replacing another, often after violent upheaval, drawing on the Heraclitean model of progress that so influenced Hegel, Nietzsche, and others—Christie posits that the true debt Romero and others owe to Matheson's vampire story lies in its cyclical focus on both destruction and regeneration. As the last surviving human on earth, the novel's hero, Robert Neville, has the audience's—or reader's—full attention and more than his fair share of sympathy, which is generally the case in a zombie narrative—the audience is focused on the harried humans who are still alive and struggling to stay that way. As Christie argues, we tend to view zombie narratives as apocalyptic because we believe that we are watching either the slow breakdown or the catastrophic destruction of human society, and we generally regard that as a negative event. But because we most closely identify with the dwindling number of living human subjects, we often miss the larger implications that what we are really witnessing in a zombie narrative is a form of violent, transformative renewal.

In Matheson's novel, Robert Neville may be the last human, but he is not the last of humanity—humanity has evolved and a new society has superseded the old one. Further, as it was the hubris and aggression of the old society that directly led to its destruction and the mutation of humans into a post-human hybrid of vampire/human, it becomes a resonating question as to whether humanity deserves our sympathy. In Romero's films, emphasis is repeatedly placed not just on the failure of society and social order to protect the populace but also on the failure of humanity to save itself. The chilling final scene of *Night of the Living Dead*, where the bodies of the first zombie we saw on-screen and the last human to survive the night in the farmhouse are both shown being tossed into the fire by the sheriff and his men, demonstrates most clearly the flaws of human judgment and its inability to discern its own capacity for inhuman behavior. Both Matheson and Romero pointedly direct our attention back to our own body politic and the weaknesses therein.

Furthering the cyclical idea is Nick Muntean's examination of "trauma zombies" in contrast with the more literal walking dead. For Muntean, the trauma zombie represents a "profoundly modern" shift in our cultural attitudes about death, where death is no longer a transition but an outcome: "something we become, rather than somewhere we go to." This shift emphasizes the dehumanization of the zombie as a product of the very same cultural institutions that previously constituted the individual as subject—now grotesquely parodied by the zombies who wander aimlessly through the mall in *Dawn of the Dead*, as well as by the traumatized humans of *On the Beach* who, cognizant of their impending death, mimic in desperation the actions of meaningful life. In the post-trauma milieu of both films it becomes increasingly obvious that what has been obliterated are not the trappings of human society, but humanity itself—returning the humanlike inhabitants to what Slavoj Žižek has called the "zero level" of humanity.

Muntean suggests that the figure of the zombie evolves in the mid-twentieth century to replace the mere loss of autonomy so emblematic of the voodoo zombie with a far more disturbing existential anxiety—"that one could continue to live, but be nothing." Drawing from historical accounts of the *hibakusha*—those exposed to the radiation from the atomic bombings of Hiroshima and Nagasaki—and the *Muselmänner*—those prisoners of Nazi war camps "so devastated by the conditions of their imprisonment that they were reduced to such a state of bare existence"—Muntean argues that the atavistic repulsion produced by the zombie is appallingly similar to the feelings of terror called forth by these uncanny survivors, outwardly recognizable but ultimately unidentifiable.

With the proliferation of zombie films that followed Romero's forays into the genre, there was an accompanying proliferation of possible causes of zombification: divine punishment, nuclear fallout, extraterrestrial invasion or contamination, biological warfare or pandemic plagues. Our next authors, Steven Zani and Kevin Meaux, address the dynamic variations of zombie genesis as represented in the films of Lucio Fulci, arguing that this very multiplicity of origins renders the origin immaterial and instead focuses our attention on the failure of social institutions and the cannibalistic nature of human interactions. According to Zani and Meaux, we fear that "the institutions holding our culture together, specifically law, family, and belief in the sacred, will break down or reveal themselves to be false in the face of catastrophe"—and thus zombie narratives become a touchstone to decipher the deep-seated fears of individual humans in the contrived plurality commonly called civilization. By demonstrating the remarkable consistencies to be found between historical and literary accounts of plague outbreaks, like Boccaccio's *The Decameron* and Defoe's *A Journal of the Plague Year*, and the more contemporary zombie scourges exemplified in Fulci's films, Zani and Meaux challenge the concept of causality as an imperative factor. Seen through this lens, Fulci appears to be deliberately confounding the human desire for order by refusing to provide resolution in terms of a consistent or sustainable explanation for why the zombies are coming to get us. "Why not?" may in fact be a more appropriate question, as both Fulci's films and the historical record of actual plague narratives substantiate the idea that humans and viruses can be equally as cannibalistic as the zombie, and they contribute just as often to similar events of destruction and renewal.

Following the willful chaos represented by Fulci, our next contributor probes the very heart of conformity—suburbia—and connects this impulse to the developing arc of zombie narratives. Bernice Murphy mines both *Fido* and *The Stepford Wives* for the depersonalizing forces of suburbia and its connection to both the post-human and the zombie. In *Fido*, the military-industrial-media complex represented by the corporation ZomCon has engineered a way to tame and effectively utilize those former humans who have been zombified as a cheap and malleable labor source. As Murphy points out, this not only resurrects some of the folkloric origins of the Carribean "zombi" and many of its racist and imperialist implications, but *Fido* also demonstrates the inherent abjection of a homogenized suburban lifestyle, which is something that Murphy also identifies in her analysis of Ira Levin's novel *The Stepford Wives*. The juxtaposition of these two narratives of suburban zombies made three decades apart but both harking back, in different ways, to the emergent suburb culture of the 1950s reveals that "keeping up with the Joneses" has evolved only tangibly in terms of cost and the speed of technology. The sterilizing effects of repetitive standardization and mimicry have found their way off the drive-in screens and into the handheld technology that comes standard on most teenage human models; what we are seeing is the transformation from "pod" people to "iPod" people, and the standard humanist concerns still apply: where does *being human* stop?

Rounding out the section, Sorcha Ní Fhlainn attempts to answer that very question in her provocative study of dehumanization, or zombification, in several postmodern films that explore the depersonalizing force of the military-industrial complex on the psyche of ordinary humans. The transformative power of the military to repress the individual is often too successful, tragically so, and the resulting "post-human soldier" exists in a liminal space between our traditional understanding of zombies and a contemporary awareness of victims of posttraumatic stress disorder. Building on the concept that Muntean initiates—that "one could continue to live, but be nothing"—Ní Fhlainn offers an unflinching analysis of "the dehumanization of the person, through the removal of individual thought, explicitly characterized by soldiers in modern warfare." The technology of warfare frequently advances irrespective of the consequences, but in the third part of the volume our authors will show how the zombie has evolved along with and in response to new technologies, often countering many of the narrative attempts to depersonalize them. In our afterword, the zombies often fight back.

Heraclitus wrote, "Where there is no strife there is decay: The mixture which is not shaken decomposes." What we see in this second group of essays is a kind of evolution—a rising up, if you will, of the product of human conflict. Looking past the zombies within these zombie narratives reveals the kind of cyclical struggle between opposing forces that Heraclitus described. Out of the apocalyptic struggles, the wars between zombies and non-zombies, or just the acrimony between different types of beings coming into conflict, we see new societies form, new species evolve, new civilizations solidify. Out of strife, in the form of the human's encounter with the zombie's decayed corpse, comes, perhaps surprisingly, renewal.

This renewal gives us the opportunity to take a second look at the zombie, to consider its status as post-human, or as an antagonist that facilitates our own accession to post-humanity, and prompts us to ask ourselves whether post-human is an improvement. Many of the offerings in this section, in a variety of ways and for a variety of reasons, give us the opportunity to examine not just what is threatened or lost by the apocalyptic scenarios that give rise to zombies, but also to see what survives or replaces that which we have known—even if we are the ones being replaced.

CHAPTER 5

A Dead New World: Richard Matheson and the Modern Zombie

Deborah Christie

Under the old government man exploited man, but since the revolution it's the other way around.

RALPH FIENNES in *Land of the Blind* (2006)

The only society more frightful than one run by children . . . might be one run by childish adults.

PAUL SHEPARD, *Nature and Madness* (1992)

He laughed at his earlier idealism, his schoolboy vision of a brave new world in which justice would reign and men would be brothers.

ÉMILE ZOLA, *Germinal* (1885)

My route to the study of zombies was circuitous, but essentially it was very much the same one that the famed zombie auteur George A. Romero took: we were both big fans of Richard Matheson's *I Am Legend*. That Romero took his inspiration for the walking dead from Matheson's 1954 novel and the subsequent film based on it (*The Last Man on Earth*, 1964) is a well-documented bit of cinema lore. Other than generally acknowledging Romero's indebtedness to Matheson, however, few writers have probed this connection beyond assuming that it begins and ends with the obvious visual cues of the shuffling, blank-eyed dead banging on the windows and doors of a house, trying to get in and eat the inhabitants.[1] The living dead in question were not even zombies originally: Matheson writes of vampires and Romero originally called them "ghouls."[2] Regardless, the stiff shambling and insistent hunger of altered corpses stalking humans became an iconic representation of modern zombie fiction and film, one that has continued to evolve.

In interview after interview Romero maintains that he was especially interested in Matheson's representation of one civilization replacing another, and this is perhaps the more significant and ideological debt that Romero channels into his films, that of "a new society coming in and devouring the old."[3] This apocalyptic version of "the more things change, the more they stay the same" is the extremist theme that runs through both the novel *I Am Legend* and the film *Night of the Living Dead*—that of social and political structures "enduring in the afterlife of [their] chaotic implosion."[4] It may sound counterintuitive to suggest that a return to the same actually represents a revolutionary—perhaps even *evolutionary*— change, but what I argue in this essay is that because we as the audience identify with the living human subjects, we never step back far enough to see the larger implications of either a vampire plague or a zombie apocalypse.

In Matheson's novel, the audience is focused on Robert Neville as the lone survivor, the last human on earth, and we tend to read the novel as apocalyptic because we see the destruction of human society down to its very last member. Unfortunately—and this is where the 2007 film version of *I Am Legend* gets it completely wrong—Robert Neville is not *legend* because he represents human society, nor because he somehow saves humanity; Robert Neville is legend because he is the single largest threat to a *new society*, one that has superseded humanity. Society has evolved beyond humanity, mutating to accommodate a new life-form that both is and is not identifiably human, which proves most clearly that it is our definition and even prioritization of *humanity* that has been flawed from the outset. This is where I see Matheson's and Romero's texts engaging with the humanist/post-humanist debate most directly, as they both offer examples of vastly transformed human landscapes wherein that change is, as Katherine Hayles has often suggested, both nightmarish *and* liberating.[5] Further, as Neil Badmington suggests, "apocalyptic accounts of the end of 'Man' ... ignore humanism's capacity for regeneration and, quite literally, recapitulation,"[6] leading unwary spectators to focus solely on the restoration of the human status quo rather than considering the potential for advancement in both mind and body that are often the focus of post-humanist considerations. If we are to consider whether the zombie is or can be representative of the post-human state, we must first purge ourselves of the very binaries that defined the old Cartesian model. If zombies are both alive and dead,[7] if they retain portions of both mind and body, then they force us to rethink the foundational philosophies that have informed our interactions with birth, life, death, and the hereafter.

Robert Pepperell in his book *The Post-Human Condition* uses the term "post-human" in a variety of contexts: (1) to designate an end to the era of social theory dubbed humanism, (2) to indicate that our conceptual construction of what it means to *be human* is undergoing a profound transformation, and (3) to account for the conflation of emerging technologies that "show that the balance of power between humans and machines is altering."[8] The first of those contexts is problematic, because, as a number of scholars have convincingly countered, anything saddled with a "post" in its name is irretrievably caught up in whatever it is that it is "posting,"[9] so it becomes nearly impossible to discuss *post*-humanism without engaging in a discussion of the relative pros and cons of *humanism*. Meanwhile, Pepperell's third context focuses on the nexus of the organic and the technological. Robotics, prosthetics, and even neural networks aside, once one engages with the concept of nanotechnology—of *living* machines—it becomes even more difficult to ignore the specter of humanism, which could prioritize the organic transformation of *machines into humans* as evidence of human superiority. Katherine Hayles, in *How We Became Posthuman*, compellingly warns against the dangers of apocalyptic or "complacent" post-humanism, arguing that in a scenario based on the death or replacement of humans we should beware the "grafting of the posthuman onto a liberal humanist view of the self."[10] The Syfy channel's series *Battlestar Galactica* appears to be traveling down this path, but while I think it's a fascinating issue worthy of further examination, it isn't the one I want to explore here. It is specifically Pepperell's second context of the word post-human—the profound transformation of humanity's conceptual definition of itself—that I am interested in applying to the *dead/Other* rather than the technological/Other, to consider whether "reading the zombie as an ontic/hauntic object"[11] reveals our own denial of that which is *inhuman* in all of us. Thus I begin my examination of both the vampire and the zombie, Matheson and Romero, with a brief look at an alien.

In "Pod Almighty!; or, Humanism, Posthumanism, and the Strange Case of *Invasion of the Body Snatchers*," Neil Badmington focuses on the scene in Don Siegel's 1956 movie where the protagonist, Miles Bennell, has a confrontation of sorts with the "people" growing inside the four pods beside his greenhouse. There are two significant ideas proffered in this scene; the first is that when the pods are first discovered discharging their vaguely human contents, Miles is restrained from destroying them by Jack, who insists that they don't pose any danger until they are fully formed. This seems like a definite shout-at-the-screen moment because the viewers already know that those four pods have given birth to alien replicas of the two men and two women, replicas who will then dispose of their human counterparts. One could argue that the best time, in fact, to destroy them is *before they are fully formed*, but no one seems ready to destroy something that is *vaguely*, or perhaps *potentially*, human. When

Jack returns to the greenhouse alone a short time later, however, four shapes are now distinctly recognizable as Miles, Becky, Jack, and Teddy. Herein lies the conflict, because while Miles destroys his own replica with nary a second thought, he simply cannot bring himself to destroy an alien body with Becky's face. He knows it is not Becky—it is even a threat to Becky—but he cannot destroy that which he identifies as/with his lover. This moment of alien/human cathexis is what prompts Badmington to argue that this scene delineates the "invasion" of post-humanism into humanism; more specifically, he argues:

> Because the alien reminds him of Becky, Miles cannot avoid acting as if it/she were the true object of his desire. His uniquely human feelings for Becky lead him to place her in a position which threatens her very existence, her very future as a human being. Although "[s]exuality and sexual difference," as Cyndy Hendershot has pointed out, "are *the* measures of humanity in the film," it would seem that they are at once the measures of posthumanism. To be human is to desire, to possess emotions, but to desire is to trouble the sacred distinction between the human and the inhuman. Miles loves Becky, but Miles also appears to love an alien legume. Humanism has been invaded by posthumanism.[12]

Ultimately, *Invasion of the Body Snatchers* upholds basic humanism by maintaining the pretext that there is some ineffable human quality that cannot be copied or reproduced, thus forever demarcating the line between human and nonhuman. As Badmington suggests, however, "A seemingly straightforward humanism secretes its own alternative,"[13] or as Pepperell more stridently argues, "No finite division can be drawn between the environment, the body and the brain. The human is identifiable, but not definable."[14] This latter sentiment returns us to the second context of Pepperell's use of the word post-human that I acknowledged previously—the profound transformation of humanity's conceptual definition of itself—because there is also a way of interpreting Miles's reluctance to destroy *the body* of the alien Becky as indicative of a reluctance to recognize or acknowledge the Cartesian mind/body separation at the heart of traditional humanism. To borrow loosely from Donna Haraway's "A Cyborg Manifesto," if "there is nothing about being female that naturally binds women together into a unified category," and even the status of "being" female is "itself a highly complex category constructed in contested sexual scientific discourses and other social practices,"[15] then can we not consider whether there can be a unified category called *human*—and if so what, then, are those unifying characteristics, because Descartes's old mantra of

"I think, therefore I am" seems woefully solipsistic in light of today's scientific and technological advances. This, of course, is too voluminous a topic to be adequately addressed here, but I would like to borrow a bit from the psychological dualism implicit in determining *self*-identification and negation, or that which is me and that which is not me. This is what the zombie incarnates: our discomfort with that boundary space that exists in us all, that objectness of our inherent material makeup whereby we transition from human to post-(as in no longer)-human.

Matheson's I Am Legend *and the Problem of Identification*

In 1954, just nine years after the Trinity Test,[16] Richard Matheson published his novel *I Am Legend*—with the guiding premise that the human race was doomed to extinction. In the novel, widespread use of bombs causes a viral pandemic that virtually wipes out all traces of humanity on earth; the resulting apocalypse leaves Robert Neville as the sole surviving human engaged in a continuous battle against hordes of Darwinian mutants: a vampiric, photosensitive group of undead, driven by an instinctual desire to feed on human blood. Of course, texts like Matheson's make the distinction between living, dead, and "undead" harder to demarcate, especially when a plethora of film adaptations have interpreted these creatures differently—from the shambling ghouls of *The Last Man on Earth* (1964) to the white-haired technophobes of *The Omega Man* (1971) to the red-eyed "Darkseekers" of *I Am Legend* (2007). The creatures were even still called vampires in *The Last Man on Earth*, but as Peter Dendle has noted, we "know a zombie when we see one."[17] Furthering the confusion is the fact that Matheson slowly reveals that there are, in fact, two kinds of vampires in his novel: one living and one dead. Thus normative categories are problematic, but this very variety reinforces Robert Pepperell's claim that "the human is identifiable, but not definable";[18] we identify the sameness of these creatures across a variety of interpretations, but we define them according to context rather than construct.

For the most part, both Neville's daily experimentations on the sleeping undead and his nightly antagonism with the hordes outside his house are devoid of personal attachment—the dead/undead are anonymous and impersonal, with only two exceptions (to be discussed in more detail below).[19] He reflects dispassionately on the "eleven—no, twelve children that afternoon"[20] that he had destroyed, and he tosses a young woman outside into the sunlight to die a painful, drawn-out death because he wanted to see how long it would take. Neville is our touchstone in this apocalyptic landscape; he is our viewpoint and, as such, determines in large part the direction and scope of our understanding of this dead new world. Because Matheson strategically alternates scenes of Neville's brutal pursuit of the vampires with flashbacks of the life Neville had before the plague, readers are placed in a position where they identify with Neville's despondency and the wretchedness of having lost the very things that gave his life meaning. After both his wife and his daughter fall victim to the plague that has produced the vampires, Neville, and by extension the reader, regains some measure of meaning in the methodic destruction of what we perceive as *the enemy*. More important, Matheson's narrative maneuvers allow us to identify with the man that Neville once was and to imagine how we might react to the traumatic circumstances that transform him into what he becomes.[21]

Robert Neville was once a conscientious citizen, one who obeyed the dictums of law and order; when his daughter, Kathy, succumbs to the spreading plague, Neville takes her to the appointed place where her body can be safely dealt with, thus preventing the further spread of the plague. What he doesn't know then is that this place of disposal is nothing more than a huge fire pit where the bodies of the infected are burned indiscriminately. The reader cringes when the full horror of what will happen dawns on Neville: "The great fire crackling, roaring yellow, sending its dense and grease-thick clouds into the sky. Kathy's tiny body in his arms. The man coming up and snatching her away as if he were taking a bundle of rags. The man lunging into the dark mist carrying his baby. Him standing there while the pile driver blows of horror drove him down with their impact."[22] Few of us can comprehend the pain of losing a child, much less the horror of watching that child immolated in the depersonalizing conflagration of a mass fire pit. For a man still grieving the death of his beloved daughter to be complicit in the utter destruction of her remains becomes a moment of transformation for Neville. When the time comes for Neville to dispose of his wife's remains, he cannot bring himself to consign her as well to "a bonfire a hundred yards square, a hundred feet deep."[23] All societal recognition of death as an emotional, symbolic event has been superseded by mass fear of infection: morticians are banned from performing their body preservation services, cemeteries are barred and guarded, "men had been shot trying to bury their loved ones."[24] The body, post-death, has become a liability that neither society nor the individual can afford to treat sentimentally. Logically, the body is no longer a symbolic representation of the life that was once housed there, and instead represents a highly contagious source of infection, but Neville refuses to recognize the mandates of reason and medicine. As he secretly buries his wife in an out-of-the-way, high-weeded lot, Neville works swiftly—not out of fear that he will pay the consequences, but out of fear that Virginia will: "If he was seen they would come out and get him. Being shot was nothing. But she would be burned then. His lips tightened. No."[25] The corporeal remains of his wife represent not simply the person it was once, but also Neville's own ability (and inability) to recognize himself: "Time was caught on hooks and could not progress. Everything stood fixed. With Virginia, life and the world had shuddered to a halt."[26] For Neville, the destruction of Virginia's body is an idea so horrible that he acts against law and logic to prevent it, to preserve her body intact as a representation of life—the life they *used to have*. Unfortunately for Neville, symbols do not always retain their meaning, and the dead do not always stay buried.

Two days, or rather two nights, after he buries his wife's body, a sleepless Robert Neville is startled by the sound of someone turning the knob on the front door. In terms of time, this is way before it becomes necessary for Neville to fortify his home—on this night, the windows are open and the front door is unlocked, but at two in the morning he isn't expecting any visitors. In a scene reminiscent of Poe's *The Fall of the House of Usher*, and I would hope recognizably similar to Badmington's example of the greenhouse scene in *Invasion of the Body Snatchers*, Neville is forced to confront a revised and referential body that is both drastically altered—and thus unfamiliar—yet simultaneously and horrifically familiar:

> He moved into the living room slowly, his heartbeat thudding heavily. The door rattled as another fist thudded against it weakly. He felt himself twitch at the sound. What's the matter? he thought. The door is open. From the open window a cold breeze blew across his face. The darkness drew him to the door. "Who . . ." he murmured, unable to go on. His hand recoiled from the doorknob as it turned under his fingers. With one step he backed into the wall and stood there breathing harshly, his widened eyes staring. Nothing happened. He stood there holding himself rigidly. Then his breath was snuffed. Someone was mumbling on the porch, muttering words he couldn't hear. He braced himself; then, with a lunge, he jerked open the door and let the moonlight in. He couldn't even scream. He just stood rooted to the spot, staring dumbly at Virginia. "Rob . . . ert," she said.[27]

Later in the story, in what is almost an aside, we learn that Neville's confrontation with she-who-is-not-his-wife has a violent end, that he is forced ultimately to destroy her body despite—even because of—what it signifies for him. Even though her death from the plague represents a cessation, an end, where "everything stood fixed," he acts to preserve her body in direct conflict with the old Cartesian model of mind/body separation, as if ensuring that her body remain intact will ensure that her essence remain intact. He is proved frighteningly correct in that enough of Virginia is intact to enable her to crawl her way out of a sewn-up blanket and several feet of earth, find her way back to the home she remembers, and even to call him by name. In the end, Neville's failure to separate mind from body, memory from corpse, results in his having to destroy precisely what he had hoped to preserve. His memories now include his having to be the architect of Virginia's final destruction—her second death.

Neville's confrontation with the reality of Virginia's death—and undeath—is demonstrably part of what causes his reversal from identification to negation; his lack of emotional involvement in his daily confrontations with the other vampires over the next ten years is the product of his having cut off the part of himself that cathects with the world around him. Everything is at his disposal; the malls, the libraries, the grocery stores are all completely open for his personal use, and he treats the vampires in much the same way—as depersonalized scapegoats for the release of his personal frustrations. This nihilistic viewpoint is challenged only by the appearance of a living dog, the named vampire Ben Cortman, and Ruth—a vampire who can walk about during the day.

The social bonds of friendship are distorted in *I Am Legend* so that rather than sustaining life, they become emblematic of its destruction—a connection that is made outside Robert Neville's house every evening when his neighbor and friend Ben Cortland, now a vampire, stands on the front lawn and shouts for Neville to come out so that he can have him for dinner. Their former friendship transmutes into a kind of perverse game of hide-and-seek—Cortman harasses Neville on a nightly basis and Neville hunts for Cortman's corpse daily: "It had become a relaxing hobby, hunting for Cortman; one of the few diversions left to him. . . . Neville felt certain that Cortman knew he was singled out for capture. He felt, further, that Cortman relished the peril of it. If the phrase were not such an obvious anachronism, Neville would have said that Ben Cortman had a zest for life. Sometimes he thought Ben Cortman was happier now than he ever had been before."[28] The fact that Cortman is named, is *known* to Neville, makes him a kind of foil against which Neville thinks to measure his relative humanity, and while the reader is under the impression that Cortman is representative of all vampires it is easier to agree with Neville. But that binary understanding of vampire/human—dead/not-dead—is most directly challenged when Neville encounters Ruth, who appears to be a human female walking about during the daytime. Readers, like Neville, are caught between their hopes that all is not lost—that this Adam and Eve scenario can repopulate Eden as we knew it—and fears that this is just another cruel twist of fate that Neville must endure as the last remnant of human life.

Dennis Giles has argued that a central theme of horror is the existence of "delayed, blocked, or partial vision,"[29] and in this case the revelation conflates the fatal flaw in Neville's, and our, conceptions of humanity—of self and Other. Ruth represents the *other survivors* of the pandemic virus; the dust storms that infected everyone but Neville resulted in two separate mutations: the animated corpses we are familiar with, and a group of mutated humans who do not die but who suffer from side effects that result in our dismissive labeling of them as vampires. Neville, whose characteristic detachment toward the vampires he killed seemed so reasonable before, is now revealed to be singularly closed-minded; he had been indiscriminately killing those he considered the enemy, some of whom had been living beings engaged in an effort to restore order and rebuild society.

By the time Ruth makes an appearance, a new society has emerged, albeit a primarily nocturnal one, and steps have been taken to bring back a certain amount of order and communal responsibility. Unfortunately for Neville, he has become an impediment to the very social order he thought he was single-handedly maintaining. In the note that she leaves him after knocking him unconscious, Ruth explains:

> When I was first given the job of spying on you, I had no feelings about your life. Because I *did* have a husband, Robert. You killed him. But now it's different. I know now that you were just as much forced into your situation as we were into ours. We *are* infected. . . . What you don't understand is that we're going to stay alive. We've found a way to do that and we're going to set up society again slowly and surely. We're going to do away with all those wretched creatures whom death has cheated. And, even though I pray otherwise, we may decide to kill you and those like you.[30]

As proof of what she says, Ruth leaves Neville one of the pills that she had been surreptitiously taking all the while she was with him: "a combination of defibrinated blood and a drug"[31] that enables Ruth to fight her hunger for blood and survive in the daylight. The horrific truth overwhelms Neville as he realizes that what Ruth suggests is indeed possible: that a mutation in the bacteria could allow some of those infected to adapt and survive.

Matheson makes a concerted effort to show the relative humanity of some of the vampires alongside the increasing inhumanity of Robert Neville; the survivors of the pandemic virus that turns them into vampires are actively rebuilding society, organizing a provisional government, forming a communications network, and establishing a military police force, one whose chief goal is the capture of the last human. Neville's failure to recognize his wife's transformation pales in retrospect as it becomes clear that he has failed to recognize his own too-narrowly-defined classification for humanity, and in his error he has been the agent of humanity's destruction. He has become the threat, the virus, the social contaminant that must be removed like a tumor before the social body can re-form and heal. Capturing and destroying Robert Neville has become the new society's foremost goal, and it becomes apparent to the readers that we have been identifying *humanness* within an outdated context; Neville has become the monster and the vampires have become representatives of the post-human.

Neville's final reflection in the novel is to realize "with an inward shock that he could not recognize in the rush of the moment . . . that he felt more deeply toward the vampires than he did toward their executioners."[32] The differences between human and nonhuman, or rather post-human, conflate in the final scene of the novel as recognition comes too late to save Robert Neville.

George Romero's Night of the Living Dead *and the Problem of Negation*

Gregory Waller, in *American Horrors: Essays on the Modern American Horror Film*, marks the "modern" era of horror film as beginning in 1968 with George Romero's *Night of the Living Dead* and Roman Polanski's *Rosemary's Baby*, calling prior films of the 1960s formulaic and safe, but crediting these two with redefining "the monstrous—thereby redefining the role of the hero and the victim as well—and [situating] horror in the everyday world of contemporary America."[33] Certainly, Romero's flesh-eating ghouls defy whatever safety audiences may have expected from the film, replacing it with an "open-eyed detailing of human taboos, murder, and cannibalism."[34] In fact, I would argue that *Night of the Living Dead* is demonstrative of what the film critic Adam Lowenstein has called *shock horror*, or "the employment of graphic, visceral shock to access the historical substrate of traumatic experience."[35] Lowenstein combines the theorist Walter Benjamin's idea of the "dialectic of awakening"[36] with this concept of shock horror, and theorizes that the "pain of . . . shock horror is the agony of awakening—to the body, and to history."[37] While Lowenstein was specifically discussing the films of Georges Franju,[38] I believe that Romero also intended to effect an *awakening*—to reflect the trauma of a nation suffering—and this interpretation is supported in a number of unexpected ways. The Museum of Modern Art was one of the first institutions to screen *Night of the Living Dead*, recognizing its cultural as well as historical value, and the installation grounded the film as follows:

> Released at a time when disillusionment was running rampant in the country—spurred by the Vietnam War and the recent assassinations of Martin Luther King Jr. and John F. Kennedy—Americans identified with the film's most shocking suggestion: death is random and without purpose. No one dies for the greater good or to further the survival of others. Instead, people die to feed faceless, ordinary America. A metaphor for societal anxiety, the sight of America literally devouring itself and the representation of the desecration of the wholesome American family . . . served as a release for the country's repressed trauma.[39]

Where I suggest *Night of the Living Dead* intersects with the issue of post-humanism is in an adaptation of Plato's theory of anamnesis—a process of remembrance or recollection of the past. Anamnesis, however, also has the medical application of referring to the body's response to a previously encountered antigen—a *remembrance* of that antigen that prompts a more focused physical response. Films, like zombie films, that project a futurity of events—even apocalyptic events—are by necessity utilizing recaptured, revised, restructured visions of the past—past anxiety, past trauma, past hysteria. They are a form of social vaccination that revisits the horror of disease or trauma in order to prepare the social body for some future contamination or event.

The spectacle of horror both familiarizes and distances the audience from the traumatic event depicted, seeming to depict something new but effectively redirecting the public's attention to past events from which they have become desensitized by repeated exposure.[40] Considered in this light, the depersonalization that is a characteristic of the zombie—bodies without souls—can be reconceived as a problem of identification, an unwillingness to recognize both similarity *and* difference. Robert Neville fails specifically to recognize the reality of his wife's physical transformation, but more universally he fails to differentiate the *living* vampires from the *dead* ones; he cannot overcome the differences manifested by the plague to identify the post-human state of the living vampires. The ephemeral yet supposedly determining essence of humanity is just as difficult to distinguish in *Night of the Living Dead*.

In the opening scene, Johnny jokingly teases his sister by saying "They're coming to get you, Barbara!," but the joke is soon decidedly not funny as it becomes apparent that they are indeed coming to get them. When her brother falls victim to the graveyard zombie, Barbara flees in the car only to have to abandon it and seek the relative shelter of a nearby farmhouse. Inside, she finds a motley assortment of humans, including the home's resident family, gathered inside for exactly the same reason. Barricading the doors and windows, the humans in *Night of the Living Dead* create for themselves a similar prison to the one Robert Neville existed in; the home becomes not a place of refuge so much as a place of confinement and restriction. Whereas *I Am Legend* takes place over several years, the events of *Night of the Living Dead* consist of just that—a single night. Thus the physical and cognitive interactions of the inmates become charged with a sense of immediacy, and the audience is swiftly engrossed in the struggle of the living against the forces of the dead.

But just like our eventual disillusionment with Robert Neville, humanity in *Night of the Living Dead* ultimately disappoints the audience and shrinks the ideological gap between themselves and the instinct-driven corpses that plague them. Those inside the marginal sanctuary of the house are as much a risk to each other as are the zombies hammering at the windows. Everything that was familiar has been inverted: familial bonds prove deadly for the Coopers, as they do for Barbara, because these figures cannot reconcile themselves to their loved ones becoming the *Other*. If the problem in *I Am Legend* was one of faulty or incomplete identification, in *Night of the Living Dead* it seems that the prevailing issue is rather a failure of negation; the characters fail to appropriately categorize the *difference* between themselves and the zombies, and thus fail to protect themselves. Barbara, though demonstrably passive through much of the film, seems to surrender entirely when she sees her brother Johnny—now a zombie—reaching through the door, giving herself over to him as if it were impossible to resist the familial bond between them. Mrs. Cooper quite nearly resigns herself to being eaten by her daughter—perhaps because she is simply too deep in denial about the changes wrought in her family, or perhaps she acts *despite* her recognition of her daughter's transformation. Her perception of her own role as mother is paramount in either scenario; regardless of whether her daughter is still human, or even still *her daughter*, she conceives of herself as mother to the recognizable form of her daughter and she cannot act contrary to this identification. Thus she cannot act to protect herself.

Neither love nor personal integrity offers any measure of protection, as the zombies themselves don't care whether they are eating a "good" person or a "bad" person, someone's sister or husband. Not even Tom and Judy are spared, despite our certainty that the young couple represent the transcendent hope of youth and love, and neither is Ben, arguably the strongest living character in the film—the one we think most likely to survive. The transformation of human into food arguably begins at death itself when, as Shakespeare most famously pointed out, the body becomes mere food for worms, but in *Night of the Living Dead* the natural order of the process is reversed, as the still living become food for the dead.

Traditionally, critiques of *Night of the Living Dead* have focused on its nihilism, its utter negation of humanity itself. As R. H. W. Dillard argues, "the plot is . . . one of simple negation, an orchestrated descent to death in which all efforts toward life fail,"[41] demonstrating what the cultural critic Slavoj Žižek in *Welcome to the Desert of the Real*[42] calls the United States' deep psychological attachment to images of catastrophe. Certainly, the shocking portrayal of cannibalism, animated corpses, and the amount and specificity of gore displayed make *Night of the Living Dead* a radical narrative for its time, but more shocking, more frightening even is the way that the film systematically takes apart the constructs of social order and human value. Death is, from the very first frames, no longer a state of being that has meaning, as demonstrated by Johnny's irreverence in the graveyard; conversely, if death no longer has value—sacred or otherwise— how are we to consider the value of life? Throughout the film, "the deaths . . . are all to no purpose; they do not finally serve the practical cause of survival, nor do they act to the enhancement of larger human value."[43] Drawing from Giorgio Agamben's concept of a permanent state of exception, Meghan Sutherland argues that "in [zombie films], death asserts its immanence in the living and life asserts its immanence in the dead," thus death becomes a continuing state of being—a post-life existence that defies normative categories.[44] Dying itself has no purpose anymore, for those who die rise again as monstrous doppelgangers of their living selves.

Night of the Living Dead dramatizes the bewildering and uncanny transformation of human beings into nonhuman forms. Yet the most callous treatment of the human form is not the result of a zombie attack, at least not directly; Ben, weary and dispirited, sits visibly motionless at daybreak as the local sheriff and his men approach the house, indiscriminately killing all the zombies in their path. Our survivor, Ben, is no longer recognizable as human, and he is shot and killed by the sheriff. Whether one chooses to see this final act as the result of racism—Ben was an African American actor cast in a leading role in the late 1960s—or indicative of a far more universal blindness or apathy, the notion that there is ultimately no discernible difference between the living and the dead suggests that the corpse of traditional humanism is as fluid and mobile as the walking corpses of the dead.

The chilling final scene of *Night of the Living Dead*—where the bodies of the first zombie we saw on-screen and the last human to survive the night in the farmhouse are both shown being tossed into the fire by the sheriff and his men—demonstrates most clearly the flaws of human judgment and its inability to discern its own capacity for inhuman behavior. In both *I Am Legend* and *Night of the Living Dead*, the surviving human is sacrificed because he represents a body that is simultaneously too similar and too different; Neville and Ben are social corpses, representative products of the "inherent and inseparable thing-character of human existence . . . not only our future but our present"[45] in that they exist in the state toward which we all advance with the same inexorable motion known as human life. Both Matheson and Romero pointedly direct our attention back to our own body politic and the weaknesses therein, and seem to ask us why, with the consequences of humanity's *humanness* making themselves blatantly apparent all around us—global warming, resource depletion, warfare—is it so difficult to consider that we might all be, well, better off dead?

CHAPTER 6

Nuclear Death and Radical Hope in *Dawn of the Dead* and *On the Beach*

Nick Muntean

Many zombie narratives, given the nature of their subject matter, take place within apocalyptic or postapocalyptic settings; as the living, sentient humans that populated the globe die and become the undead, the societies they once composed disappear, creating a world without formal governments, religions, or cultures. The possibility of such a post-human epoch on Earth looms large as one of the most salient threats in zombie narratives, along with a fear of being devoured (and that of devouring others) and the terror of losing one's sense of identity while nevertheless remaining (somewhat) alive.

As one might expect, then, many of the zombie narrative's thematic elements are not limited to this genre. One such example is Stanley Kramer's 1959 film *On the Beach* (an adaptation of Nevil Shute's 1957 novel of the same name), wherein a global nuclear war has killed most of the world's inhabitants, sparing only the residents of Australia, who are now made to face the grim fate of slowly waiting for their deaths to be delivered by trade winds imbued with the bombs' radioactive fallout. The general narrative conflict of this film—that of a small group of survivors set against near-global forces of death—is strikingly similar to that of George Romero's 1978 *Dawn of the Dead*,[1] save for the crucial difference that the antagonists in the latter film are allegorical, while those of the former are all too real. Rather, in *On the Beach* it is the plight of the protagonists themselves that is allegorical, as their lonely, doomed postapocalyptic existences offer no source of hope or meaning, such that the characters' psychic annihilation precedes their physical destruction, and life itself becomes a state of waking death.

It is in this sense that we may call the characters in *On the Beach* "trauma zombies," as their normal symbolic processes of meaning-making (that is to say, ideology) are so disrupted that they are unable to maintain a coherent identity and thus enter a muted, dazed state of being not unlike that of the traditional zombie. The trauma zombie, as suggested by its appellation, is born of a traumatic incident or injury—typically a confrontation with a massive rupture or collapse of their social order—and becomes, like the zombie itself, both victim and perpetuator of its affliction. Of course, catastrophic events do not equally affect all characters within a film; for instance, in *Night of the Living Dead* (1968), Barbara (Judith O'Dea) is deeply traumatized by her first altercation with the zombies, leading to an unsettling catatonia that unnerves many of the other characters, such that her eventual willing submission to the crowd of flesh-eating undead comes as little surprise, for she had essentially become a zombie some time before.

The similarities between the respective narrative functions of the zombie and the trauma zombie—as well as their homologous psychic states—are expressive of the shared sociohistorical origins of these two figures, and indicative of two similar strategies for narrativizing certain facets of our social reality that elude easy articulation or ready categorization. Much as some of these collective anxieties expressed through the zombie center around the disturbing dialectical reality of modern social progress—that society's technological development is only attained by a concomitant increase in the potential for society's own self-destruction—so, too, is the zombie creature itself a liminal figure, simultaneously both life and death, and yet not really either, a monstrous "degree zero" of humanity that defies easy categorization or explanation (which is perhaps, partly, what makes it so terrifying).

Stories that focus on these transgressive creatures may also constitute liminal narrative spaces, vexing interstices of fantastical horror and realist social critique that test the bounds of our conceptions of what constitutes the human. The same can be said for the social function of the trauma zombie, and the consistency of its signification, though its specific narrative function often varies among different texts. Regardless of the different processes through which the trauma zombie is engendered, or the various ends to which it is deployed, the nature of the trauma zombie itself is quite consistent: a state of being that is both that of undeath and unlife. As will be shown, the trauma zombie articulates a profound—and profoundly modern—shift from older cultural attitudes about death: the process of dying no longer means the conveyance of our eternally unchanging soul to another, more timeless realm; rather, death becomes a state that we inhabit within our own earthly vessels, something we become, rather than somewhere we go to. What makes these figures most terrifying is that, despite the extremely brutal, and uniquely modern, conditions that have produced them, we can nonetheless recognize something of ourselves in them. That is, what might be most horrifying about these creatures—both the modern zombie and the trauma zombie—is the unspoken realization that these are the contours of our contemporary cultural nightmares, the conceivable ends reached by our collective capacity for self-disgust.

This emphasis on the "modern"—specifically, post–World War II—concerns embodied by the zombie and the trauma zombie requires some explanation, as the zombie has been a part of Haitian culture for centuries, and has been a fixture of American culture since the early 1930s. Thus, in the interests of analytic clarity, it is necessary to introduce the periodizing concept of the "modern zombie." This term, referring as it does to the flesh-eating, master-less zombie figure introduced most memorably by George Romero in *Night of the Living Dead*, is meant to distinguish the Romero zombie from the earlier, Vodou zombie, in which a single (usually white) sorcerer figure would extend his will through the mesmeric command of (usually black) laborers. In contrast, the modern zombie figure lacks any such centralized figure of agency and control, and it is considerably more gruesome in appearance and behavior than the earlier Vodou zombie. Whereas one of the principal terrors in the Vodou zombie narratives was the loss of self-control and self-identity through the imposition of the will of another individual, the modern zombie is terrifying precisely because no singular agent acts to possess the victim's mind. Rather, it is society itself—the very same cultural, ideological, and material institutions through which an individual realizes him- or herself as a subject—that is ultimately responsible for the zombie's terrifying dehumanization.

It is my contention that the modern zombie arose after the allegorical powers of the earlier form were exhausted, and more specifically, that the cultural impact of the atrocities of World War II (i.e., the Nazi concentration camps and the aftermath of the atomic explosions in Hiroshima and Nagasaki) rendered the psychological threat of the Vodou zombie (that of losing one's autonomy to another) obsolete, replaced instead by the far more disturbing possibility of an existential anxiety (that one could continue to live, but be nothing), which is also articulated by the trauma zombie.[2] These events, and their repercussions in our society's collective memory, have, for the zombie genre, functioned much like a Freudian traumatic scene, arresting the normal flow of psychic energy (e.g., the common tropes and patterns of the "premodern" zombie films), such that the genre became fixated on re-creating and re-presenting this original transformative moment.

We will return to the zombie genre's traumatic wounds at the end of this essay, as only then will we have all the appropriate evidence and arguments. At present, a brief summary of the two films will set the stage for a consideration of the ways in which they foreground the traumatizing collapse of ideological systems as centrally catalyzing narrative events. The post-ideological anxieties expressed by these films will lead to an exploration of the cultural antecedents of the modern zombie and the trauma zombie, and the allegorical value of such figures for our society.

In *Dawn of the Dead*, the isolated zombie outbreaks introduced in *Night of the Living Dead* (caused by radiation emitted from a returning space probe) have swelled to critical levels, rendering entire cities into little more than charnel houses of the undead. In a besieged news station in Philadelphia, two television reporters, Stephen (David Emge) and Francine (Gaylen Ross), join with two SWAT unit members, Peter (Ken Foree) and Roger (Scott H. Reiniger), and flee the city in the station's helicopter, ultimately landing on top of a shopping mall. After clearing out the zombies roaming its stores, they turn the mall into their own fortified residence. A zombie bites Roger while he is securing one of the mall's entrances, and Peter is forced to shoot him before he transforms into a zombie. Over the passing months, broadcasts from the outside world gradually cease, and the group settles into a comfortable, if bored, lifestyle. Their delicate homeostasis is violated when a group of motorcycle-riding looters break through the mall's fortifications, with the zombies soon following suit. Stephen attempts to fight off the bikers but is attacked by zombies, and, upon becoming a zombie himself, leads a cadre of his undead brethren to Francine and Peter's hiding spot. Peter kills Stephen, and Francine and Peter head to the helicopter on the mall's roof; while Francine prepares the helicopter for takeoff, Peter appears ready to commit suicide-by-zombie, finally deciding at the last moment to join Francine in her flight to safety.

Similarly, *On the Beach* features a small cadre of survivors set against an environment that has abruptly become sinister and strange. The year is 1964, and a global nuclear war has obliterated nearly all the world's population. While Australia's geographic isolation and political neutrality saved it from direct destruction, deadly radioactive fallout has engulfed much of the Northern Hemisphere and is now slowly but inexorably advancing on the lives of the Australian survivors. An American submarine and its crew arrive in the port of Melbourne, whereupon the ship's captain, a recent widower, Cmdr. Dwight Lionel Towers (Gregory Peck), begins an ostensibly platonic affair with a local woman, Moira Davidson (Ava Gardner). Their relationship is interrupted, however, when the Australian Navy receives a radio signal emanating from somewhere around San Francisco. Hoping that the transmission might signal the continuing existence of life in the Northern Hemisphere, Towers quickly readies his crew and is accompanied by Lt. Cmdr. Peter Holmes (Anthony Perkins) of the Royal Australian Navy and the scientist Julian Osborne (Fred Astaire). After their long journey reveals that the signal was little more than a soda bottle knocking against a radio transceiver, the crew glumly returns to Australia to wait out their final days on Earth. Some, like Osborne, choose to spend their days living out the wild fantasies they would never have previously pursued (he competes in auto races), while others, such as Holmes, with his wife and young child, struggle to maintain familial cohesion and purpose. Towers tries to come to terms with the knowledge that his family and everything he knew in the United States is now gone, and he vacillates between a desire to live out his final days in the company of Moira, and an austere sense of duty to honor the memory of his family. As the radioactive gales move immanently near, the Australian government, in one of its final official acts, distributes suicide pills to those who would prefer not to suffer through the slow, anguishing death of radiation poisoning. Finally, the winds arrive and reduce everything, and everyone, to silence. In both of these (nearly) post-human environments, the characters are suddenly faced with a crisis of ideology. If we accept Louis Althusser's suggestion that ideology is "not the system of the real relations which govern the existence of individuals, but the imaginary relation of those individuals to the real relations in which they live,"[3] then it is clear that both the zombies and the characters in the *On the Beach* are post-ideological in some sense. The zombies are beyond ideology due to certain neurochemical changes in their brains, and the characters in *On the Beach* can be considered post-ideological insofar as there is no longer an extant system of larger "real relations" through which they can derive meaning. In both scenarios, ideological subjects are forced by external conditions into mental states in which it becomes impossible to imagine oneself as a deliberative, conscious agent—the gap between one's interior mental state and the real relations of the world become an impassable chasm, such that ideological meaning-making ceases to function.

While both films depict the mental circumstances that engender these post-ideological subjects as occurring under (or causing) extreme disruptions in the social order, the type of psychological state they invoke also occurs in the real world, and is typically diagnosed as schizophrenia. Schizophrenia is characterized by the subject's profound detachment from the larger world, from a sense of helplessness or lack of agency that becomes sublimated into the creation of a new internal reality over which the subject, as its maker, has complete control. According to the psychohistorian Robert Jay Lifton, "At the ultimate level, [the schizophrenic's] absence of connection beyond the self, the sense of being cut off from the chain of being, from larger human relationships, leaves him with the feeling that life is counterfeit, and that biological death is uneventful, because psychic death is everywhere."[4] Lifton's remarks were made regarding the common psychological reaction to the threat of global nuclear warfare, though others have argued that this schizophrenic state is not specific only to the threat of nuclear weapons, but is more subtly induced simply through the experience of being human in the twentieth century.

The Frankfurt School theorist and practicing psychotherapist Erich Fromm shared Lifton's concern about the psychological consequences of the threat of nuclear annihilation, as he believed that a future global thermonuclear war was "perhaps [the] most likely possibility."[5] Yet even if a nuclear war did not occur, he was not particularly optimistic about the possibilities for humankind's future, as he believed that the next hundred years would simply be a continuation of the alienation and automatization that defined modern life in the early twentieth century: "In the nineteenth century the problem was that God is dead; in the twentieth century the problem is that man is dead. In the nineteenth century inhumanity meant cruelty; in the twentieth century it means schizoid self-alienation. The danger of the past was that men became slaves. The danger of the future is that men become robots. True enough, robots do not rebel. But given man's nature, robots cannot live and remain sane, they become 'Golems,' they will destroy their world and themselves because they cannot stand any longer the boredom of a meaningless life."[6] For Fromm, the centralization and automation of managerial societies limits opportunities for self-expression and autonomy, but it does not fundamentally alter human nature. In his view, there is a fundamental kernel of "the human" inside each person, which may be repressed or otherwise truncated but will nevertheless persist, no matter how contorted it may become. It is on this belief that he makes his claim that "schizoid self-alienation"—humanity's fractured estrangement from its own "natural" beliefs and desires—has in the twentieth century supplanted cruelty as humankind's defining problem.

As detailed before, this psychological state is clearly evidenced by the characters in *On the Beach*, though it is conspicuously absent from the behavior and manifest emotions of the characters in *Dawn of the Dead*—rather, it is manifested by the zombies. The near-overwhelming presence of the zombies has seemingly the opposite effect on *Dawn*'s protagonists, as their predicament emboldens them toward action, making them crave more life, not less. Perhaps this disparity might be due to a different ground state for the films' respective characters: in *On the Beach*, the characters were in love with life before the catastrophic events that led them to become half-dead, whereas in *Dawn of the Dead* the characters were merely sleepwalking through their existences before their social order was disrupted by the zombies.

What these arguments regarding the schizophrenic state of modern humans fail to account for is the fact that the characters in both films are experiencing cataclysmic reorderings of their material environments, and, consequently, their ideological systems. Schizoid self-alienation is the response to a general state of affairs in the world, which, in these two films, are hyper-attenuated and brought to the most extreme conclusions, such that the relationship between the experience of viewers and those of the characters is that of metaphor, not mimesis. Indeed, considering the radically destabilizing circumstances experienced by the characters in the films, their responses are better understood not as those of schizophrenics, but of traumatized individuals.

The cause of trauma, argues Cathy Caruth, is "a shock that appears to work very much like a bodily threat but is in fact a break in the mind's experience of time."[7] This notion of a rupture in temporal order is usually understood as occurring in a flash of fleeting subjective experience—the traumatic event itself—though with respect to *Dawn of the Dead* and *On the Beach*, we can conceive of this traumatic event as extending to cover all the characters' post-social lives. Indeed, this interpretation seems consistent with Freud's views on trauma, as he held that the most salient element of the traumatic event was not that of temporality, but rather of the economics of stimulus and release, as the traumatic experience is one that "within a short period of time presents the mind with an increase of stimulus too powerful to be dealt with or worked off in the normal way, and this may result in permanent disturbances of the manner in which energy operates."[8] While the source of this traumatically overwhelming stimulus varies, it is often some form of confrontation with immediate physical harm or violence; crucially, though, for Freud the traumatic incident is one in which the victim does *not* experience physical injury, as he believed that the source of traumatic obsessional neurosis is the near-experiencing of the event, and that actual injuries directed energy away from the development of the traumatic neuroses.[9] The zombie's infectious bite, then, can be understood as both physically and psychologically implicating the victim into the traumatic event of the zombie outbreak.

For those not bitten, however, or those who have survived the instantaneous flash of global nuclear war only to then await their own belated annihilation, the "missing" of the event—both temporally and physically—is an insuperable rupture, such that they will never be able to "fully know" it.[10] In response to this alienation, the traumatized individual begins to relive the event through such cathexes as trauma dreams and the compulsive repetition of certain acts, in an attempt to retroactively gain control of the traumatic stimulus, and thereby reassert a sense of control over the traumatic event.[11]

There are strong parallels between the epistemological severance that occurs through the traumatic experience and the ideological vastation of the post-social environment, as well as that of schizoid self-alienation, as in all three scenarios the individual finds him- or herself in a world where the larger social structures through which we maintain our identities on a daily basis are either absent, inaccessible, or malicious. Given such a state of affairs, it is not surprising that the characters in both films then resort to patterns of behavior that might be considered a sort of "obsessional neurosis."

In *Dawn of the Dead*, the human characters maintain an internal sense of distinction from the undead hordes surrounding them through an outward display of accumulated cultural goods; hi-fi stereos, elegantly appointed living quarters, and meticulously prepared meals all serve as means through which the characters attempt to cohere and inhabit the patterns of the society of which they were once a part. While they are seemingly composing these symbolic structures anew, they are doing so using previously existing components, and in accord with the conventions and ideologies of the pre-catastrophic period. But they do so not out of a belief that they are really living the same lives they once led—for all this occurs in a small, windowless complex of storage rooms inside a shopping mall—but as an attempt to stave off the otherwise crushing alterity of their new environment by constructing a microcosm of the ideologies of their old existence.

Unlike the world of Romero's film, the characters in *On the Beach* are, as they wait for the radioactive winds to slowly envelop them, already dead. Just as the living dead in Romero's film are drawn to the shopping mall by what Stephen (David Emge) calls "some kind of instinct... memory, of what they used to do," the characters in *On the Beach* maintain nearly *exactly* the same lifestyles and routines as they did before the nuclear war, such as enrolling in secretarial school or purchasing gifts for family members they know to be dead. While some characters in the film are able to find a certain freedom in their imminent fate—Osborne fulfills a lifelong dream by entering highly dangerous car races—most are unable to accept their new reality, so much so that Towers ultimately decides to leave Moira and travel back to the United States in the submarine with his crew, despite knowing that such a journey will only allow him to die in a nation that no longer exists.

In *Dawn of the Dead*, the survivors engage in the cultural patterns of pre-apocalyptic society as a means of generating their own positive identity, of distinguishing themselves from the culture-less undead that surround them. In *On the Beach*, these cultural patterns are employed not as a mark of differentiation but of sentimental solidarity: their behaviors are one with those of the deceased. In light of this, it comes as no surprise that all the characters in *Dawn of the Dead* make personal decisions in favor of life extension; indeed, the film's climactic moment is realized when Peter decides against suicide and pulls the gun from his temple to fire the bullet into the brain of an oncoming zombie. In contrast, the characters in *On the Beach* choose to administer government-issued cyanide capsules in lieu of attempting to outlive the radioactive winds. Perhaps it is that these characters, already made half-dead through their atemporal delusions, find themselves consigned to Antonin Artaud's articulation of suicide: "If I commit suicide, it will not be to destroy myself but to put myself back together again.... By suicide I reintroduce my design in nature, I shall for the first time give things the shape of my will."[12] For the characters in *On the Beach*, it is only through self-destruction, and the manner in which it is performed, that they can erase their traumatic wounds and be at one with the meaning they desire.

Yet given the difference in the nature of the antagonists in the two films, it is unclear how the characters in *Dawn of the Dead* might hope to achieve a similar symbolic wholeness or unity. While trauma theory and ideology help to explicate the plight of the survivors in both films, it does little to advance our understanding of the zombies themselves, who, being beyond consciousness and ideology, are beyond such theories as well. Rather, the zombie exists as pure drive—though the zombies perform a gruesome caricature of our ideologies, they do not, and cannot, believe in them or realize themselves as subjects through them[13]—and are therefore resistant to psychological probing.

The real-world anxieties about death by radiation poisoning expressed in *On the Beach* were not the product of idle worry or the overly speculative minds of science fiction writers, as the horrible consequences—both physical and social—of extreme radiation exposure were demonstrated by the plight of the *hibakusha* in postwar Japan. The hibakusha—those affected by radiation generated from the atomic bombs dropped by U.S. forces on Hiroshima and Nagasaki—became a pariah class, unable to find employment or housing, with this discrimination often extended to their children as well.[14] As they wandered amid the ruined streets in the days following the bombings, survivors described themselves as being like "walking ghosts" and "not really alive." Dr. Michihiko Hachiya, a Hiroshima physician who survived the initial blast, described the residents' behavior as they moved through the burnt-out city:

> Those who were able walked silently towards the suburbs in the distant hills, their spirits broken, their initiative gone. When asked whence they had come, they pointed to the city and said, "that way": and when asked where they were going, pointed away from the city and said, "this way." They were so broken and confused that they moved and behaved like automatons. Their reactions had astonished outsiders who reported with amazement the spectacle of long files of people holding stolidly to a narrow, rough path when close by was a smooth easy road going in the same direction. The outsiders could not grasp the fact that they were witnessing the exodus of a people who walked in the realm of dreams. One thing was common to everyone I saw—complete silence. . . . Why was everyone so quiet? . . . It was as though I walked through a gloomy, silent motion picture.[15]

In the immediate aftermath of the explosions, witnesses described seeing the wounded "near-naked, bleeding, faces disfigured and bloated from burns, arms held awkwardly away from the body to prevent friction with other burned areas."[16] Many of the most severely injured hibakusha soon died from their injuries. Philip Morrison, a Cornell physicist who had worked on the Manhattan Project and was one of the first American civilians to visit Hiroshima, described how, because of radiation, "the blood does not coagulate, but oozes in many spots through the unbroken skin and internally seeps into the cavities of the body."[17] The similarities between this account and the spectacle of the gruesome modern zombie introduced by George Romero are quite apparent, though such images are conspicuously absent from the decidedly more mainstream *On the Beach*.

In no small part, this omission may be due to the tight controls exerted by the American military and government on information released to the American public regarding the long-term effects of the bombs (in fact, they went so far as to deny the possibility of radiation poisoning in the initial months following the bombings).[18] When the government did release photos of Hiroshima and Nagasaki, they were panoramic images of destruction; human victims were almost entirely absent. American public opinion surrounding the ethicality of using nuclear weapons was decisively in favor of the government's decision throughout much of the 1940s, in no small part thanks to the extensive censorship campaign aimed at "Japanese propaganda" concerning radioactive fallout and its attendant diseases. Despite this early censorship, Soviet atomic weapons testing soon led the American government to publicize the effects of radiation in great detail, such that the general public was well aware of the general effects of radiation by the time *On the Beach* was released in 1959.[19]

At the end of World War II, however, the United States was far more aware of a similar degradation of the human condition occurring on the other side of the globe, where the horrors of the Nazi concentration camps produced the *Muselmänner*, those prisoners so devastated by the conditions of their imprisonment that they were reduced to such a state of bare existence that, years later, many survivors remained uncertain as to whether one could properly refer to these individuals as being fully human. Indeed, Giorgio Agamben notes that the title of Primo Levi's concentration camp memoir, *Se questo è un uomo*, literally means "if this is a man" (this text was first published in English as *Survival in Auschwitz*), suggesting that "in Auschwitz ethics begins precisely at the point where the *Muselmann*, the 'complete witness,' makes it forever impossible to distinguish between man and non-man."[20]

While the Muselmänner (literally "Muslims")[21] were a small subset of those imprisoned in the concentration camps, their extreme condition had a profound impact on prisoners and guards alike. Jean Améry, a concentration camp survivor, provides a brief description of these individuals: "The so-called [Muselmann], as the camp language termed the prisoner who was giving up and given up by his comrades, no longer had room in his consciousness for the contrasts good or bad, noble or base, intellectual or unintellectual. He was a staggering corpse, a bundle of physical functions in its last convulsions. As hard as it may be for us to do so, we must exclude him from our considerations."[22]

The excluded position of having given up and been given on by comrades places the Muselmann in a liminal category—they constitute "the untestifiable, that to which no one has borne witness,"[23] yet they are, as suggested before, the "complete witness" of the inhumanity that lurks in man. But even then, this meta-witnessing would be partial and incomplete, as it could tell only of the inhuman side of the Muselmann, while another, separate account would have to be made of the human elements. The Muselmann, like the zombie, is a line, heterogeneous and indivisible, more terrifying in its unassimilable liminality than the dark region it delineates: "I remember that while we were going down the stairs leading to the baths, they had us accompanied by a group of *Muselmänner*, as we later called them—mummy-men, the living dead. They made them go down the stairs with us only to show them to us, as if to say, 'you'll become like them.'"[24] The Muselmänner resembled the living dead not only in the unsettling blankness of their psychological states, but also in their outward appearance. While the physical process of becoming a Muselmann began with generalized malnutrition and starvation, it was only in the second stage that the transformation, both mental and physical, truly began to take hold.[25] The physical similarities between the Muselmänner and the modern zombie are uncanny—even the language employed by survivors to describe them ("living dead," "staggering corpse") immediately denotes zombies. Yet the metaphysical similarities between the Muselmann—the complete witness—and the zombie are somewhat less immediately apparent. It is precisely because he is unable to tell of the nightmarish conditions of the concentration camps that the Muselmann becomes the complete witness of those horrors, just as the sublation of ideology into instinct simultaneously renders the zombie as both completely blank and the totalizing instantiation of the ideologies of late capitalism. The experience of the camps have so completely overwhelmed and annihilated the Muselmann's capacity to make sense of them that this silence itself serves as a testament to the unspeakably appalling nature of the camps, the reduction of unique individuals into pure symbols. In this sense, then, the modern zombie's mute lack of consciousness performs a similar function for modern society writ large, embodying the terrifyingly rapacious yet autonomous mechanisms through which subjects' consumption is purposed as a (re)productive act, the end point of the ideological and material processes through which late capitalism predicates its growth and stability on autophagic strategies of debt and credit.

Taken more figuratively, this description would also seem quite apt for the characters in *On the Beach*, who, with each passing day, spend an increasing amount of time staring blankly at the landscape that will soon become toxic with radioactivity. Yet their experience is a sort of doubling of this notion of the "complete witness," for not only does their predicament symbolically condense the logical outcome of the prevailing ideologies of their day, but it also places them in a scenario where even if they possessed the language to articulate their experience, they would be unable to make an act of witnessing, as there would be no one alive to hear their stories. In this way, *On the Beach* forces the audience to directly confront its characters with a mixture of dread and pity (and perhaps a dash of schadenfreude), offering no safe positions of secondary identification through which we might find momentary respite. *Dawn of the Dead*, on the other hand, displaces the terror of the post-ideological subject onto the zombies, thereby providing the audience with a somewhat safer zone of secondary identification in the film's principal human protagonists; we feel safe because, in witnessing their horror and anxiety, we know that we are not alone in our emotions, that these are shared, "natural" responses to such scenarios.

If we are to take but one lesson away from that of the Muselmänner and hibakusha, perhaps it should be the radical new conception of death that they suggest. For unlike the traditional mode of dying, in which the cessation of biological and psychic processes occurs roughly simultaneously, the Muselmänner and hibakusha embody a gruesome reimagining of the process, in which physical death, believed to be preordained and imminent, becomes a prolonged process, both producing and produced by the psychic death, which precedes the nearly invisible moment at which the body's life functions cease. In this formulation, the modern zombie functions as the obverse of the necro-psychic processes of the characters in *On the Beach*.

Yet in identifying the ways in which the modern zombie and the characters in *On the Beach* reveal the dormant potentiality of the hibakusha and Muselmänner lurking within each and every one of us, we are made to confront the question of whether this is a uniquely modern condition, or some more universal aspect of humankind. For if the madness that produced the horrors of World War II was an isolated aberration from the prevailing behavior of modern societies, a fugitive perversion of human nature, then perhaps the zombie is little more than a token reminder of this lamentable moment. But if this madness was, in fact, an inevitable manifestation of the developmental path of industrialized societies, of the trajectory of human evolution, then the zombie becomes a quite different figure altogether.

That is, if this madness is inherent to the human condition—and the continuing existence of nuclear proliferation suggests that, at the very least, it is a condition inherent to our modern epoch—then the modern Romero zombie, both in appearance and in its psychosocial meaning, presents a damning choice: either this potentiality is always already inherent within our conception of "the human," or it is some type of supernumerary element that has somehow affixed itself to human nature, perhaps parasitically, as a bacterium might function, or insidiously, by altering the very fabric of our nature, as radiation alters that which it comes into contact with. *On the Beach* presents a similarly ambiguous scenario: has it always been possible for this profound, collective loss of hope and sense of humanity to arise (as perhaps could be found in medieval plague narratives), or is this new zero-level of humanity a uniquely modern development?

Slavoj Žižek's writings on the Muselmänner may help to answer this question, as he argues that these figures are

> the "zero-level" of humanity in the precise sense of what Hegel called "the night of the world," the withdrawal from engaged immersion in one's environment, the pure self-relating negativity which, as it were, "wipes the slate" and thus opens up the space for specifically human engagement. To put it in yet another way: the Muslim is not simply outside language . . . he is the absence of language *as such*, silence as a positive fact, as the rock of impossibility, the Void, the background for speech to emerge against. In this precise sense, one can say that in order to "become human," to bridge the gap between animal immersion in the environment to human activity, *we all, at some point, have had to be Muslims*, to pass through the zero-level designated by this term.[26]

If we understand this "Void" in the language of ideology, then the hibakusha and Muselmänner function as the potentiality inherent in the pre- and post-ideological human, the bare margin of difference between humans and animals that allows the former to become symbol-using creatures. For Žižek, the existence of the Muselmänner and hibakusha reveals the traumatic kernel of inhumanity in us all, one that is timelessly and essentially human. The feelings of terror called forth in the presence of the

Muselmänner and hibakusha are those of atavistic revulsion, a reminder of the nonself from which consciousness blossoms, and subsequently denies. In confronting this repressed primordial form, schizoid self-alienation is called forth in the space created between nonself and self, between the truth of that which everyone carries somewhere inside of them, and the cultivated sense of identity that can only stably function through the denial of that truth's existence. Thus, while the Muselmänner and hibakusha function to actuate these universally human anxieties, the means through which they do so—by recasting death as a state of being, rather than as a realm to which we pass, and the instrumentalized processes through which this is achieved—mark these figures as quintessentially modern expressions of this ancient anxiety. If we were to consider this in the terms of literary analysis, we might say that the anxiety is the story, while the Muselmänner and hibakusha are its modern emplotments.

On the Beach, then, presents a scenario in which the characters are made to inhabit circumstances strikingly similar to those of these World War II atrocities, especially those of the hibakusha—a double emplotment, of sorts, of this age-old anxiety. Given the profound traumatic injuries inflicted on the hibakusha, it is not surprising that the characters in *On the Beach* are similarly affected. Extending the application of trauma theory beyond the film to the United States' cultural self-identity, *On the Beach* can be understood to function as a sort of trauma dream, a subject that Caruth argues perplexed even Freud "because it cannot be understood in terms of any wish or unconscious meaning, but is, purely and inexplicably, the literal return of the event against the will of the one it inhabits."[27] *On the Beach*'s bleak conclusion is fitting, then, as it does nothing to ameliorate its aura of fatalism and refrains from offering its characters (and the audience) any ersatz sense of hope.

Yet because the trauma zombie is a less figurative category than the modern zombie, it consistently retains a critical potential that the real zombie may, at certain times, lack. Upon being traumatized, sundered from their ideological and semantic systems, the trauma zombie is reduced to bare drives, that "untamed root that exists prior to all cultural development,"[28] a state of death in life that is the perverse obverse of the modern zombie's life in death. And yet it seems as though precisely what is lost in the characters of *On the Beach* is the belief in that essential kernel of the human, perhaps because the very act of belief itself is a cognitive luxury available only to those who possess a sustaining ideological and psychological schema through which they can imagine themselves as conscious, deliberative agents. Indeed, the characters in *On the Beach* act as though (perhaps rightly so) their deaths will also be the destruction of all humankind, such that they retreat into the obsolete habits and ideologies that sustained them in their pre-apocalyptic lives. This suggests that, for these characters, what makes us human is not anything inherent to the individual human itself, but rather is only accrued in the nexus of social relations through which we maintain ourselves and our systems of production (both material and conceptual). The most despairing element of the trauma zombie, then, is its own inability to recognize itself as being human, a negative feedback loop of dehumanizing anguish and alienation.

Both films seek to grapple with the implications of World War II—the heralding of the atomic age and the horrors of the concentration camps—though both their generic forms and their period of production profoundly influence the ways in which these anxieties are articulated and narratively resolved. Given the temporal proximity to the events and the urgency with which they resonated at the time, in addition to its more realist style and the use of the trauma zombie, it is not surprising that *On the Beach* directly confronts these issues in its narrative diegesis. Given the interval between World War II and the mid-1970s, and the sequence of displacements that occur, it is not surprising—though by no means inevitable—that *Dawn of the Dead* sublimates these anxieties into the figure of the zombie. Beyond this initial displacement (of atomic fears away from radiation or culpable humans per se to that of the fantastical zombie figure) is the question of what narrative possibilities are then circumscribed or overdetermined as a result.

In *Night of the Living Dead*, for instance, the confrontation between humanity and its abject double could be considered, at best, a stalemate, and at worst, humans ultimately destroy themselves in the process of attempting to destroy that which threatens them.[29] In either event, the narrative possibility is provided for humans to triumph over the zombie threat through further violence—no deep soul-searching or self-criticism of the events that promulgated the zombie outbreak are required. *Dawn* takes this one step further by asserting that narrative resolution can be achieved without any final reckoning or culling, that the possibility of survival is reason enough to continue to hope. The full ideological and political import of this maneuver is, of course, open to debate, but it is important when discussing zombies to bear in mind that it is a trope that is both transgressive and self-limiting in equal measure.

Ultimately, the fact that *Dawn of the Dead* posits the possibility of social continuation is what sets it apart from *On the Beach*. That this optimism might only be possible through the use of the "fantasy bribe"[30] of the zombie figure is perhaps secondary to its ultimate optimism about the fate of the human race. Despite the chaos wrought by the excesses of consumerism and the military-industrial complex, *Dawn* suggests that humans do have the capability to adapt and change, that the zombie will not haunt humankind forever as its dark abject Other, but that, given the proper response, the undead will eventually be regarded as indicative of an extremely trying developmental period. That *On the Beach* expresses an opposing view on human nature is not a refutation of *Dawn*'s position, but, rather, reveals that the question is ultimately not whether this zero-level potentiality is inherent within us, but whether we *believe* that it is. For if we do, then this belief fully overdetermines our actions, rendering us without hope or the conviction that we can change our material existence, a state that renders us as little more than the walking dead.

The trauma zombie then functions as a conceptual twin of the modern zombie, complementing the critical (yet ultimately optimistic) function of the flesh-eating undead with a character that is less figurative yet more fatalistic. Bridging the gap between the allegorical horrors conceived by our collective imaginations and the actual horrors of the real world, the trauma zombie is a compelling character that serves to reveal more about the nature of zombies and the societies that deploy them as myths. What is most terrifying about these traumatized survivors, however, is not that they envy the dead, but rather that they are no longer even capable of envy, or any other human emotions. Instead, they inhabit a psychological realm of such unremitting barrenness that it is as though humankind never existed at all.

CHAPTER 7

Lucio Fulci and the Decaying Definition of Zombie Narratives

Steven Zani and Kevin Meaux

No cinematic monster has experienced as many reinventions or taken as many forms as the zombie. The word "zombie" originally connoted a shuffling, glassy-eyed automaton who, having no will of his or her own, existed only to carry out the commands of the voodoo master. Early films like *White Zombie* (1932) and *King of the Zombies* (1941) exemplify this image. During the 1950s, a different kind of zombie narrative emerged, seen in films like *Creature with the Atomic Brain* (1955), *Invasion of the Body Snatchers* (the Jack Finney novel in 1955 and subsequent film version in 1956), and *Invisible Invaders* (1959). The zombies featured in these movies bear only a passing resemblance to their predecessors. In fact, *Invasion of the Body Snatchers* presents the audience with zombies who are virtually indistinguishable from ordinary humans. Unlike previous zombies, with their origins based in voodoo and folklore, atomic age zombies had pseudoscientific as well as extraterrestrial origins.

The most significant change in zombie cinema occurred in 1968, with George Romero's *Night of the Living Dead*, loosely based on Richard Matheson's 1954 vampire novel *I Am Legend*. Consequently, it is fair to argue that the blueprint for modern zombie cinema is Matheson's novel. Crucially, though, Romero contributes two enduring conventions in his adaptation of *I Am Legend*: he turns zombies into flesh eaters, and he gives them their one weakness, a bullet in the head. Romero's innovations change the zombie's need to feed into an exemplar of basic human consumption while simultaneously situating a functional brain as a core zombie feature, both metaphorically suggesting that human consciousness and human identity are the real concerns in an encounter with the monstrous. In *Dawn of the Dead* (1978), Romero would incorporate another crucial element, the religious or eschatological, with the tagline "When there's no more room in hell, the dead will walk the earth," implying a theological condemnation as the origin of the zombie—if the dead are among us, it is because we have filled the coffers of hell too quickly with our immoral behavior, and therefore have prematurely initiated the world's end.

With these precedents and varying examples, what are the constitutive elements that inform zombie texts? In order to clarify the essential issues that are at stake in a zombie narrative, this chapter will take a brief look at the history of zombie cinema and investigate its literary past, which includes the plague narratives and images of premodern and modern Europe, finally using the work of the Italian director Lucio Fulci as a contemporary template for understanding the genre. As we will argue, the choice of Fulci is not incidental; he represents the epitome of the zombie narrative precisely because the paradigms and defining elements of zombies in his multiple zombie films are never consistent. Fulci's films, where zombies constantly vacillate between biological and theological in origin, corporeal and spectral in substance, and individual and collective as threat, enable us to see that zombies represent more than just a blank template for some historically particular anxiety about death.[1] Asking why Fulci's zombies have such fluidity to them, and what that fluidity means, allows us to ignore superficial details of zombie speed, vulnerability, questions of etiology, and so forth, which characterize many other zombie critiques, in order to pursue a more substantive understanding of the genre. His oeuvre offers a touchstone for the meaning of zombie narratives because it contains a constant, repetitive decay and dissolution of origin, order, and understanding. In these films, the things we hold to have meaning—even the very logic of narrative order—all become meaningless. Fulci's zombies represent the fallacy of human understanding, and the terror or trauma that comes of realizing that fallacy. Fulci is the quintessential director of zombie gore horror, but his technique makes him different from any other director because he uses the zombie as a tool for subverting narrative itself, along with our presumptions about what narrative is, and the sense of order and meaning inherent within the narrative framework.

To understand what Fulci is responding to, subverting, and expanding, we must look at the literary and cinematic traditions that precede him. Arguably, the zombie is a relative latecomer in monstrous literature, and a cursory look at that genre is helpful to our purpose in that it reveals that the traditional definition of the zombie (on the most basic level, a corpse that is somehow animated) actually tells us very little about why people might be fascinated by them, or why certain animated corpses are considered zombies but others are not. For example, few scholars consider Odysseus's conversation with the dead Achilles in *The Odyssey* to be a zombie narrative, nor is the brief reference to flesh-eating undead in *Gilgamesh* enough to lead many scholars to celebrate it as a zombie text.[2] Even the reanimated pieces that constitute the *Frankenstein* monster are only loosely accepted as representative of the genre by most. One of the earliest modern tales that might be understood as a zombie narrative is the W. W. Jacobs 1902 short story "The Monkey's Paw." In this "be careful what you wish for" horror narrative, the parents of a recently deceased boy use a wish granted to them to make their son alive, only to wish him once again dead when they hear his approach, realizing that their son has returned to them in his newly dead, mutilated condition. Even here, however, the "zombie" itself never appears in the story except as a knock on the door.

Why are these texts not celebrated or commonly recognized as zombie narratives? With a few near misses and a knock at the door as our earliest trace, following the history of zombie literature to the beginning of the twentieth century leaves us with very little in terms of understanding why these previous texts, though featuring animated dead, did not inspire the creation of a genre, at least not the pervasive and successful one that we have seen in the modern era. With these earlier presentations, there is nary a traditional, shuffling, brain-eating zombie in sight. In literature, the genre is illusive at best, or nonexistent at worst, and the lack of substance might lead some to conclude that the zombie is predominantly a cinematic monster, and that it is only in film that the zombie has truly thrived. But before dismissing zombie literature as insubstantial, or attempting to locate the genre entirely in film, it is worth considering that the equivalent of zombie narratives *are* rampant in literature, in the form of plague narratives that arose in Europe during the medieval period. These narratives were repeated and transformed in various genres over several hundred years, and a close look at them reveals a surprising detail—the messages and themes of zombie texts are quite compatible with these plague narratives.[3] At its essence, the zombie film contains lessons already available in

Giovanni Boccaccio's *The Decameron* (depicting Europe's bubonic plague of 1348) or Daniel Defoe's eighteenth-century *A Journal of the Plague Year*.

Seen in this context, questions about whether zombies are the supernatural living dead rather than the biologically infected, or a product of an alien invasion rather than a voodoo curse, are not revelatory. Rather, significance rests in how plague and zombie narratives explore anxieties that extend beyond localized historical fears. In plague and zombie narratives, we fear, for example, that the institutions holding our culture together, often specifically law, family, and belief in the sacred, will break down or reveal themselves to be false in the face of catastrophe. But it isn't the specifics of an individual breakdown that are essential, but rather the very idea of breakdown, the dissolution of certainty and meaning that zombies represent. Every essay in this book addresses some aspect or reoccurring zombie characteristic, but what zombie narratives represent at their core isn't something that can be located in a particular characteristic. Zombie narratives do not have something at their "core" at all, but rather something at the limits of understanding, something that undoes or threatens the core, not just threatening the core of society, or the human, but of knowledge or meaning itself.[4]

These threatening elements have been present in plague narratives for centuries, and they have been absorbed into the zombie genre to the point where they have become its very conventions. Before looking at Fulci, where this idea of dissolution is in full bloom, the early plague narratives can give us an insight into how the genre began and where it is heading. In the opening pages of *The Decameron*, the earliest significant plague narrative other than the book of Exodus, Boccaccio narrates, "And in this great affliction and misery of our city the revered authority of the laws, both divine and human, had fallen and almost completely disappeared, for, like other men, the ministers and executors of the laws were either dead or sick or so short of help that it was impossible for them to fulfill their duties; as a result, everybody was free to do as he pleased."[5] Interestingly, Boccaccio notes that during the plague social codes are just as ignored as the law. The undoing of these bonds becomes an enduring topic in the narrative. Boccaccio further writes that a woman, "no matter . . . how attractive or beautiful or noble she might be, . . . did not mind having a man servant (whoever he might be, no matter how old or young he was), and she had no shame whatsoever," he continues, "in revealing any part of her body to him."[6] Boccaccio suggests that this practice was the source of looser morals in the times that followed the plague. He further states that at the height of the Black Death, "brother abandoned brother, uncle abandoned nephew, sister left brother, and very often wife abandoned husband, and even worse, almost unbelievable—fathers and mothers neglected to tend and care for their children as if they were not their own."[7] Michele da Piazza, a medieval Franciscan friar who witnessed the plague, concurs with Boccaccio's fictional account, writing that the illness "bred such loathing that if a son fell ill . . . his father flatly refused to stay with him."[8] Though unconscionable, actions like these proved lifesaving in some circumstances due to the highly contagious nature of the plague. Accounts of the 1665 plague describe houses where healthy families were forcibly quarantined along with the sick, predictably resulting in entire families infected and dead within days. Thus the early plague narratives are governed by their own paradoxical morality. Even as the chronicler subjectively disapproves of family members abandoning one another, his own narrative objectively bears out the prudence of such behavior.

For reasons we will elaborate on when treating Fulci's work in more depth, these kinds of contradictions are what his films exploit to an almost obsessive extreme. For now, it is worth pointing out that the same sensibility can be found in many zombie texts, in which the obligations of familial duty, and the conflicts that result because of it, are highlighted and become major elements of the story. Loyalty to infected family members becomes a dilemma in any number of zombie films, and virtually always results in a further spreading of the plague. The plot of Juan Carlos Fresnadillo's 2007 film *28 Weeks Later* is constructed entirely around this concept. In one of the film's major plot points, the young brother-and-sister protagonists, Andy and Tammy, who are living in a fortified city with their father, break quarantine, drawn to the idea of returning to their home. Given that they can only expect an empty home to return to, their action emphasizes the psychological stake that they (and by extension we, the viewers) have in the idea of home, with all that it implies about family, a shared past, and the value of community. The psychological power of home is such that it is more important to the children than the relative safety of the fortified city. In attempting their return, they inadvertently discover and rescue their infected but asymptomatic mother from the ruins of London. A kiss between reunited husband and wife results in the transmission of the disease, quickly followed by hoards of the infected overrunning the city. In the film's final moments, we find that the sibling protagonists have brought the infection from England to Paris and, presumably, to the rest of Europe as well. While *28 Days Later* touches on the subject of family, this sequel brings family to the forefront. Because the family unit is considered an integral component of social order itself, family bonds can be said to be a matter of ingrained human behavior. The film's central characters cannot resist the instinct to remain a family, no matter that familial loyalty is antithetical to the survival of the human race in the postapocalyptic world. One might also consider the most recognizable image from George Romero's *Night of the Living Dead*: the close-up of the zombie child as she prepares to kill her own mother. The girl's face, which can be seen on posters and T-shirts around the world, is a kind of shorthand, communicating a range of emotions, including not only horror but also wry amusement. The image's power rests in the fact that it represents the destruction of the family as well as the annihilation of order itself.

Boccaccio's plague narrative is not the only one to promote this annihilation of meaning, and a look at other early plague narratives reveals that family is not the only source of confusion or conflict. Thomas Dekker's 1603 plague narrative pamphlet "The Wonderfull Yeare" is tellingly not just about the coming of the plague, but also about the death of Queen Elizabeth that same year. Dekker does not explicitly connect her death and the loss of order it entails with the attendant plague, yet it is not surprising that these two events are the foci of the pamphlet. The plague itself, when introduced, is labeled an "*Anthropophagized* plague"[9]—that is, the plague is cannibalistic, referencing a classical myth, inspired by Herodotus, which tells of the *androphagi*—headless flesh eaters living on the Black Sea.[10] The central lament of the pamphlet, however, is not the physical ravages of the plague, but rather its consequences for morality:

> If some poore man, suddeinly starting out of a sweete and golden slumber, should behold his house flaming about his eares, all his family destroied in their sleepes by the mercilesse fire; himselfe in the very midst of it, wofully and like a madde man calling for helpe: would not the misery of such a distressed soule, appeare the greater, if the rich Vsurer dwelling next doore to him, should not stirre, (though he felt no part of the danger) but suffer him to perish, when the thrusting out of an arme might haue saued him?[11]

Disaster is all the more horrible, the pamphlet asserts, when it reveals not just a natural calamity befalling a man and his family but also the subsequent failure of others to alleviate or prevent the suffering. Man's inhumanity to man, of course, is a relative mainstay of many different literary genres, not just plague and zombie narratives. But Dekker's narrative is like Boccaccio's in that it is reminiscent of modern zombie texts. The pamphlet touches on virtually every element that we will find in future cinema. The preceding passage already argues that the plague destroys the sanctity of families, but Dekker continues in that vein, describing the difficulties of a father attempting to give his son last rites and a proper burial:

> All thy golde and siluer cannot hire one of those (whom before thou didst scorne) to carry the dead body to his last home: the Country round about thee shun thee, as a Basiliske, and therefore to *London* . . . to fetch from thence those that may performe that Funerall Office: But there are they so full of graue-matters of their owne, that they haue no leisure to attend thine. . . . With thine owne hands must thou dig his graue, (not in the Church, or common place of buriall,) thou hast not fauour (for all thy riches) to be so happie, but in thine Orcharde, or in the proude walkes of thy Garden, wringing thy palsie-shaking hands in stead of belles, (most miserable father) must thou search him out a sepulcher.[12]

Witness the dissolution of various institutions, including government, church, and family. Class distinctions unpleasantly evaporate as men whom one did "scorne" can no longer be swayed by money. The clergy fails to provide its services. Bodies no longer have a proper place to be buried. Zombie narratives provide obvious counterparts for all of these themes. For example, in an early scene in *28 Days Later*, the film's main character wanders through the deserted streets of London and enters a church desecrated with rotting corpses. There, a zombie priest attacks him. Significantly, this is the first of the infected the protagonist encounters, and the darkly humorous message is apparent: not even the sacred is sacred anymore. One might also consider another one of zombie cinema's stock images, that of zombies plundering empty malls or supermarkets (the scene first appearing in Romero's 1978 *Dawn of the Dead*) and how the image represents the collapse of the consumer-based economic system. Likewise, a brief glimpse of the undead invading the White House—a succinct way to symbolize the dissolution of the government—is a requisite scene for many of today's higher-budget American zombie films, like Zack Snyder's 2004 *Dawn of the Dead* remake.

Are zombie narratives, then, about family, religion, and government? They are about that and more, or specifically they are about the dissolution of that and more. Moving forward yet again chronologically in plague narrative history, one of the most often cited texts in plague narratives is Daniel Defoe's *A Journal of the Plague Year*, a 1722 novel about the plague of 1665, though it followed on the heels of a 1720 outbreak of the plague in France and was a response to very immediate fears of the English public that the plague would soon ravage their country as well. Multiple passages in the *Journal* attribute the plague to divine order, a ubiquitous attitude in medieval and Renaissance Europe, and one that Defoe shared with the contemporaries who still supported the idea. Yet, confusing the issue, Defoe's work contains multiple suggestions for combating the plague, many of which seem to have little grounding in religious practice, and Defoe had produced *Due Preparations for the Plague*, a nonfiction preventative manual, shortly before the *Journal*. In the *Journal*, he is fixated on measures and regulatory practices, with multiple headings and descriptions of those practices, such as "every visited house to be watched," "the streets to be kept clean," and "care to be had of unwholesome fish or flesh."[13] Defoe's reliance on, and trust in, the social order, and the guidelines for behavior that will maintain it, will show up again in our contemporary zombie anxieties, often with a didactic message ingrained in the narrative by a simple plot device: namely, that violations of those rules and the abandonment of the social space (whether through attempts at individual self-preservation or by small communities walling themselves off from the community at large) invariably results in the deaths of the protagonists involved.[14]

But what is most interesting about Defoe, and what will again show up in Fulci, is not simply his reliance on questions of the social. What Defoe shares in common with a contemporary figure like Fulci is a relative confusion of terms. While Defoe is not beyond relying on theological justifications for the plague, his arguments for stopping it are relatively scientific or biological in nature. That is, the plague may come from God, but Defoe seems to be relying more on throwing away rotten food than he is on ensuring that everyone says their prayers. In short, these literary accounts of plague narratives offer, as will Fulci, competing narratives of origins rooted in divine justice versus biological or natural accounts, side by side, without any clear or precise resolution.

One of the reasons this debate over theological and natural origins is so prevalent in Defoe's work is that, at the time, Enlightenment attitudes privileging reason and rationality began to offer counter-narratives to traditional religious discourses. One Defoe analyst remarks that when the *Journal* was written, "The more widely accepted view, at least in intellectual circles or among those with any pretensions to authority, was that the deity did not intervene in the natural order, that miraculous intervention was a thing of the past (though possible if the deity wished), and that plagues, like other diseases, were explicable in terms of natural or secondary causes."[15] But the question of biblical or theological influence or origin for the plague was certainly not decided at the time, nor perhaps is it even now. As a culture, we easily backslide into pre-Enlightenment rhetoric to explain our own widespread illnesses, even in the face of a great deal of scientific or secular rhetoric to the contrary. For example, according to another Defoe commenter, "in 1988 Cardinal Siri of Geno called AIDS 'a holy plague to punish sinners' and the Soviet Health Minister termed it 'a disease of decadence.'"[16]

The debate between these two poles of understanding is a long-standing one, existing in many plague narratives outside of Defoe's, and its origin lies in the Old Testament affirmation of plague as punishment from God. The plague literature critic Rebecca Totaro describes the problem: "The Latin *plaga*, meaning to strike or blow, does not differ much from the term 'scourge.' Once dispatched, God's blow could easily level an entire population. God alone might choose to relent, to spare his people from potential genocide, but although God promised Noah that there would be no future flood, God never removed plague from his arsenal of scourges. The early modern paradigm for the human condition had a permanent place for plague and no one—writer, doctor, king, or priest—was able to think beyond it."[17]

The issue is compounded further by the fact that a study of divine origins was often conflated in the past with basic scientific study in the form of astrology. In a world where the movement of the stars was understood as both predictive of terrestrial events and an example of divine authority, such questions of origin become even more layered. The historian Johannes Nohl, compiling multiple plague narratives, explains that these ideas were pervasive and extended from antiquity, from no less than Aristotle:

> Above all, it was the constellations which determined the destiny of man, and particular positions of the planets were regarded as the direct cause of the plague. For this, support was found in the principle authority of the medieval ages—in Aristotle, who regarded the conjunction of Mars and Jupiter as specially menacing. Thus the outbreak of the great plague of 1348 was preceded by the conjunction of Saturn, Jupiter, and Mars under the fourteenth degree of Aquarius, on March 20, 1345, at 1 p.m. Later on this conjunction has always been regarded as the true cause of the plague.[18]

Before we decry the ludicrous specificity of a "science" like astrology, which verifies its authenticity with little more than groundless claims about times and degrees, it might be best to remember that astrology still thrives today, and these star-born narratives of disease and illness are still being written. Recall minor zombie films such as *The Night of the Comet*, in 1984, or more significant attempts such as the film *The Andromeda Strain* (released in 1971, based on the 1969 novel). While not a zombie narrative per se, the latter film, a virus-from-outer-space narrative, reveals one of its more frightening moments when a Sterno-addicted[19] old man lurches, inarticulate and stumbling like a zombie, onto the screen. Note, too, the similarity between films like *The Andromeda Strain*, where the virus is extraterrestrial in origin but has come to Earth only because of a military research attempt to harvest biological weaponry, and the *Resident Evil* film series, where the root cause of the virus, and its subsequent zombie apocalypse, is similarly the overreaching effects of corporate greed and militarism.

We would be remiss in addressing the literary history of plague narratives without referencing the only major account written in the modern era, Albert Camus's 1947 novel *The Plague*. It should be no surprise that we find all our previously mentioned plague narrative tropes in the novel, where there are characters representing various philosophical or ethical positions in relation to, again, government, family, and church. The character Joseph Grand struggles to find the correct words to say to his wife; Bernard Rieux battles against the ineptitude of the bureaucracy around him and its failure to deal with the plague in a timely manner; Father Paneloux argues at various moments that the plague is a punishment from God. While no critics would define *The Plague* as an outright zombie narrative, understanding the connections between this plague account and the themes we have been discussing explains why many critics understand the novel as "among much else, a disguised account of the European struggle against fascism."[20] The reason that a struggle against a biological disease has been so easily seen as a political metaphor by critics is that, on a metaphorical level, the plague represents a threat very similar to those of fascism and zombie narratives alike: the threat of the mob, which like a plague either absorbs or destroys everything in its path, including individual identity.

To be sure, there is more to be said about *The Plague* and other plague narratives. From this brief literary history, however, it is clear that a number of insights can be gleaned from exploring these anxieties about the collapse of familial, governmental, or sacred institutions, essential elements present both in the history of plague narratives and in modern zombie cinema. More important, as we are arguing here, the fact that these elements are entangled and confused in plague narratives is the more significant discovery, and the one we will explore as similarly significant in zombie film. Many zombie films can be invoked to clarify this conjunction even further, but the filmmaker who puts it in most stark relief is Fulci.

Although he is not a well-recognized filmmaker today, and he had less influence on other filmmakers in the genre than did Romero, Fulci was one of the most popular zombie filmmakers in the 1970s and 1980s. He serves our understanding of zombie films best not only because he is representative of international zombie cinema, but also because his work continually provokes its audience by generating plague anxieties in contradictory or ambiguous ways.

What is most fascinating about the films of Fulci is that he is not afraid to throw aside logic or narrative consistency in order to produce the desired effect of stimulating anxiety. The result is precisely our point in this article—that the central concern of zombie films has nothing to do with any manifest point plot (such as battling a literal virus or biological contagion), discovering the ultimate cause of the catastrophe (whether originating as moral censure from God, or the result of militarism or corporate greed), or some obvious political/moral agenda (such as fighting fascism in *The Plague* or as one might find, for example, in Romero's later, directly "political" work). Instead, these texts generate anxiety precisely because even the very fears they articulate are neither stable nor consistent. They refuse to become concrete and containable, and that lack of consistency, as such, is precisely what operates as a standard for zombie narratives.

Fulci's most famous zombie production is the 1979 film *Zombi 2* (also known as *Island of the Flesh Eaters* and by a number of other titles—Fulci's work often had multiple titles depending on translation and distribution). Despite the title, the work is not a sequel to a preceding Fulci film, though it seems clear that the intention was to market it as a sequel to Romero's *Dawn of the Dead*, which was entitled *Zombi* when released in Italy. The film opens in New York Harbor, with a sailboat aimlessly adrift until stopped by the harbor patrol. The flesh-eating zombie aboard the boat raises a number of questions and prompts the protagonists—Peter and Anne, a newspaper reporter and the sister of the boat's missing owner, respectively—to journey to the tropical island of Matool. Along the way they enlist the aid of two boating enthusiasts, Brian and Susan, who help them find the island, though only reluctantly, because as Brian remarks, "Natives claim it is cursed; they avoid it like the plague." After one bizarre yet extraordinarily memorable scene involving a fight between a zombie and a shark, the protagonists reach the island and eventually find a doctor, David Menard, involved in research attempting to cure the zombie plague that is the apparent source of the recent uprising of the dead.

Just what is the origin of this zombie plague? The answer to that question remains ambiguous. On the one hand, as already noted in Brian's comment above, the source of the zombie outbreak is potentially supernatural in origin, a "curse" on the island. But on the other hand, the film seems intent on demonstrating that zombies arise due to contagion. In one scene, the film's point of view is that of the doctor peering into his microscope at some kind of bacteria or virus, apparently the source of the infection that is killing the villagers and bringing them back to life. "I'm sure there's a natural explanation," the doctor remarks, "and I'm determined to find it." It is also clear by the end of the film that, as in many zombie narratives, the bite of a zombie will infect its victim and result in his or her transformation into another zombie. Yet a bacterial or viral infection would do little to explain why, at one point in the film, zombies rise out of an ancient conquistador graveyard when the fleeing protagonists arbitrarily stumble into it. A "natural" blood disorder would have caused the ancient corpses to rise centuries ago, immediately after their burial, and hence it seems obvious that the transgression of sacred ground, the graveyard, must be the immediate cause of their rising.

So, which is it in this film, are the zombies supernatural or natural in origin? We argue that the popularity achieved by Fulci's films lies precisely in the fact that such questions are only to be raised rather than answered. The narrative not only refuses to answer its own questions, but it continually vacillates between multiple questions, positions, and concerns. In our previous example, it was unclear whether zombies arose because of viral infection or the transgression of sacred ground. Family tradition is invoked for yet another explanation when one employee of the doctor, an island native, produces his description of the outbreak in broken English: "The father of my father always say, when the earth spit out the dead, they will come back to suck the blood from the living." When the doctor dismisses his comment, and reassures him that there is a natural cause for the apparent zombie curse, the native replies, "Yes, you are right. You know more things than we do." Here, institutional authority conflicts with assertions of the family. Again, though, instead of choosing which of these narrators (the native, or the white colonizer who comes to examine and dismiss the island's traditions) has the correct understanding of zombies in the film, it is best to understand that in Fulci's films there is no grand narrative that will explain all events, rather only a web of possibilities.

Virtually every cinematic narrative device common to zombie films can be found in *Zombi 2*. Yet instead of resolutely focusing on one or two such elements, the familiar themes of family, church, and state all blend together in a tangle of unresolved and unfocused discursive threads. The doctor's hospital (which serves as a temporary fortress against the zombie mob that eventually overruns it) is also the island's church. The narrative involves graveyards desecrated, the church/hospital overrun, and even a subplot between the doctor and his wife (who is eventually eaten by zombies) where he chastises her for depression and neurosis, and she replies that he is performing unspeakable experiments (on zombies?) in his obsession to cure the plague, and argues that his scientific research is no research at all: "You call fooling around with superstition and voodoo rites research?" Is the film highlighting the breakdown of family caused by zombies? Is it critiquing the transgressions of the doctor in overstepping morality? Showing a conflict between Western medicine and voodoo? None of these issues becomes clear. Tangling things even further, the demands of community/family versus those of self-interest are highlighted when Susan is bitten by a zombie and her boyfriend, Brian, is himself bitten because he refuses to distance himself from her, a narrative anxiety highlighted repeatedly in the film when the doctor is reluctant to shoot his own zombie-infected friend, and when Peter and Anne refuse, at the film's end, to kill Brian, who has also been infected by the bite of Susan.

It should be obvious, then, why Fulci is an excellent choice for understanding what lies at the heart of zombie cinema (. . . unbeating though it may be), which is that his films are themselves the breakdown of order and understanding, repeating in their form (or rather, in their breakdown of form) the same thing that they represent in their content. A look at Fulci films other than *Zombi 2* reveals much the same. For example, *The House by the Cemetery* was released in 1981 in Italy as *Quella villa accanto al cimetero*, or *Zombie Hell House*, and by other titles in the United States. The film's protagonist, Dr. Norman Boyle, moves with his wife and son, Lucy and Bob, from New York City to a small New England town, to continue the research project of his predecessor, Dr. Eric Peterson, who killed himself there. Eventually, it is revealed that Peterson was researching something unrelated to his initial project, which leads to the discovery that the basement of the house contains the zombie corpse of the original owner, Dr. Freudstein, who is killing people and using their bodies to maintain his own life—albeit an unnatural, desiccated life, with maggots for internal organs. The plot may seem straightforward, but it has a great deal of additional twists and turns within it. Again we can find the familiar themes of family, church, and state from the preceding plague narratives, and again those narratives are left unresolved as the film progresses.

Family tensions abound from the beginning, as Lucy complains about the move from upscale New York City to the rural town, only to have Norman reject her complaints and occasionally remind her to take her pills to cure her anxieties. Throughout the film there is an undercurrent of trouble between the couple. But even more interesting is a strange theme of infidelity or deception that Fulci introduces but never fully explains. On multiple occasions in the story, it is suggested that Norman has visited the town sometime previously. Each time he is asked about his visits—for example, "Of course, you've been there before, haven't you Dr. Boyle?"—he refuses to acknowledge them. The idea that he has been to town before is supported by the introduction of the babysitter, Anne, who shares a curious glance with Norman when first standing in the kitchen with him and his wife. Norman and Anne stare at one another briefly yet pointedly, demonstrating that some connection exists between them, but both immediately turn their gaze aside before Lucy can observe it. The film, however, leaves this thread dangling. By the movie's end, when most of the protagonists have been murdered, including Norman, Lucy, and Anne, it is never explained whether Norman had visited town before, why he might have done so, or even what his connection is, if any, to the babysitter.

Although this unresolved family tension is present in the film, it would be unfair to say that "family" is the central agenda of the film. Just as other plague narratives lament the inefficiency of the state, law, or government to provide aid or solace, so does this film. When Norman tries to discover the research of Dr. Peterson, he looks for the tomb of Dr. Freudstein only to discover that it isn't where it is supposed to be. Cornering a cemetery caretaker, Norman asserts, "According to the official records, he's buried here," only to hear in response that "the official records don't mean a thing." The tomb is not locatable because Freudstein isn't dead, a detail that the entire narrative hinges on, because to some degree the film's entire aura of tension and dread is due to any number of different, competing problems, whether they be the tensions of family, the failures of government bureaucracy, or, ultimately, the fear of violating the sacred. The last of these is represented by the fact that the house is not only near a cemetery, but is in fact a kind of cemetery itself—it contains the living dead. This detail is true not only because Dr. Freudstein still lurks in the cellar, but also because it contains a grave on the main floor, a grave placed there, Norman asserts, as in many houses in New England towns, because for previous generations the ground was too cold to allow outdoor burials in winter.

The suggestion seems to be that it is the family's mistake to have violated the sacred grounds of the house, because in doing so they are violating the dead. But, then again, Fulci's narrative is not so singular or easily understood. The other apparent "cause" of the evil may not be the family at all; the film also asserts that the zombie Freudstein still lives its horrific afterlife because he had an unnatural obsession with extending his own existence, and hence he violated a religious or sacramental taboo. Just as in Fulci's *Zombi 2*, where it is unclear what the exact origin or cause of the malevolence might be, here we have a tangle of various mistakes, failures, and transgressive possibilities to consider, where virtually everyone in the community may be complicit in some fashion, and, given the high body count by the end of the film, everyone has the possibility of being overcome. In the end, the only major character to escape Freudstein's wrath is the (innocent?) child, Bob, although he only does so by virtue of slipping into a strange otherworld, accompanied by ghosts who are related to Freudstein. The point of such an ending, and how it might relate to anything that preceded it, is unclear. In Fulci's world, however, the lack of clarity is so evident as to be the predominant theme.

For Fulci, zombies always represent many possibilities. We have already seen that zombies can be singular products of scientific experimentation gone wrong, or violations of sacred space, or the result of native islanders being exploited by Western colonizers. They are threatening in the form of a single hundred-year-old zombie, or in the form of shuffling zombie hordes. Fulci's deliberate inconsistency continues in any number of other films. Take, for example, his 1980 work *The Gates of Hell* (*Paura nella città dei morti viventi*, also known as *City of the Living Dead*). The zombies in this film have an array of unusual abilities. As in *Zombi 2*, where the distinction between biological contagion and voodoo became so blurred as to be irrelevant, in *The Gates of Hell* the corporeal versus non-corporeal nature of the zombie is called into question. In one scene, a zombie priest causes a woman to bleed from the eyes and vomit forth her own intestines, an action taken from a distance, without any physical contact. In the same scene, that zombie instantly vanishes, only to reappear directly behind another victim, whose brains he physically pulls from the back of the victim's head. Here zombies have any number of potential characteristics, but any possibility for discovering some essential character of the zombie remains impossible. Fulci's films, with zombies that are physical and not physical, who have conflicting etiological explanations and subplots that go nowhere, deliberately raise questions that are beyond answering.

The temptation in watching Fulci films is to attempt to track down the answers to these questions. Why is a shark fighting a zombie and what are the larger implications of that for the plot? Did Norman previously visit the town and what is his relationship to the babysitter? Answering these questions, if such a thing were possible, misses the point. It is the fact that the reader must confront these unanswerable questions and be forced to remain uncertain about them that gives them their meaning. Another way to state this point is that zombie narratives do not mean what they mean. Rather, zombie narratives represent the failure of meaning altogether, and they depict in repetitive detail the problems that occur both on the individual and social level, what the decay of such meaning entails.

Fulci's other zombie works reveal many of the same anxieties of decay, but in conclusion it is worth looking for a brief moment elsewhere, just to reiterate the pervasiveness of these themes in virtually all zombie narratives. Take, for example, *28 Weeks Later* (2007) and *Land of the Dead* (2005), which both theoretically explore relatively fresh territory, based as they are on the idea of a reconstructed civilization. Some reviewers have given the easy interpretation of *28 Weeks Later* as an allegory for America's military occupation of the Middle East. Like the contemporary Middle East, in the film England is a land occupied by an American-led military force. Ostensibly, the military's function in the movie is to rebuild as it maintains law and order, but the occupying Americans consistently gaze at those they are protecting through the sniper-scopes of their rifles, and the tension between the Americans and the survivors, as well as the impossibility of American success, is apparent throughout the film. Likewise, *Land of the Dead* could easily stand as allegory for George W. Bush's United States, with the walled-off community an allegory for his administration's support for building a wall across the entire U.S.-Mexico border.

But the message-based political treatment of each film seems much less interesting than the message that the very attempt to rebuild the social order reveals that order can be as horrifying or problematic as what it is meant to replace. If, as George Romero may be suggesting, *Land of the Dead* represents contemporary America, then civilization—its value and its meaning—is illusory and sustains itself by narrating its own empty fable. In Romero's film, this narration takes the form of television advertisements for "Fiddler's Green," the upscale and fortified city center where the rich have retreated for supposed safety from both the poor living and the hungry dead. The commercials represent a new mythology, literally selling us on the very idea of the world itself as well as our place in it. During the movie's climax, when zombies overrun civilization once again, we understand that the world is merely revealing the underlying disorder that has been with us all along. In *28 Weeks Later*, the mythology of order is narrated not by television commercials but through the ever-present sniper-scope and security camera POV shots, which convey the American military's sense of control over the reconstructed society.

Even if these other films maintain more narrative consistency or cohesion than those of Fulci, the point is that loss of control, loss of meaning, is constant in the zombie narrative. These texts reveal the failed hope of understanding, gazing on, or controlling the chaos of the world. For another example, some of the most disturbing scenes in Zack Snyder's *Dawn of the Dead* appear in the first few minutes of the film, before and during the opening credits. On the eve of world's collapse, the protagonist, Anna, drives home from her job at a hospital. An aerial camera looks directly down at her car. The shot emphasizes the strict and geometrical order of the Wisconsin suburbs through which she travels. From above, one notices the clean, straight lines of the grid-like streets, the neat rectangles of the rooftops, the uncanny sameness of each yard and driveway. The next morning, an aerial view of that same neighborhood creates a parallel image, though now the neighborhood is under attack by zombies. The camera rises above the rooftops to show us the destruction of the suburbs as columns of smoke rise into the air. Instead of structure and the clear, geometrical patterns created by the streets and houses, we now see their opposite: chaos and a devastation that appears to extend all the way to the horizon. We see how far and how quickly the infection has spread. Through their juxtaposition, the two scenes communicate the fragility of the social structure we take for granted each day.

Also in the first minutes of the film, a speeding ambulance runs over Anna's neighbor as he fearfully aims a gun at her. Then, as she escapes the neighborhood, a police cruiser skids out of control and nearly crashes into her car. Moments later the radio can be heard announcing that "several military personnel have fallen ill." After the film's initial scenes, the opening credits begin. While Johnny Cash sings the apocalyptically themed song "The Man Comes Around" above the credits, we see fragmentary scenes of global chaos. One of the final images reveals the White House under attack by zombies. And so in only minutes, we have seen chaos metastasize across the planet, and the message is clear: no one is in charge of the world any longer. Nearly every zombie film contains the obligatory scenes of similar disorder as the authorities looked to for protection themselves fall victim to the chaos.

Fulci, who does very little in the way of creating any examples of zombie phenomena not seen in these other films, is the quintessential zombie director precisely for that reason. Fulci's work uses the standard narrative tropes to question the nature of narrative itself, pointing out that the logical conclusions and resolutions are not essential. "Narrative," as most people understand it, consists of a chronological sequence of events following a pattern, eventually reaching a resolution, in which plot elements are concluded and questions, which the story itself poses to the reader or viewer, are answered. In Fulci, however, there is often an almost arbitrary sequence of events that does not contribute to a comforting resolution. In the course of multiple films, Fulci violates virtually every narrative convention. In *The Gates of Hell*, for example, he even violates notions of setting, overlaying mysterious jungle noises (monkeys and tropical birds) into a scene that takes place in Dunwich, Massachusetts. The film's setting further violates common knowledge of history and geography by claiming that Dunwich was constructed on the ruins of Salem, Massachusetts, which is odd given that the original Salem still exists today. Contemporary zombie narratives often do something that Fulci's films do not: maintain a consistent explanation and narrative structure. In these movies, origins are revealed and timelines are consistent (and explicitly labeled, in fact almost obsessively so: *28 Days Later*, *28 Weeks Later*, *Night of the Living Dead*, *Dawn of the Dead*, *Day of the Dead*, etc.). Messages, whether political, theological, social, or otherwise, are unambiguous.

These texts, each in their own way, continually treat the same sets of themes and anxieties, arguing on one side or another about our individual relationship to civilization, God, and the family. These are the phenomena that make up what we have come to recognize as a traditional zombie narrative. But it is not the phenomena themselves that are the essential elements of any given tale. Instead, it is the ways that those elements, which we have composed, sustained, and trusted in, meet with collapse, decomposition, and decay.

CHAPTER 8

Imitations of Life: Zombies and the Suburban Gothic

Bernice Murphy

Meet John and Mary Drone

Andrew Currie's 2006 movie *Fido* is an ambitious satire that combines elements of Sirkian melodrama, George A. Romero's Living Dead series, and the "Timmy's down the well" plotting of heroic dog films such as *Lassie* and *Old Yeller*.[1] The parameters of the film's wry premise—a kind of parallel-universe reimagining of a 1950s suburban community in which zombies are part of everyday life—are outlined in the amusing newsreel opener that alludes to Romero's *Night of the Living Dead* (1968).[2] A cloud of cosmic radiation containing particles that can reanimate the dead led to the zombie wars, in which the last remnants of humanity desperately tried to eradicate the undead (as opposed to the red) menace. Thanks to the discoveries of a scientist named Reinhold Geiger (who figured out that zombies could be killed for good if you shot them in the head), the distinctly Halliburton-style "ZomCon" corporation managed to contain the outbreak and "tame" wild zombies for use as cheap labor during the reconstruction of society. The much-diminished new world that emerges from the ashes of the old is one in which time, it seems, has all but been suspended. We are told that it is several decades since the end of the zombie wars, but this is still a stagnant, stiflingly restrictive society in which there seems little hope of substantive change: it appears to have been the 1950s for quite a while. What makes the film even more interesting is the fact that it resurrects the folkloric origins of the Caribbean "zombi," which of course had its roots in anxieties surrounding slavery, racial inequality, and the economic exploitation of the underclass. In Currie's film, "tame" zombies in steel control collars carry out all the menial and unpleasant tasks the white middle classes would prefer not to tackle themselves. Fido's lead character is a young boy named Timmy Robinson (K'Sun Ray), whose life is transformed when his status-conscious mother, Helen, (Carrie Anne Moss), overrules the objections of her zombie-phobic husband, Bill (Dylan Baker), and buys one to help around the house so that they are not "the only ones on the street without one!" As one reviewer put it, the film's depiction of "an undead chattel class hits an authentic socio-political nerve. It seems to capture perfectly what 1950s upper-class suburbia might have looked like had slave labor still been available."[3] By projecting Romero's vision of zombie apocalypse slightly backward into a twenty-first-century vision of 1950s suburbia, Currie's film also manages to make some pertinent points about the containment culture of both that period and our own. The film evokes the upscale suburban developments of the present that rely on cheap migrant labor in the form of underpaid and often-illegal nannies, housekeepers, gardeners, and workers. Further, the security obsessed and manipulative conflation of the military-industrial complex epitomized in ZomCon evokes much-criticized elements of the presidency of George W. Bush.[4]

Willard, the suburban town in which the film takes place, is fenced off from the dangerous "Wild Zone" outside by a vast steel fence that keeps the millions of "untamed" zombies outside from getting in. Other pockets of "civilization" are sparsely dotted around the countryside like army bases amid hostile territory. And yet, the odd brutal killing aside, Willard—a tongue-in-cheek microcosm of postwar United States—exists in a kind of tenuously peaceable bubble, insulated from the threatening world outside. The film functions therefore as an imitation on two different levels. On the most obvious level, it seeks to recreate an idealized vision of 1950s suburbia. Willard is a town of white picket fences, neatly mown lawns, gleaming cars, and secretly dissatisfied housewives: apart from the zombie presence, it is an extremely familiar take on the era of the kind seen in movies such as *Pleasantville* (1998) and *Far from Heaven* (2002). The way in which *Fido* depicts the suburban milieu brings to mind Frederic Jameson's comments at the beginning of his 1989 essay "Nostalgia for the Present":

> There is a novel by Philip K. Dick, which, published in 1959, evokes the fifties: President Eisenhower's stroke; Main Street, U.S.A.; Marilyn Monroe; a world of neighbors and PTA's; small retail chain stores (the produce trucked in from outside); favorite television programs, mild flirtations with the housewife next door, game shows and contests; sputniks distantly revolving overhead, mere blinking lights in the firmament.... If you were interested in constructing a time capsule or an "only yesterday" compendium or documentary-nostalgia video film of the 1950s, this might serve as a beginning ... the list is not a list of facts or historical realities (although its items are not invented and are in some sense "authentic"), but rather a list of stereotypes, of ideas of facts and historical realities.[5]

As Jameson goes on to suggest, the idyllic small-town setting evoked in the novel—which also functioned as an allegorical expression of Eisenhower America itself—no longer exists in the present day: "The autonomy of the small town has ... vanished. What was once a certain point on the map has become an imperceptible thickening in a continuum of identical products and standardized spaces from coast to coast."[6] Complicating matters considerably is the fact that the setting of Dick's novel ultimately turns out to be a genuinely inauthentic space: "a reproduction of the 1950s—including induced and introjected memories and character structures in its human population—constructed in 1997, in the midst of an interstellar atomic war."[7] As Jameson observes:

> Dick also takes pains to make it clear that the 1950s village is also very specifically the result of infantile regression on the part of the protagonist, who has also, in a sense, unconsciously chosen his own delusion and has fled the anxieties of the civil war for the domestic and reassuring comforts of his own childhood during the period in question.... The novel is a collective wish fulfillment, and the expression of a deep, unconscious yearning for a simpler and more human social system and a small-town utopia very much in the North American Frontier tradition.[8]

In a rather similar manner, therefore, Willard serves as a kind of reassuring yet fundamentally counterfeit home for the protagonists of Currie's film. The pretty, suburban town represents an attempt by the survivors of a devastating catastrophe to create for themselves a halcyon, family-centered world. It is a place in which women (and children) know their station and one can depend on zombies to serve as a cheap workforce, while attempting to ignore the fact that much of the rest of the world has been completely overrun by flesh-eating corpses. Willard is itself an imitation of an outmoded and hyper-idealized way of life destroyed in the war, just as the setting of Dick's novel is a sham recreation of a time and a place that has long since passed. Despite the period trappings, we have no real way of knowing if Willard exists in the 1950s at all: one gets the sense that change within this deliberately static community happens very slowly or not at all. Indeed, the film's conclusion (in which Helen, Timmy, and Fido create a happy alternative family structure following Bill's death) seems to make it clear that while change is possible at the level of the nuclear family, society at large isn't going to alter all that dramatically anytime soon.

This attempt to recreate or hang on to an idealized yet bygone way of life is a crucial facet of the texts I will discuss in this article, and it is dramatized (as the notion that suburbia is an inherently repetitive, repressive milieu that dehumanizes its residents) through the appearance of the zombie or zombie-like figure. I will discuss Jack Finney's 1955 novel *Invasion of the Body Snatchers* (made into a film in 1956) and the films *Dawn of the Dead* (both the 1978 original and the 2004 remake) and *The Stepford Wives* (1975, based on Ira Levin's 1972 novel).

It is important to note before I begin that zombies in the more traditional "living dead" sense of the word feature in only three of the texts cited here—*Fido* and the two versions of *Dawn of the Dead*. The other works, *Invasion of the Body Snatchers* and *The Stepford Wives*, feature alien "pod people" and androids, respectively, and therefore rightly cannot be said to feature zombies in the strictest sense of the term.[9] But the relationship between Romero's shambling corpses, Jack Finney's relentlessly unemotional and conformist alien invaders, and Ira Levin's house-proud androids is stronger than it appears. First of all, crucially, depersonalization is a key aspect of each.[10] The classical (i.e., dead) zombie is generally portrayed as humanity reduced to its most mindless level, no longer capable of emotional engagement, an animated husk that may look like the deceased but (generally) lacks all remnants of personality. Finney's pod people similarly lack human emotion (this is indeed their most terrifying characteristic), and Levin's androids are incapable of feeling at all. Androids, zombies, and alien invaders alike look like people (albeit very unhealthy people, in the case of the zombie) yet are fundamentally inhuman in their own way. They all "take over" or otherwise replace those whose appearance they have taken on. Finney's pod people have assumed the form of normal Americans killed during the replication process, while the men of Stepford murder their troublesome wives and replace them with submissive android look-alikes. Further, they all violate time in some respect: the zombie lingers on after death, Finney's alien invaders live for only five years, and Stepford's android homemakers will never age in any conventional sense because they are mechanical, not biological. As we shall see, each of the texts I will discuss here presents suburbia (or proto-suburbia) as the setting for narratives in which attempts to recreate or otherwise cling to older, outmoded ways of living can never be anything other than essentially inauthentic imitations of life, just like the zombie or zombie-like figures who play such an important role in each narrative.

In *The City in History* (1961), Lewis Mumford outlined what he considered to be the purpose of the original, pre-twentieth-century suburb, stressing the desire for individual freedom and expression that lay at the heart of the concept. Before its present-day incarnation, therefore, the aim of the classical suburb was to allow one to "be your own unique self; to build your unique house amid a unique landscape: to live in this Domain of Arnheim a self-centered life, in which private fantasy and caprice would have license to express themselves openly." But in the mid-twentieth century, he famously claimed, everything changed: "In the mass movement into suburban areas a new kind of community was produced.... A multitude of uniform, unidentifiable houses, lined up inflexibly, at uniform distances, on uniform roads, in a treeless communal waste, inhabited by people of the same class, the same income, the same age group, witnessing the same television performances, eating the same tasteless prefabricated foods, from the same freezers, conforming in every outward and inward respect to a common mold, manufactured in a central metropolis." The ultimate effect, Mumford concluded, was to create "a low-grade uniform environment from which escape is impossible."[11] Mumford's characterization of 1950s suburbia as a shoddily constructed, repetitive, joyless hell was by no means the first or the last time the locale was considered in such terms. In his best-selling diatribe *The Crack in the Picture Window* (1956), John Keats described suburbia as a nightmarish vista of "identical boxes spreading like gangrene" inhabited by mindless, materialistic automatons whom he memorably characterized as John and Mary Drone.[12] One of the key aspects of the anti-suburban tract, as expressed by Mumford, Keats, and others was condemnation of the physical sameness of the milieu, and of the manner in which it rapidly spread across the countryside, destroying the old small-town model of rural existence. Keats's suggestive likening of suburban spread to gangrene is one that, though extreme, does capture a certain sense of futile horror experienced by certain postwar commentators. For them, suburbia was a disease spreading unchecked throughout the body of the nation, infecting new territory with breathtaking and unprecedented rapidity.

The postwar era in general saw a preoccupation among many Americans—particularly more liberal-minded cultural commentators and intellectuals—with the alleged erosion of individuality and uniqueness taking place amid the era's climate of unprecedented social and economic development. Alongside the "Creature-Features" of the 1950s and early 1960s, the body-replacement narrative—in which loved ones, friends, and neighbors are invisibly "taken over" or "replaced" by threatening, usually alien forces who seek to overthrow everything that God-fearing, freedom-loving Americans hold dear—became one of the most obvious tropes in American horror and science fiction. While Cold War anxieties undoubtedly form part of the explanation for such narratives, it was also becoming increasingly clear to many commentators that unease at the rapidity of the nation's social, political, and economic change was just as significant. As one of the most visible manifestations of the unprecedented manner in which everyday life in the United States was changing, suburbia was always going to be of particular significance.

With the establishment in 1947 of the first "Levittown," the development that virtually invented the postwar suburb, the single-family dwelling became the American norm. But not everyone was pleased by this innovation. As one critic has noted, "The rows of virtually identical $10,000 dream homes that marched across the once-rural landscape in the 1950s made suburbia an easy target for nay-sayers quick to equate stylistic sameness with middle-class conventionality and intellectual conformity." There was also the fact that the availability and affordability of homes in these new developments (along with the generous federal grants awarded to ex-servicemen after the war) seemed to "doom traditional hierarchies of wealth and class: if anybody could afford a house, and all houses were pretty much the same, what distinguished the occupants of one little box from their next-door neighbors."[13] As critics of the suburban project loved to point out, suburban neighborhoods tended to attract upwardly mobile young families of roughly the same age, class, and ethnic background. It is perhaps unsurprising, then, that the milieu was seen by some as a genuine threat to long-standing social and economic boundaries.

In his spirited defense of suburbia in *The Suburban Myth* (1969), Scott Donaldson, much as Herbert J. Gans had done in his groundbreaking sociological study *The Levittowners* (1967), attempted to address and overturn many of the most vigorous attacks on the milieu and its inhabitants produced in the previous decade. A particular target for both authors was John Keats, who had railed against suburbia and suburbanites in the strongest possible terms. Keats painted a nightmarish portrait of a land rapidly colonized by "Jerry Built," identikit slums thrown up by unscrupulous developers interested only in making a fast buck and moving on to the next site. Then there was the alleged psychological and emotional damage wrought on those foolish enough to inhabit such homes: Keats claimed that intolerably standardized dwellings created intolerably standardized people. The suburban home apparently had the power to turn its heedless occupants into mindless, materialistic, unhappy automatons. Keats and many of his fellow detractors of suburbia depicted suburbanites as feckless "drones" hopelessly in thrall to their own greed: in other words, as zombies in all but name.

The fear of the mindless masses fundamental to the modern American zombie movie can also, at least in part, be traced back to this particularly American anxiety regarding the deadening effects of industrialization and mass production. What made the suburbs so affordable and so easy to erect was the fact that prefabrication techniques developed during the war meant that preassembled homes could be put up much more quickly and cheaply than traditional homes built from scratch. For as little as a hundred dollars down, a young couple could secure their own piece of the American dream, often with all "mod cons"[14] and suitable furnishings thrown in as well. But efficiency and affordability did have its drawbacks: the choice of homes was usually limited to a carefully selected range of models.

Indeed, along with peripheral location and relatively low density, architectural similarity was one of the major (and most maligned) characteristics of the American suburb. As Kenneth Jackson explained in his history of the milieu:

> A few custom houses were built for the rich, and mobile homes gained popularity with the poor and the transient, but for most American families in search of a new place to live some form of tract house was the most likely option. In order to simplify their production methods and reduce design fees, most of the larger developers offered no more than a half-dozen basic house plans, and some offered half that number. The result was a monotony and repetition that was especially stark in the early years of the subdivision, before the individual owners had transformed their homes and yards according to personal taste.[15]

It is hardly surprising then that the very repetition of the suburbs should have aroused condemnation, especially in a nation that prided itself on facilitating the expression of individual freedom and uniqueness. Although the work of Donaldson and Gans, alongside that of later students of the suburban lifestyle such as Jackson, has helped to redress many of the more exaggerated critiques of the milieu and its residents and highlighted "the need to study suburbia without preconception,"[16] the fact remains that in the decade or so following World War II a unique confluence of environmental, economic, political, and cultural factors helped create the perfect environment for fictions concerned with alienation and depersonalization. The heated debate about the relative merits and supposed dangers of the suburban environment was therefore by no means confined to the work of sociologists and cultural commentators. Such anxieties would also find vivid expression in horror, gothic, and science fiction narratives, in which the kind of alarmist rhetoric so often aimed at the locale would be luridly dramatized.

From Pod People to the Living Dead

Prior to the Second World War, American horror and science fiction had more typically focused on terrifying external threats, generally personified in alien or supernatural menaces. In the years following the war, however, a significant strand of genre writing and moviemaking began to focus instead on dangers that were literally much closer to home. The type of narrative that seeks to make the everyday and the "normal" into something somehow alien and threatening derives its visual and emotive effectiveness from the unnerving contrast between a commonplace, ordinary setting and the quietly aberrant behavior of those who wish to subvert normality.[17] After all, what could be more terrifying than suddenly realizing that those around you have gradually been "replaced" by someone or something else? In the fifties, films such as *Invaders from Mars* (1953), *It Came from Outer Space* (1953), *The Brain Eaters* (1958), *The Brain from the Planet Arous* (1958), *I Married a Monster from Outer Space* (1958), and, most famously, Jack Finney's novel *Invasion of the Body Snatchers* (1955), relied on this basic premise. Though Finney's book (and the 1956 film adaptation of the same name) is a tale of a particularly insidious form of alien invasion, it is also a commentary on the death of an old way of life, and of the ways in which the apparently unstoppable forces of modernity and technology change an idyllic little town into something strange and unfamiliar. Ostensibly set two decades in the future (1976), the tone of *Invasion of the Body Snatchers* is from the outset one of nostalgia for an idealized way of life that is gone forever. At the time that Finney wrote *Body Snatchers*, thousands of small towns all over the United States were being gradually infiltrated by ruthlessly modern outside forces: but the threat did not come from alien pods, rather from the relentless expansion of the suburbs, which many feared would replace small-town charm and character with soulless conformity and sameness.

Finney's novel, therefore, dramatizes the anxieties aroused by the immensely rapid changes that were taking place in American culture and society at the time. The pod people who quietly and efficiently take over Miles Bennell's hometown of Mill Valley (Santa Mira in the film) may ultimately be defeated by good old American moxie, but the cozy, insulated place that he grew up in will never be the same again.[18] Like thousands of other small communities all over the United States during the postwar era, the outside world had irrevocably encroached on Mill Valley. To suburbia's most vociferous critics, the rapidly erected, identikit housing developments spreading across the country like wildfire were, like the aliens in Finney's novel, a very real threat to the core values of American culture and society. Further, for some the upwardly mobile young families who populated those suburbs were a horde of frighteningly homogenous invaders who cared nothing about the cities they left behind or the once-pristine countryside that was bulldozed in order to make way for affordable, modern homes. Given the frequency with which Finney's hero rails against the unfeeling, overtly technological focus of modern society, it seems clear that the novel's critique of conformity has at least as much to do with anxieties such as these as with fears aroused by Cold War tensions (the latter being a common interpretation of Finney's book and of Don Siegel's 1956 film adaptation). It is perhaps no coincidence then that the first patient to suggest to Miles that something is very wrong in Mill Valley lives in "an unincorporated suburb just outside the city limits."[19] There could be no more appropriate starting point for a narrative in which individualism and nonconformity come under such a powerful threat.

Given the postwar era's preoccupation with issues of creeping conformity and depersonalization, it is no surprise that the usurpation of "traditional" American values of home, family, and community would continue into the 1960s and 1970s and find further expression in one of twentieth-century horror's most iconic representatives: the zombie. George A. Romero's *Night of the Living Dead* (1968) took a supernatural threat that had previously been located in the Caribbean and associated with black magic, and instead depicted zombies roaming around the American countryside as shambling parodies of their former selves, able only to devour any living thing that crosses their path. Like the "pod people" in *Invasion*, Romero's living dead are soulless eating machines fit only to consume: Keats's John and Mary Drone reduced to their crudest components.

The reborn, reconfigured figure of the Romero zombie—no longer "native" or otherwise foreign, no longer the product of voodoo or black magic, but instead distinctively white, American, and, above all, hungry—is therefore the missing link between the paranoid alien-invasion films of the 1950s and the loaded sexual and cultural mores of narratives such as *The Stepford Wives*. As Jamie Russell noted in *Book of the Dead* (2005), "As the small town American setting and doppelganger scenario of *Invasion of the Body Snatchers* suggested, the monsters might not be readily identifiable as bug-eyed aliens. Much worse—they might look like our friends and neighbors. In some ways, the Zombie was perfectly suited to this paranoid fear as the living dead looked so ordinary: they looked like us; heck, they once were us. . . . Romero takes the paranoid fears of Invasion—in particular its vision of the mass as a terrifyingly homogenous entity—and multiplies them several times over."[20] The links between "us" and "them" was further reinforced in Romero's follow-up, *Dawn of the Dead* (1978), in which a quartet of survivors—television station employee Fran, her boyfriend, Stephen, and SWAT team members Peter and Roger—fly a stolen helicopter into the countryside and take shelter in a shopping mall in order to escape the chaotic inner city. The catch, of course, is that their new sanctuary is itself infested with zombies, who, as Tony Williams puts it, are "still fascinated by an environment which is now really redundant in terms of their new appetites."[21]

Romero's scathing take on contemporary society becomes only more unsettling as the parallels between his living protagonists and their undead counterparts become increasingly obvious. In no time at all, the mall, the ultimate haven from the world outside, is theirs, and the protagonists unwittingly set about recreating a lifestyle that functions as a tellingly claustrophobic parody of the dysfunctional world they just left behind. Finally free to take possession of anything they could possibly desire, the group gleefully satisfies their material desires, turning their attic hideaway into a kind of rough approximation of the ideal suburban home, filled with tasteful contemporary furnishings, the centerpiece of which is a large television set that eventually shows only static yet still remains mindlessly switched on. Like Miles Bennell, the protagonist of *Invasion of the Body Snatchers*, they cling to the old ways of life even though the world has changed beyond all recognition. Inevitably, their initial glee soon gives way to boredom and deadening ennui, for they are living in a place in which time itself, save for the pregnant Fran's swelling stomach, seems to be suspended. Once they have settled into their new home, as Williams notes, "the group essentially becomes a middle-class family"[22]—with the pregnant Fran and self-centered Stephen as the unhappily attached parents, and Peter and the injured (and subsequently infantilized) Roger as their children—a bitterly ironic reenactment of the destructive mores of the old world. Gradually, it becomes clear to Fran and Peter, as it does to us, that the mall, while seemingly a safe haven, is a gilded cage.

The climactic invasion of this poisoned sanctuary by a psychotic biker gang, which allows the excluded zombies to once more gain entrance, is therefore inevitable, and to some extent perhaps welcome, even if it brings death, for it has at least breached the deadening bubble in which the protagonists had willingly surrounded themselves. The film ends on a typically uncertain note as Fran and Peter fly away in the helicopter to seek a new beginning elsewhere. The final shots, however, are of the interior of the mall, and of the zombies mindlessly trooping round the shops once more, to the accompaniment of ironically lighthearted Muzak: they have reclaimed their kingdom once more.

Significantly, in Zack Snyder's 2004 remake of *Dawn of the Dead*, the original movie's oblique connection between suburban mores and the zombie apocalypse is highlighted from the outset. The film opens in the hospital in which the female lead (and Fran equivalent), Ana (Sarah Polley), works. The first intimations of the unfolding disaster come when a series of patients exhibiting unusual strength and aggression are admitted to the emergency room: they are of course early victims of the rapidly escalating zombie outbreak. Tired after a long shift, Ana fails to realize the gravity of the situation. On the drive home, she rapidly dials past increasingly fraught radio broadcasts in favor of some easy listening, and drives home to spend some quality time with her husband, Louis. Theirs is clearly a quiet, family-centered neighborhood, as Ana's warm exchange with Vivian, the little blonde girl who lives next door, testifies. Safely enclosed within her cozy home and within the arms of her husband, Ana remains completely unaware of the crisis gripping the outside world, until the next morning when the couple awaken to find little Vivian standing stock-still in the their tastefully appointed bedroom.

It is at this point that suburban insularity is violently and irrevocably disturbed. Vivian attacks them like a wild animal, ripping out Louis's throat as he tries to fend her off with a bedside lamp. He rapidly bleeds to death, and then immediately comes back to life as a zombie himself and lunges at Ana, who manages to scramble out the bathroom window and into her car. As she flees with her suddenly monstrous husband running after her, we see that the formerly peaceful suburb has in a matter of hours descended into anarchy and bloodshed, as the infected have turned against their loved ones and neighbors, who themselves then immediately become zombies.

The quartet of survivors in Romero's original film fled a rapidly disintegrating inner city (Philadelphia) and attempted to establish a rough approximation of middle-class life within the confines of an out-of-town shopping mall (thus paralleling the move from the cities to the suburbs that characterized housing patterns during the 1950s). The more numerous protagonists of Snyder's "reimagining"—about a dozen survivors make it to the mall this time around—seem to have no such interest in recreating the suburban way of life, perhaps because, like Ana, they have already seen the milieu tear itself apart. Significantly, while Romero's characters went out of their way to renovate their attic hideaway so that it resembled a family home, and thus maintained a distinction between their living quarters and the mall itself, Snyder's protagonists make no such distinction and seem happy to live within the very stores that constitute the mall.

The fact that there are many more characters in this version of the film also means that they never gel as a "family" in the way that their predecessors do. Indeed, the only real family in the place—Frank and his pregnant wife, Luda—quickly hole themselves up in a maternity store, away from the rest of the survivors. The reason for this retreat is revealed toward the end of the film when we discover that Luda has been bitten and that her unborn child has been infected too. The result is a hideous zombie infant that must then be destroyed, unlike Fran's unborn child in the original, which provides at least some hope of new life amid the oceans of death that surround her. In contrast to the vaguely optimistic conclusion of the original, the climax of the remake is even more obviously downbeat. While Ana and a few remaining survivors do manage to flee the mall, their efforts are fruitless: as the end credits roll, the zombies finally overrun them.

The Towns That Time Forgot

Of course, perhaps the most famous conflation of suburban mores with submissive mindlessness is that found in Ira Levin's 1972 novel *The Stepford Wives*. What makes the Stepford concept so resonant is the way in which the story dramatizes contemporary anxieties regarding the changing role of women in the home and in society at large.[23] As Bobbie Markowe, the soon-to-be-replaced best friend of the heroine Joanna Eberhart, puts it in one of the novel's most significant lines, "Something fishy is going on here! We're in the town that time forgot!" Bobbie has unwittingly recognized a fundamental truth about her new community: that it is a place in which a concerted effort to stave off modernity and the change in gender relations brought about by the women's rights movement is taking place. This effort to turn back the clock and reestablish a much more conservative model of family life owes so much to idealized notions of 1950s suburban life, and specifically that way of life as magazines and advertisements depicted it: this is itself an imitation of an imitation.

Indeed, Levin's novel reads like an obviously exaggerated fictionalization of Betty Friedan's *The Feminine Mystique* (1963). Famously, Friedan compared the lot of the typical suburban housewife to that of prisoners in a concentration camp, arguing that "there are aspects of the housewife role that make it almost impossible for a woman of adult intelligence to retain a sense of adult identity, the firm cores of self or 'I' without which a human being, man or woman, is not truly alive," and suggesting that these conditions resembled those which destroyed the "human identity" of so many during the Holocaust: "For in the concentration camps the prisoners were forced to adopt childlike behavior, forced to give up their individuality and merge themselves into an amorphous mass. . . . They were manipulated to trap themselves; they imprisoned themselves by making the concentration camp the whole world, by blinding themselves to the larger world of the past, their responsibility for the present, and their possibilities for the future."[24] It isn't difficult to see the obvious connection between Friedan's deliberately hyperbolic rhetoric, which is, above all else, concerned with the erosion of individual identity, and the preoccupation with the dehumanizing effect of postwar life and the suburban lifestyle expressed by commentators such as Keats and Mumford. What differentiates Friedan, of course, is her sustained focus on the lot of American women, and in particular the fate of the average middle-class housewife. But she does use language and imagery already familiar to us from our discussion of Romero's zombie movies and of the "invisible invasion" films of the 1950s and early 1960s. When explaining the psychic stresses caused in the woman who does her best to "conform inwardly to one reality, while trying to maintain inwardly the values it denies," Friedan states that she becomes "an anonymous biological robot in a docile mass."[25] It is a striking analogy, and one that clearly has parallels with Levin's premise, for his docile and submissive homemakers literally are "biological robots," uncannily realistic living dolls who have long since replaced their more demanding human counterparts.

So while Friedan knowingly made use of extreme metaphorical comparisons in order to effectively and memorably dramatize what she saw as the intolerable lot of the middle-class, suburban housewife, in Levin's novel and in the film adaptation that followed, that striking metaphor becomes fictional reality. It is a comparison that Levin was obviously well aware of: the novel opens, after all, with a highly pertinent quote from Simone de Beauvoir's *The Second Sex*, while his doomed heroines are more than familiar with the rhetoric and aims of the then-emerging women's rights movement.[26] Indeed, we are pointedly told in the film that both Bobbie and Joanna "dabbled" in the "movement" before they were married. Yet ironically, their very self-consciousness about the nature of their own situation—the fact that they belong to the second generation of American women to move to suburbia and that they both possess the language and the intelligence with which to articulate their growing sense of unease regarding the Stepford way of life—actually does them no good at all: both Joanna and Bobbie are murdered and then replaced by the end of the story.

One of the most disturbing things about the novel's premise is the fact that Joanna and Bobbie and all the other women who have been "replaced" literally find themselves unable to escape a trap which they had already spotted. The novel even suggests that it was the growing independence and self-awareness of the women of Stepford that precipitated the terrible actions undertaken by the Men's Association, a group of local men who have decided to replace their wives with submissive automatons. Carol Van Sant, the Stepford wife who seems most prominent in both the novel and the film as a ridiculous exemplar of docile femininity, was actually once one of the leading lights of the local women's group—a group that once hosted Betty Friedan, as we are pointedly informed.[27] The minute Joanna Eberhart left behind the messy, chaotic, and stimulating environs of the city and sacrificed her nascent professional ambitions in order to move to orderly, family-oriented Stepford, Levin seems to suggest, her fate was sealed.

Initially, at least, Joanna and Walter Eberhart seem to have a secure, "modern" relationship: they apparently make all the household decisions together, and Walter seems to have no problem with washing up after dinner or minding the kids while Joanna works in the darkroom on her photographs. But he is still a fairly typical suburban husband, not all that different in many respects from the "corporation man" of a generation ago: he commutes to the city for work as a lawyer every day, while Joanna, despite her college degree and ambition to become a professional photographer, remains at home to look after their children. The move to suburbia has ostensibly been made for the children's sake, and for that of the entire family, but from the outset it is clear that Joanna is experiencing some ambivalence about the decision. It soon becomes apparent that Walter was the main impetus behind the move, and that his motives were less than selfless.

Stepford itself, in both the book and the film, is obviously an affluent, comfortably middle- and upper-middle-class suburb—not a destination for couples who have just gotten their start in life, but rather a large step up the ladder for the slightly older and more upwardly mobile kind of family. The movie adaptation was filmed in the wealthy, picturesque Connecticut neighborhood of Westport, a popular location for movies and television shows (it was also the setting for Wes Craven's 1972 horror film *The Last House on the Left*). Levin's novel states that the Men's Association headquarters—the most traditionally gothic-looking building in the film—was built in the nineteenth century by a railroad tycoon, which suggests that Stepford was founded during a much earlier cycle of suburbia than the less-exclusive postwar developments, something highlighted by the fact that the members of the men's club are almost all affluent professionals. They include an illustrator, a psychiatrist, lawyers, electronics executives, a linguist, and the manager of the local mall. This roll call of professions, as well as the fact that the outskirts of Stepford are home to a number of industrial plants (such as a plastic factory and an electronics company), of course takes on a more sinister significance as the plot develops.

As she begins to settle in to Stepford, Joanna gradually realizes that most of the women she encounters there have an unusual attachment to their roles as housewives and mothers. For example, the eerily submissive next-door neighbor Carol refuses to come over for coffee because she has to wax her living room floor, and when Joanna is in the supermarket she notices that the intimidating domestic perfectionism of the suburb's housewives extends even to the neatness with which they arrange their shopping carts. It's with relief then that she finally encounters the cynical, wisecracking Bobbie Markowe, herself a newcomer, whose house is even more untidy than Joanna's. Soon the two women are best friends, each helping to reassure the other that the behavior of Stepford's other women is most definitely not normal. At times the two of them seem like nothing so much as a pair of self-consciously cynical teenage girls, attempting to disguise their own gnawing insecurities by mocking those around them. It is an impression reinforced in the film by the fact that Katharine Ross (Joanna) and Paula Prentiss (Bobbie) are almost always seen dressed casually, in shorts, T-shirts, and jeans, while the other Stepford wives are costumed in Laura Ashley–style dresses, aprons, and large-brimmed hats.[28] Bobbie at times almost seems to function like Joanna's irrepressible alter ego: it is she who first puts into words the steadily accumulating but unacknowledged suspicions that Joanna has yet to admit to herself. For what is most obviously wrong about the women of Stepford is that they act as if they are taking part in a commercial. It's a preoccupation that arises even in the opening paragraphs of Levin's novel, when the old woman who welcomes newcomers to town compliments Joanna and Walter on moving to Stepford in the first place: "It's a nice town with nice people! You couldn't have made a better choice!," and follows this up by thrusting a basket of free samples at Joanna, exhorting her in much the same tone, "Try them, they're good products!"[29]

Even during their opening conversations with each other, Joanna and Bobbie cannot help but ironically converse in the language of advertisements: as Bobbie says upon their first meeting, "Given complete freedom of choice, wouldn't you just as soon not squeeze the Charmin?"[30] In a sense, the women bond because of their own wry awareness of the fact that their homes and their lives do not resemble those in a commercial. It's hardly surprising then that both the novel and the film consistently highlight the seeming artificiality of life in the suburbs: the fact that once again we have a community that is in itself an imitation of a hyper-idealized vision of middle-class life grounded in a nostalgic and inherently problematic vision of the 1950s.

While visiting the other women in Stepford in the hopes of starting up a new women's club, Joanna and Bobbie find themselves becoming increasingly demoralized by the fact that home after home is as perfect as a TV ad, and all the women decline the invitation because they "simply have too much to do" around the house. It is while she is sitting in one of these perfect homes that Joanna experiences an epiphany that, unbeknownst to her, is the key to understanding Stepford. Watching Kit Sunderson fold laundry into perfectly neat, color-coded piles, Joanna realizes that her new neighbor is behaving just like an actress in a commercial because "that's what she was, Joanna felt suddenly. That's what they all were, all the Stepford wives: actresses in commercials, pleased with detergents and floor wax, with cleansers, shampoo, and deodorants. Pretty actresses, big in the bosom but small in the talent, playing suburban housewives unconvincingly, too nicey-nice to be real."[31]

It's the kind of implication that will arise again and again in suburban-set literature and film: an acknowledgment of the fact that in many respects the suburban home has from the outset been a stage on which a drama of perfect family life should ideally be played out; it is a recognition that for many people buying into the suburban dream, they are purchasing not just a home, but hopefully an entire way of life. The artificiality of it all is further heightened when Kit, asked if she feels that she is living a "full life," responds in a vacant, blank manner, much like that of a "reeducated" prisoner of war praising his captors during a show trial: "Kit looked at her and nodded. 'Yes, I'm happy,' she said. 'I feel like I'm living a very full life. Herb's work is important, and he couldn't do it nearly as well without me. We're a unit, and between us we're raising a family, and doing optical research, and running a clean, comfortable household.'"[32]

Indeed, much of the novel, even more so than the film, is spent detailing Joanna's hectic but ultimately unfulfilling daily routine: the everyday chores and events that punctuate the life of the busy young wife and mother. Typically, it is Bobbie who again articulates the dreadful sense of anxiety that Joanna is beginning to experience regarding life in the suburbs, though given that this is the eco-aware 1970s, she initially seeks an environmental explanation for Stepford's oddness:[33] "In the ground, in the water, in the air—I don't know. It makes women interested in housekeeping and nothing else but. Who knows what chemicals can do?"[34] Bobbie goes on to use language that deliberately harks back to the kinds of concerns we have seen in earlier portraits of suburban-related dehumanization: "There's something here, Joanna! I'm not kidding! This is Zombieville!"[35] Soon, she's sensibly looking for a new house, her disquiet having blossomed into full-blown paranoia. When Joanna asks about the potential upheaval this move will cause to the children, Bobbie is forcefully unapologetic, and once more the Stepford wives are compared to zombies:

> "Better a little disruption in their lives than a zombie-ized mother," she said. She really was drinking bottled water, and wasn't eating any locally grown produce. "You can buy bottled oxygen, you know," Joanna said.
>
> "Screw you. I can see you now, comparing Ajax to your current cleanser."[36]

Note that once again, Bobbie and Joanna communicate in a fashion that ironically mocks a commercial: repeatedly, both novel and film reference the visual and verbal rhetoric of the advertising industry. It is another deliberate reference to Friedan's scathing analysis in *The Feminine Mystique* of the housewife's ultimate purpose. As Peter Knight has observed, Friedan's book is also an attack on the contemporary culture industry, and in particular on the advertising industry, which grew to unprecedented prominence in the postwar era, and on women's magazines, which Friedan accused of deliberately perpetuating the domestic ideology for their own commercial gain: "The crowning moment of realization in *The Feminine Mystique* comes with the discovery that during the postwar period of rapid suburban development, women spent three quarters of the household budget."[37] Popular magazines, television sitcoms, and even the discourses of pop psychology and sociology were "filled with admonitions—ranging from the subtle to the absurd—designed to persuade suburban housewives to accept a domesticated role."[38] As Betty Friedan asked pointedly, "Why is it never said that the really crucial function, *the really important role that women serve as housewives is to buy more things for the house?*"[39]

What's more, "the housewife is often an unaware victim" of such sinister machinations, subtly maneuvered into "buying things that neither fulfill her family's needs nor her own."[40] It makes sense then that the women who have already been replaced in Stepford should behave as though they are acting in a commercial: according to Friedan's bitter analysis they already are, they just don't know it. Indeed, one of the funniest yet most unnerving scenes in the film is that in which a supposed "consciousness-raising" session becomes a sales pitch for household cleaning products" as housewife after housewife extols the virtues of "Easy-On spray starch" while Joanna and Bobbie watch in appalled fascination. Thus forewarned, the reader of the novel or viewer of the film, like Joanna, knows from the moment that Bobbie's home is described as looking like "a commercial" that she has quietly been replaced.

Even as Joanna desperately struggles to uncover the truth about Stepford, and to escape this fate herself, she is unknowingly playing right into the hands of the Men's Association, allowing her voice to be recorded and permitting the 1950s magazine illustrator Ike Mazzard to sketch her. Actually, Joanna has already, unconsciously stumbled on the truth early in the novel when a revealing little poem suddenly pops into her head: "They never stop, these Stepford wives. . . . They work like robots all their lives."[41] The truth, in fact, is so close to home (literally) that by the time Joanna realizes that she need look no further than her own husband for answers, it is too late for her to escape. It turns out that the entire move to suburbia—a move made largely at Walter's behest—was made for the purpose of replacing Joanna with a fancy new model. As Joanna angrily exclaims, "Is that why Stepford was the only place to move? Did somebody pass the message to you? Take her to Stepford, Wally old pal, there's something in the air there; she'll change in four months."[42]

It is the kind of scene familiar to us from many an earlier novel: the heart-stopping moment when the naïve heroine suddenly realizes that the most powerful male figure in her life has been involved in a terrible conspiracy against her all along. As so often was the case in the classical gothic of writers such as Walpole and Radcliffe, the real danger here lies at home. In this case, the evil mastermind behind the dastardly plot is Dale "Diz" Coba, the president of the Men's Association. Diz came by his nickname, we soon discover, because he was an electronics whiz formerly employed at Disneyland: his specialty, naturally, was "audio animatronics," the creation of lifelike automatons to take part in the theme park's historical tableaux. His wife was also a founder member of the Stepford women's club. It is while she haltingly explains to a sympathetic female psychiatrist the reasons why she can no longer abide Stepford that Joanna again comes tantalizingly close to putting all the pieces together: "'If only you could see what Stepford women are *like*. They're like actresses in TV commercials, all of them. No, not even *that*. They're—they're like—' She sat forward. 'There was a program four or five weeks ago,' she said. 'My children were watching it. The figures of all the presidents, moving around, making different facial expressions. . . .' 'Disneyland,' Joanna said. 'The program was from *Disneyland*.'"[43]

Even the manger scene erected in Stepford at Christmas is described as "a mite Disneyish." Aside from providing a plausible explanation for Dale Coba's prior familiarity with the creation of lifelike automatons, the obvious Disney references are resonant in other ways as well. As one commentator has noted, the connection between suburbia and Disneyland during the 1950s and 1960s was a suggestive one: "While postwar Americans, not unlike Walt Disney himself, were forsaking their small-town roots for the 'good life' that burgeoned on the suburban periphery of American cities, the rush to suburbia was fuelled in part by the kind of vision that Disney celebrated in film and ultimately enshrined in Disneyland."[44] Indeed, one of the most famous attractions in Disneyland is Main Street, USA, a highly idealized three-quarter scale celebration of the kind of small town that was rapidly becoming extinct, there to be nostalgically viewed by visitors who had never actually known this kind of life, or had already forsaken it for the affordability and convenience of suburbia. Is it mere coincidence then that Levin should have named Joanna's husband "Walter," given that he willingly sacrifices his living, breathing wife for an animatronic stand-in who conforms to an outmoded and deeply nostalgic ideal of American womanhood? The Disneyland connection also brings to mind Jean Baudrillard's meditations on the theme park as an imaginative space: "Disneyland is presented as imaginary in order to make us believe that the rest is real, whereas all of Los Angeles and the America that surrounds it are no longer real, but belong to the hyperreal order and to the order of simulation."[45] Within the context of Levin's novel, the Disney references also serve to remind both Joanna and the reader that Stepford is itself a simulation, a desperate and murderous attempt to recreate a regressive and conservative ideal of suburban living, which itself owes much to the machinations of advertisers and the culture industry.

The novel comes to a climax as an increasingly frantic Joanna finally demands that the family must leave at once, only to be betrayed by Walter, who has sent the children away so that she cannot leave. Joanna returns to Bobbie's pristine house in an effort to find them, only to be murdered by the robotic double of her best friend. The climax of the film differs slightly, in that here it is Joanna who kills the Bobbie replicant, stabbing her in the abdomen with a kitchen knife, while desperately asking, "Do you bleed?!" It is at this point that Joanna's paranoid fears are entirely vindicated, for the android then begins to malfunction, stumbling around her orderly kitchen, asking Joanna over and over if she would like some coffee (the perfect hostess even to the last). But here, too, there can ultimately be no escape for our imperiled heroine: as in *Invasion of the Body Snatchers* and many other body-replacement narratives, the forces of law and order are arrayed against her, and even her own husband cannot be trusted. In this case, as Robert Beuka has put when comparing the two films, "Stepford is a fantasy world of patriarchal control"—something highlighted in the film by the heavy police presence suggested throughout. The main difference from Finney's premise is the fact that here, "the threat of takeover is no longer imagined as alien, but rather comes from a community fractured by a legacy of gendered inequality and insecurity."[46] Further, as we have seen, Levin's indictment of the advertising industry further differentiates his narrative from Finney's novel.

It is eerily fitting that in the film, after Joanna arrives at the Men's Association (here rendered like a typical haunted house, all dark, shadowy corners illuminated by sudden crashes of lightning), she is finally murdered not by her husband or any of the other men, but by her own robotic double, and in a room mocked up to look just like her own. The fact that the real Joanna is finally dispatched by a technological creation that looks just like her (save for her enlarged breasts and black eyes) is something that is foreshadowed even in the opening scene of the film, when she is first seen somberly gazing at her own reflection in a mirror, presumably worrying about the fact that she has agreed to move to Stepford in the first place. In this respect, *The Stepford Wives* functions as a satiric but ultimately chilling dramatization of fears that would have been familiar to many women during the 1970s. These anxieties were founded on the fact that the growing prominence of the women's rights movement meant that contemporary women—particularly those who had been college educated, like Joanna and Bobbie—would have been well aware of the kind of powerful rhetoric espoused by Friedan and others. Yet despite this foreknowledge, many would still find themselves drawn into the "trap" represented by motherhood, marriage, and a nice house in the suburbs, and according to this logic could therefore hold themselves in no small way responsible for any unhappiness that resulted.

Significantly, both the novel and the film adaptation conclude with a scene set in a bright, dreamily lit supermarket, and a sequence showing the "new" Joanna gliding around the aisles, carefully filling her shopping cart with groceries, and exchanging bland pleasantries with the other Stepford wives to the accompaniment of Muzak. It is a scene in which, once again, we see dramatized in suitably exaggerated form Freidan's frightening vision of the suburban housewife's restricted, mind-numbing existence. It also anticipates the closing shot of Romero's *Dawn of the Dead*, for while the Stepford wives are not, strictly speaking, zombies, they are ultimately mindless consumers, an adman's dream and a feminist's worst nightmare. Once more, imitations of life have triumphed over the real thing.

The years following the success of the 1975 movie version of *The Stepford Wives* saw the release of no fewer than three rather obscure made-for-television sequels, and a poorly received 2004 "reimagining" of the original film, also called *The Stepford Wives*. Directed by Frank Oz and starring Nicole Kidman, the remake is notably confused: the screenwriters appear undecided as to whether the Stepford wives are robotic doubles or ordinary women with computer chips in their heads. Further, the problematic nature of the new film's final revelations, which suggest that the entire Stepford project was the brainchild of a deranged ex–career woman seeking to reestablish an excessively idealized version of 1950s suburban life, means that any pretensions toward genuine sociological commentary remain unfulfilled. Though essentially unsatisfying, these revelations do make overt one of the original novel's most significant preoccupations: the fact that replacement of the town's housewives by android doubles is all part of a concerted effort to turn back the clock to a somehow "simpler" period in which gender roles were more clearly defined (and much more restrictive for women, of course).

More than sixty years since the development of the first postwar suburban settlement, depictions of this setting as a place where alienation thrives and individuality is under threat are still remarkably common. This suggests that the unease that many of suburbia's first critics voiced has yet to disappear, but has merely changed form. The persistent belief that homes tell us a great deal about the people who live there lingers still, as does the suspicion that beneath the seeming order and neatness of the suburban neighborhood lurks something nasty, if dangerously indefinable. Though films that depict alien takeover, flesh-eating zombie hordes, and eerily submissive androids may not initially seem to have all that much in common beyond their obvious preoccupation with the fear of being "taken over" or "replaced" by powerful forces beyond rational understanding, each of the texts I have discussed here directly (or indirectly) indicts suburbia and the relentless tide of economic and social development that drives it.

As Robert Beuka has suggested, such texts broach in their own powerful way "the possibility that something in the suburban experience fosters the erosion of personal autonomy."[47] It is this suggestion, as prevalent now in many respects as it was at the beginning of the postwar era, that makes narratives of dehumanization, alienation, and imitation one of the most powerful strands of the suburban gothic. As we have seen here, time and time again the depiction of zombie or zombie-like figures in texts that deal with suburban mores is associated with inherently problematic efforts to recreate a way of life that has either disappeared already or never quite existed in the first place. The first waves of mass suburban development were at least partially motivated by the belief that the move from the cities and into the countryside would result in a better, more family- and community-focused way of life. The ironic thing was, of course, that the rapid spread of suburban housing developments meant that the kind of small-town idyll many Americans sought was being destroyed or irrevocably altered by this very effort to recreate such an environment and lifestyle. Similarly, the "traditional" zombie can come about only when someone dies and is resurrected, Finney's "pod people" take the places of the humans whose empty husks they dispose of once the transformation process is complete, and the women of Stepford are murdered before being replaced by their android doubles. In each instance, the process of imitation or "takeover" results in the demise of the person (or the place) being duplicated or replaced altogether, which further suggests that the efforts to suspend time and the forces of modernity are in themselves deeply harmful. The suburban zombie (or zombie-like) figure therefore raises some fascinating questions about the ways in which Americans view both themselves and their most common living environment.

CHAPTER 9

All Dark Inside: Dehumanization and Zombification in Postmodern Cinema

Sorcha Ní Fhlainn

When we approach different versions of the modern zombie, we often tend to categorize them in (and against) the traditional modes set forth by classic zombie cinema, such as *White Zombie* and George A. Romero's "Living Dead" series. The success and powerful cultural influences of these films have, in many ways, shaped and defined zombie cinema, often discouraging any attempt at redefining the zombie as a figure outside the strict rules of the established genre. As charted most clearly in this volume, however, zombies are among us in various and multiple incarnations: We are among the living dead, the reanimated corpse, the brain-dead and the brain-seeking; the psychotic and unresponsive body detached from the rational and reasoned thought; the automaton and the slave. Beyond the realm of the familiar zombie, we are constantly among some configuration of the undead. This horrific spectacle of the familiar zombie takes hold when the "human" aspect is removed, leaving only a reactionary piece of meat in its place. The zombies discussed here (though largely not described as such in the texts) can be categorized as combining at least two features of the nine identified permutations of the zombie as listed by Kevin Boon.[1] The soldiers herein are mostly cultural, biological, and psychological zombie manifestations. In the strictest sense, they are not all dead; they have not been reanimated by any specific spell or magical enchantment. Rather, they are typically presented as average people who are experiencing severe mental anguish, leading eventually to their very specific expressions of psychological zombification. Two later examples on the development of the post-human soldier look to other means of depicting the psychological manifestation of the cultural zombie ("Homecoming") and the tech zombie (*Universal Soldier*). However different their manifestations seem, they are members of the zombie trope: "In the horror of their changed world, they become like zombies, 'all dark inside.'"[2]

Looking at different yet linked film versions of zombies, in which specific dialogues on the undead through different prisms are present, *28 Days Later* (2002), *Full Metal Jacket* (1987), *Universal Soldier* (1992), and *Jacob's Ladder* (1990) merge to form narratives on the dehumanization of the person through the removal of individual thought, explicitly characterized by soldiers in modern warfare. As an epilogue to this chapter, I look to Joe Dante's *Masters of Horror* episode "Homecoming," which grapples with zombie soldiers who have perished in the Iraq war, only to be inadvertently resurrected in time for the presidential election. To be clear, the post-human, zombified soldiers discussed here are in various stages of liminality, but they are not always, in the strictest sense, wholly corpselike. They are, in varying degrees, zombified through the processes of dehumanization, mental breakdowns, and self-annihilation, hybridized, transfigured, and mutilated to the point where all rational thinking and reason is abandoned or removed, leaving a destructive and destroyed shell in its wake. My immediate interest in this chapter is to locate zombification at work within the realm of cinema that does not, at first glance, specifically use the term zombie. Of course, much like other tropes in horror cinema, it is not the term explicitly used that defines the monsters present in the narrative, but rather the actions and intent of the monsters that categorizes them into a specific, recognizable form. My interest in looking at soldiers in specific war scenarios such as Vietnam and Iraq is rooted in a study of personalized horrors, dehumanization, and violence that targets others and the self, which psychologically alters, damages, and annihilates the soldier, and depicts them, subtly or overtly, as zombified bodies.

Soldiers are trained to dehumanize themselves when in combat, and their subjects are terrorized by the actions of the dehumanized combatant. The zombies herein present narratives of primal rage and violence inflicted on their person and on the community. While films such as *28 Days Later* delineate between the violence of disease in the modern world by reducing human action to animal rage (which the disease itself is named) and placing us within the inner world of an infantry unit acting as a microcosm of the outside world, *Jacob's Ladder* explicitly focuses on the horrors of the world after drug treatments were given to soldiers in Vietnam without their knowledge, altering them into bio-zombies. Blurring the boundaries between reality and horror fantasy, both films seek to engage the audience in the horrors of war and warfare, the primal violence promoted in the army, and the zombification necessary to surrender to its horrors. This psychological "break" from reality featured in both films is a chemically induced form of zombification: The chemical (or, indeed, biochemical) form of pure rage acts as a frightening reminder of the body driven to violence when reason and order have collapsed or have been (temporarily) eclipsed.

In *28 Days Later*, which can rightfully be categorized as a bio-zombie film—where zombification is induced through chemical and biological means—moments of true horror primarily concern the living survivors rather than the infected "undead." By comparing Romero's *Day of the Dead* (1985), where soldiers turn on civilians as well as themselves, with *28 Days Later*, Jen Webb and Sam Byrnand identify the key aspect of fear among the survivors of an apocalypse, which in turn instigates a mental break from all modes of social order. That the zombie is in itself a break in the symbolic order proves not to be enough in postmodern fiction—the break must occur within the confines of the sane mind, and the projection of this break is simultaneously thrust outward (onto others) and inward (self-annihilation) when dealing with the threat. Jim, the hero of *28 Days Later*, remains uninfected by the virus that grips England's population, but he emulates certain traits that are associated with the infected bio-zombies. When confronted with the psychological horrors of his situation, both universalized (apocalypse) and localized (his imprisonment at the barracks, where an infantry keeps him and his group of survivors captive), Jim's rage becomes completely primal and, at certain moments, indistinguishable from the infected zombies outside the compound: "The zombies in [*28 Days Later*] are infected with a viral rage; Jim avoids the infection but can't avoid or control his innate, personal rage. The effect in either case is practically identical: for all intents and purposes, in the moments of his rage Jim is [a] zombie.... He sides with the zombies to kill his human tormentors, and even the zombies can't tell he's not one of them."[3] Another trait follows in this primary instinct for survival: Survivors in zombie narratives generally do not empathize with their fellow survivors. In many zombie films, not only is there a struggle against the reanimated, but there is a vicious power struggle between the survivors, who barely distinguish themselves from the initial threat. This repeated pattern is revisited in many films that concern cultural and psychological zombies representing the body politic, namely the American government's role in the Vietnam War. Personal integrity (which I chiefly locate as the moment when the "zombie" literally speaks) is found at moments before the breakdown occurs—revealing to the audience the level of intensity and fragility felt by the subject prior to the horror of zombification. Interestingly, both *Jacob's Ladder* and *28 Days Later* deal with the anxieties and primal fears concerning life after death—by characters who are surrounded by violent and explicitly abject depictions of death and physical destruction or deformity. Indeed, both films, and other intertextual examples of both individual and collective zombification, illustrate the overwhelming impact that apocalyptic acts and political wars have on the psyche, and draw on two key moments in American history—the Vietnam War (1963–75) and the September 11 terrorist attacks in 2001 (in *28 Days Later*, an abandoned London relocates the apocalyptic horrors by standing in for post-9/11 New York, which, though not a deliberate decision on the part of the director, Danny Boyle, is invoked throughout the film). For all the resonance of apocalypse and doom these events have become layered with—by historians, journalists, and eyewitnesses—these cinematic representations of the end of the world, or indeed, the breaking point of the mind (which, in philosophical terms, *is* the end of the world), are crucial if we are to fully understand the underlying raw emotions of terror, rage, and needless destruction which have accompanied the chronicling of these historic moments.

It is appropriate to label this understanding of the zombified state as inherently postmodern, for it illustrates an awareness of the historical importance of the landscape where the events have occurred (be it Vietnam or an abandoned London), and looks back, in an attempt to recreate the anxieties from the perspective of altering history by reentering a point where it is simultaneously culturally familiar and frighteningly detached and foreign. Under the weight of cultural reflexivity and familiarity, postmodernism, as Fredrick Jameson describes it, "looks for breaks, for events . . . after which it is no longer the same; for the [moment] 'When–it-all-changed.' "[4] This definitive "break" is important as it seems to be preoccupied with moments of Western cultural anxieties. It can also work individually or collectively, based on the severity of the dehumanization at work. Located here, the break we may commonly identify with concerns the horrors of war catalogued during the Vietnam era. The films discussed reenter the Vietnam war to examine the "zombification" of the human solider.

Full Me(n)tal Jacket

First, we may look at this zombification in Stanley Kubrick's powerful Vietnam film, *Full Metal Jacket* (1987). The film, based on the novel *The Short-Timers* by Gustav Hasford, is constructed to give two different perspectives on the Vietnam experience, by way of splitting the film into two distinctive parts: The first is set at the barracks at Parris Island, South Carolina, where a team of newly drafted recruits are introduced to their new drill instructor, Gunnery Sergeant Hartman (R. Lee Ermey), and begin their training before being sent to Vietnam; the second reveals the horrors of the war on a grand scale and the fate of the infantry in Da Nang and Hue. Both sections of the film are linked through Private Joker's (Matthew Modine) narrative (muted in the first section and animated in the second) and seek to expose the horrors of dehumanization, both in the training of new recruits who will be turned into "killing machines" and in their subsequent experiences in Vietnam. From its very first shot, that of the incoming trainees having their hair shorn off, to their renaming by their drill instructor (both acts are highly de-individuating by themselves), the film presents individuality as something that must be broken down and ruthlessly destroyed.[5] Horror and abjection are linked closely in the film through the repeated depictions of dehumanization and humiliations suffered, particularly by the character of Private Leonard Lawrence (Vincent D'Onofrio)—renamed Gomer Pyle—at the hands of the horrific Sergeant Hartman. Pyle's experience of recruit training reveals the depravity of the barracks, its hellish environment and punishing schedule coupled with Hartman's desired goal to transform Lawrence into a brutal and dehumanized killer. While Private Joker survives the narrative primarily because of his ability to use humor as a defense mechanism, Private Pyle undergoes a complete transformation; starting as a seemingly sensitive, chubby, and possibly intellectually underdeveloped young man, his evolution dominates the first half of the film, culminating in his total break from reality and his becoming a detached killer, devoid of all hope or will to live. It is important to recognize that Pyle is degraded in every possible manner—from being slapped and physically tormented to being forced to perform emotionally degrading tasks (in one scene he is made to imitate a child by waddling behind the marching infantry sucking his thumb with his trousers at his ankles). While we are constantly reminded of the torment of the entire infantry drafted into the military, it is the specific dehumanization of Private Pyle that acts as a barometer for the destruction of the mind and soul in the film.

Collectively, the infantry are taught a specific prayer to recite at bedtime, in perfect unison, giving us insight into their new form of collective identity and relationship with death and destruction. During one recitation, in a chilling close-up on Private Pyle, we begin to see his transformation into a zombified shell:

> This is my rifle. There are many like it but this one is mine. My rifle is my best friend. It is my life. I must master it as I must master my own life. Without me, my rifle is useless. Without my rifle, I am useless. I must fire my rifle true. I must shoot straighter than my enemy who is trying to kill me. I must shoot him before he shoots me. I will. Before God I swear this creed. My rifle and myself are defenders of this country. We are the masters of our enemy. We are the saviors of my life. So be it until there is no enemy but peace. Amen.[6]

The climax of Pyle's transformation occurs in the toilets of the barracks, where Private Joker discovers Pyle loading live rounds into his rifle (a full metal jacket). Kubrick's deliberate use of the barracks toilets is interesting to note, as many of his previous films also use toilets as sites for psychological breaks (or breakdowns).[7] In *Full Metal Jacket*, Hartman's speeches constantly refer to disgust and filth and incite scatological comparison, reducing the unit to consider themselves also as mere filth. In Pyle's pivotal scene, in the barracks toilet, his transformation becomes evident; his speech is slurred, slow, and deliberate, his gaze both ominous and dead. Though Joker attempts to reach out to Pyle by using his real name and reminding him of Hartman's punishments, it is of no use: "Leonard, if Hartman comes in here are catches us, we will both be in a world of shit . . ." "I *am* . . . in a world . . . of shit," he deliberately replies. When Hartman discovers Pyle and Joker in the bathroom, and finds Pyle unresponsive to his orders, the dehumanization process resumes: "What is your major malfunction, Numb-nuts? Didn't Mommy and Daddy show you enough attention when you were a child?" This is the breaking point in Pyle's mind, and he shoots Hartman in the chest, killing him. Kubrick reinforces the horror and zombification of Pyle's actions by capturing Pyle's face partly in shadow, emphasizing the interior darkness of his mind after the torment he has suffered. The pace of the scene also changes to slow-motion shots of Hartman's death to emphasize the enormity of

Pyle's actions, and the film sustains a brief silence after the gunshot is heard with reverb—an acoustic signifier of the zombified trance that has engulfed Pyle. By killing Hartman, Pyle realizes he has become a cold-blooded killer and commits suicide. In many ways, the entire film is set up to illustrate the pursuit of order over chaos, and how this relentless dehumanization ultimately undoes all sense of order in the world at large. This scene in particular illustrates the horror of the loss of the self, which Hartman deliberately removes to make his soldiers "men" for his "beloved corps."[8] As James Naremore notes of Private Pyle's responses to Hartman's often grotesque orations and humiliations, "Though Pyle's reaction to Hartman seems slow-witted, it's much like the reaction most viewers are likely to have—a bewildered mingling of amusement, fear, and disgust that turns into outright shock. . . . In contrast [to the others,] Pyle's reaction is sensible and sane; only when forced to deny his feelings does he later turn into a murderer and a suicide. His confusion and bewilderment, moreover, are built into the very structure and texture of the film, which is designed to create a world that is both absurd and verisimilar."[9] The murder-suicide committed by Pyle becomes the pinnacle of violence in the first half of the film, the watershed catalyst that "unleashes the savagery and chaos of the second half."[10] Further, Mark T. Conard highlights examples of Pyle's individuality that illustrate the futility of order sought by Sergeant Hartman to make the soldiers equal—"equally worthless maggots"—and the chaos that ensues once Pyle's sense of self is destroyed. Pyle's suicide illustrates the sickness of dehumanization, which leads to violent ends. And Kubrick's infantrymen depict similar chaos. They do not represent the cohesion and solidarity usually depicted and promoted in war cinema; they come together only when directed to whip Private Pyle into shape, beating him in a punishing manner in order to "break" what remains and to awaken the killer within. Because his own peers turn on him in such a brutal manner, Pyle internalizes the violence, which unleashes a brutal, self-destructive, psychological zombie, now reborn to kill his psychologically destructive master Hartman. James Kendrick furthers this reading of *Full Metal Jacket* by viewing it as an ironic depiction of war itself, where the first casualty is innocence, closely followed by humanity and sanity: "Although the soldiers do not kill each other in the second half of *Full Metal Jacket*, their actions in battle do not carry the heroic charge of an externally violent film but rather the sinking feeling that what has truly been killed is their own humanity."[11]

Oliver Stone's *Platoon* (1986) uses a similar story arc to convey the split identities of soldiers (human/zombie) during the war. Through the eyes of the new recruit Chris (Charlie Sheen), we meet a platoon consisting of soldiers who are deathly afraid, some psychotically broken by the violence that surrounds them, and those who are pathological, enjoying the killing spree that their sense of rage "entitles" them to. As Bunny (Kevin Dillon) says, "I told the troops, man, I like it here, you get to do what you want, nobody fucks with you, the only worry you got is dying, and if that happens you won't know about it anyway."[12] Bunny and Barnes (Tom Berenger) in particular enjoy the killing of Vietnamese civilians that symbolically replicates the massacre of My Lai in 1968.[13] In a scene where Bunny bludgeons a Vietnamese teenager to death, his fascination is mainly trained on the gray matter that spills out of his victim's shattered skull: "Holy shit, you see that head come apart man? I never seen brains like that before." While Chris sobs when he becomes aware of his own temporal lack of humanity, aimlessly firing a gun at prisoners' feet in order to make them dance, Bunny, disgusted at Chris's remorseful reaction, unleashes his frustration by bludgeoning the prisoner, cementing his zombification on-screen.

One platoon member comments on Barnes's near immortality; his zombification is so totalized and wholly evident that it can be undone only by self-annihilation: "Barnes been shot seven times, he ain't dead, does that mean anything to you? Barnes ain't meant to die. The only thing that can kill Barnes is Barnes." Further still, when Barnes attempts to bludgeon Chris during a final and brutal napalm attack, his eyes briefly glow red with absolute rage (a feature that repeatedly appears in *28 Days Later*), revealing, for a mere second, the dehumanized raging zombie contained within his wounded flesh. In the final moments of the film, as Chris is being choppered out of the war zone, he reflects on the battle that has been waged, and its effects on his very soul:

> I think now, looking back, we did not fight the enemy, we fought ourselves and the enemy was in us. The war is over for me now, but it will always be there for the rest of my days, as I am sure Elias will be, fighting with Barnes for what Rhah called the possession of my soul. There are times since I have felt like a child, born of those two fathers, but be that as it may, those of us who did make it have an obligation to build again, to teach to others what we know, and to try with what's left with our lives to find a goodness, and meaning, to this life.[14]

As James Kendrick highlights in his study on cinematic depictions of the Vietnam War, there were two specific types of film that emerged between the late 1970s and late 1980s, both acting as a catharsis for the psychological issues brought into focus by Hollywood cinema: the externally violent film, which seeks to engage the audience in a mantra of "we can still win the war effort," such as *Hamburger Hill* (1987), *Missing in Action* (1984), and *Rambo: First Blood Part II* (1985); and the internally conflicted films, which concern the internal collapse of the American narrative during (and due to) the war, such as *Rambo: First Blood* (1982), *Full Metal Jacket* (1987), *Platoon*, (1986), *Taxi Driver* (1976), and *Casualties of War* (1989).[15] As Kubrick's film is split literally in two (one could comment on this being a very appropriate method in breaking up our understanding of, partial empathy for, and interaction with the troops in its first section, which is obliterated in its second half), it is, like Joker's peace button and "Born to Kill" scrawled on his helmet, the duality of man at war. When this balance is lost to total darkness, we see its terrifying results in the actions of Private Pyle and *Platoon*'s Staff Sergeant Barnes.

Tissue with Memory

It is with this vision of hell on earth, of a world devoid of hope, that we encounter the dehumanized person who has lost meaning or a sense of self. Vietnam, in particular, is a common arena of horror and sickness in these films concerning the tech- and bio-zombified state of the body—perhaps to illustrate the shell shock and meaningless self-destruction many veterans vehemently vocalized upon returning home. Further, the levels of psychological conditions and traumatic disorders reported in the decade following the war indicate that, for some, the war continued within: Michael Bibby states that "according to a 1982 report, 110,000 [more than the Americans killed in battle during the war] died from 'war-related' problems after returning to the U.S.—of those, 60,000 were suicides."[16] Many veterans were dismissed for their traumas, often including paralyzing flashbacks, which would recapitulate their traumas as a cyclical experience; some indeed felt they had never truly escaped the war. As Myra MacPherson notes, "When Vietnam veterans tried to explain this, doctors misdiagnosed them as hallucinating schizophrenics and numbed them with damaging Thorazine, known to veterans as 'Gorilla Biscuits,' which turned them into slow moving and stumbling zombies. Veterans caustically called it the 'Thorazine shuffle.'"[17] A similar theme is evident in two other films exploring the bio-zombified state—Adrian Lyne's *Jacob's Ladder* (1990) and Roland Emmerich's *Universal Soldier* (1992), where medical practice and experimentation are used to enter, exit, or relive the traumas of Vietnam. While *Universal Solider* is primarily concerned with tech-zombie/bio-zombie fusions (and for some commentators, cyborg fusion), it shares the same textual platform with *Jacob's Ladder*; the body functions as tissue with memory, "the cadaverous 'physicality of memory' itself."[18] Indeed, "if today's zombies are the postmodern, timeless creatures of remakes and sequels, it is in part because they have their origins in narratives of erasure";[19] much like the remade and sequel-led zombies of Romero's vision and other incarnations of the undead, narratives of erasure are of primary focus here, because the flesh—dead, dying, or recycled—remembers hell and is in the process of self-eradication.

Jacob's Ladder opens in the Vietnamese jungle, where a group of soldiers at their camp relax and await orders. The protagonist, Jacob Singer (Tim Robbins), is among the group of vets and notices that his platoon suddenly become ill; many in the troupe begin to shake violently, vomit, and scream in pain, but they are unaware of the cause. They then seem to be under attack in an enemy ambush and Jacob is bayoneted in the stomach. We flash forward to modern-day New York, where Jacob awakes on an empty subway train, far away from the Vietnam nightmare. But Jacob's New York is a hostile environment—the subway trains are populated with unresponsive people, and many of the city's inhabitants often appear to have horns, tails, or blurred anamorphic faces that are grotesque, disorientating, and sickening. Everything seems overwhelmingly abject in the city. Time is disjointed and dislocated in *Jacob's Ladder* as we flash forward and back between the Vietnamese jungle and Jacob's life in New York. As we the audience are unable to locate ourselves within the narrative structure of the film because it constantly relocates, fluctuates, and alters our concept of what is the present and the past, the environment of each scene is pivotal in understanding the direction of the plot: "The film's narrative structure resembles Chinese boxes, with 'several' diegetic worlds fitted inside each other,"[20] where the environment becomes a projection of the mind. On the subway, when Jacob awakens, he sees two posters offering narratives of drug use and altered states: one that reads, "Hell . . . but it doesn't have to be that way," and an advertisement offering "Ecstasy."

As we are led through a kaleidoscope of imagery, both hopeful and horrific, we are unsure whether Jacob is losing his mind or actually witnessing the abject horrors of Vietnam superimposed onto his modern life via traumatic flashbacks. His girlfriend, Jezebel, screams in his face, "Anybody in there? Anybody home?," which reaffirms our perspective that he is in a deep, posttraumatic-stress-induced trance. When contacted by a former veteran in his platoon, Jacob realizes that he is not the only one experiencing these hellish manifestations; before he can find or share any solace, however, his comrade is killed in a mysterious explosion. The traumas continue to resemble hell as Jacob attempts to find meaning and answers to what happened to his platoon the night they were attacked on the Mekong Delta. After being mugged by a Salvation Army Santa Claus, Jacob is transported to an asylum, where his hellish vision further manifests, as he witnesses bloodied floors, torn body parts, and monstrous, demonic patients. Jacob, freed from the asylum, is contacted by a renegade chemist who admits that the U.S. Army used mind-altering drugs to make soldiers more efficient killers. The drug, manufactured in Saigon, is named "The Ladder," designed to infiltrate and isolate the dark side of the human psyche, to produce feelings of fear and rage so violent that it would act as a primal trigger for the mind: "The fast trip straight down the ladder right to the primal fear, the base anger."[21] In this altered state, the platoon reacted to the drug unexpectedly—rather than fight the enemy abroad, they violently turned on one another. Psychologically, the trip down the ladder is akin to a hysterical psychological collapse, and the altered state becomes a terrifying disembodiment of the self: a postmodern, chemically induced zombification.

In many ways, *Jacob's Ladder* is a film loaded with several meanings, duplications, and religious configurations. It is a terrifying indication of the primal forces located in the mind, and a spiritual awakening for Jacob as the victim of this primal rage. Just as Private Pyle becomes psychologically detached from his own sense of individuality and identity, so too do Jacob's comrades, in a violent detachment from reality, become biozombified and fatally destructive. Upon the revelation that the platoon was biologically poisoned to become more effective, psychologically absent killers, Jacob's visions transform from hellish to angelic manifestations. Jacob's guardian angel/chiropractor Louis (a healer of both the disjointed body and soul) paraphrases the philosopher Meister Eckhart von Hochheim to illustrate the function of his manifestations: "Eckhart saw hell, too; he said, 'The only thing that burns in hell is the part of you that won't let go of life, your memories, your attachments. They burn them all away. But they're not punishing you,' he said. 'They're freeing your soul. So, if you're frightened of dying and . . . you're holding on, you'll see devils tearing your life away. But if you've made your peace, then the devils are really angels, freeing you from the earth.'" Just as Louis has described the function of seeing the true meaning behind the demonic faces that haunt Jacob's psyche, we also uncover the split that has formed the narrative of the biological experimentation gone awry: Jacob's narrative, a disjointed collection of thoughts at the point of his death in Vietnam, is located entirely in his brain, while his body fights to survive the fatal attack on him by his own bio-zombified platoon. In effect, *Jacob's Ladder* acts both as an allegory for the horrific disconnection between brain and body, and as a depiction of physical and spiritual purgatory. It is a frightening visual representation of "life-in-death."[22]

Equally representing the malfunctions of the detached (or severely limited) brain, this time in the form of the reanimated tech-zombie of the Vietnam War, is Roland Emmerich's film *Universal Soldier* (1992), in which the bodies of expired elite Vietnam veterans are technologically reanimated to make "super-soldiers." I argue that the two main characters of *Universal Soldier*, Luc Deveraux (Jean-Claude Van Damme) and Andrew Scott (Dolph Lundgren) are reanimated post-human tech-zombies, elaborating on the postmodern divide between the zombie who remains enslaved by psychological and technological means, and the one who can transcend the status of tech-zombie by redeveloping brain function post-zombification. In essence, Deveraux regains his mind slowly by removing his artificial technology, while Scott remains largely static because the technology permanently scrambles his thought process. Scott (renamed GR-13 as a tech-zombie) repeats his final kill of an innocent man in Vietnam when the same conditions are revisited later with two American reporters. He also continues to collect trophies from his victims as he did during the war, stringing the ears of his victims onto a necklace he wears with pride. While Deveraux (GR-44) "sees" the flashbacks and is aware that something is ultimately wrong, Scott kills unquestioningly. Deveraux, by embracing his artificiality (in that he knows he is "dead" but continues to live in reanimation), becomes post-human/tech-zombie; however, while both tech-zombies recall (and recycle) their dying thoughts, Scott remains, repeats, and relives his final moments in Vietnam over and over (much like posttraumatic stress) to a greater degree, and finally disintegrates into his zombified brain by enhancing his own strength and detachment by self-administering the biochemical serum that keeps his body functioning and his brain suppressed.[23] Scott, like so many veterans who suffered horrific flashbacks, remains a zombie—his flesh remembers who he is (or was) as though it were caught in an unbreakable liminal cycle, but he does not configure new cognitive processes beyond his murderous appetite. As Michael P. Clark notes of *Jacob's Ladder* and *Universal Soldier*, "Both of these films portray Vietnam veterans as victims of an omnipotent bureaucracy that has literally invaded the very cells of their bodies and reconfigured their biochemistry to fit military needs."[24]

The creator of the universal soldiers, Dr. Gregor (Jerry Orbach), describes a reanimation process that is both technological and biochemical: "By hyper-accelerating the bodies . . . [I could] turn dead flesh into living tissue, but to make the process work, the bodies ran at dangerously high temperatures. They needed to be constantly cooled and the brain sedated, controlled." He states that Scott is suffering from "regressive traumatic recall; trauma inflicted at the time of death. In Luc's case, he wanted to go home. When he awoke as a 'uni sol,' he returned to that single emotion. In Scott's case, he still thinks he's in Vietnam, fighting the insurgents. He doesn't realize he's alive."[25] But Luc recognizes himself primarily as dead flesh: "He's [Scott] not alive—he's dead, just like me." This awareness of self, in life and death simultaneously, makes the tech-zombies of *Universal Soldier* postmodern, in that it alters the level of consciousness and potential that the tech-zombie can have, here plotted as such because Luc is primarily heroic, whereas Scott is sadistic (and possibly a serial killer). However simple the diegetic split, the placing of Luc and Scott as respective heroic/sadistic soldiers is highly relevant in reading the film, as it provides an idealistic platform where the zombified and dehumanized subject, if noble or morally worthy, can recover from the trauma of war: Luc exclaims that he is now "alive" once he has bested Scott, as though he has conquered a distilled, nightmarish embodiment of the war in the same way the nation chose to view itself as healed in later decades. Scott's death removes the "curse" of Vietnam and narratively removes all traces of the zombification both culturally and visually. It is also a cultural reflection of the political feeling in the early 1990s when the issues surrounding the Vietnam War, utterly dissected and presented though the prisms of left- and right-wing politics in the 1980s, were perceived to be exhausted topics: "Like *Universal Soldier*'s initial set of images, [the] early sequences assume audience familiarity with the conventions of the Vietnam War movie iconography."[26] The audience recognizes and relates to the images on-screen, not only because Vietnam was a televised war, but also because they have seen it all before—in the 1980s alone, Vietnam was featured either as both a central or marginal plot topic in various war movies, moral tales, comedy-horror films, television shows, and action-adventure narratives. Undoubtedly, Emmerich's film engages the conventional narrative of Vietnam merely to facilitate the greater spectacles of action, martial arts, and hard bodies around which the film was largely plotted and marketed.

The tech-zombies featured in Emmerich's film are often perceived to transcend into the realm of their post-human cousin, the cyborg. Although *Universal Soldier* is categorized by many critics as a cyborg science fiction film, the cyborg rarely exhibits malfunction due to mental will or mental illness, as the tech/bio-zombies do. So complete and seamless is the construction of the cyborg that it renders the concept of free will by a machine with flesh drastically implausible, by its sheer capacity to work too well.[27] These tech-zombies are chosen because they are the best of the soldiers who were killed in Vietnam—it is because of their specific abilities and organic tissue that they are used, while the technology revivifies the body and only maintains the portions of the brain necessary for bodily function and the following of orders. The cyborg, being based on a CPU (central processing unit) brain,[28] is brain/machine with fleshed body; the tech-zombie is body with suppressed brain. The flesh is paramount in *Universal Soldier*, as it must be kept cool to remain stable (delaying decay), whereas for the cyborg, the fleshy exterior is a superfluous camouflage, frequently torn away during battle, eventually exposing the essential machine endoskeleton underneath.

Postmodern Zombies

For some commentators, the subjective version of the zombie is highly problematic. If zombies are denied agency and mental faculties, problems concerning will, agency, subjectivity, and rebellion occur; however, this may also be the very "break" with convention that Jameson defines as postmodernity at work. If we conceive of the zombie as a body without agency, and accept that it is a culturally represented figure of repressed fears and social issues, the postmodern "break" may be located not only in the fact that they physically change from shuffling bodies to military "hard bodies"—which in itself indicates that they are up-to-date with a vengeance—but that they are no longer silent. Postmodern zombification now extends to zombie subjectivities. If the vampire's subjectivity can be traced as a definitive account of cultural history from a liminal being, then what is preventing certain zombies from gaining this subjectivity also?[29] Further, if the zombie gains such subjectivity, can temporary zombification, like half-vampirism, also be removed, similar to the zombie curse previously seen in *White Zombie* (1932), where one simply "wakes up"? The combination of such developments certainly gains momentum when considering postmodern embodiments of cultural monsters.

In their article "A Zombie Manifesto," Sarah Juliet Lauro and Karen Embry explore the boundaries that the zombie (or, indeed, their posthuman "zombii") inhabits in our modern nightmares—infectious diseases, mind control, and capitalist consumption run amok: "Zombies, like all things that are feared, are the products of the culture that shapes them and bear within their myths the imprint of existing social conditions."[30] Rightly, they argue that "we must not disconnect the zombie from its past,"[31] because the zombie represents not only a lineage of enslavement, from Haitian history to modern warfare, but also the current enslavements of capitalism, governmental power, and technology. The zombie is infused with history—it has no other agency so immediate than to resurrect an important historical narrative that must return because it has been suppressed/repressed in the cultural dialogue. While Lauro and Embry locate differing categories of the zombie, they refute the zombie's ability to generate any thought. Subjectivity is removed entirely, displaced to the role of the master (human witch doctor or cybernetic technology). I contend that when the zombies discussed here do speak (which varies from text to text), they reiterate their orders or thoughts through the memories stored in their flesh—that which has been said, learned, performed, and known before the psychological/technological mental break has taken place—or rise to speak in defiance when they have been misrepresented by their master. The military is the ultimate zombie master, the destructor of free will, and the creator of ultimate violations—moral, physical, psychological, individual, and national. This notion of the zombified soldier has been narrated before. Tom Ruffles states that this concept of zombification and the military had been utilized in zombie cinema of the 1930s: "*Universal Solider* follows the pattern of *Revolt of the Zombies* [1936] in which a regiment of dead Indochinese soldiers are brought back to life and utilized by the French in the First World War."[32]

By the time we uncover narratives that deal exclusively with the legacy of the Vietnam War, military zombies have manifested in and proliferated across multiple texts, but many commenters do not go so far as to categorize these damaged soldiers as zombies at all. For some, the experience was firsthand and evident: Glenn Adams, a psychologist, wrote of his experiences of dehumanization during his military training in an e-mail to Dr. Philip Zimbardo, leader of the Stanford prison experiment[33]:

My interest in social psychology began when I was a cadet at the USAF Academy and read about (or saw the video of) the SPE [Stanford prison experiment] study in my intro psych class. It spoke to what was going on all around me in the indoctrination of promising young minds into killing, dehumanizing, abuse machines. Your analysis is dead on: it is not a question of getting more moral soldiers. Instead it is a question of recognizing the situation of war (and the cultural/institutional practices of the military that we have designed to "prepare" people for that situation) creates monsters out of us all.[34]

Those who are damaged are disavowed by their masters; the military recognizes the horrors and the untold cognitive and human damage at the heart of war, but it will not concede that the personal destruction inherent to such activity should be subject to scrutiny.[35] As Jennifer Fay states, "The zombie, in sum, is a form of possession by one and dispossession by another that becomes visible in that temporary state of possession called military occupation."[36] Fay's comments also account for the liminal place the zombified soldier occupies—he is disavowed by his sheer existence. While the occupation of Iraq certainly makes this example clear in Joe Dante's "Homecoming," and in doing so recalls the horrors of Vietnam as a distinctly repeated pattern, it is the occupation of foreign lands that brings about this trauma and zombifies the participants. From Haiti to Vietnam to Iraq—under the "degenerating magic of the tropical sun,"[37] where "Marines go mad like rabid dogs, become violent toward the natives, then turn suicidal"[38]—psychologically and biochemically violated veterans return as zombies in a myriad of forms, becoming cultural embodiments of the empty reasons and rhetoric for such wars.

Coming Home

Joe Dante's *Masters of Horror* film "Homecoming" (2006) brings this connection to the fore. Called zombies or "the living impaired" because they represent the zombie of Romero's lineage, the zombified soldiers returning from the Iraq war are collectively postmodern broken combatants. The clever plot reimagines the re-election of George W. Bush in 2004 when, accidentally summoned, soldiers begin to rise from their graves in Arlington National Cemetery. Expecting to be massacred, the public sentiment is initially one of panic, yet the zombies are peaceful, quiet, and thoughtful. When asked why they have returned, they simply state that they want to vote, to be represented. By having the Bush campaigners killing their own zombified fighters again (but this time on American soil), Dante underscores the role of the president as zombie master desperate to regain control. The president's very use of the words "If I had one wish, it would be to have those brave American soldiers come back"[39] literally reanimates his legion in an act of democratic rebellion. The zombified soldier, disavowed at home (lacking treatment or sympathy for serious physical/psychological/chemical illnesses) and abroad (for occupying a country and fighting a war based on a lie), becomes a disposable slave, deemed worthless beyond the immediate needs of combat. One memorable moment highlights such disavowal and disregard, when a reanimated soldier, literally in bits and pieces, writhes on a military operating table while being inspected by the government officials David Murch (Jon Tenney) and Kurt Rand (Robert Picardo). David, who initially expressed the magical revivifying wish to see his brother and resolve his guilt about his brother's death and participation in Vietnam, is increasingly horrified by the political truths these zombies represent:

> David: Oh my god, Kurt, he actually feels pain.
> Kurt: Ah hell, he volunteered.
> David: What do you think they want?
> Kurt: Well, it couldn't be the disability benefits.

This reoccurrence is evident in Dante's film by shadowing the lost generation of the Iraq war with the lost soldiers in Vietnam—the site of both social and mental breakdown narratives, and later as narratives of heroism, in collective American memory.[40] Interestingly, when a reanimated soldier speaks on camera about his need to vote against "this evil war [in which] we were killed for a lie," an immediate cultural inversion occurs: The arrival of the reanimated undead, initially hailed as a divine blessing by the New Right, is quickly denounced and derided as the coming of an apocalypse because of these "satanic, spawn devils" who speak out against the president. This is at variance with the reception soldiers received returning from Vietnam—vilified at first and later legitimized in popular cinema.[41] Dante's film also reverses the role of the undead in their subjective representation. They speak in soft, low tones with dignity, commanding respect—an embodiment of the return of the repressed/suppressed guilt of the current presidential administration. The representation of the political wing is one of savage inhumanity and immorality. Jane Cleaver (Thea Gill), a tough, self-styled "Bush babe" campaigner, shoots and screams at the zombies because they have risen to vote against her incumbent presidential candidate—"We are not giving up, and we are definitely not giving up to a bunch of crippled, stinking, maggot-infested, brain-dead zombie dissidents." For the Bush administration, the return of the undead is highly problematic—they are neither terrorists nor dissidents, but, actually, seeking to honor those who have died in previous and current wars (not that this matters to the master, who incarcerates some of the zombies in a Guantanamo Bay–style enclosure, complete with orange jumpsuits)—sins of the past that must remain dead and buried. For Dante, the zombies who return physically illustrate the horrors and futility of war, and speaking out against their leader/master has become their sole purpose. Once their vote has been cast, they promptly collapse and die (again). They represent both the damaged soldier returning wounded and broken from war, promptly forgotten by the political wing, and the literal configuration of the body and brain (and soul of the nation) in bits and pieces; torn apart, the dead rise because they have been dishonored and wrongly debased: "Then they were among us, these dead young men, these monsters, demanding only that we look at that face and acknowledge what we have done."

Dante's film concludes with David confronting a suppressed childhood memory—his accidental shooting of his suicidal and Vietnam veteran brother Phillip. His mother describes Phillip as "different, he wasn't Phillip anymore" after the war. The outer violence of Vietnam invades the home, the sanctuary, and brings about the utterance of David's wish to see his brother again. Interplaying with the presidential elections of 2000 and 2004, David suppresses the zombie veterans' votes and helps engineer a win for the incumbent president. Outraged, legions of zombified veterans from all the United States' previous wars invade Washington, D.C., seeking to find and hold David responsible for the zombies' politically suppressed rights. Dante ends the episode on a postmodern and thoughtful note: Washington, D.C., is overcome by outraged zombified veterans in protest, but the true dehumanized zombies continue to rule the nation—the postmodern zombie veterans possess more humanity, dignity, and integrity than the zombie master in the White House.

At the heart of this chapter lies the true darkness located in the body that has lost its soul. The souls of the dead become broken, torn away, and mercilessly disassembled to protect the soul of the nation. Whether the zombified soldier is altered through technological, biochemical, or psychological invasions, he is "neither fully alive nor fully dead, in a state on anomie degree zero, disaffected to the point of numbness."[42] Abandoned in their trauma, we see a monster that has been created for the sake of power and control. They are uncomfortably familiar, stirring feelings of remorse and abjection by reminding us that "a zombie once was someone like you and me."[43] Perhaps this is the closest we can get to witnessing our (d)evolution toward the post-human plane, as we perilously slip, ever closer, into the devouring darkness.

And the Dead Shall Inherit the Earth

Part introduction by Peter Dendle

> They looked, to all intents and purposes, like living men and women. But then wasn't that the trick of their craft? To imitate life so well the illusion was indistinguishable from the real thing? And their new public, awaiting them in mortuaries, churchyards, and chapels of rest, would appreciate the skill more than most. Who better to applaud the sham of passion and pain they would perform than the dead, who had experienced such feelings and thrown them off at last? The dead. They needed entertainment no less than the living; and they were a sorely neglected market.
>
> CLIVE BARKER, "Sex, Death, and Starshine"

Zombies have undergone remarkable transformations over the course of their varied representations in folklore, film, and literature. The story continues to unfold in the new millennium, with fresh zombie iterations catering to the audience of a globally connected, technological world. The essays in this section focus on such fresh zombie iterations, which represent the creature in new media and which reinvent the zombie for the millennial generation—those who shall inherit the earth. Even more, the lens of the cinematographer or artist is sometimes turned around, to focus on the zombie audience and on the interplay of audience and monster. The essays highlight a range of tensions between zombie narratives and zombie audiences, which illustrate how the zombie is uniquely situated to articulate questions about life mirroring art, and death mirroring life.

Lynn Pifer analyzes Simon Pegg and Edgar Wright's 2004 film *Shaun of the Dead* as a parable for the Generation X "slacker" society, in which an over-talented, under-ambitious generation of youth shapes its identity through the deliberate protection of leisure time rather than through traditional upward mobility. The deterioration of the London public into zombies casts the numbing effect of modern employment options and conformist workplace culture into greater relief. The slacker antihero, ridiculed at first for "feeding off society," proves in the end to be the best equipped, temperamentally, to fend off the zombies now trying to feed off him and his friends. Pifer notes that in its emphasis on wage work and the deadening effects of contemporary capitalist values, *Shaun* implicitly recalls the zombie's origin in Haitian folklore as a parable of slavery and the commodification of humanity.

The zombies in *Shaun of the Dead* hark back to the classical slow and shambling undead type familiar from George A. Romero's movies. Such slow and witless undead are also standard in the low-budget home movies that proliferated in the 1990s and 2000s, even while the zombies in many major studio productions were getting faster, nimbler, and even smarter. Dendle explores this intersection in terms of the Generation Y audience and filmmakers. These "millennials" represent a tech-savvy, sense-saturated, multitasking cohort whose relationship with the torpid, tunnel-visioned zombie is dynamic and complex. Further, this proliferation of zombie narratives in new genres and distribution formats—such as the streaming or downloadable online short, catered toward consumption on the home computer or handheld device—has ushered in an era of fractured narratives and amateur video production that problematizes traditional notions of what constitutes a complete and integral movie. Finally, the ready availability of friends and neighbors to serve as zombie extras in many home-produced videos and shorts—and the fact that in many cases, that pool of people probably represents a significant proportion of the audience who will ever see the production, outside immediate friends and family—obscures the line between zombie and audience in an intimate way.

Elson Bond and Margo Collins explore the new-millennium zombie in a number of books and movies, such as Max Brooks's *The Zombie Survival Guide: Recorded Attacks* and *World War Z: An Oral History of the Zombie War*, Seth Grahame-Smith's *Pride and Prejudice and Zombies*, Michael and Peter Spierig's *Undead*, Jonathan Maberry's *Zombie CSU: The Forensics of the Living Dead*, Kim Paffenroth's *Dying to Live*, and Ryan Mecum's *Zombie Haiku*. In these recent texts, a malaise that is not simply post-human but also post-zombie seems to have set in for an audience apparently bored with traditional zombie narratives. Even as zombies have trickled down to LOLcats.com, Christmas cards, and Facebook pages giving updates on zombie-apocalypse preparedness, zombie narratives continue to explore the uncomfortable place of individuation in a society that values method, systematization, and institutional responses. The zombie embodies "our fear of loss of identity," even while global zombie apocalypse continues to serve as the crucible for heroism and the testing ground for human values.

The millennial zombie, according to Bond and Collins, portrays "the idea that humans and zombies have little to distinguish them from one another and that only a savior that partakes of the nature of both the living and the undead can possibly save post-humanity."

Beyond fan fiction, genre shorts, video games, revisionist history, campy haiku, and popular movies, the tenacious zombie has succeeded in infiltrating high art, and—as with so much cultural production in the twentieth and twenty-first centuries—has called into question what is and is not art. Sarah Juliet Lauro contrasts Jillian Mcdonald's provocative video installations (such as "Zombie Loop," shown in 2006 at Brooklyn's artMovingProjects Gallery), with the growing trend of "zombie walks." During such events, enthusiasts gather in tattered clothes and gruesome face paint to shamble through downtown areas. The zombie has thus "stepped into the real world" through "a strange process of narrative collaboration." In San Francisco zombie flash mob performances, Lauro explains, some participants will come as zombies, while others will come as victims, with a small strip of duct tape on their backs to indicate to zombies that they are fair game. Since bystanders may not be aware of this code, the spectacle of zombies attacking fellow observers may heighten the drama. Spectators will not necessarily know they are safe from being targeted as victims themselves, and thus may feel drawn in, perceiving themselves to be part of the act. "Zombie walks" inhabit a murky border space between "legitimate" art (such as some of Mcdonald's installations, which receive corporate sponsorship) and illicit—even seditious— manifestations of "performance art" that reclaim the public space for unauthorized or unintended uses.

Zombie walks have also trickled over into related zombie activities, such as the "Assassins"-inspired "Humans vs. Zombies" game played on a number of college campuses. Armed with Nerf dart guns, the last few survivors of the human race (bands of students with bandannas on their arms or legs) try to stave off the assaults of hideous, cannibal zombies (bands of students with bandannas on their foreheads, for instance). After the game sparked a shooter scare and campus lockdown at New York's Alfred University in 2008, some have questioned the appropriateness of such a shooting game after Columbine and Virginia Tech.[1] This raises broader questions concerning some of the more disturbing themes associated with zombie narratives and audiences such as firearm obsession, survivalism, individualist ethic, and the glorification of violence against human bodies taken to a scale well beyond that found in traditional war and adventure movies.[2]

The essays in this section, then, are acutely aware of the blurring between the crisis of a zombie apocalypse in imaginative space and the very real concerns of a new millennium in which global interconnectedness is a given, identities are as much virtual as physical, bioengineering is commonplace, and violence in society often seems to come "from within." The texts are intersected by the consistently collapsed binary of us and them, and illustrate some of the ways in which zombies seem to bleed over—insidiously but relentlessly—into real life. They also document the diversity of audiences engaging with these narratives, and reinforce the ways in which the zombie can mean different things to different people. The zombie-like ghouls in the 1964 Vincent Price movie *The Last Man on Earth* shunned the mirror that Price hung on his door, loath to witness firsthand what they have become.[3] The lead zombie eventually figures out how to knock the mirror off the door by approaching it from the side. The unambitious, unprepossessing zombie—however simplistic, however ugly, however unself-conscious—is itself a mirror for us, one we cannot knock off so easily.

CHAPTER 10

Slacker Bites Back: *Shaun of the Dead* Finds New Life for Deadbeats

Lynn Pifer

Zombies and slackers get the same bad rap: unproductive deadbeats feeding off society. But Simon Pegg and Edgar Wright reveal another side to these societal monsters in their 2004 film *Shaun of the Dead*. In *Shaun*, the zombie functions as the Other who is, nonetheless, uncannily familiar, and the slacker, rather than feeding off society, becomes its hero. If a society's monsters expose the deepest anxieties of the culture that created them, then Pegg and Wright's zombies follow George Romero's tradition of critiquing capitalistic culture by revealing the life-sucking effects of modern urban culture on working-class London. But *Shaun of the Dead* does not conform neatly to typical portrayals of the monster any more than it conforms to the zombie conventions we've come to expect from Romero's popular films, particularly *Dawn of the Dead*, which *Shaun*'s title parodies. Rather, *Shaun* both reflects and deflects established monster theory and depictions of the conventional hero by representing its zombies as even more familiar than the uncanny familiarity we've come to associate with the zombie, and portraying its hero, Shaun, as an ironic defender of slacker values rather than the next zombie slayer.

Pegg and Wright take an existing cultural monster, the zombie—specifically the classic Romero zombie—and show that these horrible monsters are not all that different from the people desperately trying to avoid or kill them. Critics such as Jeffery Cohen have noted that the monster is "difference made flesh,"[1] and thus eligible for destruction. But when the monster is a zombie, it is not altogether alien, as Barbara notes in Romero's *Night of the Living Dead*: "They are us. We are them." *Shaun of the Dead* likewise plays up the similarity between *us* living workers and *them* zombies, and it takes this notion a step further in the conclusion of the film, when the zombies are incorporated into the "living" society rather than overrunning the living or being dispatched with a blow to the head. This unsettling similarity between worker and zombie is evident even in the original British trailer for the film, which juxtaposes a series of quick clips from the film with a wry voice-over narration:

> Do you ever feel that modern *life* is not for you?
> Do you do the same *dead*-end job every day?
> Is your romance *dying* on its feet?
> Have you ever felt that you are turning into . . . a *zombie*?
> Maybe . . . you're not alone.
> [words flash on the screen:] IN A TIME OF CRISIS
> A HERO MUST RISE
> FROM HIS SOFA
> THIS YEAR
> FEAR
> HAS A NEW ENEMY
> AND COURAGE
> HAS A NEW NAME
> [Liz's nervous voice:] "Shaun!"[2]

The trailer clearly portrays the film's protagonist as a disaffected slacker/couch potato, playing up the humor of his lack of heroic attributes. The last four screens are meant to be ironic, as the images show Shaun running frantically or crying in fear while the words on the screen proclaim his the new name of courage. The trailer prepares us for a film that will not feature the stereotypical tough-guy Hollywood hero, the next Terminator or Rambo.

Shaun is, in fact, the anti-Rambo. He is not particularly strong or skilled in self-defense. He tries to arm himself with kitchen implements, record albums, a cricket bat, a pool cue, and, finally, a rifle that he has no skill in firing. His attempt to give the zombies "the slip" only leads them back to his hideout, and he is unable to defend his mum or his friends. He tries his best with the resources he has at hand, but is unable, in his own words, to get a "fucking break" the way typical film heroes do.

The first part of the trailer, in fact, articulates Shaun's position as an Everyman character. The repeated use of second-person pronouns implicates the audience, indicating that *we* may be turning into zombies due to our dead-end jobs and the effect of "modern life." The last statement, that we are not alone, indicates that this "zombie" condition may affect many members of our society. In addition, this part of the trailer accentuates the living/dead dichotomy: modern *life*, *dead*-end job, romance *dying*. When you put them all together, the lines begin to blur: modern life becomes a living death in the realm of the zombie. This rhetoric is consistent with Cohen's theory, which, in part, emphasizes that monsters live at the crux of dichotomies.

In *Monster Theory: Reading Culture*, Cohen explains that "the monstrous body is [. . . a] construct and a projection [that] exists only to be read: the monstrum is etymologically 'that which reveals,' 'that which warns,' "[3] and it appears that *Shaun of the Dead*'s zombies reveal and warn against the deadening effects of modern life. Even in the first minutes of the film's opening sequence, we can see that working "life" kills all but the outer shell of the grocery cart jockeys, the cashiers, and every commuter in London. As *Shaun*'s opening music plays, teens slowly push carts through a parking lot; the check-out girl, Mary, monotonously scans item after item while gazing, unfocused, at nothing in particular; commuters ride the bus without talking to or making eye contact with one another; and pedestrians plod down the sidewalk in an automaton shuffle that resembles the slow, stumbling steps of early Romero zombies.[4] The zombie-like London citizens in *Shaun*'s opening resemble *Dawn of the Dead*'s mall zombies, who ride the escalators and stumble through the mall because of some preternatural memory of that place.[5] Our entire society appears to be effected. We are not alone in the zombie condition.

Even before the film's zombie crisis explodes, our protagonist appears zombified. The audience's first "zombie false alarm" occurs as a hung-over Shaun stumbles out of his bedroom and the camera slowly pans up from his stiffly stumbling feet. Is that a zombie moan we hear? No, it's just our hero yawning. And this apathetic hero fits the Generation X slacker stereotype. In the opening sequence, Shaun can barely pay attention to the "shape up or else" lecture he's getting from his girlfriend, Liz. Despite the fact that Shaun has been to college, is now twenty-nine years old, and has been dating Liz for the last three years, he has not accepted the responsibilities of a productive adult life. He still lives in a flat with his college mate, Pete, and his childhood best friend, Ed. He continues to work as a clerk in an electronics store—Foree Electronics, a nod to the actor Ken Foree of *Dawn of the Dead*—despite his desire to do something else with his life. He still needs to be reminded not to forget his bimonthly visit with his mother. He steadfastly refuses to "grow up" or go anywhere without his unemployed and otherwise friendless sidekick, Ed. Shaun is a consummate slacker.

Although the term "slacker" generally denotes "apathy, aimlessness, and lack of ambition" in young adults,[6] works such as Douglass Copeland's 1991 novel *Generation X* and Richard Linklater's 1991 film *Slacker* champion the slacker lifestyle as a conscious choice for those who have no interest in being co-opted by the mainstream conception of proper work ethic and achievement. John Ulrich, for instance, stresses a more empowered interpretation of the term in his introduction to *GenXegesis: Essays on "Alternative" Youth (Sub)Culture*: "From the slacker perspective, working is not the point of living: in fact, it impedes living. Work, from the slacker perspective, marginalizes who we are; thus in the life of a slacker work must be decentered, relegated to the margins. As Linklater points out, . . . 'if [slackers] have a job, the job doesn't have them.'"[7] Characters with acceptable occupations, like Pete, with his office job, or David, with his lecturer's position, view Shaun and Ed as lazy and unambitious. In order to be taken seriously by these other characters, Shaun and Ed must convince them that their choices, such as deciding to seek shelter from the zombies at the pub rather than at a more conventional location, have merit. As he formulates his plan with Ed, Shaun imagines a number of scenarios, all of which involve Liz and his mum joyfully joining up with them and, without too much effort, finding a safe, zombie-free spot to relax with a beverage and wait for help. Once they realize that their favorite pub, the Winchester, is the perfect stronghold, Shaun imagines relaxing with pint glasses rather than tea mugs in their hands, and he exclaims, "How's that for a slice of fried gold?"[8] For Shaun does not intend to change himself by enduring *Rocky*-style training and strengthening montages; he intends to win by slacking. He chooses his "stronghold" more for its amenities—beer and snacks—than for its defensibility. Shaun's primary consideration seems to be finding a place that's "familiar," that won't take him out of his slacker comfort zone, and that fulfills Ed's requirement that he be allowed to smoke. But this first-floor pub in a corner building with large, unbarred windows soon proves insufficient at keeping out the zombie hoard.

In fact, part of the widespread appeal of *Shaun of the Dead* is the humor derived from placing a slacker in the hero's role, and various reviews of the film comment on the pleasure of watching slackers in the standard horror film scenarios. Roger Ebert, for instance, "like[s] the way the slacker characters maintain their slothful gormlessness in the face of urgent danger."[9] In a *BBC Collective* review, Skye Sherwin describes the film as "peopled by twentysomething PlayStation-obsessed slackers," and notes, "From the title it might seem like this is some spoof of the George Romero classic. In fact, it's truer to the spirit of Romero's vision of comatose consumer society than the straight remake also released this month."[10] *Dawn of the Dead* features zombies who return to their favorite activity: hanging out at the mall; *Shaun*'s zombies return to their favorite activity: hanging around the neighborhood pub.

In addition, Shaun's world consists of willing workers and defiant slackers. Workers such as Mary the cashier have been deadened by their jobs. Workers like Pete—who is willing to report to work on a Sunday, despite his own exhaustion—have been overcome by a sense of responsibility to their work. But slackers like Shaun, who has never fully given himself to the job he doesn't want—or Ed, who has never accepted a job—resist the deadening affects of capitalist society. The problem with being a slacker, however, is that the workers disparage the slacker's life, which leads to a sense of powerless isolation within society. In his review of the film, Marty Mapes acknowledges Shaun's sense of powerlessness, arguing that while "Romero's *Dawn of the Dead* was a . . . satirical look at the growing materialism and mall culture of the 1970s[,] *Shaun of the Dead* says that this generation can't be bothered with current events. . . . It's not so much that Shaun's generation is selfish or shallow . . . rather it's that they assume they can't change the world. News is what happens to other people, important people. Clerks and the unemployed just don't feel empowered enough to be a part of the world."[11] Mapes's assertion is only partly right. Shaun may not feel empowered enough to keep abreast of current events, including the present unfolding zombie disaster, but Pegg and Wright's story does provide disenfranchised slackers like Shaun and Ed with a situation where they can not only survive, but also succeed in winning others' respect. In the course of the film, the already-deadened workers become actual deadened zombies. Those who are living must have a plan of action, as Shaun's friend Yvonne emphasizes when she meets up with Shaun during the zombie invasion: "Have you got a plan?" Faced with this character-building crisis, Shaun develops the ultimate slacker plan: gather those he loves and head to his favorite pub. Yvonne looks dismayed when she hears his proposed course of action, but, by surviving, Shaun intends to rise above his denigrated reputation and succeed. According to Joseph Campbell, an unlikely hero such as Shaun would go through a series of trials and eventually transform himself into hero material.[12] But unlike previous film heroes such as Luke Skywalker or Daniel from *The Karate Kid*, Shaun attempts to progress from lazy slacker to slacker hero without changing himself. There is a brief moment toward the end of the film where it appears that Shaun has elevated himself into a true leader, as he rallies his mates with inspiring words from Bertrand Russell: "The only thing that will redeem mankind is cooperation." But Liz recognizes that he has recently read that quotation on a beer mat—Guinness Extra Cold, to be exact—so Shaun's slacker reputation remains untainted.

In this film, a slacker hero appears to be just what society needs. Critics have long noted that horror film monsters should be examined within the cultural/sociological matrix of relations that generate them, from Stephen King's argument that successful horror films "always seem to play upon and express fears which exist across a wide spectrum of people,"[13] to Tony Magistrale's more concise assertion that the monster "is nothing less than a barometer for measuring an era's cultural anxieties."[14] Thus *Shaun* should be examined in terms of the postindustrial, service-oriented workforce the film portrays. As Mapes notes, "*Shaun* also makes the point that many of the lower-paid workers in Western cities are practically zombies anyway. Demeaning, unimportant jobs leave them numb, and all some employers want is a body without a soul or a brain to get in the way of work, work, work."[15] This image of the enslaved zombie worker, while new to the Romero zombie audience,[16] is actually a return to the image that captured the public's imagination in the early twentieth century.

Zora Neale Hurston described zombies to the American public in her 1938 work of folklore *Tell My Horse*. For Hurston, a zombie is an individual corpse commonly believed to be raised from the dead by voodoo. Hurston also suggests that a victim could be drugged and buried alive to be retrieved later.[17] The zombie is then forced to work in the fields or do the voodoo practitioner's evil deeds. Anyone could be targeted and enslaved by a *bocor*, or voodoo priest, and the victim's family would never look for their loved one because they would assume the victim is dead and buried.[18] In fact, during her travels in Haiti, Hurston was shown the supposed zombie Felicia Felix-Mentor, who had been buried in 1907 yet was found walking about muttering incoherently in 1936. Although at first glance Felix-Mentor looked like an emaciated old woman, a closer look revealed the dreadful sight of the "blank face" and "dead eyes"; Hurston writes, "The sight of this wreckage was too much to endure for long."[19] The horror of the story is that it features a woman who was once a wife and mother, part of our familiar world, but somehow has become a "broken remnant, relic, or refuse"[20]—in other words, a monster.

The voodoo zombie has been portrayed in more recent works, such as Daniel Gruener's 1996 film *All of Them Witches*, which depicts a young woman who finds herself pursued by a Hurston-style voodoo zombie and must learn to use voodoo herself to escape not only the zombie but her own controlling husband. But the Romero trilogy effectively supplants the folklore voodoo zombie in our popular imagination with his own vision of mass zombie attacks. Romero's zombies are not, and cannot be, controlled by anyone. They do no work and exist only to terrorize and devour the living.

Critics such as Roger Ebert note that Romero's zombie trilogy has changed our notion of the zombie: "George Romeo, who invented the modern genre with *Night of the Living Dead* and *Dawn of the Dead*, was essentially devising video game targets before there were video games: They pop up, one after another, and you shoot them."[21] Pegg and Wright emphasize the notion of zombie as easy target through Ed's leisure activities. Ed, who has spent most of his life playing violent video games, now amuses himself by hitting pedestrian zombies as he drives, pretending to score points with each hit. By the end of the film, however, there are a number of zombies "saved" rather than destroyed by the living. Ultimately, Pegg and Wright are not interested in merely eradicating zombies; they seek to examine how productive members of society already resemble zombies, and how we might compartmentalize those aspects of modern life that deaden us and nourish the more playful aspects that will allow us to, in Liz's words, "live a little."

On the surface, this zombie film parody—a self-proclaimed "Romantic comedy. With zombies"—seemingly adheres to a zombie-wise audience's expectations. There are many zombies, and instead of following the most recent zombie film trend of being vicious, fast hunters, they follow in the Romero tradition of being dim, slow-moving predators one can stop with a blow to the head. And true to popular horror film tradition, they seem to provide the story with a clearly defined enemy, a monstrous Other, for our hero and his sidekick to destroy as we cheer them on, without us having to feel guilty about taking pleasure in such carnage. For instance, when Ed hits a pedestrian with Pete's car, Shaun is racked with guilt, cautiously calling out to the body in the street. When the corpse reveals its snarling zombie visage, Shaun says, "Oh, thank heavens for that," and we can all breathe a sigh of relief. We thought for a moment that our protagonists had killed someone. Thankfully, the victim was *just* a zombie.

But zombies are just the type of monsters who refuse "to participate in the classificatory 'order of things'" and are dangerous because they are "suspended between forms that threaten to smash distinctions."[22] These monsters are beings suspended between life and death. That they are not alive and thus are unable to respond to appeals to reason or emotion is noted by folklore sources such as Hurston[23] and is portrayed in popular literature such as *The Zombie Survival Guide*.[24] And yet, despite the fact that the person inside the body has died, the body is still animated and quite emphatically dangerous. Zombies seem placed squarely at the crossroads between the living and the dead. What *Shaun* emphasizes is that the simple living/dead binary is insufficient to describe the relationship between the film's zombies and the living characters; the dead walk among and threaten the living, yet the living themselves resemble the dead. At first glance, the film and its trailer appear to emphasize the binary opposition between living and dead. Living friends must be saved; dead ones must be destroyed. But *Shaun*'s zombies are like Cohen's monster, who "breaks apart bifurcating, 'either/or' syllogistic logic with a kind of reasoning closer to 'and/or,' introducing what Barbara Johnson has called 'a revolution in the very logic of meaning.'"[25] Thus the monster destroys categories because it cannot be labeled either/or—the zombie is not living or dead. In fact, upon closer examination, *Shaun*'s zombies resemble the living more than earlier film zombies do. By the end of the film, the remaining zombies have been incorporated into Shaun's society. Controlled by chains and collars, zombies perform slave labor. They are the new grocery cart jockeys and the latest hilarious contestants on humiliating television game shows. Newscasters have even adopted a more politically correct term for them, the "mobile deceased." Finally, with the image of Zombie Noel chained to his grocery cart corral, we return to the Hurston-style zombie: an enslaved worker. In Noel's case, his master is a grocery chain instead of a voodoo *bocor*.

One scene, in particular, undercuts the conventional idea, held by human characters in zombie films, that zombies no longer resemble the living. Shaun has gathered his friends and family and they are escaping in his stepfather's Jaguar. His stepfather, Philip, has been bitten and cannot drive, so Ed drives the Jag, playing heavy metal music at top volume, speeding through the streets and hitting zombies left and right, as if he's playing his favorite video game instead of taking his friends to safety. Philip, of course, cannot stand "that racket!" or the reckless way Ed is handling his beloved car, but he is too weak to intervene. When Philip dies and turns into a zombie, they stop the car and all pile out, locking

Zombie Philip inside. Shaun's mum, Barbara, is reluctant to leave Philip behind, and Shaun exclaims, "That's not even your husband in there, okay? I know it looks like him, but there's nothing left of the man you loved in that car now. Nothing!" At that moment, Zombie Philip, who has been snarling and waving his arm about, finally manages to turn Ed's music off, and he sighs and relaxes. A classic Romero zombie would have never stopped trying to get out of the car to pursue its living victims. This zombie just seems to want some peace and quiet, just as the living Philip would have. The zombies in *Shaun of the Dead* are part of a living/dead binary, yet they simultaneously deconstruct this binary, appearing to be more "and/or" than "either/or," as Barbara Johnson suggests. Likewise, when Shaun's mother becomes a zombie and the others call on Shaun to shoot her before she devours them, she looks on Shaun's face sadly, looking more mum than monster. She snarls only after David attempts to step between them. In addition to dead zombies resembling their living selves, as Philip and Barbara do, living characters seem like "zombies," due to the deadening effects of "modern life."

The monsters Shaun must battle at the end of the film were all seen going about their daily lives at the beginning of the film, and, aside from the fact that they now have opaque eyes and "some red" on them, the dead don't look that much different from their living selves. Indeed, the filmmakers play up Shaun's inability to discern when he is surrounded by zombies. He rides the bus with infected victims; he and Ed scoff at the zombie trying to enter the pub after hours; and they sing call and response to the howls of a zombie approaching them in the alley, assuming he is drunk like them. Shaun can stagger down to his local convenience store, hung over and oblivious to the car alarms, the pool of blood he slips in, or the moaning zombie in the street whom he mistakes for a panhandler. Finally, neither Shaun nor Ed is able to recognize that the girl in the garden isn't just drunk and looking for a cuddle. Even when she gets up after being impaled on a pipe, Ed's first response is not to run for safety but to wind his instant camera so he can take a picture of her.

Our protagonists' prolonged inability to perceive the monsters around them is not the only twist on conventional zombie film plots. Cohen argues that monster stories contain two narratives: "one that describes how the monster came to be and another . . . detailing what cultural use the monster serves. The monster of prohibition exists to . . . call horrid attention to the borders that cannot—*must* not—be crossed."[26] But this doesn't seem to be the case in *Shaun of the Dead*. In the first place, Pegg and Wright's film deliberately refuses to provide the narrative of how the zombies came to be. The talking heads on the television propose theories, but just before they can explain what the latest theory is, our channel-surfing protagonist clicks to the next show. Apparently, he doesn't care to know, and we never find out. Second, at the conclusion of our film, we see the monsters returning to mundane jobs or becoming the participants on TV game shows. What lesson is there here? Better them than us? Instead of warning us to proceed no further, these monsters have been domesticated and assimilated into modern life. All wear collars or are caged to prevent attacks on the living, suggesting that, although the zombie aspect of our lives threatens to destroy us, it can be restrained or compartmentalized. It might even be useful.[27]

Admittedly, our protagonist may not quite meet the Joseph Campbell–style hero's role, in which the hero undergoes a transformational journey, defeats the monster, and saves the world. Heroes from Gilgamesh to Luke Skywalker to Aang the Last Airbender have followed Campbell's blueprint for the hero's journey, but Shaun's excursion doesn't quite fit. Yes, he accepts the "call to adventure,"[28] but in his case, the initial "calls" are more like calls to grow up, such as Pete telling Shaun to "get your fucking life sorted out." Shaun and his sidekick, Ed, must transform from hapless gits throwing kitchen implements to shovel- and cricket bat–wielding warriors. One could say that they undergo the "road of trials"[29] as they get Mum and Liz and wend their way to the Winchester, although their wonderful "dream landscape"[30] is filled with lots and lots of zombies. Shaun receives his "atonement with the father"[31] during his stepfather's dying moments in the backseat of the Jag when Philip confesses that he was hard on Shaun only because he wanted him to learn to be strong. But although Shaun journeys to the underworld of Zombie London, his goal is not to defeat the monster and return to civilization with the "ultimate boon"[32]—unless the ultimate boon is the monster itself. In this story, the slacker hero is given the opportunity to rid himself of all those who would interfere with his leisure time, and, rather than destroying the monster and bringing back something to help his society, he brings the monster back into his life.

At the beginning of the film, Shaun is surrounded by characters who remind him to grow up and take responsibility for his life. His girlfriend, Liz, pleads, "I want to live a little, Shaun, and I want you to want it, too." Her flat mates David and Dianne encourage him to see life outside his neighborhood pub. His stepfather, Philip, admonishes him to "be a man," and his flat mate Pete advises him to kick out Ed and to "get [his] fucking life sorted out." It takes an "end of the world" crisis to shock Shaun into action. His first instinct is to save everyone he loves. But nearly every potentially heroic scene is undercut: Shaun tries to hop over a garden fence, only to have it collapse under him; he volunteers to check for zombies over another fence, but he has to climb a children's slide to do so; he aims the group's only rifle at the invading zombies, but he misses again and again. David bitterly calls Shaun "Captain Wow," but David cannot convince the group to break with Shaun and take over as their leader. Shaun's plan to gather everyone and go 'round to the pub is not brilliant, yet all the characters end up following him.

By the end of the film, characters who nagged Shaun to act more responsibly have conveniently turned into zombies and can thus be disposed of: Zombie Philip is locked in his car, David and Dianne have been devoured by the zombie mob, and Shaun shoots and kills Zombie Pete, who is once again picking on Ed. By taking action against those demanding beings, Shaun also wins back Liz, who is now content to make him tea (with two sugars) and go 'round to the pub later on. This film changes the standard romantic comedy plot from "boy meets girl/boy loses girl/boy gets girl again" to "boy loses girl he used to have/boy gets girl back *and* also gets to keep the slacker life that once repulsed her." What more could a slacker ask for?

A slacker could ask for a way to maintain his lifestyle. In the film's final moments, we learn that Zombie Ed, Shaun's childhood friend and social deadweight, is now kept chained in the garden shed, where he plays video games and avoids the new zombie workforce. Shaun pops out to the shed, joins in the game, and smiles at Ed as Queen's "You're My Best Friend" plays and the credits roll. Ironically, the opening line of the song is "Ooo, you make me live." In this scene, Shaun smiles sincerely for the first time in the entire film; he finally gets to sit and play with his best friend. Shaun may have appeared to have matured and entered domestic life in the earlier shot of the redecorated flat with Liz, but we now learn that he has managed to preserve the part of his life he treasures most: he has kept the friend who was "holding [him] back," and, having eliminated the voices of the socially responsible and upwardly mobile characters who used to surround him, he can remain in his regressive state.

But there is a critical difference. In the beginning of the film, Ed lives with Shaun in the flat, they play video games even when Shaun needs to be getting ready for work, and Ed's beer-drinking presence in the flat leaves it in a continual state of disarray. Even when Ed "tidies up," he rewards himself by having a few beers and making another mess. Shaun's relationship with Liz cannot grow because Shaun brings Ed along on every date. Although Shaun has found a way to keep Ed in his life, now Ed is chained in the shed, fulfilling one of Pete's earlier curses: "If you want to live like an animal, why don't you go live in the fucking shed!" Shaun holds in check the friend who formerly had held him back. The shed and the video games may beckon, but the rest of Shaun's life is Ed-free. By compartmentalizing the monster, Shaun is able to regain his relationship with Liz. He also manages to deconstruct the loser/hero binary. The loser who nonetheless wins in the end, the slacker who leads, he is always both.

CHAPTER 11

Zombie Movies and the "Millennial Generation"

Peter Dendle

The zombie is a creature of paradox.[1] It is at once familiar and alien, alive and dead, human and non-human. Barely capable of negotiating a set of stairs, the shambling, slow revenant seems an unlikely iconic villain for the cusp of the third millennium. Emerging from a relatively stable form in the 1970s and early '80s, however, the zombie has adapted resiliently to a range of new media and genres (e.g., video games and online digital shorts) sometimes organically and naturally, at other times with jarring incongruity. The ways in which it has been popularly embraced in the 1990s and 2000s can provide interesting insights into some broader social attitudes among zombie audiences. In all its artistic manifestations—film, literature, video games, graphic novels, etc.—the zombie has surfaced in the late twentieth and early twenty-first century as one of the preeminent monsters of the current generation. The zombie holds evident appeal to the technologically savvy, fast-paced generation of young people in the 1990s and 2000s, and through the creature's diverse iterations and adaptations, the zombie can serve as a mirror for some of this generation's values and notions of identity.

Among the paradoxes defining the ever-transforming zombie are conflicting portrayals of its intelligence and speed. Screen zombies were originally slow of mind and of foot. Methodical, almost robotic torpor was

175

among the zombie's most defining traits the 1980s. This is still an active genetic strand within evolving and diversifying zombie conceptualizations, and it is still the mental image most familiar to the general public (e.g., to non-fans of zombie movies or of horror). Many zombies have departed from this template, however. Some are now shown as fully capable of rational thought and language use: thus in *Return of the Living Dead* (1985), a captured zombie describes her sensations acutely, explaining to her captors that eating the brains of the living helps stop "the pain of being dead."[2] The transition to using language and learning social skills is encapsulated in Bub, the zombie from *Day of the Dead* (1985) who is the (somewhat) successful subject of behavioral conditioning that trains him to recognize objects, to interact civilly with some humans, and to gutturally parrot the phrase "Hello, Aunt Alicia." Zombies are occasionally portrayed as capable of tool use (e.g., *Night Life* [1989]), implying in some cases rational ability and in other cases stored memories. It is a tense scene in *Night of the Living Dead* (1968), when a zombie figures outs how to knock out a car's headlights with a rock, and another uses a table leg to pound on the doors and windows of the boarded-up farmhouse. The idea is brought to the surface in *Bride of Re-Animator* (1991), when stoic Herbert West (Jeffrey Combs) exclaims: "My God—they're using tools!" Beyond the continued fascination, within the narratives, of the possibility of zombies evolving to further cognitive capacities (which is really only a way of highlighting their inability to use tools), a more pronounced development has been that of zombies' speed and agility. In mainstream movies, zombies are increasingly nimble and swift in the 2000s, and this has sparked a debate within the zombie fan community.

Discussion threads on online forums often debate "do you think fast or slow zombies are scarier?" and partisans on both sides of the issue argue the relative merits vociferously.[3] Some argue that in becoming faster and more articulate, zombies cease to be what made them "zombies" in the first place (as opposed to being crazed, virus-infected cannibals, for instance). In this seemingly frivolous debate over the definition of an imaginary creature, enthusiasts are implicitly arguing, to a certain extent, what elements of humanity are the most frightening to distort or eliminate. Zombies with less mental ability asymptotically approach mindlessness, and zombies with less physical ability approach stasis. In the course of these discussions, the zombie continues to satisfy a role for which it has been well suited since its inception: to serve as an abstract thought experiment—projected at first into religion, folklore, and then eventually into film, fiction, visual arts, and electronic media—for meditation on what it means to be "human."

As an artistic portrayal of the human body itself, the zombie can be seen as reflecting shifting notions of identity in the Internet age. It is the animated body in the absence (mostly) of thought, passion, intellect, philosophy, history, and culture. This is the antithesis of the virtual body some commentators have begun to discuss in the Internet age, a "body" whose traditional corporeal boundaries are dissolved. Craig D. Murray and Judith Sixsmith, for instance, argue that "embodiment in VR [Virtual Reality] may . . . necessitate a transfiguration of the body boundaries."[4] Jonathan Marshall describes the way online presence recalls the construct of ghosts. "The lack of boundaries," he writes, "leads to the cyberbody being categorised as immaterial, in the same way as ghosts and spirits are classified as immaterial in the 'Western' world": "The number of bodies that may be squeezed into a room is not influenced by the described size of the room and it is usually impossible to interact with most of the features of a location or room, another reminder of immateriality. . . . The lack of boundary fixity in people's experience online, particularly when not interrupted by pain, creates a sense of personal immateriality, which is perhaps furthered by the loss of time sense as an organiser of experience."[5] The stereotypical zombie is essentially the opposite of such a "ghost": it is a soulless body, rather than a disembodied soul.[6] In this sense, it is the perfect complement for such a cyberbody described by these commentators, and perhaps, as a monster it is thus uniquely situated to haunt the imaginations of today's youth. In the remainder of this essay, I will illustrate this idea by showing how some recent conceptualizations of the zombie, in addition to some recent genres in which zombie narratives have thrived, reflect a dynamic relationship between these texts and the newer generation of zombie audiences.

Zombies were always slow throughout the era of classical horror movies, the 1930s and '40s—in fact, painfully slow.[7] They were slow yet relentless, and this is what made them frightening: moments of close-quarter, slow speed chases and instances of near contact can turn a room, a corridor, or an elevator into the site for scenic tension and minute exploration of domestic space and personal body space.[8] Zombies remained slow in the 1950s and '60s and in the Romero series (*Night of the Living Dead*, 1968; *Dawn of the Dead*, 1979; and *Day of the Dead*, 1985). They became maddeningly slow in such Mediterranean movies as Amando de Ossorio's "Blind Dead" series (beginning with *Tombs of the Blind Dead*, 1971) and Andrea Bianchi's *Burial Ground* (1980).[9] By 1985, however, horror movie tastes were changing. Though Romero's *Day of the Dead* appeared, a livelier and more influential movie came out as well, Dan O'Bannon's *Return of the Living Dead*. This is a quirky and kinetic movie, sustaining a frenetic pace and featuring speedy and dexterous zombies. *Return of the Living Dead* inspired a trend of increasingly fast zombies, running parallel to the traditionally slow ones.

The zombies of *Return of the Living Dead* are frightening for any of a number of reasons: they cannot be deanimated short of destroying them completely (the Romero orthodoxy that zombies can be deanimated by being shot in the head is forsaken). Also, the zombies are sentient, intelligent, articulate, and (while relatively slow in assessing an overall situation) capable over time of grouping together and forging strategy. Having devoured the crew of an ambulance, one zombie finds the CB radio and calls in the request, "send . . . more . . . paramedics. . . ." The zombie in *Return* is still ragged, putrid, shambling, falling apart from one scene to the next, and highly contagious, but it is much more dangerous than previous generations of shuffling revenants. Zombie movies in the wake of *Return* rely less on scenic tension (within a room, for instance) and more on fear of hot pursuit and swift, violent assault. This mirrors horror trends more generally, as the brooding, atmospheric, and subdued horror movies of the 1970s (such as *The Wicker Man* [1973], *Martin* [1976], *The Omen* [1976], *The Child* [1977], and *The Fog* [1979]) gave way in the 1980s to fast paced, brightly colored, increasingly gory action-horror (e.g., *The Evil Dead* [1982], *A Nightmare on Elm Street* [1985], *From Beyond* [1986], *Hellraiser* [1987], and *Beetlejuice* [1988]).

After a slew of zombie films culminating in the late '80s, zombie movies ground to a virtual halt in the 1990s. With some exceptions like Peter Jackson's *Braindead* (1992, released in the US as *Dead Alive*), studio-funded zombie movies were conspicuously in decline during this period. Zombie cult following continued to thrive throughout the '90s, however, thanks to video games such as the *Resident Evil* series and to the growth of fansites and online communities. These communities nurtured sustained discussions of narrative possibilities within the genre and laid the foundations for the next generation of more publicly visible enthusiasm for the creature. This reached fruition in 2002, when the movie version of *Resident Evil* and especially Danny Boyle's *28 Days Later* catapulted the zombie movie back to the horror movie forefront. The high-profile release and success of *28 Days Later* reinvigorated longtime fans and effectively introduced the genre to a new generation. It was the catalyst that helped secure funding for the *Dawn of the Dead* remake in 2004 and for Romero to be able to make his long-awaited fourth movie, *Land of the Dead*, in 2005. In the early third millennium, however, film has changed and horror audience expectations have changed with them.

Contemporary action and science-fiction filmmaking relies on fast-paced and heavily computer-enhanced visual effects such as "Flo-Mo" and "Bullet Time Cinematography" (speed distortion effects introduced in post-production) pioneered in such visually appealing movies as *The Matrix; Crouching Tiger, Hidden Dragon;* and *Kill Bill*. These presume an audience comfortable with visual fragmentation, multiple points of view and 360 panoramic sweeps, speeding and slowing of time sequences, and rapid-fire cuts and transitions. Even a normal conversation can be made into an action sequence using such high-adrenaline effects. The mummy—a classically slow monster, like the zombie—has been recently re-invented as such a sensory extravaganza (*The Mummy*, 1999). Though lovers of Boris Karloff's original Ardeth Bay will fail to recognize the subdued dignity and ominous understatement in this modernized version of the mummy, the series has proven commercially successful (the third installment appeared in 2008, *The Mummy: Tomb of the Dragon Emperor*). Similarly, the *Dawn of the Dead* remake in 2004 boasted state-of-the-art effects and state-of-the-art zombies. They sprint and gracefully navigate obstacles. The editing of the movie's action scenes features removed frames from motion sequences (that can give the motion a panicky, strobe-light feel), and splices the shots frenetically. There is a hyperactive energy, a continuously fevered pitch. The same is true of the infected creatures in *I Am Legend* (2007), far different from the slow, dull-witted vampire-zombies of the 1964 cinematic rendering of this Richard Matheson story. The slow zombie continues to thrive in the low-budget movie arena, but aside perhaps from *Shaun of the Dead* (2004) and Romero's movies, it is hard to find slow zombies in the new millennium among high-profile, studio-funded efforts. Clearly there has been a radical shift in the audience's relationship with this creature.

The current generation of youth is sometimes called the "Millennial Generation": those people who were born around the time MTV was launched in 1981; who were raised immersed in video games, downloadable media, and instant messaging; and who reached adulthood around the turn of the millennium. They present something of an enigma to parents and cultural commentators. Millennials are well known for short attention spans, the uncanny ability to multitask, a smattering of knowledge in an impressive diversity of unlikely areas, and—because of the unique face of violence in the modern age—an acute awareness, if not a thorough political understanding, of contemporary violence in the context of overwhelming forces such as culture wars and global biological threats. Technological changes over the past 15 years have altered the way zombie narratives are produced and consumed. The availability of affordable home videography equipment and home video-editing software has led to a proliferation of backyard movies. Many of these tend to be horror, and many of those, more specifically, tend to be zombie movies. Lists of zombie films in the 2000s run into the hundreds, with all but a handful representing amateur efforts produced on shoestring budgets by fans. Furthermore, independent zombie filmmakers can distribute their low-budget movies directly to the public through small-scale distribution enterprises (including personal webpages, eBay, etc.). Free downloads are often available of trailers, select scenes, promotional shorts, or—if the piece is short enough—of the entire movie. Many of these works are labors of love, with the aspiring director happy simply to get attention, make contacts, and begin establishing a portfolio.

The online digital short, ready for download or immediate viewing (on a Flash Player, for instance), is effectively a new genre, and one uniquely tailored to the audience expectations of the Millennial Generation. Usually it is viewed on a home computer, often in a separate window such as Real Player or Quicktime. This is not like the experience of going to the TV room, the home entertainment system, or the couch—instead the digital short *comes to us*. It is watched from the same work space (chair and desk) also used to write papers for school, Instant Message friends, and update Facebook. Rather than planning to watch the short in advance, the viewer as often as not finds it through a link and watches it spontaneously. The online digital short is usually free. It can represent a wide range of themes, budgets, and levels of background training. *Uuuugh! The Movie* (2005, around 15 minutes), a school project created by students in the Florida State University College of Communications, is available at a number of online video portals (such as WondersTV and video .google.com). *All of the Dead* (2001, Spite Your Face Productions) is a minute-and-a-half stop-motion, black and white animated zombie chase and massacre sequence, crafted out of Lego building blocks. Though incoherent and scattered, the animation work is detailed and the miniaturized zombie apocalypse is fascinating to watch. The Internet gives tremendous power and voice to the zombie fan base and to aspiring filmmakers. Even as high-budget, studio-backed features try periodically to make zombies faster and smarter (and thus, arguably, more "human"), there is a notable resistance to this trend from the grassroots. Time and again, backyard zombie massacres feature the same old shambling stiffs that hearken back to Romero's *Night of the Living Dead* and the original *Dawn of the Dead*. Thus the zombies are excruciatingly slow in Scott Goldberg's downloadable *The Day They Came Back* (2006), based on his own story "The Night They Came Back." In this 22-minute adventure shot on Long Island, a secret government genetic engineering research base unleashes a virus that turns everyone into zombies. Most of the characters, as is often the case in zombie movies, kill each other off from stress and infighting, thus saving the largely ineffective zombies a great deal of trouble. The pacing is hectic, but the zombies themselves remain slow.

More serious and ambitious productions can be found as well. Jason Tammemagi's *Detained*, available for download at www.detainedthemovie.com, is a surprisingly well-produced 14-minute feature from Ireland featuring Jarlath Conroy (William McDermott, from *Day of the Dead*). Cannibal zombies—the infected students and faculty of a prep school—overrun the school and then all of society, while hero Doyle has only a flashlight to pummel them off with. The production team for such independent works can effectively bypass all the traditional routes and hassles of distribution, making the content immediately accessible to anyone interested. The Dublin crew who created *Detained* call themselves "Zombies Don't Run Productions" (operating through the domain name www.zombiesdontrun.com). Their motto on the homepage defiantly proclaims, "We exist because running zombies don't."

Nostalgia may account for some of the lingering interest in slow zombies, as many filmmakers in their 30s or 40s reminisce about the movies that captivated their imaginations as high school or college students. Yet there is notable enthusiasm for classically conceived zombies from new filmmakers, too, including those of the Millennial Generation. This new generation of young filmmakers can provide greater insight into the relationship between history's least energetic monster and history's most energetic generation. On the whole, these efforts (like most low-budget zombie movies) are replete with self-conscious irony, while remaining lovingly loyal to all the traditions of earlier zombie movies: rampant gore, unsentimental cannibalism, and character dynamics drenched with cruel cynicism. They are often tongue-in-cheek, taking their cue from earlier zombie spoofs such as *My Boyfriend's Back* (1993) and more recent ones such as *Shaun of the Dead* (2004). The zombies in these movies remain, most notably, slow and uncomplicated.

A 2005 survey by the Kaiser Family Foundation found that Americans aged 8 to 18 spend an average of 6.21 hours/day using media, but squeeze in 8.33 hours/day of total media exposure (through overlap, presumably due to multitasking).[10] Up to a third of respondents reported simultaneously using another media "most of the time" when reading (28%), watching TV (24%), listening to music (33%), or using a computer (33%).[11] Donald Roberts, a professor of Communications at Stanford, is quoted in *Time* magazine as noting that Stanford students "can't go the few minutes between their 10 o'clock and 11 o'clock classes without talking on their cell phones. It seems to me that there's almost a discomfort with not being stimulated—a kind of 'I can't stand the silence.'"[12] The ability to multitask, localized in Brodmann's Area 10 of the anterior prefrontal cortex, is among the last areas of the brain to mature and one of the first to deteriorate with aging.[13] The inability to multitask, then, may contribute to the horror an old person—and a zombie—may hold for a young adult of today, whose social and conceptual landscape is defined by the ability to successfully navigate simultaneous stimulus and interaction.

Thus a zombie serves as the uncomplicated foil for the technology-surrounded protagonist in Kevin Strange's *Zombage!* (2005), a downloadable short produced by a Millennial filmmaker.[14] In the opening scene, a young woman breaks up with slacker anti-hero Tyler over the phone, while she sits in front of a computer screen, and while he has horror movies playing on the TV right next to his bed. For each of them, a screen is more present (both spatially and emotionally) than the other is. Tyler resumes his usual routine after that stressful phone call, playing a zombie video game on his X-Box for six straight hours until a mysterious zombie emerges from his basement and, following a chase scene, causes Tyler to be hit by a car. In the closing credits the filmmakers ask the viewer, "Why are you still watching this? Go check your myspace or something." This is a culture steeped in technology, never far away from a screen or from the digital world, yet still relishing the zombie's slowness and simplicity.

Another short piece by a Millennial filmmaker, the period piece *Unsettled* (2005) by University of Wisconsin student Sam Thompson, focuses rather on abstract historical power structures. In 1585, English settlers arrive at the forbidding sands of coastal North Carolina. Hearkening back to the starving times and the harsh circumstances of early settlers in the Americas, *Unsettled* implicitly raises questions of colonial and environmental exploitation. In this austere early landscape, the Bible-clutching colonial settlers are mysteriously turned by the land itself into zombies after they die, with something of the inexorable mystery with which human settlers turn into Martians in Ray Bradbury's 1949 story, "Dark They Were, and Golden Eyed." A zombie settler bites off a woman's fingers while she prays to God; another walks around with a Native American arrow sticking out of him. The muskets and crosses brought by the settlers are of no use. In the face of European settlers perceived as extreme, irrational, and invasive of a land they have no business in, the zombies—though slow and simple—are attuned to the moral integrity of the landscape in visiting their vengeance upon the new inhabitants. The unspoiled landscape of colonial America serves as an emblem of simpler times: the raw necessities of food, shelter, and safety are constant anxieties, and here there is no pastoral or Edenic sentimentality about the horrible imagery of the human animal alone in nature.

In many zombie movies, the gore is more prominent than the violence, and this is not an accidental feature of the genre. In an increasingly disembodied—virtual generation, the zombie is becoming increasingly biological. Few cinematic monsters (not even serial killers) so reliably offer the implicit promise of highly visceral scenes featuring dangling limbs, rotted flesh, open wounds, dripping fluids, and entrails spilling out. The zombies not only reveal human protagonists to be made of flesh, sinew, and bone by unraveling them unceremoniously, but wear in their own features the biological anatomy of the human animal. The zombie is a mass of tissues, limbs, and organs, loosely integrated under simple cognitive drives (such as eating human flesh), but largely falling apart.[15] The creature represents an unsentimental study of our underlying composition and of our base biological needs. Even more pointedly, in the cracked, leathered skin, sunken eyes, and limited mobility, the zombie is also a specter of old age. At the dawn of the third millennium life expectancy is increasing dramatically, while quality of life in the senior years is not necessarily keeping pace. The world of a senior citizen may be perceived as one of unfamiliar smells and mysterious assistance devices, and life is often perpetuated only through continuous medication and intervention. The thought of becoming increasingly dependent on others for even the simplest of daily activities, combined with the possibility of ongoing pain and discomfort (the pain of being *alive*), extended indefinitely with periodic medical advances, can provoke meditation on what the situation may be like in another forty or fifty years' time. This is the physical imagery suggested by the shambling zombie. Old age has never held such potential anxiety for a generation of young people. The aged become an increasingly visible and vocal sector of society, and one also increasing in relative proportion to the overall population (like the contagious zombie, they could be seen as "taking over").[16]

Furthermore, the perceptual and conceptual worlds of the aged—often narrowed to a small range of interests or activities—may appear frighteningly limited to fresh young minds. A zombie is like an aged person, and like an infant, in that it is limited to a small range of selfish needs and to the perceptual scene immediately around it. If this is threatening to a generation for which technological savvy and extended networking are often the currency of social acceptability, there is another sense in which it may also represent a welcome escapism. In a world in which increasing demands are placed on young people's time and attention, and in which the amount of information and stimulation available seems to increase exponentially, there may be an attractive simplicity to the zombie's diminished internal mechanisms. The zombie's mental world does not extend beyond what it can see or hear in its immediate vicinity. Barely sentient, it is reduced to a reptile brain. Its choices are simple. In Goldberg's *The Day They Came Back*, "kill the brain" remains the implacable mantra, as it is for many of these films and shorts. This apparently resonates with a generation finding their cerebral limits taxed with a continuous bombardment of stimulus.

In a generation accustomed to immediate response and instant gratification, the slow zombie's patience must represent something of a conundrum. Increasingly, students who find they can access many full-text articles through ProQuest are unlikely to order in a book from off-campus, or to bother with articles that must be acquired through Inter-Library Loan. Answers to almost any question (whether or not they are good answers) are available through Google or Wikipedia, and if anyone is talking about a scene on TV or from a movie, that can usually be found right away on Youtube. In this context, the original *Dawn of the Dead* makes an interesting contrast with the 2004 remake. In the 1979 version, a certain Hare Krishna zombie discovers the door at the end of a corridor leading to the protagonists' hideout suite of rooms in the zombie-infested mall. It takes almost eight minutes of screen time (with some half a dozen cuts back to this thread from the main action, to mark his progress) for the zombie to enter the door, shuffle up the stairs and down another corridor, and finally corner protagonist Fran (Gaylen Ross) before he is shot. Similarly, after SWAT team member Roger (Scott Reiniger) is bitten by a zombie, the contagion takes a long time to kill him, and his death scene is drawn out to some four minutes ("Peter . . . Don't do it [shoot me] till you're sure I am coming back. I'm gonna try not to . . . I'm gonna try not to come back . . . I'm gonna *try* . . . *not* to . . . "). Peter (Ken Foree) sits and watches over him with a bottle of whiskey and a gun, until at last Roger rises slowly, a zombie. This suspense is typical of that film, and of pre-1980s zombie movies in general. On the other hand, upon the death of sympathetic truck driver Norma (Jayne Eastwood) in the 2004 *Dawn of the Dead*, protagonist Ana (Sarah Polley) asserts that she died of gunshot wounds and must not have been bitten by a zombie: if she had, she would have risen again by now. This, however, is only within twelve seconds or so of the character's death. This script presumes instant turn-around, catering to an audience accustomed to immediate results. There is no counterpart in the 2004 remake to the Hare Krishna zombie's protracted expedition; that would presumably not work as well for a contemporary audience.

Zombies in the early decades were inscrutable, unpredictable. It was the outward appearance of a human, combined with a complete opacity of thoughts or intentions within, that made the screen zombie a chilling figure. In *White Zombie* (1932) and other early movies, a zombie was as likely to walk right past a character as do anything else, in pursuit of some dark errand for the voodoo master. Recent zombies have become much more outwardly violent and animalistic, and this has also made them more predictable. The characters know what the zombies want (usually human flesh or, in some instances, brains), and so know exactly how to respond and to prepare. This can provide a comfort level, arguably, for zombie audiences in an age of random, chaotic violence. It also contrasts with willful, intelligent cinematic villains such as Freddie Krueger or Hannibal Lecter, who may have some predictable motives but who delight in cat-and-mouse games with potential victims. Millennials have grown up in a world in which violence is often spontaneous and inexplicable, and—in an age of instant news and global connectedness—one in which even geographically distant violence can seem close. The case of Finnish student Pekka-Eric Auvinen and American teenager Dillon Cossey, for instance, is instructive. The two chatted online about the Columbine massacre, before Auvinen went on a school shooting spree in November of 2007. Cossey was then arrested for plotting a similar copycat massacre at his own school. Clearly, geographic boundaries are dissolving as protective bulwarks.

Young people have a different relationship with public violence than in past generations. Whereas there may have been nuclear strike preparation drills in schools in the 1960s, the sources of potential danger were geopolitical forces that seemed impossibly remote. Those impersonal and distant dangers are still as real as ever, following 9/11, but rather than a single, obliterating strike, the danger now is of dirty nuclear weapons, chemical poisons, or biohazard attacks, that could be localized anywhere, and that would most likely manifest slowly and hideously. There is the added danger of homegrown terrorism, too. Following the Oklahoma City bombing in 1995, and the Columbine and Santee school shootings in 1999 and 2001, young people may now perceive terrorism as arising not only from distant regions, but from suburban schools, and perpetrated by disaffected youths that do not look or sound remarkably different from them. Often equipped with metal detectors, surveillance cameras, and highly vigilant faculty and staff, schools now resemble the defensive compounds that play such a large role in many zombie movies. The zombie as outwardly human and familiar—but completely alien within, and capable of immediate, unanticipated aggression—may well resonate with millennial youths.[17]

Here then is the paradox: a highly stimulated, technologically saturated, and fast- paced generation has fixated on a monster known especially for its slowness, its unidimensionality of thought and action, its simplicity of character, and its inability to use even the least technologically sophisticated of tools. It seems to me that zombies must both attract and repulse such a contemporary audience, in the way the creature reflects core notions of identity. The zombie suggests a simpler, freer, and more biologically attuned psyche—one so reduced to primal evolutionary urges that it is uninterested even in sex, hearkening back to primordial eras of protists and worms. For the zombie, choices are easy and the world is uncomplicated. For a potential victim, out-lashes of violence are countered (whether successfully or not) through manageable steps that the individual can take, using items easy at hand, without the need for organized institutional response or for complicated bureaucratic diplomacy. The slow, dumb zombie—visible and eminently predictable—appeals to a generation with enough real monsters to worry about whose motives and methods are constantly changing. This part is fantasy, not horror: there is comfort in the zombie's relative incompetence. However, for a generation increasingly reliant on technological savvy and sophistication in their day-to-day lives, there is horror as well in this same incompetence, in this exaggerated luddite regressivisim. It will be interesting to see, in another twenty years' time, how the current generation reminisces back nostalgically on the current zombie conceptualization when some of them become professional filmmakers, and how the generation of young moviegoers at that time responds.

CHAPTER 12

"Off the page and into your brains!": New Millennium Zombies and the Scourge of Hopeful Apocalypses

Margo Collins and Elson Bond

> You run because zombies are slow but inevitable, and also because they're right. There are worse things than life, and zombies are better with everything.
>
> HANNAH WOLF BOWEN

The pop-culture zombie has evolved. The archetypal zombies in George Romero's zombie films, for example, were generally considered revenants of conspicuous consumption, and late-twentieth-century depictions of zombies illustrate spreading anxiety over both social atomization and the loss of individual identity. The millennial zombie, however, makes guest appearances in classic novels, is regularly "blogged" about, and even lends a dismembered hand by participating in events like "zombie walks" for charity. Much like Count Chocula or perhaps (depending on one's point of view) the Twilight series has attempted to make the vampire ridiculous and, thus, no longer scary, new millennium zombie-ism demonstrates an apparent divergence into what initially appears to be two distinct categories: zombie-as-comedy and zombie-as-threat. But as we argue in this chapter, time and again these two categories overlap, and, ultimately, depictions of both kinds of zombies come to function as monstrous placeholders for potentially dangerous human interactions in an anomic society. Accustomed to instant communication with virtual strangers, insulated from the natural world and dependent on fragile transportation, communication, and power networks, millennial audiences have good reason to fear the chaotic anonymity of zombies. In many of the examples considered here, this threat from the reanimated dead has supplanted individual conscience and volition with a collective but (usually) uncalculating malice. In a significant shift from earlier depictions, zombies are now more often presented as beings from which we recoil utterly, rather than as blighted humans in whom we are intended to recognize grotesque reflections of ourselves. The new millennium zombie described here often challenges audiences to become more fully "human": more reflective, and simultaneously more cooperative and more self-reliant. In posing this humanizing challenge as one that humanity successfully meets, many new millennium zombie stories adopt a more hopeful and less misanthropic tone than their sometimes nihilist predecessors.

Max Brooks's 2006 postapocalyptic novel *World War Z* focuses on the discovery of a common, even improved, humanity against the potentially annihilating threat of the undead. Brooks subtitled *World War Z* "An Oral History of the Zombie War." He acknowledges the expected debt to George Romero, but also more tellingly, and perhaps surprisingly, the inspiration he drew from populist historian Studs Terkel, particularly to Terkel's 1984 World War II history *The Good War*, which chronicles the conflict from personal accounts. Brooks creates his own collection of these survivors' memoirs of what is variously known as "The Crisis," "The Dark Years," "The Walking Plague," "World War Z," or "Z War One." Ten years after the worldwide zombie war, Brooks's narrator, who works for the United Nations, has salvaged and compiled oral histories omitted from the final draft of the large-scale, emotionally detached accounting of the official United Nations Postwar Commission Report. The audience, as readers of only the "oral history" and not the report itself, read about the decade-long war through a global mosaic of voices that recount more than twenty years of worldwide devastation and partial reconstruction. This history assumes readers' familiarity with the larger outlines of the war, whose course the interviews trace chronologically. Brooks sets his collection in a world that has "been at peace about as long as we were at war."[1] Unlike the bleak endings of many of its predecessors, ultimate human victory is never in doubt here. Even as the novel gleefully parodies some of the greed and cowardice that aided the plague's spread, human ingenuity and resiliency have triumphed, though pockets of infected territory, known as "White Zones," remain.

In the new post-plague world order, practical survival skills eclipse the more rarefied expertise associated with a sophisticated but highly fragile information-based society found in developed nations before the war. Unlike more nihilistic zombie stories, however, the zombie apocalypse depicted in Brooks's novel ends much more hopefully—the world as the survivors had known it has ended, but the zombies have not won. The hardened survivors are instead reclaiming their countries—and telling their stories in their own voices. The book cannot quite be described as a series of "recollections in tranquility," but even in the most harrowing reminiscences, the narrator has survived. In this collection of individuals' oral history, the more enduring reanimation is not of the world's dead, but of its living. As humanity regroups to fight, the better angels of our natures, brought into stark relief against the relentless, unthinking zombies, tend to assert themselves, making for a curiously hopeful story set against what most of us would see as a background of catastrophe. In defensible enclaves, survivors early in the war share housing, organize armed patrols against looting and zombie infiltration, and raise their own livestock and crops. These sanctuaries are not Fiddler's Green.[2]

Though it ends far more happily than Romero's films or most of their descendants, Brooks nonetheless seizes the writer's generic apocalyptic opportunity to offer implicit social criticism of a range of topics. Unlike Romero, whose largely pessimistic social commentary tended to linger on American failings, Brooks's accounting acknowledges distinctive American virtues and praises a reborn country whose leadership changed the war from a defensive series of rearguard actions to a united global offensive. *World War Z*'s scope allows a broader range than Romero's more local focus. The first account recorded in the book comes from an interview with an elderly Chinese doctor, Kwang Jing-shu. The first victim Kwang saw had been diving illegally with his father at the site of their ancestral village, Dachang, now being flooded by the rising water impounded by the Three Gorges Dam on the Yangtze River. The first zombie Brooks shows us, a twelve-year-old boy, has lost his right big toe, but neither this wound nor the others on his body bleed. Dr. Kwang recalls his examination of the bound-and-gagged child:

> At first the villagers tried to hold me back. They warned me not to touch him, that he was "cursed." I shrugged them off and reached for my mask and gloves. The boy's skin was as cold and gray as the cement on which he lay. I could find neither his heartbeat nor his pulse. His eyes were wild, wide and sunken back in their sockets. They remained locked on me like a predatory beast. Throughout the examination he was inexplicably hostile, reaching for me with his bound hands and snapping at me through his gag.[3]

Through the testimony of an old woman at this relocated village, Brooks offers almost the only hint of the plague's origins. The old woman blames the disease on the destruction of Fengdu, the City of Ghosts, "whose temples and shrines were dedicated to the underworld."[4] Despite this passing reference to supernatural explanations, Brooks premises this plague as an entirely biological, if mysterious, epidemic. But *World War Z* never explicitly describes the plague's etiology, beyond identifying it as a virus spread solely through bodily fluids. In Brooks's prior work, *The Zombie Survival Guide*, in contrast, he takes pains to distinguish viral zombieism from voodoo or other varieties, even naming its virus, Solanum.[5]

Direct human-to-human contact has been revitalized for most of the individual survivors in *World War Z*, yet those nations that have best survived the war and prospered most afterward often shared a besieged history. As with many individual survivors, outside existential threats fostered strong identities founded on preparing to resist invasion or internal rebellion. The successful responses of three of these nations, postapartheid South Africa, Cuba, and Israel, to the spread of the plague warrant particular consideration. In all three instances, racial, political, and religious divides that had separated the nation's peoples are forgotten. Indeed, Cuba, initially protected from infestation by its relative isolation and military preparedness, ultimately emerges as what one Cuban survivor describes as the "winner" of the zombie war; both non-Cuban American refugees and ethnic Cubans from the North American mainland slowly transform Castro's prison island into a capitalist showplace and rallying point for the effort to reclaim the mainland. Brooks's narrator, a native-born Cuban, savors the irony of formerly communist Cuba's transformation into the "Arsenal of Victory." This narrator even playfully analogizes Cuba's metamorphosis into a capitalist democracy as infectious: "You couldn't see this infection at first, not when we were still under siege. It was still behind closed doors, still spoken in whispers. Over the next several years what occurred was not so much a revolution as an evolution, an economic reform here, a privately owned newspaper there. People began to think more boldly, talk more boldly. Slowly, quietly, the seeds began to take root."[6] Zombies, and apocalyptic fiction generally, can function as jeremiad, a warning to its audience to repent and reform. In this sense, the new millennium zombies share a similar role with their shambling predecessors as social critiques. But rather than ending with a nearly extinct humanity, these newer zombie apocalypses depict a regeneration following the plague's scourging.

Though often prematurely aged and scarred after a decade of war, Brooks's survivors have become, in a sense, more fully human. Technologies whose prewar use had fostered a superficially connected, but essentially anomic, society, now conduct information essential toward rebuilding those aspects of the prewar world that seem worth reclaiming. In an especially compelling interview with Kondo Tatsumi, a Japanese survivor, the narrator contrasts Tatsumi's testimony with a before-and-after description: "The old photo of Kondo Tatsumi shows a skinny, acne-faced teenager with dull red eyes and bleached blond highlights streaking his unkempt hair. The man I am speaking to has no hair at all. Clean-shaved, tanned, and toned, his clear, sharp gaze never leaves mine. Although his manner is cordial and his mood light, this warrior monk retains the composure of a predatory animal at rest."[7] Prewar, Tatsumi had been an "otaku," an outsider, who enjoyed closer exchanges in cyberspace than with his own parents, to whom he never speaks and whose absence he notes only after his mother fails to leave his dinner outside his room. Alienated from his family and nation, Tatsumi's most immediate benchmarks of the zombies' advance come from the dwindling number of e-mail replies from other otaku exchanging facts on the government's evacuation plans. Now, however, as a warrior monk, he is the epitome of the postwar survivor.

In a new struggle that has almost no racial component, the postapartheid South African government adapts the so-called Redeker Plan from the apartheid era of the 1980s to address the zombie plague. This fictional plan, originally designed to counter a large-scale black uprising against the minority white government, proposed a retreat from much of South Africa's territory into much smaller, defensible, self-sustaining bastions from which counterattacks could be organized. The abandoned outposts of the old government would then draw attacking forces away from the core defensive zones and could serve later as stepping-stones toward reconquest. Most nations that survived in any recognizable form adopted some version of the Redeker Plan's strategic withdrawal into heavily defended quarantine zones. Israel's rigorous prewar security measures and its broad base of military veterans enable the small country to resist the plague. In fact, Israel even welcomes "home" uninfected Palestinians to defend the country.

Those nations that lacked the military preparedness or armed populations necessary for an effective defense, such as Iceland or Japan, essentially cease to exist, becoming completely overrun, though in Japan's case the Korean peninsula and Russian Kamchatka provide a refuge for many citizens. Ultimately, however, those societies that are both authoritarian and have porous borders, notably mainland China, fare almost as badly because they restrict the free flow of information needed to resist the undead, while their lax security simultaneously allows the plague to spread.

In contrast, some authoritarian and closed states with more secure boundaries, such as Cuba, survive comparatively unscathed because they successfully contain the plague's spread.

Brooks's fictional version of the United States prevails under the leadership of a president who might be identifiable as Colin Powell, and with a vice president, fondly referred to as the "Whacko," clearly modeled on the former Vermont governor and Democratic presidential hopeful Howard Dean. In another bipartisan touch, a fictional version of Rudy Giuliani has served as U.S. attorney general. As ravaged as the United States has been, reduced largely to a rump state west of the Rocky Mountains, the country restores its territorial boundaries while slowly redeeming itself from social traits, such as self-absorption, excessive materialism, and a dangerous faith in advanced technology as a panacea, that had left the nation initially ill-prepared to resist the zombie menace.

Brooks describes himself as a "fanatical patriot"[8] though his novel's patriotism remains clear-eyed in acknowledging national shortcomings and never descends to simple jingoism. Congruent with his debt to the populist historian Studs Terkel, Brooks's own politics in *World War Z* seem close to those of a New Deal Democrat. In the book's penultimate chapter, called "Total War," Brooks presents a theatrical turning point in the conflict; aboard the recommissioned aircraft carrier the USS *Saratoga*, off the Chilean coast and now serving as a temporary UN headquarters, a Chilean diplomat recalls the American ambassador's rallying cry that "the United States intended to go permanently on the offensive . . . 'until every trace [of infection] was sponged, and purged, and, if need be, blasted from the surface of the Earth.'"[9] This cinematic moment somewhat disrupts the more matter-of-fact recollections that make up the bulk of *World War Z*.

Responding to an interviewer's question about whether he worried about possibly offending non-American readers in presenting the United States as instrumental in humanity's victory, Brooks replied, "Some people might question the 'heroic' stance of the American approach to the zombie war. That is not chauvinism, that's simply how my people are. We're still a young country, and we have very 'young' ideals. We can be naïve, ignorant, and as arrogant as any adolescent who thinks he has the power to change the world, but we're an 'artificial country' founded on the highest ideals. I'm proud of those ideas and that we aren't afraid to stand up for them."[10] In contrast to Brooks's more idealistic statement above, most of *World War Z*'s fictional interviewees recount their—and their nations'—more quotidian efforts to negotiate a viable path between the ephemerally interconnected, technologically dependent prewar status quo and the isolated, Hobbesian existence that most of the world endures, at least for a time, after the war. Brooks sets his frame story, a postwar set of recollections, at a point in which the surviving humans have drawn closer together in more cooperatively providing for their own food, shelter, and defense. The degree of professional specialization, and sometimes isolation and alienation, allowed by the prewar world has been replaced. Through air travel, porous borders, illegal commerce in organs, and ordinary global trade, the world as it was allowed the plague to spread quickly. As one online reviewer noted, "Mr. Brooks is not one for political correctness, and, if he's not a conservative politically, the results of the war remind one of Irving Kristol's famous observation (perhaps apocryphal?) that: There's nothing wrong with America that another Great Depression wouldn't fix."[11]

Not surprisingly, given Brooks's inspiration from Terkel's World War II history, highly advanced technology occupies an ambivalent place in the survivors' narratives. Though the Internet disappears, an Australian astronaut on an international space station helps maintain a satellite network that permits global communication. The inhuman nature of the zombies themselves, whom Brooks describes as shambling "guided missile[s]," stymies initial efforts to defeat them through characteristically American high-tech military solutions. One interviewee, Todd Wainio, has survived the Battle of Yonkers, a disastrous early set-piece battle planned largely for its public relations value. He analyzes the failure of U.S. military firepower at the battle:

> What did we call the first round of Gulf War Two, "Shock and Awe"? Perfect name, "Shock and Awe"! But what if the enemy can't be shocked and awed? Not just won't, but biologically *can't*? That's what happened that day outside New York City, that's the failure that almost lost the whole damn war. The fact that we couldn't shock and awe Zack boomeranged right back in our faces and actually allowed Zack to shock and awe us! They're not afraid! No matter what we do, no matter how many we kill, they will never, ever be afraid![12]

In the rethinking of military strategy after the Yonkers debacle and in light of the country's severely limited fuel and manufacturing capacity, most of the U.S. Air Force, excepting prop-powered cargo planes, is grounded. Much of the fighting against "Zack," the "Gs," or the "G-heads" eventually takes on a decidedly old-fashioned ethos. Armies move at marching pace carrying simplified rifles. They fight the slow "charges" of their undead foes with unhurried, relentlessly regular head shots, training with the aid of metronomes to hit a moving bulls-eye at the rate of one shot per second. When surrounded, their units form reinforced squares, as done in the pre–World War I British Army. Most iconic of this low-tech warfare is an improvised handheld weapon made from a heavy steel shaft "ending in what looks like a fusion of shovel and double-bladed battle-axe."[13] These weapons, invented by the U.S. Marines and recycled from junked cars, are called "lobos" after their anti-zombie use as "lobotomizers."[14]

As the survivors' accounts shift toward the humans' still-incomplete victory, the narrator's journalistic tone contrasts vividly with their retelling of the frantic days that the survivors call the Great Panic. Even here, however, Brooks maintains an almost absolute separation between humanity, no matter how degraded, and humanity's reanimated corpses. The "quislings," humans who have buckled under the zombie onslaught and attempted to act the part of zombies, are devoured as readily as those who resist.[15] To the extent that the war's trauma prompts a re-evaluation of humanness, that revision arises from the living's fight against the dead rather than any identification with the zombies. To identify with the zombies rather than to contain and destroy them proves fruitless.

The eventually pragmatic American response to the zombie plague recalls Brooks's description of the Romans' attitudes toward the reanimated dead in his 2003 work *The Zombie Survival Guide*. The phlegmatic Roman chronicler, writing in A.D. 177, adopts an attitude that Brooks aptly describes as one of "no fear, no superstition, just another problem requiring a practical solution."[16] Brooks maintains a mock-serious tone throughout *The Zombie Survival Guide*; even the ostensibly more serious *World War Z*, despite its often-unsettling scenes, ultimately offers a basically hopeful worldview—one that departs from the utter destruction prevalent in many earlier zombie depictions. What might have appeared to be zombie-as-threat turned out to be not much threat at all. In Brooks's postapocalyptic world, humanity has ultimately prevailed and, in a Nietzschean twist, is all the stronger for it.

Given that zombies are more commonly associated with destruction—individual if not complete apocalypse—it is positively incongruous to see zombies represented as comedy, and yet the millennial zombie is quite often, well, funny. This begs the question: Why are funny zombies funny? On one level, of course, it's simply the juxtaposition of unexpected elements—as in, say, cheerfully cute kittens cast as zombies on LOLcats.com, an "I saw Mommy eating Santa Claus" Christmas card, or even *Pride and*

Prejudice and Zombies, "The Classic Regency Romance—Now with Ultra-violent Zombie Mayhem!," which billed itself as "the original text of Jane Austen's beloved novel with all-new scenes of bone-crunching zombie action." As this new edition illustrates, one strain of zombie-as-comedy can be found in the human response to the walking undead—though admittedly more of these are presented as how-to guides rather than retellings of great literature. Max Brooks's *Zombie Survival Handbook*, for example, discusses, in absolutely serious language, the best ways to take up arms against a zombie uprising, offering advice on everything from how to modify a house, to which weapons to use, to how to move from one location to another. Ultimately, the guide advocates constant vigilance, as in this section on how to move a group of survivors from one location to another: "Watch for any movement. Don't ignore shadows or distant humanoid forms. During breaks and while on the march, pause to listen to your surroundings. Do you hear footsteps or scraping sounds? Are the undead moaning, or is it just the wind? Of course, it is easy to become paranoid, to believe zombies are around every corner. Is that bad? In this instance, no. It's one thing to believe everyone's out to get you, quite another when it's actually true."[17] The mock-serious, tongue-in-cheek tone of self-help zombie guides pushes the millennial zombie away from social metaphor and into full-on social allegory; zombies are the ultimate in politically correct fall guys because they are unlikely to bring defamation suits against you. As such, this new millennial zombie provides alternate access to allegorically consider historically charged events and ideas.

In his new graphic novel, *The Zombie Survival Guide: Recorded Attacks* (2009), Brooks offers alternate-history zombie scenarios, such as Hadrian's Wall being built to prevent another attack against the Romans by the ravening zombie horde that came from the north of Britain. Again, the narrative and visual style is intensely serious—black-and-white images of flesh-eating undead create a stark vision of a past abounding with zombie attacks. In their earliest incarnations, the sheer mindless inexorability of zombies, along with the truly horrific idea that anyone could become the walking undead and turn on you, added to their horror. As James Gunn, a screenwriter for the 2004 remake of *Dawn of the Dead*, notes, "Zombie movies are horrific on every level—they bring up the fear of the paranoid (having the ones you love turn up against you), they bring up our fears of carnivores . . . and they bring up our fear of disease. . . . We're hardwired evolutionarily to be scared green of zombies."[18] Peter Dendle, elsewhere in this collection, has also suggested that the fear generated by the inexorable, albeit slow, approach of the zombie appeals to a new generation of millennials whose identities are compromised by dependence on instantaneous technology.[19] Treating the zombie threat with intense seriousness is both a cathartic outlet for anxiety *and* a method for dissemination of emergency response plans.

The website ZombieDefense.org—which bills itself as "the only zombie defense organization poised to buffer humanity from the impending zombie holocaust"—takes Brooks's tongue-in-cheek training guide a few steps further, offering more detailed information for the zombie-fighting do-it-yourselfer, on everything from important post-apocalyptic terminology (like "meatsnack" for someone who can't escape being eaten, "breather" for a non-zombie, or "zombulation" for the total zombie population in a given area) to tactical considerations, such as survival gear for the "necropalypse." The site rates a wide range of potential everyday weapons—such as, say, the relative merits of toilet lids versus toilet seats, chain saws, and even the actor Michael J. Fox (after all, you have to be prepared to use anything in your potential arsenal against the walking undead). With tongue in cheek, ZombieDefense.org also touts the power of Gold Bond Triple-Action Medicated Body Powder to "ultimately result in the creation of new governments to facilitate the renewed manufacture and fair distribution of" Gold Bond and "spur the creation of a new and phoenix-like utopian world from the decaying gore of the old. Provided we're not all totally 'meatsnacked' first."[20] The site's practical advice, set against an absurd threat, echoes the tone of Brooks's first *Survival Guide*. Thus the website offers at least a faint hope for postapocalyptic society—comprising those who prepared in advance against the impending zombie doom—that responds to the needs of its inhabitants, rather than a grim vision of an undifferentiated "zombulation" craving nothing but the brains of those who were unprepared: the meatsnacked.

These self-help zombie defense books and websites have, in turn, led to groups that take themselves perhaps a tad more seriously than one might expect. In organizations such as the St. Louis–based survivalist Zombie Squad, whose motto is "we make dead things deader,"[21] the familiar tropes of a possible zombie apocalypse are used to promote exactly the kind of self-reliance and community spirit that the survivors in *World War Z* demonstrated. As the "who we are" portion of the website proudly announces:

> When the zombie removal business is slow we focus our efforts towards educating ourselves and our community about the importance of disaster preparation. To satisfy this goal we host disaster relief charity fundraisers,

disaster preparation seminars and volunteer our time towards emergency response agencies. Our goal is to educate the public about the importance of personal preparedness and self reliance, to increase its readiness to respond to disasters such as Earthquakes, Floods, Terrorism or Zombie Outbreaks. We want to make sure you are prepared for any crisis situation that might come along in your daily life which may include having your face eaten by the formerly deceased.[22]

For groups like Zombie Squad, planning for the inevitable zombie apocalypse prepares them for any possible disaster, and that community-minded preparedness is no laughing matter. This idea has taken root in the popular imagination, so much so that even Facebook status updates discuss zombie-attack preparedness: "The march has traffic blocked from the mall, essentially cutting off my major escape routes. Oh D.C., how I love you so. If this were a zombie apocalypse emergency preparedness exercise, I'd get a big fail."[23] Computer hackers have also taken advantage of the populist conflation of emergency instruction and undead comedy, hacking into electronic billboards and roadside signs to warn of "zombies ahead!"[24] In all of these examples, much of the comedy comes from the juxtaposition of the horrific and the mundane: the more mundane, the funnier.[25]

Seth Grahame-Smith's comic novel *Pride and Prejudice and Zombies* offers a similarly hopeful vision of a world that incorporates the undead. By the time of the *Pride and Prejudice and Zombies*' Regency setting, Grahame-Smith's version of a zombie plague has now afflicted England for fifty-five years. The English gentry of this mash-up adaptation of Austen's novel accept the zombies as a ubiquitous affliction, but the "unmentionables" can hardly constitute a crisis two generations and several kings after their first appearance. The zombies must be dealt with, of course, but their constant presence has drained the humans of any sense of apocalyptic urgency. So thoroughly mundane have the dead become that martial arts skill has become a hallmark of the "accomplished" young lady. As Mr. Bennett observes to his foolish wife, "I would much prefer their minds be engaged in the deadly arts than clouded with dreams of marriage and fortune, as your own so clearly is! Go and see this Bingley if you must, though I warn you that none of our girls has much to recommend them; they are silly and ignorant like their mother, the exception being Lizzy, who has something more of the killer instinct than her sisters."[26] Fitzwilliam Darcy similarly maintains that "a woman must have a thorough knowledge of music, singing, drawing, dancing, and the modern languages; she must be well trained in the fighting styles of the Kyoto master and the modern tactics and weaponry of Europe."[27]

A television comedy writer, Grahame-Smith maintains a comically underplayed response to the walking dead from his characters, free of any heavy-handed social commentary that specifically addresses zombies as sui generis menace. If there is an apocalypse here, it merely shambles forward without the transformative power that marks Max Brooks's *World War Z* or Kim Paffenroth's *Dying to Live*. As in the historical sense of "comedy," Grahame-Smith's additions to *Pride and Prejudice* retain its essentially conservative nature; the social order, to the extent that it exists after decades of zombie outbreaks, is largely preserved. The right people still marry each other, mostly. So thoroughly inured have these characters become to zombies that even searching for a medical cure to the plague is dismissed as a fool's errand, akin to alchemy. Grahame-Smith adeptly plays on the nonchalance of Austen's fictional world: "That was what was so funny to me about this idea, is the fact that these people in Austen's books are kind of like zombies. They live in this bubble of extreme wealth and privilege, and they're so preoccupied with the little trivial nothings of their lives—who's dating who, who's throwing this ball, or having this dinner party. As long as there's enough lamb for the dinner table, they could care less what's falling apart around them."[28] The untidy interruptions of zombie attacks have been successfully managed for generations by the novel's setting and their menace has been smoothly integrated into the social routine. Well-heeled young men and women travel to China and Japan to study Asian martial arts, London has been fortified with a wall, and even the Bennetts' comparatively modest wealth allows them to keep a well-equipped dojo for their daughters' training.

Pride and Prejudice and Zombies keeps most of Austen's original text, inserting lively scenes of zombie combat as comic counterpoints to the novel's stately progress. The famous Netherfield ball scene, where the Bennett women embarrass themselves socially, ends now with Darcy dispatching two "unmentionables" who have attacked Netherfield's staff: "Two adult unmentionables—both of them male—busied themselves feasting on the flesh of the household staff. How two zombies could have killed a dozen servants, four maids, two cooks, and a steward was beyond Elizabeth's comprehension."[29] Grahame-Smith clearly models his revision of *Pride and Prejudice* on the ubiquitous Penguin edition. The book's cover art parodies its cover illustration of William Beechey's portrait of Marcia

Fox, substituting red eyes, fleshless jaws exposing teeth, and a bloodstained empire-waist dress for the serenity of the original. Grahame-Smith's edition even includes a tongue-in-cheek "Reader's Discussion Guide." Included among the guide's discussion questions are some of the novel's funniest lines, including the following: "Some scholars believe that the zombies were a last minute addition to the novel, requested by the publisher in a shameless attempt to boost sales. Others argue that the hordes of living dead are integral to Jane Austen's plot and social commentary. What do you think? Can you imagine what this novel might be like without the violent zombie mayhem?"[30]

Surprisingly, Charlotte Lucas's coolly calculated decision to marry the pompous and foolish clergyman William Collins after her friend Elizabeth Bennett has rejected Collins's proposal actually gains a new measure of poignancy in this mash-up edition. Charlotte Lucas contracts the zombie plague shortly before her wedding, but she manages to conceal her deteriorating health from her obtuse fiancé. Months later, Elizabeth notes that her "friend's skin was now quite gray and marked with sores, and her speech appallingly labored. That none of the others noticed this, Elizabeth attributed to their stupidity—particularly Mr. Collins, who apparently had no idea that his wife was three-quarters dead."[31] Charlotte Lucas's slow decline into zombie-dom parallels her unhappy, though uninfected, marriage in Austen's novel. Overall, the zombies in Austen's reimagined world remain contained: a nuisance to be dealt with rather than a frightening menace.

Not all recent zombie stories are so hopeful, of course. *Undead*, a movie written and directed by Michael and Peter Spierig, begins like many zombie movies: a meteorite shower over a small Australian fishing village unleashes a virus/bacteria/something that turns all the town's inhabitants into flesh-eating zombies. Enter the small-town beauty queen Renee (Felicity Mason). She, along with a few other survivors—the pregnant beauty-queen wannabe Sallyanne ("I might not look so great in a bathing suit right now, but that crown was mine!"); Sallyanne's partner, Wayne; two impotent cops; and the crazy fisherman turned weapons expert Marion (played by Mungo McKay)—fight to survive in a world gone mad. And then the aliens land and start abducting everyone. The movie is replete with impromptu weapons, big blood splats, gratuitous violence, and naked aliens, all of which add to its comic element. Nevertheless, the movie's conclusion is fairly grim: Renee and the baby seem to be the only survivors, living in a fortified house surrounded by a zombie-repelling fence.

She has survived in part because of her now-dead companions, which is a typical ending to zombie movies. But before we are so quick to attribute her continued breathing to some ephemeral human quality, we should consider her former companions who were also human and now are dead. Regardless of whether the band of persevering, plucky humans (or the human population in general) in any one particular zombie tale ultimately triumphs, many explorations of zombies seem to suggest that this ability to come together, to use our minds and our wits, is what separates us from zombies and gives us the slightest hope of saving the world—or at least ourselves—from the ravenous hordes of mindless flesh eaters. That is, you are smart, prepared, and able to work within a group, or you are a meatsnack.

In his book *Zombie CSU: The Forensics of the Living Dead*, Jonathan Maberry asserts that in the case of a real zombie epidemic, human survival would be aided—indeed, virtually guaranteed—by the emergency protocols already in place. To prove his theory, he posits a "patient zero" zombie attack and traces the emergency services responses to quell such an outbreak. In *Zombie CSU*, the inexorable zombie attack is met by the implacable police adherence to protocol and form, which lead to containment.[32]

Thus the message seems to be that when individual differences have been elided by death, the only way to meet the threat becomes the elision of human individuality. That is, to protect human individuality, you have to suppress it temporarily, much as a soldier must sublimate his own desires and identity in favor of following orders, and all the zombie prep sites argue for the "common man's" ability to defend himself and others. But the problem is that the "common man" can just as easily become the "common zombie," and if individuality has been erased, it becomes increasingly difficult to distinguish the human from the zombie. Interestingly, as the humans in zombie stories—whether online, in books, or in film—become more uniform in thought and action, we're beginning to see some individuation of zombies. Leaving aside the discussion of whether they're really "zombies,"[33] in the 2007 version of *I Am Legend* starring Will Smith, for example, Smith's character, Dr. Robert Neville, claims that the monsters surrounding him can't think. Yet one creature—listed in the credits as the "Alpha Male"—clearly shows intelligence and reasoning when he works to trap Neville, and demonstrates a remarkable capacity for memory and feeling when he targets Neville in an effort to get his mate back. Romero's 2005 film *Land of the Dead* also gives a nod toward the idea of zombies who think, albeit simplistically, and in doing so pushes the audience to empathize with the undead rather than with the living, who are depicted as rapacious, unthinking, and untrustworthy.

In Kim Paffenroth's self-consciously philosophical novel *Dying to Live*, Jonah Caine, an English professor turned zombie killer, teams up with the ex-military man Jack and the half-zombie Milton in their fortified compound (formerly a museum) to ponder the issues of life, death, and undeath—and what it means to be human in a post-human world. The narrator begins by highlighting the distinction between the anonymous, unthinking zombies and the still-human prey who hide from them. He spends the night in an old tree house, noting that "the undead are by nature incurious and almost never look up."[34] Moreover, Paffenroth emphasizes the unthinking nature of not only zombies but also the zombie apocalypse in its entirety by offering a theory—or more precisely, a non-theory—of how the apocalypse happened in the first place. In one of his many long, thoughtful passages, Caine notes:

> The most popular theory—the one I personally advocated, though without much conviction—was simply that there had been a horrible accident. Nothing malevolent or calculated, just plain old human error. Somebody dropped a test tube somewhere. A lab monkey bit through somebody's glove. The kind of thing that happens a thousand times a day for thousands of days with no fatal outcome. It was the most blackly humorous theory, I suppose, for it made the misery and violent deaths of billions of people just the result of a stupid mistake, but it has its own cold comfort. If all this was just some blunder, then maybe, if we could ever shoot every zombie in the head . . . or if they would just eventually rot and fall apart . . . then we could go back to life like it used to be. We weren't evil, just stupid and clumsy.[35]

In the end, though, it is not martial ability or even the passage of time that saves the community Caine joins; it is Milton's status as half-zombie, half-human. Milton is described as being "somehow appropriate to our particular apocalypse." According to Caine, "The world had ended in such a mundane way, with your utterly ordinary neighbors attacking you and turning you into yet another member of a mindless, anonymous mob. So maybe it made a sort of sense that the new leader or prophet of the apocalypse would be an entirely regular-looking man."[36] But of course, as "regular" as Milton might look, he is still half-zombie—bitten by a zombie dog and left rotting away but still thinking and acting as a human.

Indeed, Milton the half-zombie is much more humane than the other humans Caine and his new friends meet. While retrieving a helicopter from a local hospital, they see a column of smoke on the horizon, alerting them to the possibility of other human survivors. Jack sets out to meet these other survivors, taking Caine and a few others with him (including a small but fiercely violent child). Unfortunately for them all, the survivors are the former inmates of a local prison and Caine's group is taken prisoner. Caine says that "months of dealing with only non-human monsters had made us soft and naïve. We had forgotten about the ugliness and brutality that humans could so gleefully perpetrate on anyone weaker than themselves, imagining that ours was the worst possible hell, when we should've remembered that it wasn't. Not even close."[37] The inmates alternately beat their new prisoners and sodomize the child, participating in a bloody orgy of violence. Thus the human survivors of the zombie apocalypse become more horrific than the mindless horde of brain eaters; because they can think, humans are potentially more horrific than their undead counterparts.

Milton, the half-zombie prophet, on the other hand, can "see the moments of virtue and grace amidst the horror,"[38] an ability that leaves him in the rare position of being able to counteract both the horrors perpetrated by the humans and the inherent horror of the undead. Granted, Paffenroth's treatment of the idea is a bit heavy-handed. When Milton comes to save Caine and the others from the inmates, Paffenroth writes that "the dead stopped, swaying and letting out a rumble of discontent or alarm. The lightening went through the crowd; a path opened up in it. The crowd parted and a tall, lean figure emerged."[39] The biblical parallels are clear, but just in case we miss the point, the hero's new girlfriend says Milton "looks like some damn zombie Jesus."[40] Despite the sometimes inelegant analogies, Paffenroth's novel hits on one of the prevailing tropes of the millennial zombie: the idea that humans and zombies have little to distinguish them from one another, and that only a savior that partakes of the nature of both the living and the undead can possibly save post-human humanity.

It's that interstitial place between zombie-humans and human-zombies that has opened up an opportunity for the thinking zombie that pervades the most recent comic depictions of the walking undead, pointing to a new social anxiety distinct from the consumerist concerns apparent in movies that trap their human protagonists in malls, previously devoted to conspicuous consumption and now fortified against zombie consumption. In the introduction to this collection, Sarah Juliet Lauro and Deborah Christie set forth that there are "three . . . recognizable stages of twentieth- and twenty-first-century zombie configurations: the classic mindless corpse, the relentless instinct-driven newly dead, and the millennial voracious and fast-moving predator." We would argue that the comic zombie resists these categories, which is exactly what makes him (or her) funny; he can be a slow-moving zombie who thinks. This kind of zombie comedy most often appears when individualism reasserts itself—sometimes on the part of the human fighters, but more commonly in the zombies themselves.

Ryan Mecum's book *Zombie Haiku*, for example, is funny precisely because it is the story of a poet becoming a zombie—but still writing poetry. The book is set up as a journal, written in by two different people. First there is the journal's original, anonymous owner, who begins by vowing to "attempt to capture the earthly beauty which can be so overwhelming that I sometimes feel like I'm going to burst open."[41] On the same page, in a distinct handwriting, the character Chris Lynch writes that he is the lone survivor of a zombie outbreak, trapped in an airport bathroom, having ripped the arm off the zombie who had been carrying this journal.

The poet's haiku begin generically enough: "Joy! Magic exists!/An old dream of mine came true/and I think it's love!," but quickly turn first prosaic—"Something on the news/about people acting odd/so I switch to sports"—then oddly macabre—"I start the engine/but it's really hard to steer/with Beth on my hood"—and finally gruesome—"I loved my momma/I eat her with my mouth closed/how she would want it," and "Blood is really warm/it's like drinking hot chocolate/but with more screaming." What works in this book is the juxtaposition of the thinking zombie poet and the horrific subjects of the poems themselves. Despite the disintegration of humanity, of the poet himself, the poems maintain their form perfectly; the poet may be falling apart, but his haiku do not: "My rigor mortis/is mainly why I'm slower./And the severed foot." And as the poet himself notes, "I keep saying 'brains.'/I remember other words/but I just need one."

At the end of the journal, Chris—the character trapped in the bathroom—finally succumbs to the zombie virus (the book alludes early on to the possibility that it is spread by mosquitoes) and requests that any future readers of the journal find his wife and "tell her I loved her and that I want to eat her and SWALLOW HER BRAINS!"[42] In the end, the named character Chris Lynch has been absorbed into the zombie horde, whereas the nameless poet zombie actually retains more individuality through his poetry. The convention of associating naming and identity has been overturned by means of the comic, thinking-zombie figure.

Elsewhere in this collection, Lauro and Christie claim that "zombies in performance art and public demonstrations elucidate a further type of zombie evolution: the spectator has become participant in, and even creator of, his own zombie stories."[43] But the comic zombie somewhat complicates this claim. Ultimately, modern zombie stories reflect our fear of loss of identity. To be a creator of one's own zombie story is to claim an autonomy that every single zombie story, comic or not, disallows. In her contribution to this collection, Lynn Pifer notes that in movies such as *Shaun of the Dead* and *Fido*, the zombies are "incorporated into the 'living' society rather than overrunning the living or being dispatched with a blow to the head." Similarly, in *Pride and Prejudice and Zombies*, killing the undead becomes part of the courtship ritual. In *Zombie Haiku* and countless zombie movies, the dead simply obliterate—replace—the living. And in *World War Z*, the living survivors function in precarious safety knowing that there are still zombies in the world that need to be eradicated. But in every single case, one group destroys the other. Any simple equation in which the anomic is horrific and community means survival is undermined by the fact that, in a post-zombie-apocalypse world, to belong to either the living or the undead is to suppress one's autonomy in order to survive.

CHAPTER 13

Playing Dead: Zombies Invade Performance Art . . . and Your Neighborhood

Sarah Juliet Lauro

I

No one ever gets caught, and no one ever gets eaten.
Jillian Mcdonald, on *Zombie Loop*

In the performance artist Jillian Mcdonald's video installation piece *Zombie Loop*, the viewer is positioned between two simultaneously running screens—one on which is projected the image of a lumbering, lunging zombie, and one on which we see the hapless victim, ceaselessly running, casting nervous glances over her shoulder.[1] The two figures are clearly treading the same rural roadside, and they are plainly played by the same person. In fact, both are Mcdonald herself, wearing the same cotton frock in each video; aside from the transformative makeup and stiff gait of the zombie, the figures are identical. Much could be said about this doubling of the character of zombie and victim, for what it illustrates is the crux of the zombie's ability to terrify: its emphasis on the uncanny process of "depersonalization," whereby someone previously known to the spectator becomes something strange, foreign.[2] As we will see, both Mcdonald's work and the phenomenon of live zombie performances directly emphasize the zombie's "odd familiarity," as the Toronto Zombie Walk's founder, Thea Munster, calls it, making the zombie a cultural signifier prime for exploitation in a manner not unlike the Situationist International's practices in the 1960s, which commandeered the quotidian "spectacle" of capitalist society for the purpose of its undermining and critique. Yet, as we will see, appropriate to the zombie's perpetual trope of distorted reflection, these zombie walks defy and challenge the Situationist agenda even as they seem to resemble or resurrect it, rendering it similar and yet different.

One of the ways that Mcdonald's work investigates the zombie as an embodiment of the uncanny is by illustrating the moment of transformation, but in *Zombie Loop* we find something different: That moment is both present and absent.

Mcdonald explains that the viewer's location between two walls on which the images are projected puts him or her simultaneously in the position of both zombie and victim. One is not able to see the two screens at the same time, and must turn to look either at the fleeing damsel, and thus find him- or herself in the zombie's place as pursuer, or at the zombie, and at that moment step into the role of prey. Of course, there is a third term, and one senses him- or herself as the spectator ensconced in an ongoing

FIGURE 1. The zombie of Mcdonald's *Zombie Loop*. (Photo by Aron Namenwirth, *Zombie Loop*. 2006, video installation at ArtMoving Projects, courtesy of the artist and ArtMoving Projects.)

FIGURE 2. The would-be victim of *Zombie Loop*. (Photo by Aron Namenwirth, *Zombie Loop*. 2006, video installation at ArtMoving Projects, courtesy of the artist and ArtMoving Projects.)

drama. In its structure, then, *Zombie Loop* explores the role of the viewer. Mcdonald is known for her exploration of fandom as a social and cultural category, and her recent attention to the horror film is just the latest iteration of this theme in her oeuvre. But in this piece the spectator is pushed away as much as embraced. The climax of the piece, the anticipated attack and subsequent transformation of the victim into a zombie, is continually deferred. Because the projected images are run on a continuous loop, "no one ever gets attacked, and no one ever gets eaten."[3] As such, the viewer may experience the work as a suspension of action. But because the zombie is plainly the same woman as the victim, there is also the sense that the spectator has been deprived of the pivotal moment of metamorphosis. And thus the piece is a Möbius-like "loop" not just in technical definition, but also as a description of the effect it has on the viewer, who may feel an alternation between relief and frustration, as well as a push and pull between his or her ambivalent positioning in the (non)event.

What this piece questions is what *kind* of catharsis the zombie fan seeks. As such, *Zombie Loop* provides a perfect introduction to the zombie found increasingly in performance art in galleries and in public places. Yet there is another reason that I lead into my discussion with this artwork: this chapter is a dialectical endeavor that presents a parallax perspective of the performed zombie. As in Mcdonald's piece, the two very different zombies that I am describing here (that which calls itself art, and that which does not) do not cross paths in a hierarchically structured narrative. That is, I am not going to assign either a place of privilege, but the hope is that the reader, positioned between the two, will be able to see the cross-contamination of these figures, at one and the same time very different and the same: strange, and yet familiar. To Jillian Mcdonald's various zombies—including photographic, filmed, and live performances—I juxtapose the work of Thea Faulds, aka Thea Munster, who has been credited with sparking a phenomenon that is now global: the organization of events in which large groups of people convene in a public place and communally perform as a zombie horde.[4]

Thea Munster organized the first Toronto Zombie Walk in October 2003, and since then we have seen a cultural trend that appears viral-like in its operations and transmission, an aspect that is fitting of the zombie's most recent metaphoric instantiation: in film, the zombie has been read increasingly as an allegory for contemporary fears of disease.[5] In San Francisco zombie "flash mob" performances, participants come dressed either as zombies or plainly, as victims. The victims wear a small strip of duct tape on their backs to signal to zombies that they are willing targets. Zombies will attack these bystanders and transform them with makeup; thereafter, they join the marauding horde.[6] Implicit in these gatherings is the presence of nonparticipating bystanders, who may be unaware of this signal system and perceive themselves to be potential victims as well. Thus these gatherings uphold the cinematic convention of the zombie as infectious and maintain the illusion that all spectators are equally vulnerable.

Mcdonald notes that part of her objective in putting zombies into art is to emphasize the "manufacturing of fear as entertainment that the horror film genre accomplishes."[7] Indeed, the zombie has become a cash cow for the entertainment industry, but what does it mean that the zombie has now seemed to transgress this last border, and, through a strange process of narrative collaboration, stepped into the real world? Is a fictional entity now colonizing our real cities? And what do we make of it that this performed zombie's cultural capital aspires to be entirely divorced from commercialism? Is this zombie evolution or zombie revolution?

I read the occurrence of these zombie gatherings as the latest incarnation of the zombie narrative's evolution and an interesting display of communal narrative making. These performances continue to emphasize the zombie as uncanny by inserting this mythic figure into the quotidian and dramatizing its colonization of public space in the real world. Further, the participant's willful rewriting of the everyday may intend to obstruct the functionalism of the modern city and its facilitation of the capitalist grind. The zombie DIYers who participate in such events emphasize this aspect by dressing in clothing that makes them immediately recognizable as someone who was formerly a harmless cog in the system. There are certain clichés to look for when attending a zombie event: the woman with her hair in curlers, the cheerleader, a plethora of brides (insert your own feminist critique), and various career types, such as the zombie businessperson, zombie nurse, zombie traffic cop, and zombie soldier.

However we read this phenomenon today, zombies first started walking the city streets as advertisements. The New York premiere of the 1930 film *White Zombie* orchestrated the publicity stunt of having people dress like zombies to advertise opening night.[8] This is still a popular tactic today: I saw zombies recently on street corners in London to advertise a tour called "The London Bridge Experience, featuring the Tombs," in Toronto, to advertise the annual zombie walk, in Times Square to hype the AMC zombie series *The Walking Dead*.[9] The odd zombie out of this group is the last one, Thea Munster, who on the day I met her was passing out flyers advertising the sixth annual Toronto Zombie Walk: unlike those hawking the series, the film, and the tour, the walk costs nothing and does not accept donations. It is affiliated with no charity, corporation, or organization, and insists on its own purposelessness. People get together, dress up like zombies, and walk through town. That's it. Or is it?

Throughout this volume we have been tracing the zombie's evolution, and this is one of its most critical transformations of the past few years: the zombie has seemed to leap off the page (or the screen) and shuffle into the city, becoming an extratextual monster communally constituted. Is this a new development for the zombie, or just a turn befitting a figure that hails from Haitian folklore, and which has its roots in communally made narratives? Perhaps this figure, which many in Haiti still believe exists, was never really confined to fiction.[10] My inquiry in this chapter will investigate whether these events are truly purposeless, or if there is a hidden agenda (or even an unintended outcome) that emerges as a result of the zombie's separation of itself from commercial entertainment. Since most zombie gatherings are clearly unmotivated by profit, what propels these zombies forward?[11] Is this art, anarchy, or something else?

I want to make it clear from the outset that I am not trying to represent the whole of the walking zombie movement. I have corresponded with many organizers of zombie events, including some who might even contest that *they* were the true founders of the movement. But this chapter takes Thea Munster, whose pseudonym dubs her both goddess and monster, as my designated representative of this larger phenomenon. By no means, either, do I want to claim that Jillian Mcdonald is the only artist inviting the zombie into the art gallery.[12] These two women represent, for me, the extremes of the movement, and they delimit the boundaries of a cultural phenomenon with a wide gray area. Between these poles we find many other zombies worthy of serious critical investigation, but I am interested here in what comes out of the stark juxtaposition of their very differently framed zombies—namely, a larger conversation about the origins, agenda, and function of performance and performance art.

II

I think it's performance art.
                Stranger on the New York subway, on Mcdonald's *Horror Makeup*

Better known for her work in which she splices her own image into movies so that she can be seen interacting (and even making out) with the stars of the silver screen, Jillian Mcdonald made her first artistic foray into the world of zombies by producing lenticular images that, depending on the viewer's position to the photograph, showed the transformation of a human figure into a grotesque zombie. The central narrative of these images is the zombie transformation. Posed against an ultraviolet sky, we see a smiling figure gradually become a zombie in both physical appearance and gesture.[13] Here, too, we see the artist's play with the role of the spectator: most of the zombies are looking at the camera, and many of their exaggerated grimaces acknowledge that camp is a central feature of the zombie genre. Putting the process of transformation on display defers some of the shock associated with the zombie—the encounter of the familiar within the strange—but Mcdonald's next zombie performance directly presented the unwitting spectator with the uncanny experience of witnessing that transformation.

In the work that would draw some major attention to Mcdonald's zombies, the artist performed zombie evolution in the public arena. In *Horror Makeup*, a woman gets on a subway with her makeup kit. Over the course of her ride, she transforms herself not into a professional woman ready for work—an everyday occurrence often witnessed during a morning commute—but into a hideous, decaying zombie. This film was displayed in Brooklyn, from September 8 to October 15, 2006, and the exhibition notes explain some of the issues that are piqued by this hair-raising display: "This work takes cues from the legion of women who perform beauty rituals on the subway in a curious private zone where they are unaware of anything outside their activity, and the rising cult of zombies in popular culture, where zombie gatherings and zombie lore flourish. Locating the audience physically in the subway performance space positions them as both voyeurs and potential victims." The piece self-consciously draws on one of the most fascinating features of the zombie myth, the interruption and confusion of private and public space.[14]

As the artist suggests, this conflation is very much a feature of the recent phenomenon of zombie gatherings, but it also speaks to that definitive element of the zombie, which some critics have claimed is the basis for all art—the boundary transgression between strange and familiar.[15] Mcdonald's was a zombie performance aside from the fact that it performed a woman's transformation *into* a zombie, because it presented the viewer, particularly the first-generation audience of unwitting subway spectators, with an unfamiliar element in a familiar setting. Of course, though the performance began with the non-zombie Mcdonald, the flow of spectators was uncontrolled, and people became involved at various points in her evolution, depending on when they entered the subway car. Because the overall narrative depicts the transformation of a stranger on a train into a zombie, the sense of the strange interrupting the everyday must come more from the unexpectedness of the encounter rather than from the confrontation of change in a person one knows. This is the form that the defamiliarizing of the zombie takes in performances like the zombie walk or the zombie flash mob, where a "mob" by definition is a depersonalizing force.[16]

Mcdonald's *Horror Makeup* performance was chronicled by a hidden camera and by a journalist for the *New York Times*, who wrote, "Only when she slipped in a pair of green teeth and began daubing her face with fake blood did people start to stare, exchange meaningful glances and roll their eyes. When the train reached Morgan Avenue in Bushwick, the woman stood, grimaced delicately and staggered to the doorway. As the man with the messenger bag hurried out behind her, one of the noisy women hissed, 'I think it's performance art.'"[17] Mcdonald seems reticent to embrace this definition of her work. In a statement on her website, she writes, "My work in video, web art, and public intervention is often performative and relational," and she lists the many planned interactions with strangers that she has conducted over the years as "public works" rather than "performance art"—presumably because there is more about these interactions that is real and spontaneous than staged or performed.

Mcdonald's work could be said to be about questioning community among spectators in a way that might be directly in line with Marxist critiques of spectacle, and it deserves much more critical attention than I can give it here. She recognized that there is a community of celebrity fans who relate to their mutual obsession with a particular film star; this is acknowledged in her pieces like *Me and Billy Bob* or *Screen Kiss*, in which she digitally inserts herself into scenes alongside Hollywood's leading men. There is a very definite experience of catharsis in her work. Just by seeing the artist intrude into Hollywood's closed frame, the viewer experiences a kind of satisfaction by proxy—as if it were us, instead of her, whom we were watching kiss Johnny Depp. By identifying with the artist as someone like "us," on the outside, the viewer experiences communion with the artist and becomes aware that what we are offered by the technologically enhanced medium is a transgression of cinematic boundaries.[18]

Mcdonald's urge to create a cathartic experience in her work is equally visible in her play with the horror film, and it often reads as feminist revision. In *The Screaming*, she encounters famous movie monsters and screams in place of the hapless heroine—she grafts herself into classics like Lucio Fulci's *Zombi 2*, Stanley Kubrick's *The Shining*, and Ridley Scott's *Alien*—but here we find a different outcome than in the original texts: her screams have power, and she defeats her foes with those ear-piercing shrieks. Her own discomfort with the horror genre may be the impetus behind these reworkings, for she also provides a different outcome in her less visibly gendered zombie pieces, where violence is permanently deferred: No one ever gets caught, and no one ever gets eaten.

Most recently, she has filmed a work titled *Field of the Dead and Undead*, in which figures dressed from different time periods move through the same visual field, perform a death scene, and then rise as zombies. But here again, there is no interaction between the zombies, and other than the solo death sequences, no violence—definitely no blood, and no confrontation between figures on-screen.[19]

Mcdonald's interest in and development of the zombie theme in her work has turned up the volume on her dialogue with the audience, a quality for which her work has been lauded.[20] One of Mcdonald's latest projects pushed the limits of the boundary between artist and spectator. *Zombies in Condoland* was a live performance held at the 2008 Nuit Blanche art festival in Toronto. Nuit Blanche is an annual event in which contemporary artists set up installations and display their work throughout the city of Toronto, and the exhibitions last from sundown to sunup. The pamphlet describes the event thus: "For one sleepless night the streets will be bustling with activity as thousands experience a full night of contemporary art and performance in three zones across the city. Discover art in galleries, museums and unexpected places. From bridges and tunnels to warehouses and stadiums, choose from 155 destinations and chart your own path."[21] Toronto is one of many cities to host a Nuit Blanche like the one held each year in Paris, and the very nature of the event brings to mind the Situationist International's dream of transforming the experience of the city through interaction with art in unexpected places.

One might question my choice to read these movements in light of the Situationists' disruptions, rather than looking at them as a kind of site-specific art, which is emphasized by both the architecture of Jillian Mcdonald's piece and its inclusion in the Nuit Blanche festival. But one reason to do so is that the collectivity of these zombie gatherings has a much more equalizing effect even than something like the art movement's collective community projects, which, as Miwon Kwon points out in *One Place after Another*, have been read as advancing reformist agendas that necessarily separate the artist or author of the work from the local community of participants.[22] It is Kwon's intention to apply Jean-Luc Nancy's model of "un-working community" and Iris Marion Young's writing on "a politics of difference" to suggest a more effective way of conceptualizing the community.

Claiming that community "may be seen as a phantom, an elusive discursive formation that, as Nancy puts it, is not a 'common being' but a non-essential 'being-in-common,'" Kwon's intention is to reveal how we must shift from community-based art to collective artistic praxis.[23] But there is an interesting parallel to be drawn between this commentary on the need for a sense of community in art, and the zombie mob phenomenon with which this chapter is concerned. Invoking Young's appeal for "a politics of difference" that would allow for a definition of community that embraces rather than shuns difference, Kwon frames the argument as a utopian fantasy that is nonetheless useful for exposing the flaws of our real-life community-based artworks: "The ideal of community, in [Young's] view, is predicated on an ideal of shared or fused subjectivities in which each subject's unified coherence is presumed to be not only transparent to him/herself but identically transparent to others."[24] We can see this through the lens of Nancy's reconceptualization of community as a "specter"[25] and a "phantom,"[26] so why not a zombie? Nancy writes, "there is no communion, there is no common being, but there is being in common . . . [and] the question should be the community of being and not the being of the community."[27] One can see how well these zombie gatherings epitomize (and even literalize) fantasies of the unattainable community. The zombie swarm emphasizes the difference of its various participants (zombie mail carrier, zombie jock) at the same time that it equalizes all of them. The zombies are immediately legible as belonging to one community, despite differences in gender, age, race, or tax bracket. The zombie is a state of "common being," and the participants suggest the swarm identity (like the angry mob or the killer bee) of one new kind of being that comprises the composite parts of its individual bodies. What the community-based activity of zombie gatherings illustrates is that the fantasy of community is alive and well, shared by people all over the world, and yet it remains consigned to the status of fantasy. As Kwon makes clear, pure community is inaccessible to the kind of site-specific art projects that continually cast the facilitator as auteur; in Jillian Mcdonald's self-conscious play with this dichotomy between authored art and communally made project, the problem is highlighted, though not resolved.

I was fortunate to be able to attend Jillian Mcdonald's *Zombies in Condoland*, a live performance in which the artist invited the audience to participate by becoming zombies. Makeup and wardrobe were provided for those who wanted to transform themselves into the living dead. The guide to the festivities advertised Mcdonald's event thus:

> *Zombies in Condoland* is a series of night actions that mimic a film screening set for a low budget horror film such as the type made famous by George Romero whose latest film, [*Diary of the Dead*], was filmed in Toronto.[28] Anyone can participate and be a zombie. People are encouraged to come in character—nurse zombie, business person zombie, geek zombie, sports zombie—and are also encouraged to do their makeup en route, in cafes, bars, and mass transit. There will also be make-up tents and zombie clothing available on site.[29]

Playing the part of the director, Mcdonald wore a cream-colored corduroy suit and gave direction to the actors, whom she affectionately called "my zombies," through a megaphone. Interestingly, her own makeup depicted her as a zombie with a bullet-hole in her forehead, which (as every good zombie film fan knows) is the most surefire way to de-animate the undead. Perhaps this signified that the director had been freed from her zombie state, and thus Mcdonald was positioned outside the throng, able to steer the zombie horde. Mcdonald had several "scenes" scripted: zombies rising from the ground, zombies lumbering, zombies attacking a building, and so forth. As there was a wide range of participants, there was also a great diversity to the type of zombies portrayed. Some growled and lunged after the large crowd of spectators that gathered to witness the event, some drooled and wheezed, "Brains!," circa 1985's *The Return of the Living Dead*, some adopted the somnambulistic style, arms outstretched—but even though it has become the latest trend in zombie cinema, I personally didn't see any fast zombies among the crowd. In this way, Mcdonald gave over creative control to an audience of nonperformers, invited them to make themselves strange, to perform; thus she played her role as director, but simultaneously, she was as much of a neutral witness as the camera lens. As such, it was an event that pushed at the boundary between art and experience, and for this reason it called into question the nature of performative art and its historical intersections with a revolutionary agenda. For many citizens of Toronto, however, *Zombies in Condoland* may just have been a dress rehearsal for the zombie walk slated to take place only a few weeks later.

Toronto, of course, is no stranger to zombies: as the Nuit Blanche program notes, many zombie films have been shot in the area, and Thea Munster's annual zombie walk, the first of its kind, has been a staple since 2003. Mcdonald coordinated with Munster to try to bring out her base, and she had an open call for participants on her website for months in the hopes of drawing out Toronto zombie regulars.[30] Mcdonald has acknowledged how much her interest in zombies was and continues to be informed by the zombie mobs and zombie walks that people have organized in cities across the world. This overlap between Mcdonald's accepted brand of performance art and these other zombie events resurrects questions about the definition of art, and the boundary lines established between performance and protest, with which the Situationist International struggled in the 1950s and 1960s. True to the ultimately unsatisfying, irresolvable duality of the zombie—which is immortal, but also dead and decaying; which is clearly a metaphor for slavery, but is also historically tied to the only successful slave rebellion in history—the zombie mob phenomenon seems to resurrect some of the techniques of the Situationists, if only to defer the prospect of actual revolution. In a frustrating "détournement" of the Situationist apparatus itself, consumerist spectacle, in the form of the Hollywood zombie, becomes the unifying force that takes over the urban landscape, yet it may only demonstrate our own mute impotence against the capitalist machine.

III

We never called what we were doing "art," but big movements usually don't.

Thea Munster, on Toronto Zombie Walk

In *The Society of the Spectacle*, published in 1967, Guy Debord describes the detriment of capitalist culture to society; "spectacle" is defined as "capital accumulated to such a degree that it becomes an image." Debord writes of the epistemic turmoil of the artist amid this social climate: "Art in the period of its dissolution, as a movement of negation in pursuit of its own transcendence in a historical society where history is not yet directly lived, is at once an art of change and a pure expression of the impossibility of change. This is an art that is necessarily avant-garde; and it is an art that *is not*. Its vanguard is its own disappearance."[31] As we will see in the following section, the Situationists' conundrum is very zombie-like in its dialectical struggle with antinomies: It is both absent and present, (not) occurring in a time that both is and has not yet begun; it is an art that is not an art. Currently, we are experiencing a strange confluence of zombie events and zombies in the arts that not only calls to mind the rhetoric of Situationists like Guy Debord and Asger Jorn, but may also signal the second coming of a movement that never truly arrived.

Thea Munster has been running the Toronto Zombie Walk since 2003, and she has seen her ingenuity give rise to a host of imitations. I met up with the self-proclaimed founder of the zombie walk phenomenon in a little coffee shop in Toronto. She was easy enough to identify: at a corner table in the back sat three young zombies, two men in mostly white face paint with some black circles hollowing their eyes, and with them a young woman (who with her slight frame and dyed orange hair appears much younger than her thirty-odd years), wearing a white eyelet blouse splattered with blood underneath her zipped-up hoodie. Her makeup betrayed the six years of experience that she has at playing dead: some sort of putty was used under her makeup to give the effect of open wounds; there were marks on her neck that looked like bloody fingerprints; purple bruises played on her cheeks, just as, in the later stages of rigor mortis, coagulated blood will puddle underneath the skin. This is someone who knows her zombies.

On the day I interviewed Thea she was dressed the part to advertise her upcoming zombie walk, and she would also be making an appearance at Mcdonald's event later in the evening. Despite multiple overtures from Mcdonald to collaborate for Nuit Blanche, and an acknowledgement of

Munster's zombie walks in the Nuit Blanche pamphlet, the physical and temporal proximity of Mcdonald's installation to Munster's own scheduled event seemed too close for comfort. In fact, Munster was rather upfront about feeling disrespected by the festival and its coordinators. This candor about her bruised ego seemed somewhat incongruous in a woman who spends so much of her time playing a being without consciousness or a sense of self. Still, there are many immediately noticeable differences between the style and approach of the zombie works of Thea Munster and Jillian Mcdonald. Unlike Mcdonald, whose interest in the zombie came out of disbelief that anyone would *want* to watch this type of film, Munster has had a lifelong love affair with the horror genre. Further, whereas Mcdonald's work is widely recognized as participating in a genre of contemporary art, Munster's events are harder to define. She is vague on the details of her education, saying instead that she situates her background as "punk rock/death rock." The impulse that led her to organize the first zombie walk in Toronto, in October 2003, came out of an anarchic impulse to disrupt, to "shake things up." "I was always saying to my friends, let's dress up like zombies . . . so I started putting flyers up to see who else would come, and only six people came to the first one."

Thea's annual zombie walk has grown in size with each passing year, and on the day of our interview, she was expecting 2,200 zombies at her upcoming event. She seems to have all the facts at hand. She can tell you exactly how many people attended each event, and how much she has raised in funds, which she and her "zombies" (read: volunteer assistants) call "fiend-raisers." They sell T-shirts to raise *only* enough to pay for insurance for the event and the cost of the flyers that she passes out in the weeks leading up to the walk.

Although at least initially pure disruption was the goal, defining her motivations and the ramifications of the event is becoming more complicated for this unwitting founder of a movement. Much like the history of punk rock, there is palpable tension surrounding the issue of other zombie organizers not giving credit where credit is due, and the acceptance of corporate sponsors by other zombie walks, something that Munster denigrates. She is particularly vexed by the fact that the City of Toronto, which has never before been a help to her as she tried to facilitate the walk, is now sponsoring Mcdonald's event. "Why?!," she demanded rhetorically, handing out flyers in full zombie drag. "'Cause it's labeled 'art'? Sponsored by Scotiabank and the City of Toronto? This is art, in the streets!"[32]

In many ways, this seems a fair question, and one with which artists and critics have struggled since the beginning of the twentieth century. What is the difference between an event like Jillian Mcdonald's and that organized by Munster, except for the acceptance of the art community and the embrace of the definition of the performance as "art"? While Mcdonald's installation is not high-tech per say, she does have the assistance of makeup artists; she has lights and several cameras, a megaphone, and tracking shots, and yet the event is close in tone to, and admittedly inspired by, the playfulness of a DIY zombie event like those Munster coordinates. Nonetheless, there are elements of Mcdonald's spectacle that, for me, distinguish hers and Munster's zombies as accomplishing two very different agendas.

The flyer that Thea is passing out on the day of our interview reads, "The 6th annual Toronto Zombie Walk 2008. Sunday October 19, Shuffling Starts at 3 pm. Starting Point: Trinity Bellwoods Park, Destination: Bloor Cinema." Munster coordinates "walks" only in that there is a starting and an end point. There are participants, and undoubtedly observers; thus such an event directs and deflects the normative gaze. There is doubtlessly both an individual and a collective experience fostered—and true to the zombie narrative, these categories are sure to bleed one into the other. Individual participants each bring new narratives to the walk with their choice of costume and gestures, and they continue this narrativizing as they interact with others. The artistry of the individuals' makeup, as well as their performance, qualifies this as collectively produced street art. One has only to peruse the photos of the Toronto Zombie Walks and you will see the lengths to which people go to make their zombies every bit as convincing as Hollywood's: One man has a fake eyeball dangling from a hollow socket; another carries his own detached and bleeding arm; another portrays a bizarre tennis instructor fatality with multiple balls lodged in his chest.

In comparison, Mcdonald's play with spectacle betrays much more nuance just by virtue of the interface of the cameras and the illusion of the film shoot, which allows her to "play" director without becoming the *author* of the spectacle. On the level of audience, the most removed is the second-generation viewer, who may see the film or the stills that come out of this night's performance at a later date and in a different venue. At the performance on October 4, 2008, there were many different kinds of participants and the roles were constantly in flux. Mcdonald was both conductor and observer; her zombies were both artists themselves and—at the same time—volunteers in someone else's project. The non-zombie witnesses both were and were not participants.[33] Even while dressed as a zombie, I felt there to be many different levels to the performance and the

Zombies Invade Performance Art

FIGURE 3. 2009 Toronto Zombie Walk, "grunge zombies." (Photo by Bryan Weiss, reprinted with permission.)

FIGURE 4. 2009 Toronto Zombie Walk, zombies in Trinity Bellwoods Park. (Photo by Lara Willis, reprinted with permission.)

experience of it: at times I perceived myself to be a non-active participant, observing the other zombies in between "takes," or when I would momentarily slip out of character. I felt there to be the experience of performing zombie, when I was self-consciously trying to act like a zombie, thinking about how a zombie would walk, lean, moan; I felt myself to be myself when I caught my analytical eye at work. And yet there was a third state of being that I experienced, what I would say was the most authentic zombie, when I would sort of lose my own consciousness and just be a part of the lumbering mob. I really tried to expand into the collective, sensing myself propelled forward by the motion of the crowd more than by my own will, and, odd as it sounds, I do think I achieved, albeit temporarily, a kind of walking meditation, a zombie Zen.[34]

Of course, from Elias Canetti's description of the depersonalizing effects of the crowd, we might argue that all mobs are zombies: individual consciousness abates, and the one collective drive (in "baiting crowds" it is thirst for blood; at Mecca or in a revival tent, it is desire for communion or transcendence) overtakes the participants, inducting them into a kind of swarm experience.[35] Do these types of coordinated zombie events afford the kind of revolutionary shift in consciousness that earlier avant-gardes hoped would come out of collective or Situationist art?

Certainly not, for Munster's events have the shape and form of insurrection, but, like a zombie, are just contour, devoid of sense. Is the zombie event therefore a hollow spectacle, or is its emphasis on spectacle revelatory of the nature of collective awakening? Is there room, within the performance of the brainless horde, for political commentary? Pardon the paradoxes here, but if Guy Debord were a zombie, what would he think? Has Thea Munster started a zombie revolution or just reduced revolution to dramatic spectacle?

IV

> We must try to construct situations, that is to say, collective ambiances, ensembles of impressions determining the quality of a moment.
> Guy Debord, "Report on the Construction of Situations and On the International Situationist Tendency's Conditions of Organization and Action"

The group that called themselves Situationist International was led by Guy Debord and Asger Jorn. They were affiliated with the earlier Lettrists, and like them, the Situationists yearned for the kind of disruption they associated with the century's earlier movements like Surrealism (minus the emphasis on individual consciousness) and Dada (minus the nihilism and with more of a Marxist influence).[36] Simon Sadler's *The Situationist City* depicts the Situationist movement of the 1960s as coming out of a fundamental distrust of the way that capitalism and institutions like the government and the Church had organized modern cities. Functionalism, like that seen in Haussmann's Paris, was considered particularly objectionable, and they advocated for the disruption of the normative flow of traffic and the making of new narratives within the cityscape.[37] The Situationists called for the "détournement," or diversion, of everyday elements of the city.[38] But most important here, the SI called for the coordination of and collaboration on situations that would take place in public, thereby challenging notions of what constituted art by moving it from the gallery to the street.[39] Inspired by theories of dialectical materialism, the central tenets of the movement also questioned the boundaries separating art and revolution, and above all, had the aim of illustrating that the ideology of modern functionalism and capitalist spectacle were covert mechanisms for control of the populace.

As such, the SI, a movement that was ill defined even in its own time, would likely applaud Jillian Mcdonald's artistic hijacking of the subway car, and perhaps even her *Zombies in Condoland* for its insertion into the public space of a collaborative performance that calls spectacle into question. But to an even greater extent, the agenda of diversion espoused by SI is not so dissimilar from the punk-rock credo of disruption of the mainstream that inspires Munster.[40] But over and above these points of comparison, there is also something inherently zombie-like about Situationist discourse and its key texts that lead me to draw the comparison.

In 1959, Asger Jorn would describe his "Modifications," in which he painted over the paintings of others, in a way that suggests the living dead: "Painting is over. You might as well finish it off. Detourn. Long live painting."[41] This description of artistic resurrection has been explicated by Hal Foster as exhibiting the afterlife of the carcass more than the zombie potential of the transcendent signifier: "Like the old king, Jorn suggests, painting may be dead; but like the new king it may live on—not as an idealist category that never dies but as a materialist corpse that rots subversively."[42] Herein we see the revolutionary reframing of the Situationists' practices (repossess, redirect, reuse) in light of its commonality with the walking dead. What is the zombie, after all, if not a dead thing put to new, and infinitely stranger, uses?

The paradox of modern life illuminated by SI also recalls the zombie's contradictory nature. In *The Situationist City*, Simon Sadler quotes Debord's 1961 film *Critique de la séparation*: "Until the environment is collectively dominated, there will be no individuals—only specters haunting the things anarchically presented to them by others. In chance situations we meet separated people moving randomly. Their divergent emotions neutralize each other and maintain their solid environment of boredom."[43] Until the formation of a collective identity (one that is not the false unity presented by the capitalist spectacle), freethinking individuality will not be available to the masses. Elsewhere, particularly in Debord's important text *The Society of the Spectacle*, everyday life is further characterized as a kind of zombification from which we should strive for liberation: "When the real world is transformed into mere images, mere images become real beings—dynamic figments that provide the direct motivations for a hypnotic behaviour."[44]

I recognize some of the difficulties posed by my assertion that we should read Munster's zombie walks as the kind of collective ambiances that the SI was describing in the 1960s. I take these inconstancies not as problematic, but rather as suggestive of the usefully irresolvable dialectic of the zombie's ambivalent position—opposing life and death, subject and object, human and nonhuman, individual and collective. For Jorn, even time was out of joint: "Our past is becoming, one needs only to crack open the shells."[45] We might claim then, that at its core the Situationists were as dialectical (and perhaps at times as paradoxical) as the zombie. We should always remember that the zombie's simultaneity as living and dead makes it a figure that defies temporal law: the zombie exists always outside of time.

One of the Situationists' practices was itself a kind of *détournement* of an earlier artistic practice: *le dérive*, or "drift," having its predecessor in the flaneur's idle and purposeless wandering through the city, was considered by Ivan Chtcheglov (author of *Formulary for a New Urbanism*, a text that was a major inspiration to Guy Debord) to be a therapeutic technique.[46] Taking up what was formerly associated with the leisure culture of the bourgeois class, the Situationists' *dérive* involved "radical rereadings of the city—what Michel de Certeau was to call 'a pedestrian street act.'"[47] Drift rests somewhere between the personal and the collective, the private and the public, and it resembles the sort of dialectical discovery the SI posited would come from opposing terms like revolution/art, performance/life, individual/group.

That we could call Thea Munster's zombie walk a "pedestrian street act" cannot be doubted. In this elucidation of some Situationist tenets, we see how inserting zombies into the space of the city (with or without the embrace of a definition of it as an art performance) is inherently a kind of détournement of the Hollywood spectacle that facilitates a new experience through the unpaid, non-commodified, novice performer's "drift." Yet can we call this practice revolutionary? Here it gets more complicated. One might argue that, ultimately, what the zombie walk détourns is, in fact, the Situationist practice, and that by means of remapping the city in a collectively made narrative predicated on the false unity of consumerist culture, it actually undermines the potential weapon of mass assembly (and all of Debord's careful theorizing) even as it satirizes the society of the spectacle.

The Situationist embrace of paradox had a limit. Beyond the obvious push and pull of the Situationists' seemingly contradictory concepts, like the dictum that we must "work to make ourselves useless,"[48] there was the grander notion that the goal was "to take theatre beyond entertainment and into revolution."[49] The SI was aiming for a "revolutionary transformation of consciousness," and other movements that lacked this as the agenda, like the contemporaneous New York avant-garde's "happenings" were dismissed as glib or shallow.

What attracts me to draw a comparison between these zombie events and the Situationists—rather than movements like Fluxus or Allan Kaprow's happenings, which likewise emphasize communal involvement and the use of public space—is precisely the zombie-like quality of the Situationist use of notions like "dérive" and "détournement," which give new life to existing monuments or works. Guy Debord wrote, "We can use, with some light touching up, certain zones that already exist. We can use people who have already existed."[50] The aesthetic of recycling the components of the city (and perhaps even the dead), which have formerly been used by capitalist spectacle culture to inculcate ideology, suggests a kind of zombification, a wiping clean of these signifiers in order to reveal a latent potential within the community.[51] For this would seem to be the only definite message that one might take from the zombie walk movement: that other movements might yet be possible. Ironically, and even appropriate to Asger Jorn's comment that "our past is becoming," social protests and disruptions hereafter will look to the model of these walking dead, making use of the techniques honed by zombie walk organizers, but instead using Facebook, Twitter, and texting.

All the major movements in performance art have their roots in the pure disruptive principles of the earlier Futurist and Dada movements, yet I prefer the vocabulary of the Situationists even to their close contemporaries, the kineticists, whose GRAV movement in Paris staged simultaneous disruptive events in Paris on April 19, 1966, such as the distribution of balloons and pins with which to pop them on the Boulevard Saint-Germain and whistles for art-house moviegoers in the Latin Quarter.[52] In the case of the New York happenings, audience participation would grow in importance as the movement developed, became more complex, and began be held outdoors rather than in galleries, which is admittedly akin to these zombie events.[53] But Debord criticized the movement for not being political enough, deeming it insufficient because "revolutionary transformation of consciousness among its participants was neither its prerequisite nor its result."[54] On the flip side, George Maciunas's goal for the Fluxus movement was nothing less than advancing the "socialist aspirations for the group as a viable economic and politically engaged collective."[55] But because Fluxus emphasized that everyday actions should be considered art, they tended to produce performances of the banal, such as Alison Knowles's *Make a Salad* (in which the performance consisted of the artist making a salad). One has difficulty hearing the call to arms emanate from within the safe domesticity of the housewife's kitchen: elevating the everyday to the status of art may actually seem to justify the banalization that is the reverse of spectacle.[56]

Just by virtue of the fact that these zombie gatherings mobilize thousands of people in their city streets (never mind the fact that many of them hold potential weapons, like golf clubs and tire irons, and are covered in fake blood) is more suggestive of the possibility of revolution than many of the now-classic performances of the 1960s and 1970s that were truly iconoclastic in the world of art. Of course, a revolutionary transformation of consciousness akin to that advanced by Debord is not the goal for either Jillian Mcdonald or Thea Munster, but it may be an unforeseen result. Many participants who play dead feel the experience reveals something about the material conditions of our society: namely, that the commercialized spectacle that normally surrounds us has an anesthetizing effect. (Debord might say, How do you do an impression of a zombie? Just imagine yourself watching TV.) Thereby the Zombie Walk phenomenon ironically fulfills Debord's dictum that there will be no individuals until the collective is formed: but that which is subjected to détournement is not just the modern city, but also the figure ensconced in the commercial spectacle; belonging to the B movie, the zombie wrested from Hollywood and taken to the streets is thus made to stand for the liberation of consciousness, rather than its diversion.

But once again, the zombie metaphor returns us to us, this, its frustrating dialectic: In playing zombie, one becomes aware of the subject/object duality of our everyday existence, that which specifically inhibits the success of revolution. For Debord, when we confront the spectacle we sense ourselves as the object in a large matrix of Capital. But in general, the zombie is a reminder of the inherent duality of the human condition: as thinking subjects, and as future corpses. In playing zombie, we make visible the thingness of our body as that recalcitrant object from which we do not hurry to separate, and which real revolution endangers. In zombie makeup, we see our own distorted reflection: we perceive that as mortals, we are already split between object and subject. Simultaneously, the zombie mob's ultimate failure to live up to this comparison to the SI is analogous to the figure's larger insufficiency as a symbol for revolution. A figuration of both the slave and slave rebellion, the zombie always connotes the annihilation of revolution at the same time that it embodies revolutionary drive; likewise, these zombie mobs are antirevolutionary even as they illustrate the concept's latent potential. In playing dead, in trying to become blank, one becomes aware that some kind of subjectivity is nonetheless alive and well within us, be it the higher consciousness of the swarm identity, or the realization that we are seeing the surface of spectacle exposed as a screen onto which false consciousness is projected. This kind of frustrating paradox seems endemic to the living dead trope of the zombie, and perhaps it is only natural that such complexity arises when playing dead. Put simply, we become zombies to discover what we *are* as much as what we *are not*.

V

CONCLUSION: LA REVOLUTION EST MORTE. VIVE LA REVOLUTION!

Interest in Situationist *practices* (for as Foster clarifies, "the result was not intended as art or antiart at all," but merely a "'dialectical devaluing/revaluing of the diverted artistic element'") did not end with the dissolving of the SI into component groups scattered across the globe, though the group's fracture was caused in part by disagreement over Debord's staunch affirmation that Situationist art and politics "could not be separated."[57] Rather, various groups have carried on the tradition of "anart" (anarchist art), or art with a political agenda. In the compendium titled

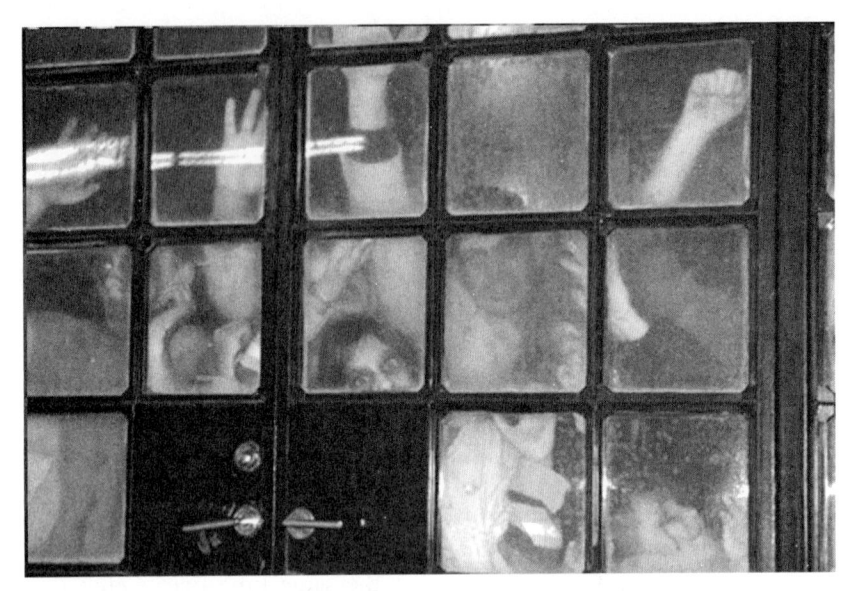

FIGURE 5. *Zombies in Condoland* (detail), Jillian Mcdonald. 2008, performance at Nuit Blanche, Toronto. (Courtesy of the artist.)

The Interventionists: User's Manual for the Creative Disruption of Everyday Life, Gregory Sholette and Blake Stimson write specifically on collectivist art that involves the disruption of the smooth everyday workings of the capitalist machine: "The desire to speak in a collective voice has long fueled the social imagination of artists. Futurism, Constructivism, and Surrealism shared this early aim in the 20th century, as did collectives such as CoBrA, the Situationist International, Gutai, and the Lettrists after World War II." In this same volume they define contemporary Interventionism as kind of "art activism," the goal of which is "to create situations in the world at large"; many of these groups, like the Situationists, emphasize collectives or collectivism. Sholette and Stimson write, "New collectivism gathers itself around decentered and fluctuating identities that leverage heterogeneous character of any group formation."[58] The authors here are most likely thinking of artists that question the stability of categories like race and gender. There is no mention of zombie gatherings among the pages describing the Interventionists, but perhaps there should be. For what is a more "decentered and fluctuating" identity than that of a collective zombie performance? In this regard, another advantage of these amorphous zombie events is that they do not seem to have embraced one set identity; it is indeterminable whether they are art, anarchy, play, or protest. Thus the zombie event remains, like the zombie identity, ever decentered and fluctuating.

Zombie events emphasize the collective, and not just on a local level. The organizer of the Chattanooga zombie group was first to propose a "Zombie World Invasion Day," originally set for May 25, 2007. Organizers in cities across the world would plan simultaneous events.[59] The people who coordinate these events call them by different names and no doubt think of them differently, and overall, there is no uniform agenda (aside from dressing like zombies and occupying public spaces) and there is no universal message to convey.[60] The zombie gatherings that most interest me are those that are neither organized fund-raisers nor overt protests, but rather demonstrations that communicate nothing but the participants' embrace of the zombie as a legible cultural signifier; the signified is up for grabs.[61] The mute, staggering zombies that are coming soon to a city near you do not affirm that this revolution is aimed at articulating the rights of the worker; but nonetheless, they attest to the possibility of organized rebellion, giving us the form but not the substance of insurrection. The zombie always, in some tacit sense, bears the trace of the Haitian slave and his rebellion, and these events serve as a reminder that power can be exercised by the horde. But yet, that there *is* no rebellion is only fitting of the zombie metaphor's lack of potential: the frustrated antipathy of its inherently dual state.

Regardless of whether these events are labeled "art" or "demonstration," these zombie gatherings are both of these things, and neither of them. Even something as gruesome and nonsensical as an assembly of people made up to look like oozing, bleeding, bruised corpses is not only a demonstration that citizens have the capability to organize and to assemble (and now, due to new technologies, they can coordinate at the last possible moment to prevent the intervention of authorities), but also that they will do it for no reason, for pure enjoyment divorced of any commercial impulse, and stemming from a desire to make something together.

To me these zombie happenings are, most aptly, *non*-events, *anti*-revolutions; it's not, after all, what the zombie says that is important, but rather its mere presence that communicates. The zombie presents a theoretical oddity, a frozen, irresolvable dialectic, an embodiment of opposites that displays simultaneously that which is *not there* by that which *is*: Even something as innocuous as 2,200 people convening on a street corner to moan and stumble around in fake blood and face paint is a display of the collective working together, a reminder of the Haitian revolution in which the zombie has its roots, and a veiled threat, as if to suggest what else might be possible—what dark army could rise and exact its revenge . . . if it ever comes to that.

And yet, appropriate to the frustrating ambiguity of the living dead, and just like the disappointment of predecessor movements like Situationist International (which failed to achieve its revolutionary agenda) or even punk (which was subsumed under capitalism as just another marketable "Hot Topic"), the commentary of these zombie gatherings is often too hard to read, which allows it to be co-opted by the very forces it mirrors and mocks. One of the leaders in the world of zombie organizers is "David," of the San Francisco Zombie Mob. His events have sometimes employed overt social critique, as when zombies occupy shopping centers to draw attention to the capitalist spectacle.[62] But as I alluded to at the beginning of this chapter, the zombie hordes tend to reiterate the power of spectacle and celebrate Hollywood's industry, even as they purport to denigrate the economic system that sustains the status quo. In a nutshell, the zombie détournement is too easily turned on its own head.

Recently, the SF Zombie Mob's revolutionary potential might have been dealt its deathblow. I received this e-mail on September 28, 2009:

> Undead Threat Level: Orange
> Quarantined Area: Century 9 Theater at 817 Mission St.
> Planned Activity: 6pm Zombies gather in Quarantine zone, possible security breaches subjecting innocent bystanders to zombie infection and/or digestion.
> Containment Plan: Lure the Undead to a free screening of the movie "Zombieland" at 7pm, Century 9 Theater. Placate their simple minds with Hollywood eye candy and the acting of Woody Harelson [*sic*].

Even though the movie is a "free screening," and despite the tongue-in-cheek acknowledgment that this event is contributing to, rather than effectively challenging, the culture of consumption, I am tempted to consider this as the end of the walking zombie movement—which began in the 1930s as a publicity stunt, and could appropriately end here as well. Indeed, the zombie-gathering phenomenon appears to already be destroying itself. Of course, there are Thea Munsters who will resist the temptations of corporate sponsors with their cross-promotions and merchandise tie-ins, and kindly decline the good citizens' requests that the events morph into fund-raisers. But just like zombies, these temptations to take the easier, more fiscally rewarding path can't be resisted forever; they are relentless, they just keep coming. The zombie walks that began as a playful resistance to consumer culture are becoming the very thing they set out to mock. Appropriately, they have been bit and have changed.

I would like to conclude by revisiting the words of Guy Debord, whose *Society of the Spectacle* nonetheless provides a way for us to consider these zombie gatherings in the discourse of the future, rather than just as chronicles of the failed revolutions of the past. I recognize some of the complications that arise from reading these zombie walks as the kind of revision of geography that Debord desired: First, there is Debord's indebtedness to Henri Lefebvre, who asserted in *Critique of Everyday Life* that literature should investigate the everyday rather than the magical or fantastic.[63] And second, Debord's Situationist International failed to achieve what he intended. Still, it is haunting to see how neatly his words fit here: "We have to multiply poetic subjects and objects . . . and we have to organize games of these poetic objects among these poetic subjects. This is our entire program, which is essentially transitory. Our situations will be ephemeral, without a future: passageways."[64] This seems to me to describe the ludic quality of these zombie events, and to once again flip the dialectic on itself, opening up a space to question whether the zombie mob's anti-revolution, and even its failure, *is* revolutionary after all, if only in part: a dry run, a dress rehearsal. The zombie mob's contribution is not that it models progress by looking to the future, but only that it reads our present moment's relationship to revolution as one that, like the zombie, is out of step with time. These words of Debord's echo back to me, taking on new and strange shapes when read in the light of these zombie gatherings:

> Proletarian revolution is this *critique of human geography* through which individuals and communities could create places and events commensurate with the appropriation no longer just of their work, but of their entire history. The ever-changing playing field of this new world and the freely chosen variations in the rules of the game will regenerate a diversity of local scenes that are independent without being insular. And this diversity will revive the possibility of authentic journeys—journeys within an authentic life that is itself understood as a journey containing its whole meaning within itself.[65]

In the end, though, perhaps we need to dig up even older graves, and spend a moment with the predecessor theorist who spawned Debord's description of revolution as it was imagined in the halcyon days of advanced capitalism. Henri Lefebvre wrote of his own vision of change in 1947: "When the new man has finally killed magic off and buried the rotting corpses of the old 'myths'—when he is on the way towards a coherent unity and consciousness, when he can begin the conquest of his own life, rediscovering or creating greatness in everyday life—and when he can begin knowing it and speaking it, then and only then will we be in a new era."[66] Perhaps, at this historical moment, we need to revisit Lefebvre's imagery. These events seem to me to incarnate the youth culture's lament for its lack of real social power, and perhaps signal a willingness to change this. Like the zombie as vacant shell or soulless body, the zombie mob, zombie gathering, and zombie walk demonstrated only the form of social insurrection devoid of content, yet this phenomenon illustrates the profundity of this absence by the sheer magnitude and scale of these blank cultural events. I wonder if the rise of this phenomenon, which ostensibly began in Canada in 2003 but quickly spread across the United States and then globally over the course of the first decade of the twenty-first century, might not have been influenced by the highly unpopular presidency of George W. Bush, and specifically the broad population's inability to effectively demonstrate their disapproval of the Iraq invasion in the public sphere. Maybe, when the zombie walk phenomenon has slouched toward its final resting place, we will begin knowing and speaking that which the zombie mob only played at: community, action, (r)evolution.

AFTERWORD: ZOMBIE (R)EVOLUTION

Sarah Juliet Lauro

She's not your mother anymore, she's a zombie!

Shaun of the Dead, 2004

In an unexpectedly appropriate way, it seems that the ideal place to end a discussion of what we mean by "zombie evolution" is with a film that is not a zombie movie at all—or at least, not a zombie movie on the surface. The 2008 film by M. Night Shyamalan, *The Happening*, both is and is not a zombie movie.[1] Of course, we cannot help but think of George Romero's iconic film when we watch the protagonists cross the Pennsylvanian countryside and hole up in a rural farmhouse, but aside from these similarities, in what ways can we claim *The Happening* as the kind of narrative that precisely exhibits the trends that we have articulated in our charting of the zombie's evolution?

For several reasons, *The Happening* feels uncannily familiar, not unlike a zombie. Part of this is because, to me, it seems to echo Edmund Cooper's 1965 novel *All Fools' Day*, in which sunspots cause a rash of mass suicide; also because of the general similarity to Alfred Hitchcock's *The Birds* (1963), in which an innocuous part of the natural world all of a sudden turns against humanity, as our planet's flora does in Shyamalan's film; and in part because it is not so unlike the 1978 version of *Invasion of the Body Snatchers*, which also featured plants as the dispensers of doom. (In 1978's *Invasion*, this is an alien germ that facilitates the pods' takeover, replication, and replacement of the humans.) Most of all, however, *The Happening* can be claimed as a kind of zombie film because it features the two key aspects that we have come most recently to expect of the genre: the "depersonalization," to use Peter Dendle's term,[2] of people we once knew, and a vast, sudden, inexplicable epidemic.[3] As the authors in this volume discuss at length, the zombie has changed so much over the course of twentieth-century cinema as to become nearly unrecognizable from its earliest filmic instantiation: as the sleepwalking subaltern, an unthreatening Voodoo puppet doing the bidding of an evil-minded human (and usually white) master. Yet it seems that the one constant that remains even after the zombie genre evolved to dispense with Voodoo, and then with living corpses, is the zombie's depersonalization.[4] The zombie is primarily a formerly familiar figure who has been wiped blank, depersonalized, and this is why the articles in this book have examined zombies as disparate as the vampires of Matheson's novels and the android wives of Stepford.

The second defining feature of the genre preserves the sense of onslaught, outbreak, or epidemic. No matter the zombie's origin story, whether it be the result of radiation exposure or a literal virus, zombie stories tend to involve a legion of newly transformed individuals, rather than a few lone specimens. Here again, Shyamalan's film fits the criteria: there is an *epidemic*, albeit not of brain-eating zombies, but of suicide. As with the classic zombie, the afflicted in *The Happening* do not seem to recognize loved ones any longer. Instead, they utter some nonsensical or out-of-context words, as if the brain is resetting, and then they kill themselves in whatever way seems the most immediately expedient. Like zombies, they are automatons on autopilot, but instead of doing someone else's bidding or thirsting for blood, they are the death drive incarnate. There is the same kind of mindlessness exhibited in victims here as in the classic zombie, a bleaching out of the person you once knew, to which I allude in the epigraph: "She's not your mother anymore, she's a zombie!" These words are said in the half-serious spoof *Shaun of the Dead* (2004) and echo a line from Peter Jackson's *Dead Alive* (1992), but something of the kind is probably uttered in countless zombie films. This exclamation represents the moment when the protagonist has to confront the fact that one of the people he has known best has now become this other thing called a zombie. For me, this is the definitive aspect of the zombie—the uncanny encounter with the unfamiliar, the terror from the familiar (especially when it is a family member) made unexpectedly different.

What the various essays collected here strive to do is participate in a conversation about the development of the zombie. Is this cyborg-like evolution to a kind of post-human state that frees us from the subject/

object binary by straddling the border betwixt these categories? Or is it devolution, a kind of return to the violent, primordial Man? Or, as when, in later films, the zombie epidemic becomes associated with literal virus, is it possession and puppeteering by a simpler organism? Our interest in the zombie's "evolution" is both diachronic and synchronic, general and specific: herein, our essays look at the development of the zombie myth over the course of the century and at the nature of the individual's transformation into a different kind of being.

The issue of whether we can truly say that we are witnessing a zombie evolution or devolution deserves further discussion. It would be woefully reductive to claim that the zombie has only begun to evolve since we have started seeing an increasing number of zombies using tools, as in Romero's fourth installment in his Dead series, *Land of the Dead* (2005); or since the increased prevalence of the fast zombie, especially in *28 Days Later* (2002), *28 Weeks Later* (2007), and the 2004 remake of *Dawn of the Dead*. Our interest in the term "evolution," in fact, suggests something altogether separate from the zombie's increased abilities or its having become more "human" in various narratives.[5] If we take the zombie's origin to be the folkloric Haitian figure symbolizing the culture's slave history, then the subsequent incarnations of the zombie in cinema, on radio, in comics and popular literature, and, more recently, in video games represent an altered zombie—a corruption of the original narrative that is now made to be the psychological bellhop (to adapt Elizabeth Spelman's term) of mainstream American culture.[6] Thus we might consider that what we are actually witnessing develop over the course of the century is not the progressive development of the concept of the zombie, but more aptly, a devolution or even a colonization of the original zombie metaphor. Yet to bring the term "devolution" into the conversation also seems problematic, for one of the things that we see happening is the zombie's claim to a kind of post-identity—appropriately, since the zombie, in its most basic definition, is post(mortem)—and thus we should consider it useful to examine the zombie through the lens of post-human theory as well.

It is interesting to note that the concept of evolution, as Darwin described it, did not imply a teleological trajectory. Evolution signified only adaptability, yet in today's vernacular, it is a highly charged topic. In the context of a virus, for example, the term is endowed with a sinister meaning—as another life-form rapidly evolves (something of which humans are apparently much less capable) to get the upper hand on us.[7] In many zombie films, the virus is not depicted as something completely natural that is in conflict with humans, but rather a mutation that begins with human tampering in a lab.[8] In *The Happening*, it is the evolution of the plants that is infused with danger, and this theme points to what may be the latest advance in the zombie narrative. If zombies in film and other popular media have often expressed our anxieties about humans overreaching their natural sphere (from space exploration, to the development of nuclear weapons, to biotechnologies), then it seems only natural that one of our most pressing concerns as a civilization—the environment—would also begin to be reflected in the guise of zombie film.

Increasing panic about the environment has, predictably, given rise to the eco-zombie. One manifestation of this theme can be felt in those zombie stories, or apocalypse narratives more generally, where the earth, wiped clean of its human inhabits, begins to reclaim its space. We can think here of scenes from *28 Days Later*, and the Matheson adaptations *The Omega Man* (1971) and *I Am Legend* (2007), in which deer begin to repopulate what were once human habitats (like midtown Manhattan), and grass begins to grow where formerly there were busy intersections.[9] The earth, these shots convey, would not miss us. But a more direct expression of humanity's antagonistic relationship with nature can be seen in these emerging narratives where the planet's response to our misdeeds is to foster the zombie epidemic.

The parting image of 1985's *The Return of the Living Dead* is of the polluted sky beginning to give way to rain. The protagonists have foolishly burned the zombie remains, and while this was a viable solution to the problem in Romero's *Night of the Living Dead* (1968), in this unauthorized sequel the zombie's corrupt flesh can never, it seems, be fully destroyed. The ashes that go up the crematorium's chimney turn into rain and pour down the zombifying contaminant in a most unfortunate spot: a graveyard. Made in the 1980s, this obviously alludes to contemporary fears about acid rain. In Shyamalan's *The Happening*, there is also a prominent ecological theme. The protagonists deduce halfway through the film that plants are causing the "event." In a retaliatory strike for our crimes against nature, the plants have evolved a defense mechanism that will diminish the human population. When groups of a certain number of individuals are sensed, the vegetation releases a kind of neurotoxin that kills the death-drive inhibitor, and the plants make the humans do their dirty work for them: we off ourselves. Many critics found the transparency of Shyamalan's environmentalist message cloying, but it is interesting to note that as a zombie film, this trend is far from novel. In fact, inducting the film into the zombie movie annals may even serve to justify this moral-toting narrative as

Afterword: Zombie (R)evolution

fulfilling obligations to the genre. At least since Romero, the zombie epidemic has served as a modern-day equivalent of the biblical plague; because zombies are so often raised from the dead by some misdeed of humanity, they pass judgment on our naïve vanity and Icarian hubris, delivering a punishment of mass proportions without reference to an angered deity but, nonetheless, with the implication that humanity has sinned . . . even if only against natural law.

Thus we might say that the zombie is inherently an ecological avenger. As a walking corpse, the zombie threat is one in which things of the earth, bodies that had been consigned to become a part of the planet, refuse to take it lying down. Whether the sin is man's enslavement of his brother—as in the original myths of Haitian folklore—or humanity's development of technology, weapons, and chemicals that pollute and poison the planet—as in the halcyon days of Romero's and Fulci's cinematic zombies—the living dead may be little more than the planet's messengers, raised to exact revenge. So, we might say, whether the earth sends birds, or plants, or our own dead mother to do its bidding, there may be essentially no difference.

In this collection, our contributors have discussed many permutations of the zombie and what its evolution—or revolution, if one considers its periodic uprisings—reveals about our own society. As many in the field of monster studies have noted, how better to judge a civilization than by its bogeymen? It is our greatest sins that haunt our collective nightmares—our horror films. But as we have seen here, the zombie is so prevalent in our culture today that it seems as if it has begun to stalk us in our waking life as well. My prediction is that the next wave of zombie films will further develop the eco-zombie, and that this myth is far from exhausting its cultural potential. As students of the world in which we live, we must yield to the warning posted by hackers on a digitized road sign in Austin, Texas: "Caution! Zombies ahead!"[10]

NOTES

INTRODUCTION
Sarah Juliet Lauro and Deborah Christie

1. There are far too many important texts on horror to mention all of them here, but some of the key models for us are Carol Clover's *Men, Women, and Chainsaws*, Judith Halberstam's *Skin Shows*, David J. Skal's many books on horror and the gothic, and Slavoj Žižek's attention to the genre. Others whose work on horror (if not specifically on the zombie) we emulate include Robert Latham, Rick Worland, James Twitchell, Stephen Jay Schneider, Cynthia Freeland, Stephen Prince, Adam Lowenstein, Jay McRoy, and Kendall Phillips. Some of the predecessor zombie scholarship to which we acknowledge this collection's indebtedness include Steven Shaviro's *The Cinematic Body* and Robin Wood's examination of 1970s horror films in *Hollywood: From Vietnam to Reagan*. For more expansive investigation of the zombie as cultural signifier, see Franco Moretti's *Signs Taken for Wonders* and Caleb Jefferson Smith's "Detention without Subjects: Prisons and the Poetics of Living Death," featured in *Texas Studies in Literature and Language* in 2008. For scholarship on the zombie's relationship to capitalist society, see Jean Comaroff's 2002 article "Alien-Nation: Zombies, Immigrants, and Millennial Capitalism" in *South Atlantic Quarterly* and Annalee Newitz's *Pretend We're Dead: Capitalist Monsters in American Pop Culture*. For recent collections that examine the zombie from an interdisciplinary perspective, see Richard Greene and K. Silem Mohammad's *The Undead and Philosophy*, as well as Shawn McIntosh and Marc Leverette's *Zombie Culture*. For an overview of zombie cinema, see Jamie Russell's *Book of the Dead*, Peter Dendle's *Zombie Movie Encyclopedia*, and *Zombie Movies: The Ultimate Guide*, edited by Glenn Kay and Stuart Gordon.

2. For a discussion of zombie tag, see Ben Nuckols's 2008 AP article "Humans vs. Zombies: New Sport Sweeping College Campuses," and Matthew Daneman's 2008 *USA Today* article "Dead Man on Campus: 'Zombie Tag' a Growing Game at Colleges"; for pictures of a 2009 zombie prom, see *SF Weekly* online at http://www.sfweekly.com/slideshow/zombie-prom-at-the-dna-lounge-2394l5/; for zombie road signs, see the Chris

Nakashima-Brown's 2009 blog post "Keep Austin Zombie-Free," *No Fear of the Future*, http://nofearofthefuture.blogspot.com/2009/01/keep-austin-zombie-free.html.

3. Neil Badmington, "Theorizing Posthumanism," *Cultural Critique* 53 (Winter 2003): 11.

4. For a description of how the zombie is different from the iconic model of the post-human cyborg, see Sarah Juliet Lauro and Karen Embry's 2008 essay "A Zombie Manifesto: The Non-human Condition in the Era of Advanced Capitalism" in *boundary 2*; see also Neil Badmington's *Alien Chic: Posthumanism and the Other Within*.

5. A quick nod to *Survival of the Dead* (2010) is called for here. The latest iteration of George Romero's zombie epic appears to be directly concerned with zombies as an addition to the natural world—an addition that seeks to *survive* with as much tenacity as humans so often do. The editors can only speculate at this point, but it does seems as though Mr. Romero has himself reconsidered the defining parameters of what it is to be a zombie with the tagline for the movie: "Survival isn't just for the living."

AND THE DEAD SHALL RISE
Part introduction by Kevin Boon

1. According to Dendle (*The Zombie Movie Encyclopedia*, McFarland, 2001), the Golden Age of zombie films begins with the appearance of Romero's *Night of the Living Dead* in 1968 and ends when Michael Jackson's "Thriller" video elevates the zombie to "mainstream popularity" (7–8) in 1983.

2. Our contributors use various spellings of the word "voodoo," which is more commonly spelled "Vaudou" or "Vodou" when discussing the Haitian religion. Some chapters reference the Louisiana or Creole folk religion, which is usually designated "Voodoo"; other chapters refer to Haitian "Vaudou." In some places, authors quote texts that use a different orthography than they prefer, but the various spellings can take on different resonances—in some spots, authors may be self-consciously using a spelling to suggest a particular valence of the term. We let individual authors choose the spelling of the word for themselves, thus the orthography will not be consistent across the volume, or even within each chapter. (Editors' note.)

3. Ibid., 13.

4. I mention seven categories in "Ontological Anxiety Made Flesh: The Zombie in Literature, Film, and Culture," published in *Monsters and the Monstrous* (Rodopi, 2007). I have since added two categories that I consider relevant.

5. For a fuller description of these categories and where to find examples in literature and film, please see Kevin Boon's chapter (editors' note).

1. "THEY ARE NOT MEN . . . THEY ARE DEAD BODIES!":
FROM CANNIBAL TO ZOMBIE AND BACK AGAIN
Chera Kee

1. There are two primary variations on the word: "zombi" and "zombie." For the purposes of this chapter, I will use the more popular American variation "zombie." When quoting texts and other materials, however, I will stay true to the variation used by the original authors. Likewise, there are several variations on the word "Voodoo." Again, I will use the more popular American variation of the word but will stay true to other spellings used by other authors.

2. By the second major U.S. zombie feature, *Revolt of the Zombies* (1936), zombies had been moved from Haiti to Cambodia. From that point on, zombies in U.S. film were tied to a host of exotic locales, including Cuba, Africa, and any number of unnamed West Indian islands.

3. There are many different ways to approach the concept of "the Other." It has been understood as other peoples, other cultures, those people within a culture that deviate from its ideological norms, or even other genders (typically, the female is the Other to the male). In any incarnation, though, a binary is set up contrasting the Other with an assumed norm: the Other represents that which any given group believes is its opposite (think "us" versus "them," with the Other being "them"). Thus, while on the most basic level, the Other can be understood as that which is external to the self or the group, as Robin Wood observes, "it functions not simply as something external to the culture or to the self, but also as what is repressed (though never destroyed) in the self and projected outward in order to be hated and disowned. . . . It is repression, in other words, that makes impossible the healthy alternative—the full recognition and acceptance of the Other's autonomy and right to exist." *Hollywood From Vietnam to Regan . . . and Beyond*. Rev. ed. New York: Columbia UP, 2003, 66. Thus, for any given group, the Other represents another group onto which the first group can project its most deep-seated fears and insecurities. The first group can then use these hated characteristics as a justification for repressing, dismissing, or destroying the second group. In referring to this understanding of the Other, it is common to use a capital "O" to distinguish it from other uses of the word. For a detailed explanation of the Other, see Robin Wood, above; Foucault, Michel. *The History of Sexuality*, vol. 1. Trans. Robert Hurley. New York: Vintage Books, 1985; Kristeva, Julia. *Powers of Horror: An Essay on Abjection*. Trans. Leon S. Roudiez. New York: Columbia UP, 1982; Lacan, Jacques. *The Four Fundamental Concepts of Psychoanalysis*. Ed. Jacques-Alain Miller. Trans. Alan Sheridan. New York: Norton, 1978; and Said, Edward W. *Orientalism*. New York: Vintage Books, 1979.

4. For the purposes of clarity, I should explain what I consider to be a zombie. First, I separate zombies into three types. The first is what I call

Voodoo-style zombies, which are those zombies inspired by or derived from the zombies of Haitian folklore and Voodoo. I understand this type of zombie to be a human being, either living or dead, whose will is controlled by another (the "zombie master") via Voodoo, some other kind of "native" religion, or witchcraft. This type of zombiism is potentially reversible (there is a cure or a way to break the zombie spell). I see this type of zombie as predominant in U.S. film from 1932 to 1968. The second type of zombie is the Romero-style zombie. These zombies are the dead returned from the grave, are cannibalistic, and can only be destroyed; there is no cure to restore them to their former human selves. This type of zombiism is highly infectious, and this has been the predominant type of zombie on U.S. film screens since 1968. Finally, since the mid-1990s, I have noticed a change in some depictions of the zombie. What I call the video-game or post-Romero zombie tends to be faster than traditional Romero-style zombies. These zombies may or may not be strictly cannibalistic but are driven to kill humans regardless. In these narratives there is a clear-cut reason or culprit for the zombie infection, which is, in many ways, a corporate version of the zombie master. These zombie media also envision a cure for zombiism or a means of reversing its effects. Thus, my definition of the zombie is quite broad. For instance, while there are those who do not consider *28 Days Later* a zombie film, I see it as a very good example of a video-game-style zombie film.

5. By the time of the revolts these had been outlawed, but they continued to occur—mainly because soldiers didn't want to travel into the hills to oust supposed Voodoo adherents.

6. See James, C. L. R. *The Black Jacobins: Toussaint L'Ouverture and the San Domingo Revolution*. 2nd ed. New York: Vintage Books, 1989.

7. Davis, David Brion. "Impact of the French and Haitian Revolutions." *The Impact of the Haitian Revolution in the Atlantic World*. Ed. David P. Geggus. Columbia: University of South Carolina Press, 2001, 4.

8. See James. *Black Jacobins*.

9. For example, the United States didn't officially recognize Haiti until 1862.

10. See, for example, Austin, Henry. "The Worship of the Snake: Voodooism in Haiti To-day." *The New England Magazine* (Mar.–April 1912): 170–182; Candler, John. *Brief Notices of Hayti: With Its Condition, Resources, and Prospects*. London: T. Ward & Co., 1842; "Cannibals in Hayti." *Harper's Weekly* (Sept. 2, 1865): 545; Derbighy, Pierre. "Hayti: A Crumbling Republic." *Harper's Weekly* (Aug. 29, 1908): 11–13; Harvey, W. W. *Sketches of Hayti: From the Expulsion of the French to the Death of Christophe*. London: L. B. Seeley, 1827; Prichard, Hesketh. *Where Black Rules White: A Journey across and about Hayti*. Westminster: A. Constable & Co., Ltd., 1900; St. John, Spencer.

Hayti, or the Black Republic. 1884. Source Books on Haiti no. 9. New York: Cass, 1971; and Lawless, Robert. *Haiti's Bad Press.* Rochester, VT: Schenkman Books, 1992.

11. Harvey. *Sketches of Hayti,* vii.
12. Lawless. *Haiti's Bad Press,* 48.
13. Quoted in ibid., 34.
14. See Rhodes, Gary D. *White Zombie: Anatomy of a Horror Film.* Jefferson, NC: McFarland, 2001, 72.
15. Cannibalism actually has its own chapter in St. John's text, and he asserts that "every foreigner in Hayti knows that cannibalism exists." *Hayti,* 188. Thus St. John's argument suffers from a warped a priori reasoning: because he and the other foreigners know cannibalism exists, it exists. Still, from time to time, stories of cannibalism tied to Voodoo rites would surface in American and European newspapers and magazines. One such story, related more than a year after the fact in *Harper's Weekly* in 1865, states that upon the ascension of Soulouque to power in Haiti, Voodoo sects ran wild, and that one group "after having stuffed and devoured one unfortunate child, were about to gormandize upon a second victim when justice overtook them. "Cannibals in Hayti." *Harper's Weekly* (Sept. 2, 1865): 545. Using cannibalism to critique the Haitian government, the article also places Voodoo as a threat not only to civilization but also to Haiti's future (i.e., its children). St. John refers to this same instance of supposed cannibalism in his book. See chapter 5, "Vaudoux-Worship and Cannibalism," and chapter 6, "Cannibalism."
16. Prichard. *Where Black Rules White,* 94.
17. Quoted in Trefzer, Annette. "Possessing the Self: Caribbean Identities in Zora Neale Hurston's *Tell My Horse.*" *African American Review* 34.2 (Summer 2000): 300.
18. Seabrook, W. B. *The Magic Island.* New York: Harcourt, Brace and Co., 1929, 93.
19. Ibid.
20. Ibid., 101.
21. Atkinson, J. Brooks. Rev. of *Zombie,* by Kenneth Webb. *New York Times,* 11 February 1932, clipping in *White Zombie Production Code File.* The Margaret Herrick Library of the Academy of Motion Picture Arts and Sciences.
22. Young, Elizabeth. "Here Comes the Bride: Wedding Gender and Race in 'Bride of Frankenstein.'" *Feminist Studies* 17.3 (Autumn 1991): 425.
23. Rhodes. *White Zombie,* 114.
24. The nineteenth-century explorer John Stanley described Africa as "the dark continent." In *The Question of Lay Analysis,* trans. James Strachey (New York: Norton, 1989), Freud borrowed the term to describe psychology's relationship to the adult woman's sexual life. By using this particular phrase, Freud

could be implicitly linking female sexuality to Africa and the Other, while also calling attention to the lack of clinical materials available on the sexual life of women. Women's sexuality is thus both something unexplored and something that defies easy understanding.

25. The problem with the Other, of course, is that it is always defined as that which a person or group is not. Therefore, even when it seems perfectly clear who or what the Other is to the person/group doing the defining, because it is built on a negation, the definition is always tenuous at best.

26. *White Zombie*. Dir. Victor Halperin. Perf. Bela Lugosi. Halperin Productions, 1932.

27. Given the homoerotic undertones of films like *White Zombie* and its 1936 follow-up, *Revolt of the Zombies*, it might be possible to take these claims even further, as there are moments in each film when zombified men become the implicit objects of the lust of the zombie masters.

28. Of course, another way to approach this would be to say that this line also strips zombies of any claims to manhood, effectively feminizing them.

29. Skal, David J. *The Monster Show*. Rev. ed. New York: Faber and Faber, 2001, 168.

30. Also known as *Drums of the Jungle*, *Love Wanga*, and *Crime of Voodoo*.

31. In a treatment of the film given to the Hays Office for review before filming, the screenwriters Victor Halperin and Howard Higgin noted about zombies, "Should the method of making such impregnable soldiers fall into the hands of the yellow race itself, it would doubtlessly mean the annihilation of the white race." Halperin, Victor, and Howard Higgin. *Treatment for White Zombie*. 11 January 1936, in *Revolt of the Zombies Production Code File*. The Margaret Herrick Library of the Academy of Motion Picture Arts and Sciences, 5. Although Halperin and Higgin were urged by the Hays Office to "drop the material . . . which reflects unfavorably upon 'yellow races' "—and they did—a very palpable fear of the nonwhite is still evident throughout in the film. Breen, Joseph I. Letter to Edward Halperin. 22 January 1936, in *Revolt of the Zombies Production Code File*. The Margaret Herrick Library of the Academy of Motion Picture Arts and Sciences.

32. In fact, the 1941 release *King of the Zombies* casts its zombie master as a Nazi intelligence officer.

33. *The Ghost Breakers*. Dir. George Marshall. Perf. Bob Hope and Paulette Goddard. Paramount, 1940.

34. This zombie represents one of the first examples of a zombie whose features are deformed. Interestingly, this is not a characteristic that other early zombie films would use. Up until the radical change in zombies in 1968, zombies in Hollywood films typically did not have monstrous features. (The zombies of *The Incredibly Strange Creatures Who Stopped Living and*

Became Mixed-Up Zombies [1964] are deformed, but this is not a result of zombiism, but rather of abuse and acid being thrown in their faces.) In fact, the monstrosity of early film zombies was born of their banality—an important part of early zombie discourse was the idea that "it could be you or me."

35. A similar implication that zombiism is punishment for a slaveholding past is made in Jacques Tourneur's *I Walked with a Zombie* (1943).

36. Depending on what you classify as a zombie film, there were roughly thirty-five zombie films that appeared domestically between 1940 and 1968.

37. The 1943 film *Revenge of the Zombies* could claim to be an exception to this. In the film, Lila von Altermann (played by Veda Ann Borg) has been zombified by her husband, and she eventually breaks his control and leads his other zombies in killing him. For most of the film, however, her husband does retain control over her, and when she does break the spell, she manages to gain control over all the other zombies, so they always have a zombie master.

38. Maddrey, Joseph. *Nightmares in Red, White, and Blue: The Evolution of the American Horror Film.* Jefferson, NC: McFarland, 2004, 15.

39. Dendle, Peter. *The Zombie Movie Encyclopedia.* London: McFarland, 2001, 2.

40. Ibid., 3.

41. Prawer, S. S. *Caligari's Children.* New York: Oxford UP, 1980, 69. To give a sense of how rapidly zombies entered the scene, it is worth noting that *Revolt of the Zombies*, besides being among the first major zombie films, also highlighted the very nature of the term "zombie." When the Halperin brothers announced they were making the film, the Amusement Securities Corporation (ASC), the financers of *White Zombie*, challenged the Halperins' right to use the term "zombie." Previously, the Halperins had relinquished to ASC all their rights connected to *White Zombie*, including the title and story, and the ASC felt the Halperins were now capitalizing on the prior film's success. In a refereed settlement, it was decided that the term was, in fact, a trade name. The opinion by Herman Hoffman went on to state that "zombie" was a "word which is not in common use and is unintelligible and nondescriptive to the general public. . . . The word 'zombie' has acquired a secondary meaning, suggestive of the photoplay *White Zombie*." Hoffman was, in essence, suggesting two things: that the term "zombie" was popularized by the ASC film, but that the concept was still not known widely enough to stand on its own. See Rhodes. *White Zombie*, 173. Yet by 1940, with the release of *The Ghost Breakers*, there were no such court battles over the notion of the "zombie."

42. *Night of the Living Dead* also moved zombies into the middle of rural America. As R. H. W. Dillard observes, this is one element that contributes

to the shocking nature of the film: it takes place not on a foreign island or in a mad scientist's laboratory, but at a farmhouse, an "ordinary" place. This very ordinariness was what made the film so terrifying. It created what Dillard called the "fear of the ordinary." While Haiti may have been made terrifying for Americans through claims of cannibalism, it was a cannibalism that was exotic. It was the very opposite of the mundane. *Night of the Living Dead* brought cannibalism home and set it outside an idyllic Pennsylvania farm. See Dillard, R. H. W. "*Night of the Living Dead*: It's Not Like Just a Wind That's Passing Through." *American Horrors: Essays on the Modern American Horror Film*. Ed. Gregory A. Waller. Urbana: University of Illinois Press, 1987, 17, 22.

43. It could be argued that other monster narratives allow for people to be "saved" from turning into a monster, yet this usually requires that the person in question not be turned fully or that people be saved on an individual basis. With early zombie narratives, a person can be turned fully into a zombie and still be saved, and salvation often comes to the entire group, not just the individual.

44. Further, the links to cannibalism/ghoulism can be tied to zombie fiction itself. At least one pre-1968 zombie film has hints of flesh-eating zombies. In 1941's *King of the Zombies*, a maid warns one of the protagonists, an African American man, to be in bed before midnight as "It's feedin' time—and [the zombies] likes dark meat!" Zombies, it seems, never completely shook the Voodoo-cannibalism connection of nineteenth-century discourse on Haiti. See Weaver, Tom. *Poverty Row Horrors!* London: McFarland, 1993, 38.

45. hooks, bell. *Black Looks: Race and Representation*. Boston: South End Press, 1992, 36.

46. Quoted in Brottman, Mikita. *Offensive Films: Toward an Anthropology of Cinema Vomitif*. Westport, CT: Greenwood Press, 1997, 12.

2. "WE ARE THE MIRROR OF YOUR FEARS": HAITIAN IDENTITY AND ZOMBIFICATION
Franck Degoul (translated by Elisabeth M. Lore)

1. I would like to thank Aden Atteyeh Sougal and Professor Delphine Perret from San Francisco State University for the time they spent in verifying my translation of certain passages of this article (translator's note).

2. Jardel, J-P. "Représentation des cultes afro-caribéens et des pratiques magico-religieuses aux Antilles: Une approche du préjugé racial dans la littérature para-anthropologique." p. 458, in J. Barnabe et al. (eds.), *Au visiteur lumineux: Des îles creoles aux sociétés plurielles*. Petit-Bourg, Guadeloupe, Ibis Rouge Editions. 2000.

3. Ibid. p. 459.

4. Métellus, J. *Haïti, une nation pathétique*. Paris, Denoël. 1987. p. 42: "Four successive presidents at the Palais National, from May 4, 1913 to July 27, 1915—so, in two years—dealt with the revolt of the Cacos. Permanent and universal anarchy, maintained and guided by the Americans, wore out the country. The Americans, who already insisted on assuring control over the bank of Haiti in order to favor their companies, delegated a commando of Marines that lifted, in broad daylight and with military display, the country's stock of gold, or $500,000, which was incontestably the property of the Haitian government, and transferred the contents to a warship destined for the National City Bank."

5. d'Ans, A-M. *Haïti, paysage et société*. Paris, Karthala. 1987. p. 200.

6. The details of this chapter were gleaned from a collection of articles on the subject from *Le Monde*, appearing in the Librio editions under the direction of Yves Marc Ajchenbaum. Ajchenbaum, Y-M (ed.). *Les Etats-Unis, gendarmes du monde: Pour le meilleur et pour le pire*. Paris, J'ai Lu. 2003.

7. Najman, C. *Haïti, Dieu seul me voit*. Paris, Balland. 1995. p. 251.

8. Ibid.

9. Ibid. p. 252.

10. Paravisini-Gebert, L. "Women possessed: Eroticism and exoticism in the representation of woman as zombie." p. 43. in M. Fernandez-Olmos and L. Paravisini-Gebert (eds.), *Sacred possessions: Vodou, Santería, Obeah, and the Caribbean*. New Brunswick, NJ, Rutgers University Press. 1997.

11. Najman. *Haïti, Dieu seul me voit*. p. 249.

12. Paravisini-Gebert. "Women possessed," pp. 43-44.

13. Barth, F. "Les groupes ethniques et leurs frontiers." in P. Poutignat and J. Streiff-Fenart (eds.), *Théories de l'ethnicitié*. Paris, Presses Universitaires de France. 1995. pp. 203-49.

14. Farmer, P. *Sida en Haïti: La victime accussée*. Paris, Karthala. 1996. p. 352.

15. Najman. *Haïti, Dieu seul me voit*. p. 250.

16. Colbert is one of the principle local informants for this piece, and is a lens through which to view the locals' perspective on Vaudou. The dissertation from which this article is taken cites interviews with Colbert, Claudel, Fène, and others who are knowledgeable about, and in some cases, practitioners of, Vaudou.

17. Théodat, J-M. "Haïti et la République Dominicaine: Identités et territories en partage." *Recherches haïtiano-antillaises*. Paris, L'Harmattan, 2005. p. 52.

18. Ibid. p. 50.

19. Ibid. p. 59.

20. Ibid. p. 53.

21. The piece "Nap tann yo" that Colbert speaks about here is an excerpt of the eponymous album of the very popular "roots" group Koudjay (Chancy Records, CRCD 1035). This piece broaches, in an aggressive tone, the problems that face the Haitians at the border as they leave to work as cane harvesters in the Dominican Republic. Their audience was important, since the song was destined for the popular events of Carnaval in the year 2000. In fact, it is a tradition in Haiti that each group introduces an upbeat, rhythmic piece dedicated to the carnival period, which will be diffused through thousands of watts in the streets, to be heard by a jubilant crowd. As this particular text seems key to the present discussion, I offer a Creole transcription as well as a personal translation of certain significant excerpts.

> "Sendomeng, Sendomeng, pap jwé! Nou pa ka jwé, tandé! Sendomeng, Sendomeng, pap jwé! Si gen la vi o, nap viv ansanm o! Si pa gen la vi sou frontiè-a: pap jwé! Si ou anmerde pèp-la, nap pousé sèl nan bonda'w: men lougawou vole!" [Saint-Domingue, Saint-Domingue: don't play! Us, we don't play, do you hear? If there is life, then we can live together. If there is no respect for life at the border, don't play that game! If you get on the people's [Haitian] nerves, we will get you with our wings, look, the werewolves fly already!] It is important to note here that the werewolves mentioned in this song refer to flying characters in the sphere of witchcraft. They are most often older women transformed by zoomorphism, allowing them to fly through the air to suck the blood of newborns. The Haitian "weapon" employed against the Dominican arsenal, then, consists not only of the powders that the video and Colbert allude to, but also of these types of blood-sucking creatures.

> "Mwen tandé Sendomeng ap vin okipé nou, m'pral di yo: 'nou la yé!' Nap tann yo. Yo té mèt gen ouzi: nap tann-yo! Té mèt gen cha blendé: nap tann yo! Yo té mèt gen misil: nap tann yo!" [I've heard said that Saint-Domingue is going to occupy Haiti: I'm going to tell them, "We are here!" We are waiting for them! So they have Uzis [machine guns], that is nothing. We are waiting for them anyway! So they have their armored tanks, that is nothing: We are waiting for them anyway! So they possess missiles, that means nothing: We are waiting for them anyway!]

22. See above for an explanation of Claudel.
23. Barth. "Les groupes ethniques et leurs frontières." p. 203.
24. Théodat. "Haïti et la République Dominicaine." p. 57.
25. Unnamed source.
26. Kerboull, J. *Vaudou et pratiques magiques*. Paris, Editions Belfond, Presses Pocket. 1977. pp. 108–9.

3. UNDEAD RADIO: ZOMBIES AND THE LIVING DEAD ON 1930S AND 1940S RADIO DRAMA
Richard Hand

1. Portions of this essay were originally published in *Monsters and the Monstrous: Myths and Metaphors of Enduring Evil*. Niall Scott, ed. New York: Rodopi, 2007.

2. Dunning, John. *On the Air: The Encyclopedia of Old-Time Radio*. Oxford: Oxford University Press, 1998, p. 454.

3. Grams, Martin, Jr. *Inner Sanctum Mysteries: Behind the Creaking Door*. Churchville, MD: OTR Publishing, 2002, pp. 26, 34.

4. Dunning. *On the Air*. p. 34.

5. For example, in an early instance of horror adaptation, *The Witch's Tale* broadcast *Frankenstein* (August 3, 1931), and, toward the end of the era of live radio, *The Hall of Fantasy* produced an adaptation of Poe's "The Tell-Tale Heart" (June 1, 1953). In terms of innovation and the atypical, *Quiet, Please* stands out with plays like "The Thing on the Fourble Board" (August 9, 1948), set in an oil field, and "Nothing behind the Door" (June 8, 1947), in which there is a man-made vault of pure "nothingness" that annihilates all who step into it.

6. Dunning. *On the Air*. p. 559.

7. As mentioned above, all broadcasting was live during this era. It was very rare for a play to be revived, but if it was it had to be in the form of an all-new production broadcast live once again.

8. Santo's first name alludes to the famous German military figure General Erwin Rommel (1891–1944) and his heavy German accent compounds this, making him an archetypical Prussian villain, thus revealing the context of World War Two. In addition, the fact that Rommel Santo is a scientist is a reflection of fears surrounding Nazi experimentation.

9. William Gaines, editor of EC, advised prospective writers in 1954, "We love walking corpse stories. We'll accept the occasional zombie or mummy." Quoted in Von Bernewitz, Fred, and Grant Geissman. *Tales of Terror! The EC Companion*. Seattle: Fantagraphics Books, 2000, p. 192. The titles of EC's two most famous comic books say it all: when readers opened *Tales from the Crypt* or *The Vault of Horror*, they were unleashing horrors from the domain of the grave. In the vast body of pre-code horror comics, the living dead—Gaines's "walking corpses"—are used in a number of ways. Some stories are authentic to the origins of zombie folklore and are set in Haiti, some use distinctly historical or Gothic settings for tales of the living dead, while the zombies in other stories crawl from the grave into a contemporary United States to exact their revenge or retribution. Characteristic for the undead in pre-code horror

comics is the graphic specificity: the living dead are fetid and decaying and colored in grimly lurid detail. In 1954, the Comics Code Authority dictated that scenes dealing with "the walking dead . . . are prohibited" (Sabin, Roger. *Adult Comics: An Introduction*. London: Routledge, 1993, p. 252), and this, in a single phrase, annihilated both the rich narratives and the graphic images that together constructed the 1950s horror comic zombie tales.

10. Nachman, Gerald. *Raised on Radio*. Berkeley: University of California Press, 1998, p. 308.

11. Dunning. *On the Air*. p. 608.

12. This is interesting in relation to Wade Davis's more recent and high-profile, if controversial, assertion that the zombie phenomenon in Haiti could be explained by tetrodotoxin poisoning (Davis, Wade. *Passage of Darkness: The Ethnobiology of the Haitian Zombie*. Chapel Hill: University of North Carolina Press, 1988; Davis, Wade. *The Serpent and the Rainbow*. New York: Simon and Schuster, 1985).

4. THE ZOMBIE AS OTHER: MORTALITY AND THE MONSTROUS IN THE POST-NUCLEAR AGE
Kevin Boon

1. R. P. Van Wing, *Etudes Bakongo* (Goemaere, 1921; pp. 170 ff.), as translated by Edwin W. Smith in Smith (ed.), *African Ideas of God: A Symposium* (2nd ed; Edinburgh House Press, 1950), p. 159.

2. E. Torday, "Nzambi Mpungu, the God of the Bakongo," *Man* 30 (Jan. 1930), p. 3.

3. Review of *Mutter Erde: Ein Versuch über Volksreligion* by Albrecht Dieterich, *Classical Review* 20.3 (April 1906), p. 187.

4. Anselm of Canterbury, "Proslogion," translated by David Burr, for the *Internet Medieval Sourcebook* (Fordham University), January 1996, viewed 31 December 2006, http://www.fordham.edu/halsall/source/anselm.html.

5. It is perhaps more accurate to say that origin can be external or internal, depending on whether you are a rationalist or an empiricist. Nevertheless, both positions valorize objectivity, and the truth, once realized, exists internally.

6. Peter Dendle, "The Zombie in Haitian and Southern U.S. Folklore," unpublished manuscript, 2005.

7. Irving Howe, *The Idea of the Modern in Literature and the Arts* (Horizon, 1967), p. 36.

8. Quoted in *Kurt Vonnegut Jr: Deadeye Dick*, videocassette, Wombat Productions, Altschul Group, 1984.

9. R. D. Laing, *A Divided Self* (Pantheon, 1960), pp. 79–80.

10. H. P. Lovecraft, "Herbert West—Reanimator," *The Mammoth Book of Zombies*, edited by Stephen Jones, Carroll and Graf, 1993, p. 243.

11. There is some confusion over whether the wives in the 2004 remake were robots or had implants.

12. Ksenych's story is included in *The Book of All Flesh*, edited by James Lowder, Eden Studies, 2001.

13. Clive Barker, "Sex, Death, and Starshine," *Mammoth Book of Zombies*, p. 31.

5. A DEAD NEW WORLD: RICHARD MATHESON AND THE MODERN ZOMBIE
Deborah Christie

1. To be clear, the visual similarities are prompted more by Sydney Salkow's 1964 film version, starring Vincent Price. In later film adaptations like *The Omega Man* (1971) with Charleton Heston and *I Am Legend* (2007) with Will Smith, as in Matheson's novel, the creatures can run quite fast and their complexion is merely pale. But in Salkow's film the hollow-eyed dead lurch and shamble with terrifyingly persistent slowness, and this is the recognizable image that Romero borrows for *Night of the Living Dead* (1968).

2. According to Romero, "I didn't call them zombies in the original film, you know? I didn't even think of calling them zombies. Back then, zombies were those guys in the Caribbean doing wetwork, so I called them flesh eaters or ghouls, or whatever. And it's only after people started to write about the film that they were referred to as zombies, and I thought, well, maybe they are! I don't know. I guess that I created the dead neighbor [*laughs*]." Balfour, Brad. "George A. Romero Relives His Zombies through the *Diary of the Dead*." PopEntertainment.com. February 14, 2008, http://www.popentertainment.com/romero.htm.

3. Again according to Romero, "When we originally shot the *Night of the Living Dead* thing, there were three proposed causes, and we cut two of them out.... I don't want there to be a cause, it's just something that's happening, it's just a different deal, it's a different way of life. If you want to look at it as a revolution, a new society coming in and devouring the old, however you want to look at it. That's really my take on it, it doesn't matter. And people just don't communicate to get to the core of it all, they just have their own agendas or their own concerns ... you know, Band Aids." Curnutte, Rick. "There's No Magic: A Conversation with George A. Romero." *Film Journal*. October 2004, http://www.thefilmjournal.com/issue10/romero.html.

4. Sutherland, Meghan. "Rigor/Mortis: The Industrial Life of Style in American Zombie Cinema." *Framework*. Vol. 48, No. 1, Spring 2007, pg. 72.

5. This theme is present in much of Katherine Hayles's work, but she treats it most specifically in *Writing Machines* (Cambridge: MIT Press, 2002) and *How We Became Posthuman: Virtual Bodies in Cybernetics, Literature, and Informatics* (Chicago: University of Chicago Press, 1999).

6. Badmington, Neil. "Theorizing Posthumanism." *Cultural Critique*. Vol. 53, No. 1, Winter 2003, pg. 11.

7. The relationship of the zombie to post-human theory has been addressed recently in a number of places: Sarah Juliet Lauro and Karen Embry's "A Zombie Manifesto: The Nonhuman Condition in the Era of Advanced Capitalism," in *boundary 2*, Vol. 35, No. 1, Spring 2008, engages specifically with post-human theory. Also, Martin Rogers's "Hybridity and Post-human Anxiety in *28 Days Later*" and Patricia MacCormack's "Zombies without Organs: Gender, Flesh, and Fissure" both appear in *Zombie Culture: Autopsies of the Living Dead*, edited by Shawn McIntosh and Marc Leverette (Lanham, MD: Scarecrow Press, 2008). And, in dialogue with the kind of ontological discussions associated with post-human theory, though they don't mention it explicitly, see Larry Hauser's "Zombies, *Blade Runner*, and the Mind-Body Problem" and K. Silem Mohammad's "Zombies, Rest, and Motion: Spinoza and the Speed of Undeath," which mentions Deleuze and Guattari briefly. Both of these appear in *The Undead and Philosophy: Chicken Soup for the Soulless*, edited by Richard Greene and K. Silem Mohammad (Chicago: Open Court, 2006).

8. Pepperell, Robert. *The Post-Human Condition: Consciousness beyond the Brain*. Chicago: University of Chicago Press. 2009. pg. 11.

9. Badmington. "Theorizing Posthumanism." pg. 11.

10. Hayles, Katherine. *How We Became Posthuman: Virtual Bodies in Cybernetics, Literature, and Informatics*. Chicago: University of Chicago Press. 1999. pg. 286–87.

11. Lauro and Embry. "Zombie Manifesto." pg. 87.

12. Badmington, Neil. "Pod Almighty!; or, Humanism, Posthumanism, and the Strange Case of *Invasion of the Body Snatchers*." *Textual Practice*. Vol. 15, No. 1, March 2001, pg. 9.

13. Ibid. pg. 12.

14. Pepperell. *Post-Human Condition*. pg. 3.

15. Haraway, Donna. "A Cyborg Manifesto: Science, Technology, and Socialist-Feminism in the Late Twentieth Century." In *Simians, Cyborgs, and Women: The Reinvention of Nature*. New York: Routledge. 1991. pg. 155.

16. The Trinity Test was the first full-scale test of the atomic bomb conducted in the New Mexico desert near Los Alamos. Several eyewitness accounts—now declassified—can be viewed at http://www.dannen.com/decision/trin-eye.html (U.S. National Archives, Record Group 227, OSRD-S1 Committee, Box 82 folder 6, "Trinity").

17. Dendle, Peter. *The Zombie Movie Encyclopedia*. Jefferson, NC: McFarland. 2001. pg. 100.

18. Pepperell. *Post-Human Condition*. pg. 3.

19. The exceptions are his interactions with his former neighbor and friend, Ben Cortman, and his brief association with Ruth, the apparently human survivor who turns out to be a vampire.

20. Matheson, Richard. *I Am Legend*. New York: Tom Doherty. 1995. pg. 29.

21. I hate to spoil the ending for anyone who has yet to read *I Am Legend*, but the final pages leave little doubt that Robert Neville has become a killer as prolific and indiscriminate as the plague of which he is a survivor.

22. Matheson. *I Am Legend*. pg. 70.

23. Ibid. pg. 73.

24. Ibid. pg. 74.

25. Ibid. pg. 75.

26. Ibid. pg. 69.

27. Ibid. pg. 77.

28. Ibid. pg. 119.

29. Giles quoted in Waller, Gregory. "Introduction." In *American Horrors: Essays on the Modern American Horror Film*. Ed. Gregory Waller. Urbana: University of Illinois Press, 1987. pg. 6.

30. Matheson. *I Am Legend*. pg. 154–55.

31. Ibid. pg. 155.

32. Ibid. pg. 44.

33. Waller, "Introduction." pg. 4.

34. Dillard, R. H. W. "*Night of the Living Dead*: It's Not Like Just a Wind That's Passing Through." In Waller. *American Horrors*. pg. 15.

35. Lowenstein, Adam. "Films without a Face: Shock Horror in the Cinema of Georges Franju." *Cinema Journal*. Vol. 37, No. 4, Summer 1998, pg. 37.

36. "Benjamin, like the Surrealists, believed the rapidly metamorphosing urban-industrial landscape simulates a mythic, enchanted dream state of consciousness.... [But he] wished to *transform* these dream images into dialectical images by exposing their historical content." Ibid. pg. 48.

37. Ibid. pg. 44.

38. In examining Georges Franju's film *Blood of the Beasts* (1949), Lowenstein probes the connection between horror and reality by focusing on the ways in which Franju intersperses a documentary-style montage of scenes from a slaughterhouse with the romantic lyrics of the Charles Trenet love song "La Mer," causing "the discrete elements of the song and the work [to] blur together, each infecting the other's presence to the point where the initial 'reality' of the workplace seems irrevocably altered." Ibid. pg. 42.

39. MOMA Film Exhibition. "George A. Romero's *Night of the Living Dead*." October 31, 2007. http://www.moma.org/visit/calendar/films/565.

40. Ibid. pg. 46.
41. Dillard. "*Night of the Living Dead.*" pg. 23.
42. Žižek, Slavoj. "Welcome to the Desert of the Real!" *The South Atlantic Quarterly.* Volume 101, Number 2, Spring 2002, pg. 385–389.
43. Ibid. pg. 27.
44. Sutherland. "Rigor/Mortis." 72.
45. Lauro and Embry. "Zombie Manifesto." pg. 101.

6. NUCLEAR DEATH AND RADICAL HOPE IN *DAWN OF THE DEAD* AND *ON THE BEACH*
Nick Muntean

1. The selection of *Dawn of the Dead* (1978) instead of *Night of the Living Dead* (1968) (which was made much closer to the time of *On the Beach*'s production in 1959) is due to the fact that, compared with the isolated zombie outbreaks in *Night of the Living Dead*, in *Dawn* the zombie hordes have swelled to truly apocalyptic numbers, and therefore constitute an overwhelming global antagonism much closer in spirit to the radioactive winds of *On the Beach*.
2. One can continue this argument, as I have elsewhere, that the 9/11 attacks engendered another epochal shift in the nature of the zombie form, as evidenced by the fast-moving, viral zombies of *28 Days Later* (2002).
3. Althusser, Louis. *Lenin and Philosophy, and Other Essays.* New York: Monthly Review Press, 2001. p. 111.
4. Lifton, Robert Jay. *The Future of Immortality, and Other Essays for a Nuclear Age.* New York: Basic Books, 1987. p. 154.
5. Fromm, Erich. *The Sane Society.* New York: Owl Books/Henry Holt, 1955. p. 359.
6. Ibid. pp. 359–60.
7. Caruth, Cathy. *Unclaimed Experience: Trauma, Narrative, and History.* Baltimore: Johns Hopkins University Press, 1996. p. 61.
8. Freud, Sigmund. *Introductory Lectures on Psycho-Analysis (1915–17).* London: Hogarth Press, 1959. p. 16.
9. Freud, Sigmund. *Beyond the Pleasure Principle.* New York: Norton, 1961. p. 11.
10. Caruth. *Unclaimed Experience.* p. 62.
11. Freud. *Beyond the Pleasure Principle.* p. 36.
12. Artaud, Antonin. "On Suicide." *Artaud Anthology.* New York: City Lights Books, 1965, p. 56.
13. In this way, it is almost as if the zombies are post-ideological sociopaths, as they bear an outward semblance of humanness but have no sense of morality, empathy, or any other definitively "human" qualities. Yet the sociopath, despite acting in accord only with the whims of his or her own id, can

nonetheless feign an air of—oftentimes quite charismatic—humanity, something unavailable to the zombie (but perhaps available to the vampire).

14. Boyer, Paul S. *By the Bomb's Early Light: American Thought and Culture at the Dawn of the Atomic Age*. Chapel Hill: University of North Carolina Press, 1994. p. xx.

15. Hachiya quoted in Lifton. *Future of Immortality*. pp. 150–51.

16. Lifton. *Future of Immortality*. p. 151.

17. Morrison quoted in Boyer. *By the Bomb's Early Light*. p. 78.

18. Lifton. *Future of Immortality*. p. 51.

19. Boyer. *By the Bomb's Early Light*. p. 307.

20. Agamben, Giorgio. *Remnants of Auschwitz: The Witness and the Archive*. New York: Zone Books, 2002. p. 47.

21. As Agamben extensively details in his book, the precise origins of the term are unknown, but he believes that the most likely explanation "can be found in the literal meaning of the Arabic word *muslim*: the one who submits unconditionally to the will of God," which, in the context of Auschwitz, becomes "a loss of all [personal] will and consciousness." *Remnants of Auschwitz*. p. 45.

22. Améry quoted in ibid. p. 41.

23. Agamben. *Remnants of Auschwitz*. p. 41

24. Aldo Carpi quoted in ibid. p. 41.

25. "It was possible to ascertain that the second phase began when the starving individual lost a third of his normal weight. If he continued losing weight, his facial expression also changed. His gaze became cloudy and his face took on an indifferent, mechanical, sad expression. His eyes became covered by a kind of layer and seemed deeply set in his face. His skin took on a pale gray color, becoming thin and hard like paper. He became very sensitive to every kind of infection and contagion, especially scabies. His hair became bristly, opaque, and split easily. His head became longer, his cheekbones and eye sockets became more pronounced. He breathed slowly: he spoke softly and with great difficulty. Depending on how long he had been in this state of malnutrition, he suffered from small or large edemas.... They excluded themselves from all relations to their environment. If they could still move around, they did so in slow motion, without bending their knees. They shivered since their body temperature usually fell below 98.7 degrees." Zdzislaw Ryn and Stanislaw Klodzinski quoted in Agamben. *Remnants of Auschwitz*. pp. 42–43.

26. Žižek, Slavoj. *Did Somebody Say Totalitarianism? Five Interventions in the (Mis)use of a Notion*. New York: Verso, 2001. p. 77.

27. This recurrence occurs because the mind has been unable to give meaning to the traumatic event—or, as Caruth describes it, "the outside has

gone inside without any mediation." *Unclaimed Experience*. p. 59. If we understand those mediating agencies as that of consciousness and ideology, then the parallels between our groups are brought into even sharper relief, as the traumatizing objects are literally the specter of trauma itself.

28. Ricoeur, Paul. *Freud and Philosophy: An Essay on Interpretation.* Trans. Denis Savage. New Haven, CT: Yale University Press, 1970. p. 351.

29. The uncertainty here is indicative of the ambiguity of the ending, in which it appears as though the zombie threat is being brought under control by government authorities—which would count as humans "winning," in a way—but is achieved through the destruction of non-zombies such as Ben (Duane Jones), such that the very cycles of self-destructiveness that brought civilization to that crisis point are simply re-perpetuated.

30. Fredric Jameson describes the fantasy bribe as proof of a Utopian element in all mass culture texts: "The works of mass culture cannot be ideological without at one and the same time being implicitly or explicitly Utopian as well: they cannot manipulate unless they offer some genuine shred of content as a fantasy bribe to the public about to be so manipulated." "Reification and Utopia in Mass Culture." *Social Text*. Winter 1979. p. 144.

7. LUCIO FULCI AND THE DECAYING DEFINITION OF ZOMBIE NARRATIVES
Steven Zani and Kevin Meaux

1. Examples include race anxiety as the "meaning" of *White Zombie*, or *Night of the Living Dead* understood as a reaction to American fears about the spread of Communism.

2. The text is eerily prescient of future zombie film rhetoric. Tablet VI of *Gilgamesh* contains a threat from the goddess Ishtar that she will "break in the doors of hell and smash the bolts; there will be confusion of people, those above with those of the lower depths. I shall bring up the dead to eat food like the living, and the hosts of the dead will outnumber the living. Let the dead go up to eat the living! And the dead will outnumber the living!" *Gilgamesh*. Trans. John Gardner and John Maier (New York: Random House, 1985).

3. Further development of the plague/zombie theme that extends beyond the scope of this chapter can be found in Jennifer Cooke's *Legacies of Plague in Literature, Theory, and Film* (New York: Macmillan, 2009), which treats the issue at length.

4. For thinking about zombies as a limit space for the very idea of human identity, see Nick Muntean's preceding essay in this book. While the account we are about to give here of plague narratives in literature is more attuned to questions of social dissolution on multiple levels, he addresses the same issues, and many more, on a more existential or individual register in zombie narratives.

5. Giovanni Boccaccio, *The Decameron*. Trans. Mark Musa and Peter Bondanella. (New York: Penguin, 2002), 9.
6. Ibid., 11.
7. Ibid., 10.
8. John Kelly, *The Great Mortality*. (New York: HarperCollins, 2005), 85.
9. Thomas Dekker, *The Plague Pamphlets of Thomas Dekker*. Ed. F. P. Wilson. (Oxford: Clarendon Press, 1925), 26.
10. For a more in-depth exploration of how cannibalism is both literally and metaphorically used in literature, see *The Man-Eating Myth: Anthropology and Anthropophagy* (New York: Oxford University Press, 1980), which has become famous, if controversial, in cannibalism scholarship. For the brief original account of cannibalism by the *androphagi*, see Herodotus, *The History of Herodotus*. Trans. George Rawlinson. (New York: Tudor, 1956), 236.
11. Dekker, *Plague Pamphlets*, 28.
12. Ibid., 30–31.
13. Daniel Defoe, *A Journal of the Plague Year*. (New York: Norton, 1992), 41.
14. Though obvious exceptions and parodic counter-texts exist, such as Max Brooks's *The Zombie Survival Guide: Complete Protection from the Living Dead* (New York: Three Rivers Press, 2003), which argues precisely for employing such techniques.
15. Louis Landa, "Religion, Science, and Medicine in *A Journal of the Plague Year*." In Defoe, *A Journal of the Plague Year*, 276.
16. Paula Backscheider, "Preface." In Defoe, *A Journal of the Plague Year*, x.
17. Rebecca Totaro, *Suffering in Paradise: The Bubonic Plague in English Literature from More to Milton*. (Pittsburgh: Duquesne University Press, 2005), 12–13.
18. Johannes Nohl, *The Black Death: A Chronicle of the Plague*. (New York: Harper & Row, 1969), 54.
19. Sterno is a brand name that has become the generic term for jellied cooking fuel. Mixed with other liquids, it can be strained to remove its poisonous methanol content and consumed as an alcoholic beverage.
20. Steven Kellman, *The Plague: Fiction and Resistance*. (New York: Twayne, 1993), 3.

8. IMITATIONS OF LIFE: ZOMBIES AND THE SUBURBAN GOTHIC
Bernice Murphy

1. Douglas Sirk's best-known films include *Magnificent Obsession* (1953), *All That Heaven Allows* (1959), *Written on the Wind* (1956), and *Imitation of Life* (1958). They are notable for their sentimental, soap-opera content, mannered acting style, painstakingly composed color schemes, emotive scoring, and

Sirk's tendency to reuse the same actors over and again (most famously Rock Hudson, Jane Wyman, and Lana Turner). The conflation of Sirk-style melodrama and Romero's zombie films isn't as incongruous as it at first appears. From *Night of the Living Dead* onward, Romero has time and time again presented radical critiques of both the American family and the complacency and materialism of postwar society. Further, race and its relationship between ordinary people and the supposed forces of law and order have also been a recurring preoccupation, most recently expressed in his 2007 film *Diary of the Dead*, in which the authorities are presented in a similarly unflattering light.

2. I am referring here to *NOTLD*'s use of news footage: the tone, of course, is very different from the camp knowing of Currie's film.

3. Sevin, Julia. "DVD Review: *Fido*." *Fear Zone*. February 5, 2008. http://www.fearzone.com/blog/fido-review.

4. The notion of a suburban, all-American community patrolled by aggressive security forces, fenced off by a ring of steel from the lawless and threatening "Wild Zone" brings to mind Baghdad's heavily fortified "Green Zone," as well as the growth of gated suburban communities in the United States.

5. Jameson, Frederic. "Nostalgia for the Present." In *Postmodernism, or, The Cultural Logic of Late Capitalism*. London: Verso. 1991. p. 279.

6. Ibid. p. 282.

7. Ibid.

8. Jameson. pp. 282–83.

9. Just as films such as *28 Days Later* (2002), the 2004 remake of *Dawn of the Dead*, and *[Rec]* (2007, remade as *Quarantine*, 2008) all feature "infected" antagonists with many of the characteristics of the traditional zombie except (at least initially) their undead origin.

10. See Dendle, Peter. *The Zombie Movie Encyclopedia*. Jefferson, NC: McFarland. 2001. pp. 3–4.

11. Mumford, Lewis. *The City in History: Its Origins, Its Transformations, and Its Prospects*. London: Penguin. 1961. p. 353.

12. Keats, John. *The Crack in the Picture Window*. New York: Ballantine. 1956.

13. Marling, Karal Ann. *As Seen on TV: The Visual Culture of Everyday Life in the 1950s*. Cambridge: Harvard University Press. 1996. p. 253.

14. That is, "modern conveniences," such as air conditioning, brand-new furnishings, and electronic goods.

15. Jackson, Kenneth. *The Crabgrass Frontier: The Suburbanization of the United States*. New York: Oxford University Press. 1985. pp. 239–40.

16. Shentin, James P, and Sobin, Dennis P. *The Future of Suburbia*. Port Washington, NY: Kennikat Press. 1971. p. 38.

17. Sobchack, Vivian. *Screening Space: The American Science Fiction Film*. New Brunswick, NJ: Rutgers University Press. 1999. p. 120.

18. The 1978 version, directed by Philip Kaufman, features a notably bleak ending in which the invaders triumph.

19. Finney, Jack. *Invasion of the Body Snatchers*. New York, Scribner. 1998. p. 10.

20. Russell, Jamie. *The Book of the Dead: The Complete History of Zombie Cinema*. Surrey: FAB Press. 2005. p. 69.

21. Williams, Tony. *The Cinema of George A. Romero: Knight of the Living Dead*. Middlesex, UK: Wallflower Press. 2003. p. 91.

22. Ibid. p. 63.

23. Beuka, Robert. *SuburbiaNation: Reading Suburban Landscape in Twentieth-Century Fiction and Film*. New York: Palgrave Macmillan. 2004. p. 174.

24. Ibid.

25. Friedan, Betty. *The Feminine Mystique*. London: Norton. 1963. p. 265.

26. The de Beauvoir quote is as follows: "Today the combat takes a different shape; instead of wishing to put man in a prison, woman endeavors to escape from one; she no longer seeks to drag him into the realms of immanence but to emerge, herself, into the light of transcendence. Now the attitude of males creates a new conflict: it is with bad grace that the male lets her go."

27. Levin, Ira. *The Stepford Wives*. New York: Simon & Schuster. 1972. pp. 43–45.

28. On a side note, it's worth noting that Paula Prentiss also came to a sticky end in another classic paranoid thriller of the 1970s, Alan Pakula's *The Parallax View* (1974).

29. Levin. *Stepford Wives*. p. 1.

30. Ibid. p. 16.

31. Ibid. p. 40.

32. Ibid. p. 41.

33. See also Larry Cohen's *It's Alive* trilogy (about a generation of infants mutated by environmental pollutants) and 1970s Creature Features such as *Grizzly*, *Prophecy*, and *Piranha* as well as more mainstream films such as the Jane Fonda vehicle *The China Syndrome*.

34. Levin. *Stepford Wives*. p. 53.

35. Ibid. p. 54.

36. Ibid. p. 63.

37. Knight, Peter. *Conspiracy Culture: From the Kennedy Assassination to* The X-Files. London: Routledge. 2000. p. 123.

38. Beuka. *SuburbiaNation*. p. 152.

39. Friedan. *Feminine Mystique*. p. 197. (emphasis added.)

40. Ibid. p. 202.

41. Levin. *Stepford Wives*. p. 61.
42. Ibid. p. 82.
43. Ibid. p. 91.
44. Avila, Eric. *Popular Culture in the Age of White Flight*. Berkeley: University of California Press. 2004. p. 113.
45. Baudrillard, Jean. *Simulacra and Simulation*. Trans. Sheila Faria Glaser. Ann Arbor: University of Michigan Press. 1995. p. 14.
46. Beuka. *SuburbiaNation*. p. 177.
47. Ibid. p. 183.

9. ALL DARK INSIDE: DEHUMANIZATION AND ZOMBIFICATION IN POSTMODERN CINEMA
Sorcha Ní Fhlainn

1. See Boon's contribution to this volume, "The Zombie as Other."
2. Jenn Webb and Sam Byrnand. "Some Kind of Virus: The Zombie as Body and as Trope." *Body and Society*. Vol. 14, Issue 2, 2008. p. 86.
3. Ibid. p. 86.
4. Fredric Jameson. *Postmodernism, or, The Cultural Logic of Late Capitalism*. London: Verso, 1991. p. ix.
5. While renaming a person without their consent is an obvious attempt to de-individuate at a personal level, the cutting of hair is more symbolic: "In the history of initiation, woundings, beatings, scarifications, and hair cutting represent dying by losing some part of the 'living world' to the 'other world' of death." Michael Meade. "Rites of Passage at the End of the Millennium." In *Crossroads: The Quest for Contemporary Rites of Passage*. Michael Meade, Nancy Geyer Christopher, and Louise Carus Mahdi (eds.). Chicago: Open Court Publishing, 1996. pp. 30–31. For more on the devastating effects of renaming, de-humanization, and de-individuation, especially in relation to the military and the famous Stanford prison experiment, see Philip Zimbardo. *The Lucifer Effect: How Good People Turn Evil*. London: Rider, 2007.
6. *Full Metal Jacket*. Dir. Stanley Kubrick. Warner Bros. 1987.
7. Most famously, in *The Shining* (1980) Jack Torrance (Jack Nicholson) has three distinctly horrific scenes: in the bathroom of room 237 with the reanimated corpse of a woman embracing him sexually; in the red toilets with Grady, the spectral butler, where he informs Jack of the need for him to "correct" his family situation; and in the family's bedroom suite, when he corners his family with a hatchet in his hand. Other associations with bodily functions (purity of essence) and fluids are mentioned frequently by Brig. Gen. Jack D. Ripper (Sterling Hayden) in *Dr. Strangelove* (1964), which also features scenes in bathrooms where the sense of the abject and its associations (filth, excrement, and body fluids) are highly amplified.

8. One could further a connection on Hartman's beloved "corps" as a killing unit and the dehumanisation undertaken to make these men into killing machines, or, indeed, dehumanized living *corps*es.

9. James Naremore. *On Kubrick*. London: British Film Institute, 2007. p. 40.

10. Mark T. Conard. "Chaos, Order, and Morality: Nietzsche's Influence on *Full Metal Jacket*." In *The Philosophy of Stanley Kubrick*. Jerold J. Abrams (ed.). Lexington: University Press of Kentucky, 2007. p. 35.

11. James Kendrick. *Hollywood Bloodshed: Violence in 1980s American Cinema*. Carbondale: Southern Illinois University Press, 2009. p. 132.

12. *Platoon*. Dir. Oliver Stone. Orion Pictures. 1986.

13. The My-Lai massacre in March 1968 was perpetrated by a U.S. Army unit and resulted in the murder of an estimated four hundred South Vietnamese civilians. The victims were predominantly women, children, and the elderly. Some of the murdered civilians were found to have been sexually assaulted, mutilated, and tortured prior to death. Initially, the massacre was covered up by its participants, and it was later investigated by the U.S. government only because of letters sent by soldiers who had witnessed and were disgusted by the events. Of the twenty-six soldiers initially charged with war crimes, only Lieutenant William Calley was convicted for the premeditated murder of twenty-two civilians. It has been noted that Calley was both feared and hated by his own troops and that many had conspired to kill him. We can therefore link the character of Barnes in *Platoon* with Calley through their similar attributes and murderous actions.

14. In this final voice-over, Chris designates the roles that both Barnes and Elias had in the platoon. Barnes, zombified and psychotic, is configured as the devil by consuming and devouring life, while Elias, with his Christological pose prior to death, his sense of justice and righteousness, his defiance of Barnes's murderous rampaging, and his final betrayal by his own platoon member, is clearly cast as Christ.

15. For a greater analysis on the internal/external conflict in depictions of the Vietnam War, see James Kendrick's chapter "Fighting Outward, Looking Inward: Violence in the 1980s Vietnam Film" in *Hollywood Bloodshed*. pp. 106–34.

16. Michael Bibby. "The Post-Vietnam Condition." In *The Vietnam War and Postmodernity*. Michael Bibby (ed.). Amherst: University of Massachusetts Press, 2000. p. 153.

17. Myra MacPherson. *Long Time Passing: Vietnam and the Haunted Generation*. Bloomington: Indiana University Press, 2002. p. xi.

18. Meghan Sutherland. "Rigor/Mortis: The Industrial Life of Style in American Zombie Cinema." *Framework*. Vol. 48, Issue 1, 2007. p. 69.

19. Jennifer Fay. "Dead Subjectivity: White Zombie, Black Baghdad." *CR: The New Centennial Review*. Vol. 8, Issue 1. 2008. p. 83.

20. Anna Powell. *Deleuze and the Horror Film*. Edinburgh: Edinburgh University Press, 2005. p. 176.

21. *Jacob's Ladder*. Dir. Adrian Lyne. Carolco Pictures. 1990.

22. Powell. *Deleuze and the Horror Film*. p. 179.

23. Luc also resorts to using the biochemical agent to enhance his strength during the final standoff with Scott at the film's climax (though it seems to have no impact on his brain function). This reading of the film aligns with Larry Hauser's readings of "good" and "bad" zombies in "Zombies, *Blade Runner*, and the Mind-Body Problem." In *The Undead and Philosophy*. Richard Greene and K. Silem Mohammad (eds.). Chicago: Open Court, 2006. pp. 53–66.

24. Michael P. Clark. "The Work of War after the Age of Mechanical Reproduction." In Bibby, *Vietnam War and Postmodernity*. p. 37.

25. *Universal Soldier*. Dir. Roland Emmerich. Carolco Pictures. 1992.

26. Cynthia Fuchs. "'What do we say happened here?': Memory, Identity, and the Vietnam War." In Bibby, *Vietnam War and Postmodernity*. p. 66.

27. There are examples of cyborgs coming apart (literally and figuratively) in science fiction and action cinema, but usually, when a cyborg mentally malfunctions, it is due to a revelation that their memories are fabrications in order to keep them under control, such as in Ridley Scott's *Blade Runner* (1982). Cyborgs who hold no such memories and serve as killing machines, such as James Cameron's T-101 and T-1000 Terminators (of 1984's *The Terminator* and 1991's *Terminator 2: Judgment Day*) are physically and mentally synchronized to perform their respective missions only. The brain is thus a system undertaking a required task. For more on the abject female cyborg and the problems of femininity and cyborg fusion, see Glenda Shaw-Garlock. "Abject Cyborg Woman." In *Our Monstrous (S)kin: Blurring the Boundaries between Monsters and Humanity*. Sorcha Ní Fhlainn (ed.). Oxford: Inter-Disciplinary Press, 2009. pp. 91–118.

28. A CPU's fundamental function is to execute the commands of a computer program.

29. Vampire subjectivity is the ultimate postmodern achievement in vampire literature and cinema. Beginning between 1967 and 1974 (from *Dance of the Vampires* to *Blood for Dracula*) and then manifesting fully in 1975/76 (with Stephen King's *'Salem's Lot* and Anne Rice's *Interview with the Vampire*), the vampire, in using the term "I," is immediately empowered, and provides a distinct point of view on the modern world from within our own cultural walls. For much more on this, see Sorcha Ní Fhlainn. "The Eternal Changeling: Dracula's Transformations in the 1970s." In *The Horrid Looking*

Glass: Reflections on Monstrosity. Peter Mario Kreuter and Paul Yoder (eds.). New York: Rodopi, 2011; Nina Auerbach. *Our Vampires, Ourselves*. Chicago: University of Chicago Press, 1995; and Stacey Abbott. *Celluloid Vampires*. Austin: University of Texas Press, 2007.

30. Sarah Juliet Lauro and Karen Embry. "A Zombie Manifesto." *boundary 2*. Vol. 35, Issue 1. 2008. p. 100.

31. Ibid. p. 98.

32. Tom Ruffles. *Ghost Images: Cinema of the Afterlife*. Jefferson, NC: McFarland, 2004. p. 104.

33. The Stanford Prison Experiment was a psychology experiment conducted in 1971 in which a group of Stanford University college students were treated like prisoners by another group of students playing prison guards. The two-week experiment was concluded after only six days because of the amount of abuse the elaborate role-play produced. This is now a landmark study cited as proof of the potential for abuses of power.

34. Personal e-mail communication between Glenn Adams and Dr. Philip Zimbardo, May 4, 2004. Reprinted in Zimbardo. *Lucifer Effect*. p. 249.

35. Philip Zimbardo discusses the lengths to which the military went to describe those involved with torture in Vietnam, and at Abu Ghraib in Iraq, as a "few bad apples," disavowing the extent of the pervading culture of dehumanization at work. See Zimbardo. *Lucifer Effect*. pp. 297–443.

36. Fay. "Dead Subjectivity." p. 93.

37. John Houston Craige. *Black Baghdad*. New York: Minton, Balch, 1933. Quoted in ibid. p. 96.

38. Fay. "Dead Subjectivity." p. 97.

39. *Masters of Horror*: "Homecoming." Dir. Joe Dante. Anchor Bay Entertainment. 2006.

40. Many films of the late 1970s and 1980s are haunted by a collective memory of the Vietnam War, some serious—*Coming Home* (1978), *Apocalypse Now* (1979), *The Deer Hunter* (1978), *Rambo: First Blood* (1982)—and some more comedic and hypermasculine—*Lethal Weapon* (1987), *House* (1985), the two *Rambo* sequels (1985, 1988), *Wild at Heart* (1990), and (allegorically) *Predator* (1987) and *Commando* (1985) (both situated in, or concerning, South America, once considered the United States' "new Vietnam," standing in with its jungle/dictatorship backdrop). Across network television, Vietnam was a central fixation in shows such as *Airwolf*, *The A-Team*, *Magnum, P.I.*, *Tour of Duty*, *Riptide*, and *China Beach*. The war reoccurred as a theme of protest for the liberal parents Elyse and Steven Keaton in *Family Ties*, contrasting with the other programs listed, which often reified the position of the veteran as a central (and often heroic) character.

41. There are many examples of heroic portrayals of Vietnam veterans in popular 1980s cinema, as illustrated by Susan Jeffords in her study of

masculine hard bodies as Reaganite emblems. See Jeffords. *Hard Bodies: Hollywood Masculinity in the Reagan Era*. New Brunswick, NJ: Rutgers University Press, 1994. See also Bibby. "Post-Vietnam Condition." pp. 143–72.

42. Marina Warner. *Phantasmagoria*. Oxford: Oxford University Press, 2006. p. 358.

43. Ibid. p. 360.

AND THE DEAD SHALL INHERIT THE EARTH
Part introduction by Peter Dendle

1. Ben Nuckols, "Humans vs. Zombies: New Sport Sweeping College Campuses," *The Herald* (Sierra Vista, AZ), Dec. 9, 2008. See also Matthew Daneman, "Dead Man on Campus: 'Zombie Tag' a Growing Game at Colleges," *USA Today*, Oct. 6, 2008.

2. On gun fetishism and survivalism in zombie movie audiences, see Peter Dendle, "The Zombie as Barometer of Cultural Anxiety," in Niall Scott, ed., *Monsters and the Monstrous: Myths and Metaphors of Enduring Evil* (New York: Rodopi, 2007), 45–57, esp. 53–54.

3. Elsewhere in this volume, Deborah Christie discusses why we should consider Matheson's monsters and its offspring in filmed versions of the *I Am Legend* narrative, such as *The Last Man on Earth*, as zombies rather than vampires.

10. SLACKER BITES BACK: *SHAUN OF THE DEAD* FINDS NEW LIFE FOR DEADBEATS
Lynn Pifer

1. Jeffrey Jerome Cohen, "Monster Culture: Seven Theses," in Jeffrey Jerome Cohen, ed., *Monster Theory: Reading Culture* (Minneapolis: University of Minnesota Press, 1996), 7.

2. *Shaun of the Dead* trailer, *IMDb*, http://www.imdb.com/video/screenplay/vi2172780825/ (accessed November 23, 2010) (emphasis mine).

3. Cohen, "Monster Culture," p. 4.

4. For an examination of the history of zombies in the films of Romero and others, see Peter Dendle's chapter "Zombie Movies and the 'Millennial Generation'" in this anthology.

5. When Stephen thinks the zombies have entered the mall because they're after the human characters hiding there, Peter explains, "They're after the place. They don't know why, they just remember. Remember that they want to be in here."

6. *Oxford English Dictionary Online*, "Slacker," http://dictionary.oed.com/ (accessed August 3, 2007).

7. John M. Ulrich, "Introduction," in John M. Ulrich and Andrea L. Harris, eds., *GenXegesis: Essays on "Alternative" Youth (Sub)Culture* (Madison: University of Wisconsin Press, 2003), 18.

8. This one-liner is lifted from the Britcom *Spaced*, a slacker cult favorite about London working-class youth that features Pegg, Nick Frost (*Shaun*'s Ed), and other actors from the film. In addition to sounding like a goofy allusion to standard Hollywood movie catchphrases, such as "Make my day" or "I'll be back," it serves as an in-joke intended to please slacker television fans.

9. Roger Ebert, "Shaun of the Dead," rogerebert.com, September 24, 2004, http://rogerebert.suntimes.com/apps/pbcs.dll/article?AID=/20040924/REVIEWS/40913006/1023 (accessed July 2, 2007).

10. Skye Sherwin, "Zombies in North London," *BBC Collective: The Interactive Culture Magazine*, April 8, 2004, http://www.bbc.co.uk/dna/collective/A2500002 (accessed July 2, 2007).

11. Marty Mapes, "Shaun of the Dead," *Movie Habit*, September 23, 2004, http://www.moviehabit.com/reviews/sha_iw04.shtml (accessed July 2, 2007).

12. See Joseph Campbell's *The Hero with a Thousand Faces* (Princeton, NJ: Princeton University Press, 1973).

13. Stephen King, *Stephen King's Danse Macabre* (New York: Everest House, 1981), 5.

14. Tony Magistrale, *Abject Terrors: Surveying the Modern and Postmodern Horror Film* (New York: Peter Lang, 2005), xiii.

15. Mapes, "Shaun of the Dead."

16. While some critics may argue that the zombie worker has always been a subtext of Romero and post-Romero zombie films because they show zombies still dressed in their work uniforms, I would assert that there's a difference between a gas station attendant who is attacked and turns into a zombie while still wearing his gas station jumpsuit, and a zombie who, after the zombie invasion is quelled, is chained to the gas pump and forced to do menial labor, much as Zombie Noel is chained to his grocery cart corral at the end of *Shaun*.

17. Hurston interviewed two Haitian doctors who had a "zombie" patient in their hospital: "We discussed at great length the theories of how Zombies come to be. It was concluded that it is not a case of awakening the dead, but a matter of the semblance of death induced by some drug known to a few. Some secret probably brought from Africa and handed down from generation to generation. These men know the effect of the drug and the antidote. It [. . .] destroys that part of the brain which governs speech and will power. The victims can move and act but cannot formulate thought." Hurston, *Tell My Horse: Voodoo and Life in Haiti and Jamaica* (1938; repr., New York: Perennial Library, 1990), 196.

18. Ibid., 181.
19. Ibid., 195.
20. Ibid., 179.
21. Ebert, "Shaun of the Dead."
22. Cohen, "Monster Culture," 6.
23. Hurston, *Tell My Horse*, 196.
24. Max Brooks, *The Zombie Survival Guide: Complete Protection from the Living Dead* (New York: Three Rivers Press, 2003), 15.
25. Cohen, "Monster Culture," 7.
26. Ibid., p. 13.
27. See also Andrew Currie's 2006 zombie comedy *Fido*.
28. Campbell, *Hero with a Thousand Faces*, 49–59.
29. Ibid., 97–109.
30. Ibid., 97.
31. Ibid., 126–49.
32. Ibid., 172–92.

11. ZOMBIE MOVIES AND THE "MILLENNIAL GENERATION"
Peter Dendle

1. I wish to thank Sarah Juliet Lauro and Dr. Deborah Christie for their thorough and very helpful suggestions to improve this essay. An earlier version of this paper was read at the Fourth Global Conference: Monsters and the Monstrous in Oxford, England (Mansfield College, Oxford University; Sept 18, 2006).

2. Other memorable zombies who are fully articulate and capable include Johnny Dingle (Andrew Lowery) in *My Boyfriend's Back* (1993) and Julie (Mindy Clarke) from *Return of the Living Dead Part III* (1993). In *Rosemary's Baby*-style zombie movies in which everyone in the vicinity turns out at the end to be a zombie, a fairly rational and composed front has to be maintained throughout most of the movie by the majority of zombies: thus *Messiah of Evil* (1972), *Dead and Buried* (1981), and *Zombie High* (1987).

3. See, for instance, the debates at GameSpot Forums in which fast zombies win (http://www.gamespot.com/pages/forums/show_msgs.php?topicid=26534223) or at ConvinceMe.net (http://www.convinceme.net/colDebate.php?dib=29) in which slow zombies win. A recent rehashing of the issue appears on AllThingsZombie at http://www.allthingszombie.com/forums/showthread.php?t=14533&highlight=fast+slow, while musings on the topic have also appeared in Slate.com (Josh Levin, "Dead Run: How Did Movie Zombies Get So Fast?" March 24, 2004, http://www.slate.com/id/2097751/.

4. Craig D. Murray and Judith Sixsmith, "The Corporeal Body in Virtual Reality," *Ethos* 27.3 (1999): 315–43, 316.

5. Jonathan Marshall, "The Online Body Breaks Out? Absence, Ghosts, Cyborgs, Gender, Polarity and Politics," *Fibreculture* 3 (2004): http://journal libreculture.org/issue3/issue3_marshall.html. For more on the ghost or ka metaphor (an "ethereal and less dense" copy of the human body in ancient Egyptian thought) and the cyberbody, see Murray and Sixsmith 333–35.

6. It should be noted that this common caricature of the zombie is a distorted simplification of the original folkloric zombi. The zombie in West Africa, Haiti, and even in the US South originally covered a much wider and more nuanced array of manifestations and behaviors (for initial orientation, see Hans-W. Ackermann and Jeanine Gauthier, "The Ways and Nature of the Zombi," *Journal of American Folklore* 104 [1991]: 466–94).

7. Overviews of the zombie in cinema include Allan Bryce, *Zombie* (Stray Cat Publishing, 2000); Peter Dendle, *The Zombie Movie Encyclopedia* (McFarland, 2001); and Jamie Russell, *Book of the Dead: The Complete History of Zombie Cinema* (FAB Press, 2005).

8. For more on zombie narratives and domestic space, see Bernice Murphy's essay in this collection.

9. For zombies in Italian movies of the period see Jay Slater, *Eaten Alive! Italian Cannibal and Zombie Movies* (Plexus Publishing, 2005) and Stephen Thrower, *Beyond Terror: The Films of Lucio Fulci* (FAB Press, 1999); for de Ossorio, see Nigel J. Burrell, *Knights of Terror: The Blind Dead Films of Amando de Ossorio* (Midnight Media, 1985).

10. Roberts, Donald F., Ulla G. Foehr, and Victoria Rideout. *Generation M: Media in the Lives of 8–18 Year Olds*. Kaiser Family Foundation, March 2005. p.36. http://www.kff.org/entmedia/upload/Generation-MMedia-in-the-Lives-of-8-18-Year-olds-Report.pdf.

11. Roberts, et al. (2005), p. 54.

12. Claudia Wallace, "The Multitasking Generation," *Time* (March 19, 2006): 51–52; also available at http://www.time.comitime/archive/preview/0,10987,1174696,00.html.

13. Paul W. Burgess, Emma Veitch, Angela de Lacy Costello, and Tim Shallice, "The Cognitive and Neuroanatomical Correlates of Multitasking," *Neuropsychologia* 38 (2000): 848–63.

14. *Zombage!* is a twelve-minute internet downloadable short with all the parts played by the filmmaker himself (born 1980), available online at www.hackmovies.com/shorts.php.

15. See Pete Boss, "Vile Bodies and Bad Medicine," *Screen* 27 (1986): 14–24.

16. Robin Campillo's *Les Revenants* (Haut and Court, 2004; released in English as *They Came Back*) is a thoughtful deployment of the zombie in exploring anxieties of old age.

17. This contrasts with *Invaders from Mars* or *Invasion of the Body Snatchers*–style 1950s movies that represented Cold War parables of communist infiltration. Cold War movies in which a seemingly normal person has been taken over by an alien personality portray not the threat of immediate bodily violence, but of long-term social assimilation as part of the program of cultural sabotage.

12. "OFF THE PAGE AND INTO YOUR BRAINS!": NEW MILLENNIUM ZOMBIES AND THE SCOURGE OF HOPEFUL APOCALYPSES
Margo Collins and Elson Bond

1. Brooks, Max. *World War Z: An Oral History of the Zombie War*. New York: Three Rivers, 2006. p. 2.

2. A reference to the privileged enclave of wealthy survivors from Romero's *Land of the Dead* (2005) who live in the high-rise buildings known as Fiddler's Green in downtown Pittsburgh, surrounded by high walls, defended gates, and presumably impassable rivers.

3. Brooks. *World War Z*. p. 7.

4. Ibid. p. 10.

5. Brooks, Max. *The Zombie Survival Guide: Complete Protection from the Living Dead*. New York: Three Rivers, 2003. p. 2.

6. Brooks. *World War Z*. p. 232.

7. Ibid. p. 204.

8. "Exclusive Interview: Max Brooks on *World War Z*." *Eat My Brains!* October 20, 2006. http://www.eatmybrains.com/showfeature.php?id=55.

9. Brooks. *World War Z*. p. 265.

10. "Exclusive Interview: Max Brooks on *World War Z*."

11. Review of *World War Z*. BrothersJudd.com. October 18, 2007. http://brothersjudd.com/index.cfm/fuseaction/reviews.detail/book_id/1637/World%20War%20Z.htm.

12. Brooks. *World War Z*. p. 104.

13. Ibid. p. 146.

14. Ibid.

15. Significantly, the term "quislings" comes from the Norwegian military officer Vidkun Quisling, who collaborated with Nazi Germany's conquest of Norway, and whose name became a term for traitors acting in concert with occupying forces.

16. Brooks. *Zombie Survival Guide*. p. 189.

17. Ibid. p. 99.

18. Maberry, Jonathan. *Zombie CSU: The Forensics of the Living Dead*. New York: Citadel, 2008. p. 23.

19. Dendle, "Zombie Movies and the 'Millennial Generation,'" in this collection.

20. Zombie vocabulary taken from http://www.zombiedefense.org/. Accessed April 17, 2010.

21. "Zombie Squad is an elite zombie suppression task force ready to defend your neighborhood from the shambling hordes of the walking dead. We provide trained, motivated, skilled zombie extermination professionals and zombie survival consultants. Our people and our training are the best in the industry." Zombie Squad home page. http://zombiehunters.org/whatiszs.php.

22. Ibid.

23. Ben Hauschild. Facebook status update. October 10, 2009.

24. For more on zombie road signs, see the blog post by Chris Nakashima-Brown, posted on January 26, 2009, "Keep Austin Zombie-Free." *No Fear of the Future*. http://nofearofthefuture.blogspot.com/2009/01/keep-austin-zombie-free.html.

25. Pifer, L. "Slacker Bites Back," here in this collection.

26. Austen, Jane, and Grahame-Smith, Seth. *Pride and Prejudice and Zombies*. Philadelphia: Quirk, 2009. p. 8.

27. Ibid. p. 34.

28. Grossman, Lev. "*Pride and Prejudice*, Now with Zombies!" *Time*. April 2, 2009. http://www.time.com/time/arts/article/0,8599,1889075,00.html.

29. Austen and Grahame-Smith. *Pride and Prejudice and Zombies*. p. 80.

30. Ibid. p. 319.

31. Ibid. p. 120.

32. This was pointedly *not* the situation in Romero's classic 1968 film *Night of the Living Dead*, where protocol had no such comforting effect; in fact, as demonstrated by the sheriff and his men in the closing frames, it was just as scary as the undead hordes.

33. It was noted in a great number of reviews for the film that the viral outbreak resulting in the mutation of humans into "Darkseekers" was representative of the common expectations for a zombie apocalypse; as Deborah Christie argues earlier in this collection in her piece on *I Am Legend*, regardless of whether a hungry mutant is *called* a zombie, it is fairly easy to recognize one.

34. Paffenroth, Kim. *Dying to Live: A Novel of Life among the Undead*. New York: Permuted, 2007. p. 2.

35. Ibid. p. 7.

36. Ibid. p. 64.

37. Ibid. p. 146.

38. Ibid. p. 76.

39. Ibid. p. 180.

40. Ibid. p. 190.

41. Mecum, Ryan. *Zombie Haiku: Good Poetry for Your... Brains!* New York: How, 2008. p. 2.

42. Ibid. pp. 5, 18, 40, 53, 126, 118, 139.

43. We offer the theory that the "comic" zombie exists as a counter to any fundamental definition of zombie-dom. That's why it's funny.

13. PLAYING DEAD: ZOMBIES INVADE PERFORMANCE ART... AND YOUR NEIGHBORHOOD
Sarah Juliet Lauro

1. I am extremely grateful to Thea Faulds, Nick Muntean, and "David" for their input as organizers of zombie events in Toronto, Austin, and San Francisco, respectively; to Jillian Mcdonald for granting me interviews and allowing me to participate in her *Zombies in Condoland* performance; to Lindsay Riordan, Blake Stimson, and Simon Sadler for their council as art historians; to Colin Milburn and Timothy Morton for their generosity and expertise in all matters, zombies and otherwise; and to Joshua Clover and Nathan Brown.

2. I borrow this term from Peter Dendle, *The Zombie Movie Encyclopedia* (Jefferson, NC: McFarland, 2001), 4.

3. This was said at a talk the artist gave at the Headlands Center for the Arts in Marin, California, on September 4, 2008.

4. The phenomenon of zombie gatherings is increasing in scope as well as size. In 2009, a "Zombie Prom" was held in San Francisco. This is apparently not affiliated with the SF Zombie Mob, but was rather a burlesque show that invited audience participation, and attendees were encouraged to come dressed as zombies attending a prom. See Janine Kahn, "Zombie Prom, Wicked, and the Seven Deadly Sins: Your Monday Morning Hangover," *SF Weekly Blogs*, February 9, 2009, http://blogs.sfweekly.com/shookdown/2009/02/zombie_prom_wicked_and_the_sev.php. On the more violent side of the spectrum, the increasing popularity of zombie-shooter-style video games has spawned the staging of human versus zombie battles on college campuses, where students wage war against peers dressed as zombies. See Ben Nuckols, "Humans vs. Zombies: New Playground Tag for the MySpace Generation," Associated Press, December 6, 2008, http://www.pantagraph.com/news/article_4d98d5c6-7b15-5613-8d4a-d28a67d66a8a.html; and Matthew Daneman, "Dead Man on Campus: 'Zombie Tag' a Growing Game at Colleges," *USA Today*, October 6, 2008, http://www.usatoday.com/news/education/2008-10-05-zombie-tag_n.htm. For the purposes of this chapter, I am concentrating on the zombie gatherings that demand of their participants patience and endurance, and are less immediately legible as entertainment and more like a kind of performance art.

5. See Jennifer Cooke, *Legacies of Plague in Literature, Theory, and Film* (New York: Macmillan, 2009).

6. This information is culled from accounts I read on the Listservs at http://www.eatbrains.com/ and http://www.zombiewalk.com/, and confirmed in interviews with the events' coordinators.

7. Jillian Mcdonald, *Horror Makeup*, exhibition notes, Brooklyn, NY, 2006.

8. Jamie Russell, *Book of the Dead: The Complete History of Zombie Cinema*, 2nd ed. (Surrey, UK: FAB Press, 2006), 22, 75.

9. "The London Bridge Experience is a fun-filled attraction with realistic special effects and professional actors. The London Tombs section is set in a notoriously haunted part of London Bridge." Tourist pamphlet, London, May 2008 (publication information unknown). Regarding the Times Square stunt, see "Zombies Take over Times Square," BBC News, October 27, 2010, http://www.bbc.co.uk/news/entertainment-arts-11633589.

10. The *Haitian Internet Newsletter* of September 3, 2008, published a story about a zombie: a woman had been found alive after being buried by loved ones three months previously. See http://www.haitianinternet.com/articles.php/362.

11. Most of these zombie mobs have no visible ties to the commodity marketplace, though a few zombie gatherings have been held as fund-raisers. Ironically, a few zombie gatherings have been held to raise support for blood drives, though this would seem more fitting of a congregation of vampires.

12. Other zombies in art galleries include Matthew Barney's resurrected of *Cremaster 3* (2002), Debra Drexler's multimedia presentation *Gauguin's Zombie* (2005), and the Bruce LaBruce film that bridges the gap between esoteric art film and gay pornography, *Otto; or, Up with Dead People* (2008).

13. These images might be employed as a how-to for zombie walkers, as they show step-by-step how the subtle addition of eye black to the Adam's apple, or the ratting of a woman's neat coif, can take an individual from benign to bizarre in an instant. Jillian Mcdonald, "Zombie Portraits," 2007, http://jillianmcdonald.net/projects/zombie_lenticular.html.

14. It is also in dialogue with a long history of performance artists who use their own bodies. Specifically, I am thinking here of Adrian Piper, who "carried out a series of 'self-transformations' in which she intentionally disfigured herself in order to provoke responses from people in the streets, the subway, the Metropolitan Museum of Art, and the library." Gary Sangster, *Outside the Frame: Performance and the Object* (Cleveland: Cleveland Center for Contemporary Art, 1994), 51. For a detailed description of the history of performance art, which may provide more context for the work of Jillian Mcdonald and suggest many other fruitful comparisons that I do not have the space to explicate here, see RoseLee Goldberg, *Performance Art: From*

Futurism to the Present (New York: Thames and Hudson, 2001); or Manuel J. Borja-Villel, Bernard Blistène, Yann Chateigné, and Museu d'Art Contemporani, *A Theatre without Theatre* (Lisbon: Museu Colecção Berardo, 2007).

15. I am thinking here of the Russian Formalist concept of *ostranenie*. Ironically, this is the idea that art defamiliarizes life in order to prevent overautomatization, a condition in which the individual will function as though by formula. See Viktor Shklovsky, "Art as Device," in *Theory of Prose* (1917; repr., Normal, IL: Dalkey Archive Press, 1990), 4–5. In these zombie gatherings, then, we may see people play the automaton in order to prevent it from becoming a reality.

16. See Elias Canetti's *Crowds and Power*, trans. Carol Stewart (Hamburg: Claassen Verlag, 1960) for a discussion of how the crowd becomes a single organism.

17. Carol Kino, "Jillian Mcdonald, Performance Artist, Forsakes Billy Bob Thornton for Zombies," *New York Times*, July 30, 2006, http://www.nytimes.com/2006/07/30/arts/design/30kino.html.

18. At first glance, Mcdonald's celebrity cycles might just seem like celebration of the consumerist spectacle, but rendering the silver screen permeable has an equalizing effect. It illustrates that the position Mcdonald plays here, of the digitized persona capable of interfacing with the untouchables of the celebrity cult, is available to all. This work might be said to be simultaneously cyborg and socialist, but this is an argument for another time; the important point here is Mcdonald's predilection for reworking the epitome of capitalist spectacle, the Hollywood movie. Further, that this aspect of participatory spectatorship seems foreclosed to the heterosexual male might constitute a challenge to the normative male gaze, which has historically been *the* focus of cinema. See Laura Mulvey, "Visual Pleasure and Narrative Cinema," *Screen* 16.3 (1975): 6–18.

19. Another piece that was filmed at the same time, called *Slasher Cycle*, is a four-screen projection in which masked men dressed like cinema's most famous slashers (Freddy Krueger, from *A Nightmare on Elm Street*, 1984; Michael Myers, from *Halloween*, 1978; Jason Voorhees, from *Friday the 13th*, 1980; and Leatherface from *Texas Chain Saw Massacre*, 1974) stalk about what is obviously the same house, but none of them ever find one another, or a victim, and thus violence is infinitely deferred.

20. In an article for *Art Papers*, Virginia Spivey writes, "The engagement of audience is one of the greatest strengths of Mcdonald's work. In addition to its use of humor and physical involvement of the viewer, the work also enlists interactive platforms that reach beyond the confines of the artworld, such as the Internet." Virginia Spivey, "Jillian Mcdonald: Richmond, VA," *Art Papers*, May/June 2008, 72–72.

21. Nuit Blanche guidebook (Toronto: Scotiabank, October 4, 2008), 1.
22. Miwon Kwon, *One Place after Another: Site-Specific Art and Locational Identity* (Cambridge, MA: MIT Press, 2002), 142.
23. Ibid., 7. The only difference between the two seems to be more self-awareness of the distinction between artist and community; Kwon calls for "questioning of the exclusions that fortify yet threaten the group's own identity" (154).
24. Ibid., 149.
25. Ibid., 148.
26. Ibid., 7.
27. Quoted in ibid., 153.
28. This blurb from the Scotiabank pamphlet mistakenly lists the title of Romero's film as "Diary of a Zombie," not to be confused with *The Zombie Diaries*, a 2006 UK production.
29. Nuit Blanche guidebook, 18.
30. Several of the zombies in attendance at Mcdonald's performance were obviously old hands at the zombie game—several of them truly upped the makeup ante with eerie contact lenses, gelatinous blood, and exposed arteries. Zombie walks have become so popular that online one can find many different "how-to" videos with makeup tips to help you transform into your undead self.
31. Guy Debord, thesis 191 from *The Society of the Spectacle*, excerpted in Hal Foster et al., *Art since 1900: Modernism, Antimodernism, Postmodernism*, vol. 2, *1945 to the Present* (London: Thames and Hudson, 2005), 393.
32. In fact, Munster tells me, the City of Toronto has even interceded to keep the zombies' path from straying too close to churches. Thea Faulds (aka Thea Munster), interview by the author, Toronto, October 4, 2008.
33. The presence of many other types of cameras only made the spectacle feel more labyrinthine. Tourists and newspeople were also chronicling the event. Many tourists wanted their picture taken with a zombie. I started taking pictures not only of those bystanders posing with the undead, but also of the people who were taking their pictures, hoping to catch them up in the inescapable cycle of spectacle.
34. Reference to the humorous book *The Zen of Zombie: Better Living through the Undead*, by Scott Kenemore (New York: Skyhorse, 2007), is mostly unintentional.
35. Canetti, *Crowds and Power*, 49.
36. Foster, *Art since 1900*, 391.
37. Simon Sadler, *The Situationist City* (Cambridge, MA: MIT Press, 1999), 17.
38. Sadler gives a more complete list of translated nuance for the word "détournement": "rerouting, hijacking, embezzlement, misappropriation,

corruption . . . all acts implicit in the Situationist use of society's preexisting aesthetic elements." Ibid., 17.

39. One of the examples of Situationist détournement that Sadler gives is Gil J. Wolman's replacement of official street signs with lines of poetry, which might provide a literal, as well as metaphorical, *diversion* of the public (ibid., 97). Of late, we have seen zombie détournement in Austin, Texas, in the form of a road sign hacked and reprogrammed to read, "Caution! Zombies Ahead!" Chris Nakashima-Brown, "Keep Austin Zombie-Free," *No Fear of the Future*, January 26, 2009, http://nofearofthefuture.blogspot.com/2009/01/keep-austin-zombie-free.html.

40. The punk movement shared many of the SI's goals, including the diversion or reuse of capitalist "refuse" for other means, and general disruption of the smooth workings of mainstream society. See Dick Hebdige's introduction to *Subculture: The Meaning of Style* (London: Routledge, 1979) for an overview of this aspect of punk culture.

41. Elsewhere I argue that the novel *Pride and Prejudice and Zombies* (Philadelphia: Quirk Books, 2009), in which Seth Grahame-Smith inserted zombies into Jane Austen's original text, is a "modification" in line with Jorn's painted-over paintings.

42. Foster, *Art since 1900*, 397.

43. Sadler, *Situationist City*, 97.

44. Guy Debord, *The Society of the Spectacle*, trans. Ken Knabb (London: Rebel Press, 2004), 11.

45. Foster, *Art since 1900*, 397.

46. Ibid., 98.

47. Ibid.

48. Sadler, *Situationist City*, 92.

49. Sadler links the SI to experimental theatre, "the energies of which had been dedicated to the integration of players and audience, of performance space and spectator space, of theatrical experience and 'real' experience" (ibid., 105).

50. MACBA, *Theatre without Theatre*, 168.

51. Unfortunately, the zombie does not speak, and signifies only the irreconcilability of the dialectic. For a further explanation of this idea, see Sarah Juliet Lauro and Karen Embry, "A Zombie Manifesto: The Nonhuman Condition in the Era of Advanced Capitalism," *boundary 2* 35.1 (2008): 85–108.

52. MACBA, *Theatre without Theatre*, 167. GRAV saw themselves as a first stage, the second of which might be the production of "ensembles that would play the part of social incitement." But for the moment, their works strived to create "varied situations, whether they engender a strong visual excitement,

or demand a move on the part of the spectator, or contain in themselves a principle of transformation, or whether they call for active participation from the spectator. To the extent that this proliferation calls into question—even diffidently—of the normal relations between art and the spectator, we are its supporters." Kristine Stiles and Peter Selz, eds., *Contemporary Art: A Sourcebook of Artists' Writings* (Berkeley: University of California Press, 1996), 411.

53. Foster, *Art since 1900*, 453.
54. Sadler, *Situationist City*, 106.
55. Brentano, *Outside the Frame*, 40.
56. For a discussion of banalization, see Debord, *Society of the Spectacle*, 94.
57. Foster, *Art since 1900*, 395.
58. Nato Thompson, Gregory Sholette, and Joseph Thompson, eds., *The Interventionists: Users' Manual for the Creative Disruption of Everyday Life*, 2nd ed. (Cambridge, MA: MIT Press, 2006), 150.
59. Though there appear to have been some cities that participated in this event (e.g., San Francisco, Memphis), World Zombie Day has since been co-opted by charitable organizations. In 2008, the event garnered widespread attention. Simultaneous events were held in forty-six cities in North America, Europe, and Australia on October 11. But this global event was organized by a television producer, Mark Menold of Pittsburgh's *It's Alive Show*, featured on the Discovery Channel, and it involved fund-raising. Because of its direct ties to capital, I do not include it as the kind of zombie event I am profiling here. For more on this, see "World Zombie Day Bites 2009," posted by Meh, March 25, 2009, http://www.horror-movies.ca/horror_14719.html.
60. The San Francisco zombie group calls itself a "flash mob," rather than using the term "zombie walk" or "zombie gathering." But in its adoption of the name flash mob to describe itself, the SF group seems more at ease with being categorized as a kind of interventionist art. Flash mobs are typically thought of as a phenomenon arising out of new Internet and cell phone technologies. Simply put, people coordinate via online forums to meet at an appointed time and place and perform a seemingly random and usually playful act. Recent events staged by flash mobs have orchestrated the wide-scale collaboration of up to three thousand individuals. In the Paris Trocadéro, London's Trafalgar Square, and New York's Grand Central Station, flash mobs orchestrated elaborate performances called "freezes." Participants, having been given an appointed time and signal, froze in place simultaneously and held their poses for five minutes, creating the impression for the uninvolved passersby that time had just been suspended, or that one was walking through a gallery of statues.
61. Many of these flash mob events, and increasingly, the zombie gatherings, are being claimed as protests. Looking at forums online, it seemed to

me that there were about even numbers of people organizing inanity in the name of insurrection—those who name their event as a particular form of demonstration against a specific gripe—and those who do it for the mere joy of disruption, what we might imagine as a more general protest against capitalist society and the status quo. Some of the zombie-ins have been held as fund-raisers (a group called the "Obama Zombies" purportedly raised money for the 2008 presidential campaign by staging zombie events), but there have also been occasions when zombie groups had the rather ironically benign goal of "raising awareness." On FlashMob.com I even saw one call for a zombie walk to advertise safe driving to teens. The zombies wore signs that read, "Dead is forever." All the zombie organizers whom I have contacted are committed to keeping their zombies depoliticized, but this aspect of the movement may be on the rise: Thea Munster has had people encourage her to ally the event with a charitable cause, saying that it would be easier to get off work for a breast cancer awareness walk than for a zombie walk.

62. "David" is the only name he communicates by as an organizer; he is very protective of his identity and refused to divulge his real name or profession to me. See Declan McCullagh, "Brain-Eating Zombies Invade SF Apple Store," *CNET News*, May 26, 2007, http://news.cnet.com/8301-17938_105-9723086-1.html.

63. Henri Lefebvre, *Critique of Everyday Life*, trans. Michel Trebitsch (1947; repr., London: Verso, 2008), 117. I recognize, too, that the movement's taking up of the mythic zombie eerily parallels the kind of "demotion to the bizarre" that Lefebvre argues is a feature of depoliticized bourgeois literature of the nineteenth century.

64. Stiles and Peter Selz, eds., *Contemporary Art*, 706.

65. Debord, *Society of the Spectacle*, 99.

66. Lefebvre, *Critique of Everyday Life*, 129.

AFTERWORD: ZOMBIE (R)EVOLUTION
Sarah Juliet Lauro

1. At least one critic, Roger Moore in his June 13, 2008, review in *Orlando Sentinel*, calls the film a "zombie movie," but only in order to denigrate it. He writes, "We're all witness to a career that was overpraised until it imploded. The new Spielberg? The new Hitchcock? Naah. He's the new Romero."

2. Peter Dendle, *Zombie Movie Encyclopedia* (Jefferson, SC: McFarland, 2001).

3. For a different take on this same phenomenon in zombie film, see Hamish Thompson's aptly named article "'She's Not Your Mother Anymore, She's a Zombie!': Zombies, Value, and Personal Identity," in Richard Greene and K. Silem Mohammad, eds., *The Undead and Philosophy: Chicken Soup for the Soulless* (Chicago: Open Court, 2006).

4. The most recent development in zombie evolution that I have noticed is in Romero's 2007 work *Diary of the Dead*, in which the phenomenon of the dead rising seems to be something that is just . . . happening. Even those who have not been bit by zombies will reanimate after death.

5. There are a few spoof films that feature zombies as the beleaguered protagonist, such as *Zombie-Americans* (2005), a short film by Ed Helms. In the film, Zombie-Americans speak and may be said to display a more evolved specimen of living dead.

6. Spelman describes how the suffering of others is sometimes co-opted by certain groups; for example, the slave is made into a "spiritual bellhop" by suffragist rhetoric. See *Fruits of Sorrow: Framing Our Attention to Suffering* (Boston: Beacon Press, 1997).

7. For a discussion of the zombie film's treatment of virus see Jennifer Cooke's book, *Legacies of Plague in Literature, Theory and Film*.

8. See, for example, *28 Days Later*, in which animal activists release chimpanzees infected with a virus that may have been bioengineered, or the 2007 film version of Richard Matheson's 1954 novel *I Am Legend*, in which the virus is described as having developed out of the human-manufactured cure for cancer.

9. There is also a highly regarded miniseries produced by the History Channel called *Life after People* that explores the same progression of nature's reclamation of the earth in a post-human scenario.

10. The changed signs were apparently the accomplishment of hackers. See the January 26, 2009, blog post by Chris Nakashima-Brown, "Keep Austin Zombie-Free," *No Fear of the Future*, http://nofearofthefuture.blogspot.com/2009/01/keep-austin-zombie-free.html.

SELECTED BIBLIOGRAPHY

BOOKS AND ARTICLES

Agamben, Giorgio. *Remnants of Auschwitz: The Witness and the Archive.* New York: Zone Books, 2002.
Althusser, Louis. *Lenin and Philosophy, and Other Essays.* New York: Monthly Review Press, 2001.
d'Ans, A-M. *Haïti, paysage et société.* Paris: Karthala, 1987.
Anselm of Canterbury. "Proslogion." Translated by David Burr. *Internet Medieval Sourcebook* (Fordham University). January 1996. http://www.fordham.edu/halsall/source/anselm.html.
Arens, William. *The Man-Eating Myth: Anthropology and Anthropophagy.* New York: Oxford University Press, 1980.
Artaud, Antonin. *On Suicide: Artaud Anthology.* New York: City Lights Books, 1965.
Atkinson, J. Brooks. Review of *Zombie*, by Kenneth Webb. *New York Times.* February 11, 1932.
Austen, Jane, and Seth Grahame-Smith. *Pride and Prejudice and Zombies: The Classic Regency Romance—Now with Ultraviolent Zombie Mayhem!* Philadelphia: Quirk, 2009.
Backscheider, Paula. "Preface." In Daniel Defoe, *A Journal of the Plague Year.* New York: Norton, 1992.
Badmington, Neil. "Pod Almighty!; or, Humanism, Posthumanism, and the Strange Case of *Invasion of the Body Snatchers.*" *Textual Practice* 15 (2001): 5–22.
———. "Theorizing Posthumanism." *Cultural Critique* 53 (2003): 10–27.
Balfour, Brad. "George A. Romero Relives His Zombies through the *Diary of the Dead.*" PopEntertainment.com. February 14, 2008. http://www.popentertainment.com/romero.htm.
Barth, F. "Les groupes ethniques et leurs frontières." In *Théories de l'ethnicitié.* Edited by P. Poutignat and J. Streiff-Fenart. Paris: Presses Universitaires de France, 1995.

Bibby, Michael. "The Post-Vietnam Condition." In *The Vietnam War and Postmodernity*. Edited by Michael Bibby. Amherst: University of Massachusetts Press, 2000.

Boccaccio, Giovanni. *The Decameron*. Translated by Mark Musa and Peter Bondanella. New York: Penguin, 2002.

Boyer, Paul S. *By the Bomb's Early Light: American Thought and Culture at the Dawn of the Atomic Age*. Chapel Hill: University of North Carolina Press, 1994.

Brooks, Max. *World War Z: An Oral History of the Zombie War*. New York: Three Rivers, 2006.

———. *The Zombie Survival Guide: Complete Protection from the Living Dead*. New York: Three Rivers Press, 2003.

Brottman, Mikita. *Offensive Films: Toward an Anthropology of Cinema Vomitif*. Westport, CT: Greenwood Press, 1997.

Campbell, Joseph. *The Hero with a Thousand Faces*. Princeton, NJ: Princeton University Press, 1973.

Camus, Albert. *The Plague*. Edited by Tony Judt. Translated by Robin Buss. New York: Penguin, 2002.

Canetti, Elias. *Crowds and Power*. Translated by Carol Stewart. London: Victor Gollanz, 1962.

Caruth, Cathy. *Unclaimed Experience: Trauma, Narrative, and History*. Baltimore: Johns Hopkins University Press, 1996.

Clark, Michael P. "The Work of War after the Age of Mechanical Reproduction." In *The Vietnam War and Postmodernity*. Edited by Michael Bibby. Amherst: University of Massachusetts Press, 2000.

Cohen, Jeffrey J. *Monster Theory: Reading Culture*. Minnesota: University of Minnesota Press, 1996.

Conard, Mark T. "Chaos, Order, and Morality: Nietzsche's Influence on *Full Metal Jacket*." In *The Philosophy of Stanley Kubrick*. Edited by Jerold J. Abrams. Lexington: University Press of Kentucky, 2007.

Cooke, Jennifer. *Legacies of Plague in Literature: Theory and Film*. New York: Macmillan, 2009.

Crichton, Michael. *The Andromeda Strain*. New York: HarperCollins, 2008.

Curnutte, Rick. "There's No Magic: A Conversation with George A. Romero." *Film Journal*. October 2004. http://www.thefilmjournal.com/issue10/romero/html.

Davis, David B. "Impact of the French and Haitian Revolutions." In *The Impact of the Haitian Revolution in the Atlantic World*. Edited by David P. Geggus. Columbia: University of South Carolina Press, 2001.

Davis, Wade. *Passage of Darkness: The Ethnobiology of the Haitian Zombie*. Chapel Hill: University of North Carolina Press, 1988.

———. *The Serpent and the Rainbow*. New York: Simon & Schuster, 1985.
Defoe, Daniel. *A Journal of the Plague Year*. New York: Norton, 1992.
Dekker, Thomas. *The Plague Pamphlets of Thomas Dekker*. Edited by F. P. Wilson. Oxford: Clarendon Press, 1925.
Dendle, Peter. *The Zombie Movie Encyclopedia*. Jefferson, NC: McFarland, 2001.
Dillard, R. H. W. "*Night of the Living Dead*: It's Not Like Just a Wind That's Passing Through." In *American Horrors: Essays on the Modern American Horror Film*. Edited by Gregory A. Waller. Urbana: University of Illinois Press, 1987.
Dunning, John. *On the Air: The Encyclopedia of Old-Time Radio*. Oxford: Oxford University Press, 1998.
Ebert, Roger. "Shaun of the Dead." rogerebert.com. September 24, 2004. http://rogerebert.suntimes.com/apps/pbcs.dll/article?AID=/20040924/REVIEWS/40913006/1023.
"Exclusive Interview: Max Brooks on *World War Z*." *Eat My Brains!* October 20, 2006. http://www.eatmybrains.com/showfeature.php?id=55.
Farmer, P. *Sida en Haïti: La victime accusée*. Paris: Karthala, 1996.
Fay, Jennifer. "Dead Subjectivity: White Zombie, Black Baghdad." *CR: The New Centennial Review* 8 (2008): 81–101.
Finney, Jack. *Invasion of the Body Snatchers*. New York: Scribner, 1998.
Foster, Hal, Rosalind Krauss, Yve-Alain Bois, and Benjamin Buchloh. *Art since 1900: Modernism, Antimodernism, Postmodernism*. Vol. 2: *1945 to the Present*. London: Thames and Hudson, 2005.
Freud, Sigmund. *Beyond the Pleasure Principle*. New York: Norton, 1961.
———. *Introductory Lectures on Psycho-Analysis (1915–17)*. London: Hogarth Press, 1959.
Fromm, Erich. *The Sane Society*. New York: Owl Books/Henry Holt, 1955.
Fuchs, Cynthia. "What Do We Say Happened Here? Memory, Identity, and the Vietnam War." In *The Vietnam War and Postmodernity*. Edited by Michael Bibby. Amherst: University of Massachusetts Press, 2000.
Gilgamesh. Translated by John Gardner and John Maier. New York: Random House, 1985.
Grossman, Lev. "*Pride and Prejudice*, Now with Zombies!" *Time*. April 2, 2009.
Grams, Martin, Jr. *Inner Sanctum Mysteries: Behind the Creaking Door*. Churchville, MD: OTR Publishing, 2002.
Hand, Richard J. *Terror on the Air! Horror Radio in America, 1931–52*. Jefferson, NC: McFarland, 2005.
Haraway, Donna. "A Cyborg Manifesto: Science, Technology, and Socialist-Feminism in the Late Twentieth Century." In *Simians, Cyborgs, and Women: The Reinvention of Nature*. New York: Routledge, 1991.

Harvey, W. W. *Sketches of Hayti: From the Expulsion of the French to the Death of Christophe*. London: L. B. Seeley, 1827.
Hayles, Katherine. *How We Became Posthuman: Virtual Bodies in Cybernetics, Literature, and Informatics*. Chicago: University of Chicago Press, 1999.
Herodotus. *The History of Herodotus*. Trans. George Rawlinson. New York: Tudor, 1956.
hooks, bell. *Black Looks: Race and Representation*. Boston: South End Press, 1992.
Howe, Irving. *The Idea of the Modern in Literature and the Arts*. New York: Horizon, 1967.
Hurston, Zora Neale. *Tell My Horse: Voodoo and Life in Haiti and Jamaica*. New York: Perennial Library, 1990.
James, C. L. R. *The Black Jacobins: Toussaint L'Ouverture and the San Domingo Revolution*. 2nd ed. New York: Vintage Books, 1989.
Jameson, Fredric. "Reification and Utopia in Mass Culture." *Social Text* 1 (Winter 1979): 130–48.
———. *Postmodernism, or, The Cultural Logic of Late Capitalism*. London: Verso, 1991.
Jardel, J.-P. "Représentation des cultes afro-caribéens et des pratiques magico-religieuses aux Antilles: Une approche du préjugé racial dans la littérature para-anthropologique." In *Au visiteur lumineux: Des îles creoles aux sociétés plurielles*. Edited by J. Barnabe et al. Petit-Bourg, Guadeloupe: Ibis Rouge Editions, 2000.
Kellman, Steven. *The Plague: Fiction and Resistance*. New York: Twayne, 1993.
Kelly, John. *The Great Mortality*. New York: HarperCollins, 2005.
Kendrick, James. *Hollywood Bloodshed: Violence in 1980s American Cinema*. Carbondale: Southern Illinois University Press, 2009.
Kerboull, J. *Vaudou et pratiques magiques*. Paris: Editions Belfond, Presses Pocket, 1977.
King, Stephen. *Stephen King's Danse Macabre*. New York: Everest House, 1981.
Kino, Carol. "Jillian Mcdonald, Performance Artist, Forsakes Billy Bob Thornton for Zombies." *New York Times*. July 30, 2006.
Laing, Ronald D. *The Divided Self*. New York: Pantheon, 1960.
Landa, Louis. "Religion, Science, and Medicine in *A Journal of the Plague Year*." In Daniel Defoe, *A Journal of the Plague Year*. New York: Norton, 1992.
Lauro, Sarah Juliet, and Karen Embry. "A Zombie Manifesto: The Nonhuman Condition in the Era of Advanced Capitalism." *boundary 2* 35 (2008): 85–108.
Lawless, Robert. *Haiti's Bad Press*. Rochester, VT: Schenkman Books, 1992.
Lifton, Robert J. *The Future of Immortality, and Other Essays for a Nuclear Age*. New York: Basic Books, 1987.

Lowenstein, Adam. "Films without a Face: Shock Horror in the Cinema of Georges Franju." *Cinema Journal* 37 (1998): 37–58.
Mcdonald, Jillian. *Horror Makeup*. Exhibition notes. Brooklyn, NY: 2006.
MacPherson, Myra. *Long Time Passing: Vietnam and the Haunted Generation*. Bloomington: Indiana University Press. 2002.
Maddrey, Joseph. *Nightmares in Red, White, and Blue: The Evolution of the American Horror Film*. Jefferson, NC: McFarland, 2004.
Magistrale, Tony. *Abject Terrors: Surveying the Modern and Postmodern Horror Film*. New York: Peter Lang, 2005.
Mapes, Marty. "Shaun of the Dead." *Movie Habit*. September 23, 2004. http://www.moviehabit.com/reviews/sha_iwo4.shtml.
Matheson, Richard. *I Am Legend*. New York: Tom Doherty, 2007.
McCullagh, Declan. "Brain-Eating Zombies Invade SF Apple Store." *CNET News*. May 26, 2007. http://news.cnet.com/8301-17938_105-9723086-1.html.
Nachman, Gerald. *Raised on Radio*. Berkeley: University of California Press, 1998.
Najman, C. *Haïti, Dieu seul me voit*. Paris: Balland, 1995.
Nakashima-Brown, Chris. "Keep Austin Zombie-Free." *No Fear of the Future*. January 26, 2009. http://nofearofthefuture.blogspot.com/2009/01/keep-austin-zombie-free.html.
Naremore, James. *On Kubrick*. London: British Film Institute, 2007.
Nohl, Johannes. *The Black Death: A Chronicle of the Plague*. New York: Harper & Row, 1969.
Paravisini-Gebert, Lizabeth. "Women Possessed. Eroticism and Exoticism in the Representation of Woman as Zombie." In *Sacred Possessions: Vodou, Santería, Obeah, and the Caribbean*. Edited by Margarite Fernández Olmos and Lizabeth Paravisini-Gebert. New Brunswick, NJ: Rutgers University Press, 1997.
Pepperell, Robert. *The Post-Human Condition: Consciousness beyond the Brain*. Chicago: University of Chicago Press, 2009.
Poutignat, P., and J. Streiff-Fenart, eds. *Théories de l'ethnicitié*. Paris: Presses Universitaires de France, 1995.
Powell, Anna. *Deleuze and the Horror Film*. Edinburgh: Edinburgh University Press, 2005.
Prawer, S. S. *Caligari's Children*. New York: Oxford University Press, 1980.
Prichard, Hesketh. *Where Black Rules White: A Journey across and about Hayti*. Westminster, UK: A. Constable & Co., Ltd., 1900.
Review of Mutter Erde: Ein Versuch über Volksreligion, by Albrecht Dieterich. *Classical Review* 20 (1906): 187–88.
Rhodes, Gary D. *White Zombie: Anatomy of a Horror Film*. Jefferson, NC: McFarland, 2001.

Ricoeur, Paul. *Freud and Philosophy: An Essay on Interpretation.* Translated by Denis Savage. New Haven, CT: Yale University Press, 1970.
Ruffles, Tom. *Ghost Images: Cinema of the Afterlife.* Jefferson, NC: McFarland, 2004.
Russell, Jamie. *Book of the Dead: The Complete History of Zombie Cinema.* 2nd ed. Surrey, UK: FAB Press, 2006.
Sabin, Roger. *Adult Comics: An Introduction.* London: Routledge, 1993.
Sadler, Simon. *The Situationist City.* Cambridge, MA: MIT Press, 1998.
Seabrook, W. B. *The Magic Island.* New York: Harcourt, Brace and Co., 1929.
Sherwin, Skye. "Zombies in North London." *BBC Collective: The Interactive Culture Magazine.* April 8, 2004.
Skal, David J. *The Monster Show.* Rev. ed. New York: Faber and Faber, 2001.
Spivey, Virginia. "Jillian Mcdonald: Richmond, VA." *Art Papers.* May/June 2008.
Sutherland, Meghan. "Rigor/Mortis: The Industrial Life of Style in American Zombie Cinema." *Framework* 48 (2007): 64–78.
Théodat, J-M. "Haïti et la République Dominicaine: Identités et territoires en partage." *Recherches haïtiano-antillaises.* Paris: L'Harmattan, 2005.
Thompson, Nato, Gregory Sholette, and Joseph Thompson, eds. *The Interventionists: Users' Manual for the Creative Disruption of Everyday Life.* 2nd ed. Cambridge, MA: MIT Press, 2006.
Torday, E. "Nzambi Mpungu, the God of the Bakongo." *Man* 30 (1930): 3.
Totaro, Rebecca. *Suffering in Paradise: The Bubonic Plague in English Literature from More to Milton.* Pittsburgh: Duquesne University Press, 2005.
Trefzer, Annette. "Possessing the Self: Caribbean Identities in Zora Neale Hurston's *Tell My Horse*." *African American Review* 34 (2000): 299–312.
Ulrich, John M., and Andrea L. Harris, eds. *GenXegesis: Essays on "Alternative" Youth (Sub)Culture.* Madison: University of Wisconsin Press, 2003.
Van Wing, R. P. *Etudes Bakongo.* Translated by Edwin W. Smith. In *African Ideas of God: A Symposium.* 2nd ed. Edited by Edwin W. Smith. London: Edinburgh House Press, 1950.
Von Bernewitz, Fred, and Grant Geissman. *Tales of Terror! The EC Companion.* Seattle: Fantagraphics Books, 2000.
Waller, Gregory, ed. *American Horrors: Essays on the Modern American Horror Film.* Urbana: University of Illinois Press, 1987.
Warner, Marina. *Phantasmagoria.* Oxford: Oxford University Press, 2006.
Webb, Jenn, and Sam Byrnand. "Some Kind of Virus: The Zombie as Body and as Trope." *Body and Society* 14 (2008): 83–98.
Young, Elizabeth. "Here Comes the Bride: Wedding Gender and Race in 'Bride of Frankenstein.'" *Feminist Studies* 17 (1991): 403–37.
Zimbardo, Philip. *The Lucifer Effect: How Good People Turn Evil.* London: Rider, 2007.

Žižek, Slavoj. *Did Somebody Say Totalitarianism? Five Interventions in the (Mis)use of a Notion.* New York: Verso, 2001.

FILMS

28 Days Later. Dir. Danny Boyle. 2002.
28 Weeks Later. Dir. Juan Carlos Fresnadillo. 2007.
All of the Dead. Dir. Tim Drage and Tony Mines. 2001.
The Andromeda Strain. Dir. Robert Wise. 1971.
Beetlejuice. Dir. Tim Burton. 1988.
Bride of Re-Animator. Dir. Brian Yuzna. 1990.
Burial Ground (orig. *Le notti Del terrore*). Dir. Andrea Bianchi. 1980.
The Child. Dir. Robert Voskanian. 1977.
Creature with the Atomic Brain. Dir. Edward Cahn. 1955.
Crouching Tiger, Hidden Dragon (orig. *Wu hu zang long*). Dir. Ang Lee. 2000.
Dawn of the Dead. Dir. George Romero. 1978.
Dawn of the Dead. Dir. Zack Snyder. 2004.
Day of the Dead. Dir. George Romero. 1985.
The Day They Came Back. Dir. Scott Goldberg. 2006.
Dead Alive. Dir. Peter Jackson. 1992.
Detained. Dir. Jason Tammemagi. 2004.
The Evil Dead. Dir. Sam Raimi. 1981.
Fido. Dr. Andrew Currie. 2006.
The Fog. Dir. John Carpenter. 1980.
From Beyond. Dir. Stuart Gordon. 1986.
Full Metal Jacket. Dir. Stanley Kubrick. 1987.
The Gates of Hell. Dir. Lucio Fulci. 1980.
The Ghost Breakers. Dir. George Marshall. 1940.
Hellraiser. Dir. Clive Barker. 1987.
The House by the Cemetery. Dir. Lucio Fulci. 1981.
I Walked with a Zombie. Dir. Jacques Tourneur. 1943.
Invasion of the Body Snatchers. Dir. Don Siegel. 1956.
Invisible Invaders. Dir. Edward Cahn. 1959.
Jacob's Ladder. Dir. Adrian Lyne. 1990.
Kill Bill. Dir. Quentin Tarantino. 2003/2004.
King of the Zombies. Dir. Jean Yarbrough. 1941.
Land of the Dead. Dir. George Romero. 2005.
Martin. Dir. George Romero. 1977.
"Homecoming" (*Masters of Horror*). Dir. Joe Dante. 2006.
The Matrix. Dir. Andy Wachowski, Larry Wachowski. 1999.
The Mummy. Dir. Stephen Sommers. 1999.
The Mummy: Tomb of the Dragon Emperor. Dir. Rob Cohen. 2008.

My Boyfriend's Back. Dir. Bob Balaban. 1993.
Night Life. Dir. David Acomba. 1989.
Night of the Comet. Dir. Thom Eberhardt. 1984.
Night of the Living Dead. Dir. George Romero. 1968.
Night of the Living Dead. Dir. Tom Savini. 1990.
A Nightmare on Elm Street. Dir. Wes Craven. 1984.
The Omen. Dir. Richard Donner. 1976.
On the Beach. Dir. Stanley Kramer. 1959.
Platoon. Dir. Oliver Stone. 1986.
Resident Evil. Dir. Paul W. S. Anderson. 2002.
The Return of the Living Dead. Dir. Dan O'Bannon. 1985.
Shaun of the Dead. Dir. Edgar Wright. 2004.
Tombs of the Blind Dead (orig. *La noche Del terror ciego*). Dir. Amando de Ossorio. 1971.
Universal Soldier. Dir. Roland Emmerich. 1992.
Unsettled. Dir. Sam Thompson. 2005.
Uuuugh! The Movie. Dir. Dan Murrell and Erni Crews. 2005.
White Zombie. Dir. Victor Halperin. 1932.
The Wicker Man. Dir. Robin Hardy. 1973.
Zombage! Dr. Kevin Strange. 2005.
Zombi 2. Dir. Lucio Fulci. 1979.

CONTRIBUTORS

ELSON BOND holds a Ph.D. in nineteenth-century American literature from Fordham University and teaches at Tarleton State University. He is currently coediting a collection of nineteenth-century American vampire tales and writing his first book, titled "Sentiment and Race in the Struggle for American Memory and Identity, 1879–1913."

KEVIN BOON is an Associate Professor at Pennsylvania State University and English Program Coordinator for the Mont Alto Campus. He has authored eight books and edited two scholarly collections. His research in zombie mythology centers on zombie fiction and issues of identity within twentieth- and twenty-first century American culture. He has published several articles on zombies, he recently completed a comic zombie novel (*Jesus vs. The Zombies of Perdition*), and he is working on a book-length work related to zombie classification.

DEBORAH CHRISTIE earned her Ph.D. from Fordham University in 2005 and is currently an Assistant Professor of English at ECPI University in Virginia Beach, Virginia. She is also developing and teaching courses in writing and literature in several online modalities. Working mainly with late Victorian and modern texts, she takes a cultural studies approach to constructions of monstrosity and its associated tropes of exclusion and suppression. Her current project is titled "Death Is Not the End: How the Un-dead Complicate Nature and Humanist Philosophy."

MARGO COLLINS is a Visiting Professor at DeVry University. She holds a Ph.D. in eighteenth-century British literature from the University of North Texas and is the author of several articles in such journals as *Comparative Drama*, *Studies in the Literary Imagination*, and *Restoration Theatre*. She was the associate editor for the Eliza Haywood edition for Pickering and Chatto and edited *Before the Count: British Vampire Tales, 1732–1897* for Zittaw Press. She is currently coediting a collection of nineteenth-century American vampire mysteries and working on a novel.

Holding a Ph.D. in anthropology, FRANCK DEGOUL has conducted research in Martinique and in Haiti, investigating firsthand the relative imaginary of the magical-religious. His principle work concerns Creole and Caribbean modes of imagining a pact with the devil, on which he published a monograph titled *Le commerce diabolique: Une exploration de l'imaginaire du pacte maléfique en Martinique* (Ibis Rouge Éditions, 2000). He is also the author of several articles and contributions to collections on Vaudou and Creole culture. His work emphasizes the way that servitude, embedded in the social fabric of these historically servile territories, is reimagined in regard to their culture's conception of the relationship between the living and the dead, their legends about colonial treasure, and the depiction of the individual process of transformation into a (Haitian) zombie—in other words, slaves bound by sorcery.

PETER DENDLE is Associate Professor of English at Pennsylvania State University, Mont Alto. He holds a masters degree in philosophy from the University of Kentucky, a master's in English from Yale University, and a Ph.D. in English from the University of Toronto. He has published widely on cultural constructions of the monstrous in both the medieval and modern era. He has authored a monograph on early medieval demonology (*Satan Unbound: The Devil in Old English Narrative Literature*) and another on zombie movies (*The Zombie Movie Encyclopedia*).

SORCHA NÍ FHLAINN received her Ph.D. from Trinity College, Dublin. Her work focuses on the postmodern vampire and its representation in cultural history. Her interest in zombies derives from a postmodern perspective, where zombies violate previous classifications or definitions. She has edited many collections on monsters, including *The Wicked Heart: Studies in the Phenomena of Evil* (Inter-Disciplinary Press, 2007) and *Dark Reflections, Monstrous Reflections: Essays on the Monster in Culture* (Inter-Disciplinary Press, 2008). She is also a regular contributor to and board member of the *Irish Journal of Gothic and Horror Studies*, and is the current hub leader of "evil studies" for At the Interface, Oxford, UK, running five major annual conference projects on evil, fear, horror, monsters, and villainy. She lectures in Gothic studies at the Centre for Talented Youth, Ireland, and teaches American literature in Trinity College, Dublin. In particular, her research focuses on violations of categorizations, 1980s American culture, heavy metal, and cultural developments in representations of the monstrous.

RICHARD HAND is Professor of Theatre and Media Drama at the University of Glamorgan in Wales. He is the author of *Terror on the Air! Horror Radio* in America, 1931–52 (McFarland, 2006) and *The Theatre of Joseph Conrad: Reconstructed Fictions* (Palgrave, 2005), and is a founding coeditor of the *Journal of Adaptation in Film and Performance*. He has published journal articles and book chapters on aspects of performance media including theater, radio, film, graphic narratives, and digital gaming. As a collaborator, he coedited *Monstrous Adaptations: Generic and Thematic Mutations in Horror Film* (Manchester University Press, 2007) with Jay McRoy; and has enjoyed a successful partnership with Michael Wilson, cowriting *Grand-Guignol: The French Theatre of Horror* (University of Exeter Press, 2002) and *London's Grand-Guignol and the Theatre of Horror* (University of Exeter Press, 2007). Together Hand and Wilson feature in a documentary "extra" on Grand-Guignol on the DVD of Tim Burton's *Sweeney Todd*. As a theater director, Hand's productions have included the world premiere of Joseph Conrad's Grand-Guignol horror play *Laughing Anne* and the subsequent tour of the play in the United Kingdom and the United States; and Victor Hugo's bloody revenge melodrama *Lucretia Borgia* for the 2007 International Hugo Festival. An occasional actor, he features as "Father" in the award-winning independent feature film *Footsteps* (dir. G. H. Evans 2006).

CHERA KEE is a Ph.D. candidate in critical studies at the University of Southern California. She received her B.A. in mass communications and Asian studies from Oklahoma City University, her A.M. from the Regional Studies–East Asia Program at Harvard University, and her M.A. in critical studies from USC. Her research interests include the zombie in U.S. popular culture, documentary filmmaking, and Chinese-language film. Her dissertation explores the interplay of race, gender, and space in zombie media and the zombie's place in a longer tradition of the politically undead.

SARAH JULIET LAURO holds a recent PhD's lectureship at the University of California, Davis. She has published elsewhere on the zombie's importance to critical theory—with Karen Embry, "A Zombie Manifesto," *boundary 2*, Spring 2008—and her work more broadly considers the body's relationship to modern technologies. Her next project concerns the portrayal of corpses in art and literature.

KEVIN MEAUX was born in Kaplan, Louisiana, and is now teaching at Lamar University in Beaumont, Texas. His writing has received numerous awards, including a Ruth Lilly Fellowship as well as a Louisiana Division of the Arts Artist Fellowship. His poems have appeared in such journals as the *Southern Review*, *Poetry*, *Prairie Schooner*, and *Shenandoah*, and he is the author of the book *Myths of Electricity*.

NICK MUNTEAN is currently a doctoral student in the Radio-Television-Film department at the University of Texas, Austin. His master's thesis was a sociohistorical analysis of *Night of the Living Dead*, and his dissertation analyzes the generic and cultural history of postapocalyptic films. He has a forthcoming article in the *Journal of Popular Film and Television* exploring the relationship between mediated traumatic experiences and 9/11 films, and he has coauthored an essay with Matthew Payne regarding the impact of the 9/11 attacks on contemporary zombie films. In addition to his academic pursuits, Muntean organized a zombie flash mob attack on the 2005 *American Idol* auditions held in Austin, a stunt that was unexpectedly filmed by the show's crew and subsequently incorporated into the program itself. He still wonders whether he should have billed Fox for his services.

BERNICE MURPHY is Lecturer in Popular Literature at the School of English, Trinity College, Dublin. She has edited a collection titled *Shirley Jackson: Essays on the Literary Legacy* (McFarland, 2005) and authored *The Suburban Gothic in American Popular Culture* (Palgrave Macmillan, 2009), from which her chapter here is an extract. She is also coeditor and founder of the online *Irish Journal of Horror and Gothic Studies*, which can be found at http://irishgothichorrorjournal.homestead.com/.

LYNN PIFER is a professor of English at Mansfield University, where she directs the Frederick Douglass Institute and teaches American literature, including African American literature and literature of the U.S. South. Her articles have appeared in journals such as *African American Review*, *MELUS*, and *Making Connections: A Journal for Teachers of Cultural Diversity*, and in conference proceedings such as *Conflict in Southern Writing* (Troy State University, 2006). She became interested in zombies when she used *Shaun of the Dead* as a text for analysis in her Freshman Composition course in an effort to enliven an often-boring mandatory class. She called it fighting zombies with zombies, and it worked so well she decided to write about *Shaun*. Pifer is currently working on her book *Literary Legacy of the Civil Rights Movement*, but she still enjoys showing *Shaun of the Dead* to her composition students every fall.

STEVEN ZANI is chair of the English and Modern Languages department at Lamar University in Beaumont, Texas. He has publications in a number of journals and books, including the *Byron Journal*, the *Lovecraft Annual*, and *James Bond and Philosophy*. He has coauthored a literature anthology, *Inside Literature*, in the Penguin Academic Series.

INDEX

Adams, Glen, 153
Agamben, Giorgio, 79, 91
AIDS, 106
Alien (1979), 212
aliens, 21, 69, 70, 101, 119, 121, 123–25, 135, 137, 164, 175, 186, 231
All Fool's Day (1965), 231
All of the Dead (2001), 180
All of Them Witches (1996), 169
Althusser, Louis, 85
American Horrors, 76
Améry, Jean, 91
Amos 'n' Andy (1926–60), 41
anamnesis, 77
anart (anarchist art), 225
Anderson, Brad, 59
The Andromeda Strain, 106, 107
androphagi, 103
Anselm of Canterbury, 51
apocalypse, 68, 71, 141, 142, 155, 194, 198, 201, 234. *See also* zombie apocalypse
Aristide, Jean-Bertrand, 32
Aristotle, 106
arsenal of victory, 190
Artaud, Antonin, 89
ArtMovingProjects, 161, 206, 207
Atkinson, J. Brooks, 14
Auschwitz, 91
Austen, Jane, 195, 197–99
avant-garde, 216, 220, 223

Badmington, Neil, 2, 68, 69, 70, 73
Barker, Clive, 59–60
Barth, Fredrik, 28, 33
Bastide, Roger, 25
Battle of Yonkers, 193
Battlestar Galactica, 69
Baudrillard, Jean, 135
Beauvoir, Simone de, 129

Beechey, William, 198
Beetlejuice (1988), 178
Benjamin, Walter, 76
Beuka, Robert, 135, 137
Bianchi, Andrea, 177
Bibby, Michael, 147
Bill, the Galactic Hero: On the Planet of Zombie Vampires (1991), 60
bio-zombie, 8, 58, 139, 141, 148, 152
Bio-Zombie (1998), 58
The Birds (1963), 231, 235
Black Bagdad (1934), 28, 54
Black Death, 101. *See also* plague
Boccaccio, Giovanni, 63, 101–3
Bond, Elson, 3, 160, 161
Book of the Dead (2005), 125
Boon, Kevin, 3, 139
Bowery at Midnight (1942), 20
Boyer, Jean-Pierre, 13
Boyle, Danny, 142, 178
Bradbury, Ray, 183
Bradner, Gary, 57
The Brain Eaters (1958), 123
The Brain from the Planet Arous (1958), 123
Braindead (1992), 178. See also *Dead Alive* (1992)
breather, 196
The Breeze Horror, 57
Bride of Re-Animator (1991), 176
Brooks, Max, 160, 188–90, 192–96, 198
Browning, Tod, 20
Bullet Time Cinematography, 179
Burial Ground (1980), 177
Burke, Thomas, 54; "The Hollow Man," 54
Bush, President George W., 113, 117, 154–56, 230

Caligari, 7, 8, 20, 58, 59. See also *Das Cabinet des Dr. Caligari*

289

Caligari's Children, 20
Campbell, Joseph, 167, 172
Camus, Albert, 107
Canetti, Elias, 220
cannibal, 6, 16, 20–23, 57, 161, 176, 181
cannibalism, 9, 12–14, 19, 21–23, 57, 63, 76, 79, 181
cannibalistic, 9, 10, 27, 63, 103
capitalism, 92–93, 153, 221, 228, 229
capitalist, 14, 17, 153, 160, 163, 167, 190, 206, 209, 215–16, 221–23, 226, 228
Caponegro, Candace, 57
caribbean zombie, 64, 117. See also Haitian zombie
Carrion, 57
Carroll, Noel, 22
Caruth, Cathy, 87, 95
"The Case of the Living Dead," 47
Casualties of War (1989), 147
Cédras, Raoul, 32
Cell (2006), 58
Certeau, Michel de, 222
The Child (1977), 178
Christie, Deborah, 3, 61, 202, 203
Christophe, Henri, 13
Chtcheglov, Ivan, 222
The City in History (1961), 120
City of the Living Dead (1980), 112
Clark, Michael P., 150
CoBrA, 226
Cohen, Jeffery, 164, 165, 170, 171
Cole, Alonzo Dean, 41
collectivism, 226, 227
Collins, Margo, 3, 160, 161
colonial, 6, 12, 17, 25, 30, 31, 182–83
colonialism, 12, 14, 16
colonization, 209, 233
Columbine, 161, 185–86
Conard, Mark T., 145
Condon, Richard, 59
Constructivism, 226
Cooper, Edmund, 231
Count Chocula, 187
"The Country of the Comers-Back," 54
The Crack in the Picture Window (1956), 120
Craige, Captain John Houston, 28, 54
Craven, Wes, 130
Creature with the Atomic Brain (1955), 98
Critique of Everyday Life, 229
Critique de la separation (1961), 222
Crouching Tiger, Hidden Dragon, 179

Cuba, 19, 20, 26, 31, 190, 192
cultural zombie, 8, 59, 140, 187
Currie, Andrew, 116, 117, 118

Dada, 221, 224
d'Ans, André-Marcel, 26
Dante, Joe, 140, 154–56
"Dark They Were, and Golden Eyed" (1949), 183
Darwin, Charles, 1, 71, 233
Das Cabinet des Dr. Caligari (1920), 7, 58. See also Caligari
Dawn of the Dead (1978), 5, 56, 62, 81, 84, 87–89, 93, 96, 99, 104, 108, 114–15, 119, 125, 127, 136, 163, 165–69, 177–78, 181, 184
Dawn of the Dead (2004), 114, 119, 126–27, 179, 184, 185, 195, 233
Day of the Dead (1985), 5, 115, 141, 176–78, 181
The Day They Came Back (2006), 181, 184
Dayan, Joan, 13
Davis, David Brion, 10
Davis, Wade, 7
Dead Alive (1992), 178, 232. See also *Braindead*
Dead in the West, 57
Debord, Guy, 216, 220, 222, 223, 224, 225, 229
The Decameron, 63, 101
Defoe, Daniel, 63, 101, 104–6
Degoul, Franck, 3, 6, 13
Dekker, Thomas, 103–4
Dendle, Peter, 2, 3, 5, 7, 20, 71, 160, 195, 232
Depp, Johnny, 212
dérive, 222, 223. See also drift
Descartes, René, 51, 70
Dessalines, Jean Jacques, 10, 11, 13
Detained, 181
détournement, 215, 221–24, 228
devolution, 12, 157, 233
dialectic of awakening, 76
Dick, Phillip K., 118–19
Dillard, R. H. W., 79
Disney, Walt, 134, 135
Disneyland, 134, 135
Donaldson, Scott, 121, 122
Dracula, 20–21, 42
drift, 222, 223. See also *dérive*
drone, 116, 122. See also John and Mary Drone; zombie drone

Dunning, John, 42, 47
"The Dunwich Horror," 42
Dying to Live, 160, 198, 201

Ebert, Roger, 167, 169
eco-zombie, 234–35
Embry, Karen, 153
Emmerich, Roland, 147, 150, 151, 152
Escape (1947–54), 42; "Three Skeleton Key," 42
The Evil Dead (1982), 178
evolution, 1–3, 6, 50, 61, 64, 68, 94, 143, 186, 190, 195, 208–11, 230, 233–34. See also devolution; zombie evolution

Facebook, 160, 180, 197, 223
"The Facts in the Case of M. Valdemar," 59
"The Fall of the House of Usher," 73
Far from Heaven (2002), 117
Farmer, Paul, 28
Faulds, Thea, 208. See also Munster, Thea
Fay, Jennifer, 154
The Feminine Mystique (1963), 128, 133
Fiddler's Green, 113, 189
Fido (2006), 3, 63–64, 116–17, 119, 204
Field of the Dead and Undead, 212. See also Mcdonald, Jillian
Finney, Jack, 98, 119, 123–24, 135, 137
Flo-Mo, 179
Fluxus, 223, 224
The Fog (1979), 178
Formulary for a New Urbanism, 222
Foster, Hal, 221, 225
Fox, Michael J., 196
Franju, Georges, 77
Frankenstein (1819), 42, 47
Frankenstein's monster, 5, 7, 21, 100
Freaks (1932), 20
Fresnadillo, Juan Carlos, 102
Freud, Sigmund, 16, 84, 87, 88, 95
Friedan, Betty, 128, 129, 133, 136
From Beyond (1986), 178
Fromm, Erich, 86
Fulci, Lucio, 56, 63, 99, 100–2, 104–5, 107–12, 114–15, 212, 235
Full Metal Jacket (1987), 140, 143, 144, 145, 147
Functionalism, 221
Futurism, 224, 226

Gans, Herbert J., 121, 122
The Gates of Hell (1980), 112, 115
generation X, 159, 165, 166
generation Y, 160. See also millennials
GenXegis: Essays on "Alternative" Youth (Sub) Culture, 166
The Ghost Breakers (1940), 19
"The Gibbering Things," 47. See also *The Shadow*
Giles, Dennis, 75
Gilgamesh, 100, 172
Goddard, Richard E., 54; "The Whistling Ancestors," 54
Gold Bond Triple-Action Medicated Body Powder, 196
Goldberg, Scott, 181, 184
The Good War (1984), 188
Google, 184
The Gorgonzola Zombies in the Park (1994), 60
Gouch, Brad, 59
Grahame-Smith, Seth, 160, 197, 198, 199
Grams, Martin Jr., 39
Green Eyes (1984), 58
Guantanamo Bay, 156
Gruener, Daniel, 169
Gunn, James, 195
Gutai, 226

Hachiya, Dr. Michihiko, 90
Haining, Peter, 57
Haiti, 6, 9–14, 16–17, 19–21, 24–32, 34–35, 37–38, 42, 53–54, 59, 154, 168, 209
Haitian zombie, 7–8, 24, 27, 54, 56–56
Hamburger Hill (1987), 147
Hand, Richard, 3, 6
Hannibal Lecter, 185
The Happening (2008), 231–32, 234
happenings, 222, 223, 224, 227
Haraway, Donna, 70
Hare Krishna, 184, 185
Harvey, W. W., 11
Haussmann, baron, 221
Hayles, Katherine, 68, 69
Hayti, or the Black Republic, 12
Hearn, Lafcadio, 54; "The Country of the Comers-Back," 54
Hegel, G. W. F., 61, 94
Hellraiser (1987), 178
Hendershot, Cyndy, 70
Heraclitus, 61, 64

The Hermit's Cave (1935–44), 41; "Spirit Vengeance," 43–44
Herodotus, 103
hibakusha, 63, 90, 93, 94, 95
Hiroshima, 55, 63, 83, 90, 91
Hitchcock, Alfred, 231
"The Hollow Man," 54
Holocaust, 128
"Homecoming," 140, 154
hooks, bell, 22
Horror Makeup (art), 210, 211
"The House in Cypress Canyon," 42
The House by the Cemetery (1981), 110
How We Became Posthuman, 69
Howe, Irving, 55
humanism, 68–70, 80
humanist, 4, 64, 68–69
Hurston, Zora Neale, 54, 168–70; "Tell My Horse," 54, 168
Huxley, Aldous, 61

I, Zombie (1982), 58
I, Zombie (1998), 8
I Am Legend (1954), 61, 67, 68, 71, 74, 78, 80, 98
I Am Legend (2007), 68, 71, 179, 200, 234
I Married a Monster from Outer Space (1958), 123
I Walked with a Zombie (1943), 7, 27, 44, 54, 57
The Incredibly Strange Creatures Who Stopped Living and Became Mixed-Up Zombies (1964), 21
Inner Sanctum Mysteries (1941–52), 6, 42–43
"The Island of Death," 42
"The Undead," 43
insurrection, 227. *See also* rebellion; revolution; slave rebellion
Interventionism, 226
The Interventionists: User's Manual for the Creative Disruption of Everyday Life, 226
Invasion of the Body Snatchers (1956), 69, 70, 73, 98, 119, 123, 125, 135, 231
Invaders from Mars (1953), 123
Invisible Invaders (1959), 98
iPod, 64
Iraq, 140, 154, 155, 230
"The Island of Death," 42
Island of the Flesh Eaters, 108
"Isle of the Living Dead," 47–49

Israel, 190, 191
It Came from Outer Space (1953), 123

Jackson, Kenneth, 122
Jackson, Peter, 178, 232
Jacob's Ladder (1990), 3, 140–42, 147–50
Jacobs, W. W., 100
James, C. L. R., 10
Jameson, Frederic, 117, 118, 142, 152
Jardel, Jean-Pierre, 25
Jerry Built, 122
John and Mary Drone, 116, 120
Johnson, Barbara, 170
Jones, Stephen, 59
Jorn, Asger, 216, 220, 221, 222, 223
A Journal of the Plague Year, 63, 101, 104, 105

Kaiser Family Foundation, 182
Kaprow, Alan, 223
Karloff, Boris, 179
Keats, John, 120–22, 124, 128
Kee, Chera, 3, 6
Keene, Brian, 7, 58
Kendrick, James, 145, 146
Kerboull, Jean, 35
Kill Bill, 179
King, Alexander, 14
King, Stephen, 58, 168
King of the Zombies (1941), 21, 54, 57, 98
Knight, Peter, 133
"Knock at the Door," 44, 45, 46
Knowles, Alison, 224; *Make a Salad*, 224
Kramer, Stanley, 81
Kristol, Irving, 193
Ksenych, Daniel, 58; "The Other Side of Theory," 58
Kubrick, Stanley, 143–45, 147, 212
Kwon, Miwon, 213, 214

Laing, R. D., 56
Land of the Dead (2005), 113, 179, 200, 233
Lansdale, Joe R., 57
The Last House on the Left (1972), 130
The Last Man on Earth (1964), 67, 71, 162
Lauro, Sarah Juliet, 3, 153, 161, 202, 203
Layman, Richard, 58
Lefebvre, Henri, 229–30
Lettrists, 220, 226
Levi, Primo, 91
Levin, Ira, 58, 64, 119, 127–31, 134–35

Index

Levittown, 121
The Levittowners (1967), 121
Lewton, Val, 44
Lifton, Robert Jay, 86
Lights Out (1934–47), 42, 44–46, 49
"Knock at the Door," 44, 45, 46
"Scoop," 44
Linklater, Richard, 166
lobos (lobotimizers), 194
Lovecraft, H. P., 42, 57; "Herbert West—Reanimator," 57
Lowenstein, Adam, 76, 77
Luke Skywalker, 168, 172
Lyne, Adrian, 147

Maberry, Jonathan, 160, 200
The Machinist (2004), 59
Maciunas, George, 224
MacPherson, Myra, 147
Maddrey, Joseph, 20
The Magic Island (1929), 13, 14, 26
Magistrale, Tony, 168
Main Street, USA, 118, 134
Make a Salad, 224. *See also* Knowles, Alison
The Mammoth Book of Zombies (1993), 59
The Manchurian Candidate (1959), 59
Manhattan Project, 91
Mapes, Marty, 167, 168
Marshall, Jonathan, 177
Martin (1976), 178
Marxist, 212, 221
Masters of Horror, 140, 154
Matheson, Richard, 61, 62, 67–69, 71–72, 76, 80, 98, 179, 232, 234
The Matrix, 179
Mcdonald, Jillian, 161, 205–8, 210–18, 221, 224–25
Field of the Dead and Undead, 212
Horror Makeup, 210–11
Me and Billy Bob, 212
The Screaming, 212
Screen Kiss, 212
Zombies in Condoland, 212, 214–15, 221, 225
Zombie Loop, 161, 205–7
meatsnack, 196, 200
Meaux, Kevin, 3, 63
Mecum, Ryan, 160, 203
millennial zombie, 2, 3, 161, 187–88, 194–95, 202

millennials, 159–60, 175, 179, 180–82, 185–87, 196. *See also* generation Y
Missing in Action (1984), 147
modern zombie, 9, 61, 67, 83–84, 91–93, 95, 97–98, 103, 107, 139, 204
"The Monkey's Paw," 100
Monster Theory: Reading Culture, 165
Moreau de Saint-Méry, M. L. E., 53
Morrison, Philip, 90
MTV, 179
Mumford, Lewis, 120, 128
mummy, 92, 179
The Mummy (1999), 179
The Mummy: Tomb of the Dragon Emperor (2008), 179
Munster, Thea, 205, 208–10, 215–18, 220–24, 228. *See also* Faulds, Thea
Muntean, Nick, 3, 62, 63, 64
Murphy, Bernice, 3, 63–64
Murray, Craig D., 177
Muselmänner, 63, 91–95
My Boyfriend's Back (1993), 181
The Mysterious Traveler (1943–52), 42

Nachman, Gerald, 47
Nagasaki, 63, 83, 90, 91
Najman, Charles, 26–28
Namenwirth, Aron, 206–7
Nancy, Jean-Luc, 213
Naremore, James, 145
National Geographic, 12
Nazi, 19, 63, 83, 91
New Deal Democrat, 192
Ní Fhlainn, Sorcha, 3, 64
Nietzsche, Friedrich, 61, 194
The Night of the Comet, 106
Night Life (1989), 176
Night of the Living Dead (1968), 5–6, 9–10, 21, 23, 50, 56–57, 62, 68, 76–80, 82–84, 96, 98, 103, 115–16, 124, 164, 169, 176–77, 181, 234
A Nightmare on Elm Street (1985), 178
nihilism, 74, 79, 188, 221
9/11, 142, 185. *See also* September 11
Nohl, Johannes, 106
"Nostalgia for the Present," 117
Nuit Blanche, 212–13, 215–17, 226
Nzambi, 50, 51

Oates, Joyce Carol, 59
O'Bannon, Dan, 178
Oboler, Arch, 44, 46

Odysseus, 100
Oklahoma City bombing, 186
The Omega Man (1971), 71, 234
The Omen (1976), 178
On the Beach (1959), 62, 81–82, 85, 87, 89–91, 93, 94, 95, 96, 97
On the Origin of Species (1859), 1. *See also* Darwin, Charles
One Place After Another, 213
One Rainy Night, 58
Ossorio, Amando de, 56, 177
"The Other Side of Theory," 58
Ouanaga (1935), 7, 18
Oz, Frank, 136

Paffenroth, Kim, 160, 198, 201, 202
Paravisini-Gebert, Lizabeth, 27
Pascal, Blaise, 52
Passage of Darkness, 7
patient zero, 200
Paul, E. C., 25
Pegg, Simon, 159, 163, 167, 169, 171
Pepperell, Robert, 68, 69, 70, 71
Pétion, Alexandre, 13
The Philosophy of Horror, 22
Piazza, Michele de, 102
Pifer, Lynn, 3, 159, 160, 204
plague, 42, 63, 72, 74, 77, 101–2, 104–8, 188–89, 235. *See also* plague narratives; vampire plague; zombie plague
The Plague (1947), 107, 108
plague narratives, 63, 94, 99–107, 110–11
Plan 9 from Outer Space (1958), 20
Plato, 77
Platoon (1986), 145–46, 147
Pleasantville (1998), 117
pod people, 64, 69, 119, 123–24, 137, 231
Poe, Edgar Allan, 59, 73
Polanski, Roman, 76
post-human, 2, 62–65, 68–70, 77, 81, 85, 140, 150, 152–53, 157, 160, 201, 232, 233. *See also* post-human soldier; post-humanism; post-humanity
The Post-Human Condition, 68
post-human soldier, 64, 139–40
post-humanism, 68, 70, 77
post-humanity, 2, 65, 161, 202
postmodern, 64, 139, 141–42, 150–54, 156
postmodern zombie, 148–49, 152, 156
post-traumatic stress, 64, 148
Prawer, S. S., 20

Price, Vincent, 162
Pride and Prejudice and Zombies, 160, 194–95, 197, 198, 204
Pritchard, Hesketh, 12
psychological zombie, 8, 58, 139–40, 142, 145

Quarantine (2008), 58
Queen Elizabeth I, 103
Quiet, Please (1947–49), 42
quislings, 194

Rambo: First Blood (1982), 147
Rambo: First Blood Part II (1985), 147
rebellion, 13, 152, 155, 190, 215, 225, 227. *See also* insurrection; revolution; slave rebellion
Redeker Plan, 191
Resident Evil, 107, 178
Return of the Living Dead (1985), 176, 178, 215, 234
Revenge of the Zombies (1943), 54
Revolt of the Zombies (1936), 7, 18, 153
revolution, 9–12, 17, 170, 190, 208, 215, 220–25, 227–29, 235. *See also* insurrection; rebellion; slave rebellion
The Rising (2003), 7, 58
Roberts, Donald, 182
Romero, George, 2, 5–6, 9–10, 44, 50, 57, 61–63, 67, 69, 75–76, 80–83, 89, 94, 98–99, 103–4, 108, 113, 116–19, 124–28, 136, 139, 141, 148, 160, 163, 165, 167–69, 177–81, 187–89, 200, 231–35
Rosemary's Baby (1968), 76
Ruffles, Tom, 153
Russell, Bertrand, 168
Russell, Jamie, 125

Sadler, Simon, 221, 222
San Francisco Zombie Mob, 161, 208, 228
Santee school shooting, 186
Sartre, Jean-Paul, 53–55
schizoid, 56, 86–88, 95
schizophrenia, 86–87, 147
Scott, Ridley, 212
Screen Kiss, 212
Seabrook, William, 13, 14, 17, 26–28
The Second Sex, 129
Selby, Curt, 58
September 11, 142. *See also* 9/11

The Serpent and the Rainbow, 7
"Sex, Death, and Starshine," 59–60
The Shadow, 6, 46–49
    "The Case of the Living Dead," 47
    "The Gibbering Things," 47
    "Isle of the Living Dead," 47–49
    "Ship of the Living Dead," 47
    "Society of the Living Dead," 47
    "Undead," 47
    "Valley of the Living Dead," 47, 49
Shaun of the Dead (2004), 3, 159–60, 163–67, 171, 179, 181, 204, 232
Shephard, Lucius, 58
Sherwin, Skye, 167
The Shining (1980), 212
"Ship of the Living Dead," 47
shock and awe, 193
shock horror, 76–77
Sholette, Gregory, 226
Shute, Nevil, 81
Shyamalan, M. Night, 231, 234
Siegel, Don, 109, 124
The Sirens of Titan, 58
The Situationist City, 221, 222
Situationist International (SI), 206, 213, 215–16, 220–26, 228, 229
Sixsmith, Judith, 177
Skal, David, 17
Sketches of Hayti: From the Expulsion of the French to the Death of Christophe, 11
slacker, 159, 163–68, 172–74
Slacker (1991), 166
slave labor, 8, 10–11, 19, 21, 56–58, 117, 170
slave rebellion, 10, 215, 225, 227
slavery, 16, 215
slaves, 9–10, 12, 14, 16–17, 25, 27, 49, 86, 139, 153, 155, 168, 225, 233
Snyder, Zack, 104, 114, 126, 127
"Society of the Living Dead," 47
The Society of the Spectacle (1967), 216, 222, 229
South Africa, 190, 191
Spelman, Elizabeth, 233
Spierig, Michael and Peter, 160, 199
"Spirit Vengeance," 43, 44
Stanford Prison Experiment, 153, 154
Stepford Wives, 3, 63, 131–33, 136
The Stepford Wives (1972), 58, 64, 125, 127, 136
The Stepford Wives (1975), 57, 119, 136
The Stepford Wives (2004), 57, 119, 136

St. John, Spencer, 12
Stimson, Blake, 226
Stone, Oliver, 145
Strange, Kevin, 182
The Suburban Myth (1969), 121
suburbia, 63, 117, 119–24, 129–30, 133–34, 137
suburban zombie, 3, 64, 138
Surrealism, 221, 226
Suspense (1942–62), 42
    "The Dunwich Horror," 42
    "The House in Cypress Canyon," 42
Sutherland, Meghan, 79

Tammemagi, Jason, 181
Taxi Driver (1976), 147
tech zombie, 8, 58, 140, 147–48, 150, 151, 152
"Tell My Horse," 54
Terkel, Studs, 188, 192, 193
Théodat, Jean-Marie, 30
Thompson, Sam, 182
Thorazine, 147
"Three Skeleton Key," 42
Tombs of the Blind Dead (1971), 177
Torday, E., 51
Toronto Zombie Walk, 205, 208, 209, 216, 217–19
Totaro, Rebecca, 106
trauma zombie, 62, 82–84, 95–97
Trinity Test, 71
Trujillo, Leónidas, 30
28 Days Later (2002), 2, 3, 7, 58, 102, 104, 115, 140, 141, 142, 146, 178, 233–34
28 Weeks Later (2007), 3, 102, 113, 114, 115, 233
Twilight, 187
Twitter, 223

Ulrich, John, 166
"The Undead," 43, 47
Undead, 160, 199
Universal Soldier (1992), 140, 147, 148, 150, 151, 152, 153
Unsettled (2005), 182
U.S.S. *Saratoga*, 192
Uuuugh! The Movie (2005), 180

"Valley of the Living Dead," 47, 49
vampire plague, 68, 77
vampires, 3, 5, 40, 43, 61–62, 67–69, 71–72, 74–77, 98, 152, 179, 187, 232

Van Wing, R. P., 51
Vietnam, 77, 140–43, 146–48, 150–56
Virginia Tech, 161
Vodou zombie, 83
Vonnegut, Kurt, 55, 58
voodoo: and Haiti, 9–10, 12–13, 15, 18–19, 21–22, 42; as religion 6, 9–10, 12–13, 19–20, 23, 42–43, 101, 110, 112, 125, 232; and zombies, 6, 9–10, 12–13, 15, 18–19, 21, 23, 42, 49, 54, 61–62, 98, 101, 168–69, 185, 190, 232

The Walking Dead, 209
Waller, Gregory, 76
War of the Worlds (1938), 39
Webb, Kenneth, 14
Weiss, Bryan, 219
Welcome to the Desert of the Real, 79
Welles, Orson, 39, 46
werewolves, 5, 40, 47
Where Black Rules White: A Journey across and about Hayti, 12
"The Whistling Ancestors," 54
White Zombie (1932), 7, 15–18, 23, 27, 54, 98, 139, 153, 185, 209
white zones, 188
The Wicker Man (1973), 178
Wikipedia, 184
Williams, Tony, 125
Willis, Lara, 219
The Witch's Tale, 41
World War Z, 160, 188, 189, 190, 192, 194, 196, 198, 204
Wright, Edgar, 159, 163, 167, 169, 171

X-Box, 182

Yip, Wilson, 58
Young, Elizabeth, 15
Young, Iris Marion, 213
Youtube, 184

Zack, 193
Zani, Steve, 3, 63

Zimbardo, Dr. Philip, 153
Žiěk, Slavoj, 62, 79, 94
Zombage! (2005), 182
zombi, 53, 64, 117
Zombi 2 (1979), 108, 109, 110, 112, 212
Zombie (1932), 14–15, 18
Zombie (1995), 59
zombie apocalypse, 101, 117, 126, 160, 162, 180, 188, 190, 196, 197, 201, 202, 204. *See also* apocalypse
Zombie CSU: The Forensics of the Living Dead, 160, 200
zombie drone, 8, 53–54, 56, 57
zombie evolution, 1, 4, 8, 204, 208, 210, 220, 230–31, 233
Zombie Haiku, 160, 203, 204
Zombie Hell House (1981), 110
zombie Jesus, 202
"Zombie Loop," 161, 205, 206, 207
zombie mob, 225
zombie plague, 109–10, 188–94, 197–99. *See also* black death; plague
Zombies in Condoland, 212. *See also* McDonald, Jillian
"A Zombie Manifesto," 153
Zombie Squad, 196, 197
Zombie: Stories of the Walking Dead, 57
Zombie Survival Guide (2003), 170, 190, 194, 195, 196
Zombie Survival Guide: Recorded Attacks (2009), 160, 195
zombie swarm, 214
zombie walks, 161, 187, 223, 224, 228. *See also* Toronto Zombie Walk
zombie zen, 220
Zombieoo (2000), 59
Zombie Zone, The (2005), 60
zombiedefense.org, 195
zombification, 223
zombulation, 196
ZomCon, 63, 116, 117